Napoleon

From Tilsit to Waterloo

1807–1815

GEORGES LEFEBVRE

THE FRENCH REVOLUTION

(*In two volumes*)

I. From Its Origins to 1793

II. From 1793 to 1799

NAPOLEON

(*In two volumes*)

I. From 18 Brumaire to Tilsit, 1799–1807

II. From Tilsit to Waterloo, 1807–1815

Napoleon

From Tilsit to Waterloo

1807–1815

BY

Georges Lefebvre

TRANSLATED FROM THE FRENCH
BY J. E. ANDERSON

COLUMBIA UNIVERSITY PRESS
NEW YORK

Published 1969 by Routledge & Kegan Paul Ltd, London

This book is a translation of the second three parts of *Napoléon,* by Georges Lefebvre, Volume XIV of the series 'Peuples et Civilisations,' published by Presses Universitaires de France. The original work was published in 1936 and this translation is based on the fifth (1965) edition.

ISBN 0-231-03313-3

Library of Congress Catalog Card Number: 74-79193

Printed in the United States of America

10 9 8 7

Contents

Introduction

AT THE TIME when Napoleon Bonaparte assumed control of France, Europe and the French Revolution had been at war for over seven years, and except for a brief interruption, this conflict was to last until 1815. The 18 Brumaire did not in itself mark the end of an epoch. It might be more logical to say that the period of peace which followed the Treaty of Amiens was the dividing point between two eras. True, when considering the internal history of France, one sees that the coup d'état of Brumaire opened the way for the restoration of personal power. In this respect, the contrast between the Napoleonic and Revolutionary periods is well defined, but their essential unity cannot be ignored. It was to the Revolution that Bonaparte owed his marvellous destiny. He was able to force himself upon republican France precisely because an internal necessity fated that country to dictatorship as long as the partisans of the Old Regime strove to re-establish the monarchy with the help of foreign powers.

In his methods of government, Bonaparte had more in common with the Committee of Public Safety than writers are generally willing to admit. It was because he respected the social legislation of the Constituent Assembly that he was able to remain the leader of France. His military victories assured that the work of the Constituent Assembly would endure and become permanently rooted in French society. More than that, his victories enabled French ideas to sweep over the Continent with a rapidity and an efficacy which neither propaganda nor spontaneous diffusion could have equalled. Had he not implanted the fundamental principles of the modern state and society in all the countries which he dominated, no trace would have ever been left of his smashing campaigns. In vain did he attempt to create a new legitimacy and a new aristocracy. His contemporaries always saw him as the soldier of the Revolution, and it was as such that he made his mark upon European civilization.

All this notwithstanding, from the moment that Bonaparte became master of France, he was elevated to a place in the very centre of universal history. And so, despite the fundamental unities linking his reign with the tragedy that was the Revolution, the traditional dividing point—his accession—has much to be said for it, and is the one used in this work.

It is hardly necessary to point out that this book is not a biography of Napoleon. As in the other volumes of this general history, an attempt has been made to cast light not only on the essential features of the collective life of the French people and those who were subjugated by the Emperor, but also on the operation of forces independent of his will and on the distinguishing characteristics of nations which escaped his domination. England and the United States maintained their liberal tradition; capitalism continued its progress; and the bourgeoisie, growing in strength, was well on its way to assuming complete political power. Religious life followed its course, and Napoleon was unable to modify it. Nations reacted against the universal empire whose foundations he was laying. Above all in Germany, Romanticism fostered new ways of feeling, thinking, and acting; and Latin America threw off the Spanish yoke. Even the Far East, in a negative way, experienced repercussions of the great conflict, for it would have been subjected to European assaults much earlier had not the Napoleonic Wars monopolized the energies of Europe. The nineteenth century, so shifting and varied in its character, was visible beneath the apparent uniformity which Napoleon's genius tried to impose. But during the course of this period, otherwise so brief, everything seemed to yield before him. It was he who dominated history. What then could be more natural than that this volume should bear his name.

I

THE IMPERIAL CONQUESTS AFTER TILSIT (1807–1812)

CHAPTER ONE

The Continental System (1807–1809)

ALTHOUGH ENGLAND contrived to put a good face on it, it seemed for some months that the treaty of Tilsit would bear fruit. The Continent submitted to Napoleon, and the blockade, reinforced by the decrees of Milan, appeared to close it to British commerce.

But the Continental System had scarcely come into being before it was jeopardized by the defection of the East, and more especially by the rising in Spain, which Napoleon had provoked, but was then unable to put down.

ENGLAND AWAKENS

When she heard about the interview at Tilsit, England realized that the Franco-Russian *entente* of 1801 had been restored and saw the danger confronting her. After losing Germany, she now risked having the Baltic closed to her once more. But thanks to Canning's prompt decision, she stole a march on her enemies. True, Gustavus IV seemed in a secure position: he had just resumed hostilities on July 3 and Cathcart had led 10,000 men into Pomerania. But Denmark was an uncertain quantity, and there was erroneous news that she was mobilizing her fleet; besides, Bernadotte could occupy her country from Hamburg in a very few days. Canning was hot-blooded, and had the temperament of a fighter: he did not lose a single moment. Though he knew of the interview of July 16, he did not begin to get the details—and then in very incomplete form—till the 21st; and he only learnt of the treaty's signature on August 8 through a French newspaper. On July 18 Admiral Gambier was ordered to proceed to Copenhagen with a huge squadron, and arrived there on August 3, whilst Cathcart, who had evacuated Pomerania and received reinforcements, was approaching with 30,000 men. The Prince Royal at Kiel was notified that he must enter into alliance with England and supply her with ships. When he refused, his capital was blockaded and then bombarded on September 2. He capitulated on the 7th. Canning then tried in vain to win over the Danes, attempted to induce the Swedes to occupy the archipelago, and in despair of success was even inclined to leave the English troops there, though his colleagues were in favour of evacuation. But the Danish fleet was taken in possession, and the following year Moore disembarked in Scania and Admiral Saumarez was able to move freely into the Baltic and escort the merchant shipping, which was the essential thing.

On the eve of the Berlin decree, the big export industries already constituted an element of prime importance in the English economy. It could not fail to be affected by any crisis involving these industries. They depended largely on European trade with the United States for their markets, and in certain cases for the provision of their raw materials; and they were therefore particularly vulnerable to the threat of blockade, especially if accompanied by a closing of the United States to English commerce. Nor must we forget the dependence of England on Northern Europe for her naval supplies and cereals, or the weaknesses of her banking system and her balance of payments. But there is no denying the power and elasticity of the British economy. The technical progress already achieved and her capitalist system gave her an assured superiority over France. England had undergone a veritable demographic revolution, in the course of which the population of Great Britain had risen from 10,943,000 in 1801 to 12,597,000 in 1811. This acted as a stimulus to the whole economy, and in particular supplied industry with a definitely expanding home market and an abundant and cheap supply of labour. English agriculture had become the best in Europe as far as technique was concerned; and although the agricultural revolution had upset the traditional rural society, it ensured that a rapidly expanding population need only depend on imports for a smaller portion of its foodstuffs. The oligarchy constituted by the great landowners who governed England were confident of their own destiny, and gave evidence of an almost unshakable will to win. The most powerful section of the middle classes—the London bankers and merchants and big businessmen—had long been firmly linked with the aristocracy, and were as doggedly opposed to France, seeing how she threatened their commercial and colonial interests. The industrialists, however, enjoyed a much lower social status in general, and their role in politics was as yet a very minor one. The workers were the people who had most to fear from the blockade, for it might well lead to unemployment and high prices, thus making their living conditions even worse—though they were already wretched enough in all conscience. But the social framework of the country, buttressed still further by the Combination Acts of 1799 and 1800, was, as has been emphasized, 'reassuringly strong'. Nothing less than an intense and prolonged crisis had any chance of setting the middle class against the oligarchy and driving the proletariat into revolt.

Far from allowing itself to be intimidated by the Berlin decree, the Tory government reinforced the mercantile character of the British blockade at the expense of the neutral countries. Persons of importance had long been insisting on measures against them under the Navigation Acts. The builders and shipowners were indignant that their flags covered 44 per cent of the ships that had come from British ports in 1807, instead of the 28 per cent which had been the figure for 1802. The trade of the United States was more prosperous than ever, their exports in 1807 rising to 108 million dollars, almost 60 million of which consisted of colonial goods, partly from the colonies of England's enemies. The planters in the Antilles were full of complaints about the fall in the price of sugar, but the Whigs had shown little readiness to listen to these grievances. On January 7, 1807, they did not do more than extend the 1756 regulations about coastal shipping between enemy ports that excluded English ships. As from February, Perceval proposed to compel neutrals trading with France to pass through a British port, a measure of retaliation that seemed to be demanded for the honour of the country. Once in power, Perceval proceeded to act. Although all trading with the enemy was again forbidden, it was made clear that there would be no change in the licence system, which allowed traders to infringe these regulations wherever the national interest required. They were solely aimed at the neutrals, and their purpose was 'to subordinate the trade of the whole world to the development of the navy and the shipping of Great Britain'. By Orders in Council on November 11, 15 and 25 and December 18, 1807, any neutral vessel sailing to or from an enemy port would be obliged to unload its cargo in one of a number of specially designated British ports, and be subject to customs duties—which were now notably increased—and would have to take out a licence. In addition, it was forbidden to import certain articles, such as quinine and cotton, into France. In theory at any rate, neutrals were still allowed to transport direct to their own countries goods from enemy colonies and even to export grain and raw materials from their place of origin to ports under Napoleon's control. With these exceptions, it looked as though maritime trade would become a British monopoly. In taxing neutral cargoes, the English reckoned to prevent them from carrying the produce of foreign colonies whose competition reduced the profits of the British colonists; and by refusing licences they could, if need be, bring neutral shipping to a standstill. This was precisely what the shipowners and the planters would have liked to happen.

The English were delighted at Canning's exploit and at all these measures. They did not question the burdens which the government, foreseeing that England was likely to be isolated, imposed upon the country in order to enable it to face its enemies single-handed. Taxes were increased, and Castlereagh set about strengthening the army, which had been somewhat neglected by the Whigs. On April 13, 1806, Windham had thrown out Pitt's Bill, suspended the militia ballot system, and given up the recruitment of regulars from among the militia, to return to the system of ordinary enlistment. He had shown his dislike for the reliance upon volunteers. Life service had been abolished, and replaced by service contracts of from seven to twelve years. Castlereagh re-established the militia ballot and encouraged volunteers, but transformed them into a local militia under government control. He returned to Pitt's system for recruiting regiments of the line, and drew 21,000 regulars from the militia. In 1807 and 1808 it procured 45,000 recruits, at a time when the army only lost 15,000 men. At the beginning of 1809 there were 200,000 soldiers on foot in Great Britain, 30,000 being held in readiness for expeditions on the Continent. It was thus possible to resume Pitt's policy with more ample means, though the cost was heavy. By 1807 the yield of direct taxation had risen from £3 million in 1804, and £6 million in 1806, to £10 million. Expenditure rose from £76 million in 1804 and £106 million in 1806 to more than £120 million in 1808. The burden was all the heavier because exports went down markedly in 1807 and 1808, though bread remained cheap. Yet England kept a stout heart as she watched the Continent rallying to Napoleon, for she was persuaded that his success would be short lived.

EUROPE CLOSED TO ENGLAND (1807–1808)

Napoleon had come back to Paris on July 27, 1807. He was officially given the title of *Grand*, like Louis XIV after the Peace of Nimwegen, and on August 15 there were brilliant festivities in honour of *la Gloire* and *la Grande Armée*. It looked for a short while as if there would certainly be peace on the Continent, and a general peace would surely follow before long. Napoleon himself had remarked that 'the achievements of Tilsit will settle the destinies of the whole world'. And so these festivities were genuinely popular, and Napoleon once more became for a time the national leader. The creation of the kingdom of Westphalia was officially announced on August 18, and soon afterwards Jerome's marriage to Catherine of Wurtemberg was celebrated. Then in September and October Napoleon held court at Fontainebleau. As he had done after Austerlitz, he now resumed the work of administration, carrying out a purge among the judiciary in 1807, and organizing the university in 1808.

Particularly striking was his increasingly marked taste for a personal despotism and his preference for the aristocracy. On August 19, 1807, he abolished the *Tribunat*, and on the 9th he had in effect dismissed Talleyrand by decorating him with the title of *vice-Grand-Électeur*, reproaching him with his venality, and probably being unable to forgive his discreet disapproval. In October 1805 Talleyrand had presumed to advise a conciliatory line towards Austria, wishing to console her for the loss of Italy and Germany at the expense of Turkey. This policy has often since been praised, but was in fact chimerical, for Austria would have taken anything offered to her without for a moment forgetting her deeply-felt losses. At Warsaw, Talleyrand had shown contempt for the Poles, and after Friedland, he said—in complimenting the victor—that he was particularly delighted with this triumph because he was certain that it would be his last. Napoleon could no longer put up with a servant who showed such independence, and replaced him by Champagny, who was never more than a good clerk, though—most unfortunately, as it turned out—he continued constantly to consult his ex-minister. At the same time he continued to organize the new aristocracy, distributing 11 million in *rentes* to the military chiefs, re-establishing entails, and constituting finally in 1808 a fully-fledged imperial nobility.

At the same time he began to adopt a sharper attitude towards foreigners. In October 1807 there was scene after scene at Fontainebleau as he stormed at the envoys of Etruria, Bremen, and Portugal: 'If Portugal does not do what I want, the House of Braganza will no longer be on the throne in two months' time'. There was no need for these threats, for his plans were already drawn up; but he was showing himself less and less capable of self-control. 'Napoleon has not only ceased to recognize any limits,' wrote Metternich, 'he has completely thrown off the mask.' 'Now that he has made an agreement with Russia,' Champagny admitted, 'he is no longer afraid of anyone.' The world had now become his keyboard, and he could play whatever tune fancy brought into his head.

To begin with, the alliance lived up to expectations. True, Alexander was in no hurry to break with England, and allowed Budberg to receive Wilson, an amateur diplomat who came in as an intermediary. Canning did not positively turn down the possibility of mediation, reckoning that the Czar had only entered into alliance with France to get himself out of an awkward position. In fact, Alexander wanted to seek shelter for Siniavine's squadron which had remained in the Mediterranean, and was afraid of exposing Kronstadt to a sudden attack. The bombardment of Copenhagen cut the knot: Budberg was replaced by Rumiantsov and on October 31 Russia declared war. Prussia was forced to follow her example on December 1, while privately making excuses and getting her ambassador Jacobi to agree with Canning to maintain communications through Francis d'Ivernois. As far as Austria was concerned, Napoleon did just condescend to express his satisfaction at her behaviour during the recent war, but he no longer offered her an alliance, and on October 16 put her under an obligation to range herself against England. Starhemberg in London and Merfeldt in St. Petersburg protested in vain. The swift *dénouement* of Tilsit had terrified the authorities in Vienna, and there were suspicions of a projected partitioning of Turkey in which they wanted to have a share. In Paris, Metternich expressed agreement with Stadion and sketched out the line of action he was to follow later on when Chancellor. The only possible course was to wait for 'the great day when Europe will be able to put an end to a state of affairs that is essentially precarious, because it is contrary to nature and to civilization'. On January 1, 1808, Starhemberg, acting under peremptory orders, was forced to hand Canning a note that was badly received, and Austria followed suit in declaring war, though privately expressing her regrets. Denmark had signed an alliance with France on October 30, but Sweden proved obstinate till Stralsund and Rügen fell. On January 16, 1808, Alexander sent her an ultimatum and on February 21 invaded Finland, whilst Denmark also opened hostilities.

Meanwhile, Napoleon had gone to Milan and Venice on November 16 in order to arrange his Italian affairs. He was displeased with the behaviour of the Queen of Etruria, who had been regent since Louis I's death in 1803. She, like her husband, had shown entire submission to the Church, to which she had given complete liberty, declaring the property of the clergy inalienable, and handing over the censorship to the bishops. In addition she had turned a blind eye to the English dealings in contraband. By an agreement with Spain she was dethroned, and given the northern part of Portugal. Napoleon joined Tuscany to the Empire and on May 24, 1808, turned it into a Grand Duchy, as a *gouvernement général*, for the benefit of Elisa. At the same time he annexed Parma and Piacenza. With Eugène as his intermediary, he tried in vain to force the Pope to submit. In November 1807 he occupied the marches and on April 2, 1808, joined them to the Kingdom of Italy. Miollis had entered Rome on February 2. As Turkey was still friendly and Junot had taken Lisbon on November 30, 1807, the Continental federation seemed on the point of complete success.

As it progressed, the blockade became more and more of a real threat. Up to the end of the war, the Berlin decree had scarcely modified its range in any way. There had previously been confiscation of English merchandise in Germany and in the Hanseatic cities, but when he was short of money Napoleon would give it back for an appropriate payment and it would return to circulation, so that the act of seizure became a kind of fiscal expedient. As the troops advanced in Poland contraband dealings had grown up, and Holstein—and in particular the port of Tönning—provided English depots instead of Hamburg. It soon became known that a little money would procure the connivance of a good many French officers, consuls, and even customs officials since Bourrienne and Brune had set a bad example in Hamburg. Moreover, French businessmen were alarmed to see the blockade turning into a weapon of war to the extent of closing Germany, Poland, and Russia to trade and provoking a severe industrial crisis. In order to be able to import and export at their convenience, they would have liked to go on leaving neutral shipping completely free. The Berlin decree declared that they would no longer be received if they came directly from England or her colonies. But they could always claim that they had merely called in there, and as there was no threat of confiscation, they ran no risk in continuing to come to France as before. In that case, the Berlin decree would lose all meaning. Its ambiguous terms proved that Napoleon, when he made it, was still hesitating between the needs of national production and the requirements of war. The uncertainty continued for more than a year. In order to spare the Americans, he assured them that the blockade did not apply to the high seas, and as late as August 26, 1807, the Danes were dispensed from observing it. In July, he had considered whether there might not be a case for granting neutrals a licence to trade with French ports as previously, on condition that they re-exported an amount equivalent in value to their imports. This solution—which was to be taken up again in 1809—would once more have emphasized the mercantile character of the blockade.

Although the alliance of Tilsit had some effect, the course of events proved contrary. The plan was abandoned. The decree of Fontainebleau (October 13, 1807) and the first decree of Milan which renewed its terms on November 23, reinforced the Berlin decree. They declared that colonial goods and a number of products were to be considered by their nature English, unless they could show a certificate of origin, and in particular that any ships having touched in at England must be confiscated, together with the entire cargo. The Orders in Council, which had increased the subservience of the neutrals for the benefit of England, decided the Emperor to take this decisive step. The second decree of Milan (December 17, 1807) laid down that any neutral vessel submitting to the English requirements would be considered denationalized, and would be deemed British property. It would therefore be a lawful prize, not only in the ports, but also on the high seas. There was thus a reversion to the position in 1798. As the neutrals could not escape the English, the Empire became closed to them, and the blockade changed from a mercantile device to an instrument of war. Since the Continent rallied to the French cause, the blockade had a considerable effect. The troops had been sent back to Germany and the seizure of ships had been handed over to the customs officers who had a right to call for armed assistance when necessary. Austria moreover was closing the Adriatic.

Although the Baltic remained open, it could only be for contraband traffic, except in Sweden. English exports underwent a serious decline. Their customs value fell from £33·5 million in 1806 to £30·4 in 1808, and the declared value from £40·8 to £35·2. This success had a tonic effect on Napoleon's spirits. From this moment onwards his desire to perfect the blockade began to urge him to further annexations, until it finally became merged with the spirit of conquest in 1811.

Peace on the Continent being now assured, Napoleon was

thinking of resuming the war at sea. In Italy, he directed Joseph to prepare to attack Sicily, and told Ganteaume to leave Toulon and join this operation, after having replenished the food supplies of the Ionian Islands, which the French had seized together with Cattaro in August 1807. Reynier drove out the English from Reggio, but Ganteaume was only able to carry out the second part of his assignment. More and more orders went out to Decrès. Naval construction forged ahead on every hand, and on May 28, 1808, Napoleon calculated that he would soon be at the head of 77 French ships, 54 foreign ones and 300,000 men grouped at various places along the coast, from Texel to Tarento. 'It seems to me', he wrote, 'that this represents a chessboard which, without asking too much of fortune or too great skill from our sailors, ought to lead to great results.' But he did not have time enough to threaten England at sea or at home, for the Continental federation began to crumble before it had even received the finishing touches.

The first miscalculations came from the East. Napoleon's policy was bound to go wrong from the moment of his alliance with Russia, since Turkey and Persia had only made advances to him in order to keep in line with the latter. Mustafa IV having agreed to French mediation, Guilleminot arranged an armistice at Slobodzie on August 24, 1807; on October 21 Alexander rejected it on various pretexts, but in reality he wanted to keep the principalities and the Sultan thought that Napoleon was in agreement. For the present, however, war did not break out again in Europe, but fighting continued in Asia, where the Russians defeated the Pasha of Erzerum. The English used this to increase their influence in Constantinople to such good effect that Napoleon finally recalled Sebastiani in April 1808. Before long, new revolutions in Turkey completed the estrangement from France. The Bairakdar undertook to restore the Sultan Selim to power, but Mustafa IV just had time to put the latter to death before he himself was overthrown on July 28, 1808, in favour of his brother Mahmud II. In November the janissaries rose once again and massacred the Bairakdar. Mahmud, who had caused Mustafa to be strangled, was the last representative of the dynasty, and as such, his life was spared. On January 5, 1809, he made peace with England.

Events followed much the same course in Persia. Gardane

contrived an armistice, while Colonel Fabvier set about organizing an army. But here too Alexander refused to relinquish his conquests and was soon besieging Erivan. The Shah deserted France and Malcolm reappeared in Teheran. The Czar's attitude, moreover, showed that he intended to be left a free hand in the East, and this was a serious symptom, for Napoleon had already determined to allow nothing of the kind. All the same, there was worse to follow. He had taken it into his head to annex the Iberian Peninsula to the Grand Empire, and it proceeded to put up an unexpected resistance whose endless repercussions brought disaster to the achievement of Tilsit.

AFFAIRS IN PORTUGAL AND SPAIN (1807–1808)

Napoleon had been watching Portugal since the establishment of the Consulate. Almost all its trading was done with England, who had predominant business interests and large capital investments in it, especially in the vineyards. Portugal was one of the chief bases for contraband and an outpost for the British fleet and she could not break with London without being completely ruined, for more than a third of her income was from the customs, and her corn had to come to her by sea. In short, she was in effect an English colony—as British imperialism fully appreciated—who brought in a great deal and cost nothing. Even at Tilsit, Napoleon had decided to conquer her, and on July 29, as soon as he got back to Paris, he took steps to form an expeditionary corps at Bordeaux. Aranjo refused to stop the English ships and confiscate their goods; the most he would do was to close his ports and declare war, reckoning no doubt that he would only have to make a pretence of hostilities. But Canning refused to join in this farce, and the rupture took place. On October 12 Napoleon set Junot's forces in motion.

But to reach Portugal, it was necessary to cross Spain. So from the very beginning the schemes concerning this country had been dovetailed with Napoleon's Spanish policy. In 1805, Godoy had insinuated that he would gladly carve out a principality for himself in Portugal, and on May 24, 1806, he put his request into writing. But on each occasion war broke off negotiations, and he became so disillusioned that he turned against the French alliance. The loss of Buenos Aires on

June 27, 1806, seemed to be a prelude to the loss of the whole of South America, and roused strong feelings in Spain. It induced Godoy to offer to make peace with England, but the English required him to join the coalition, as the Russians and Prussians also advised. Godoy hesitated. If he did not enter into a tacit agreement with Prussia (as he has been accused of doing), he at any rate addressed a proclamation to Spaniards on October 5, 1808, announcing that they would arm. The statement was ambiguously worded, and Napoleon pretended to believe that it was a question of inviting his help; but it was certainly something he did not forget. After Jena, Godoy hastened to break with Russia, joined the blockade on February 19, 1807, and sent the Marquis de la Romana to Germany with 8,000 men, who reached Hamburg at the beginning of August. And now at last he was eager to join in the plan for a war against Portugal. By the treaty of Fontainebleau, October 27, 1807, this country was to be divided into three parts: the north for the Queen of Etruria, the south for Godoy, the centre—with Lisbon—being reserved by Napoleon, either because he wanted to hold this port until the peace, or because it formed part of his Spanish schemes.

Spain appeared to Napoleon to be badly governed, and did not provide him with all he considered she should be able to supply. For a long time he had thought Spain needed 'regeneration'—an opinion widely held in his entourage where, with Murat in the fore, there was no lack of candidates for this task, who hoped to find Spain a land even more richly 'flowing with milk and honey' than Portugal. Talleyrand, for his part, was strongly in favour of extreme measures. There was however no urgency about acquiring Spain, since it was already part of the Continental System; and there can be little doubt that it was because of his recent triumphs that Napoleon felt impelled to action in order to stimulate still further his urge for power. Nevertheless we can only conjecture how his mind worked, and it is only possible to suggest in a tentative manner the two solutions between which he seems to have hesitated.

It was in fact the divisions in the royal family that came to his assistance. Even as he was signing the treaty of Fontainebleau he already held in his hands the threads of an intrigue that gave a glimpse of one possible solution. The Prince of

Asturias was a persistent enemy of Godoy, for he suspected him of intending to usurp the crown on the death of Charles IV. His friends, the Duke del Infantado and Canon Escoïquiz, his former tutor, conceived the plan of marrying him to a French princess and so making certain of the Emperor's support. Napoleon's ambassador, who was a Beauharnais, probably saw the chance of advancing the family fortunes by putting forward a cousin of Josephine's as a suitor for the Spanish throne, and took it upon himself to get in touch with Escoïquiz. Champagny, learning of this possibility, and clearly acting on his master's orders, asked for a letter from Ferdinand, who produced it on October 11. As Napoleon's protégé, he could be used as a tool, and would perhaps have had to cede Spanish provinces as far as the Ebro in exchange for Lisbon. At all events, a scheme put forward by the Spanish agent Izquierdo on February 29, 1808, mentioned the possibility of this annexation.

Meanwhile, Junot was advancing by forced marches over appalling roads, in terrible weather. As usual, he had set out with no provisions or transport. Spain was expected to provide everything, but in fact provided very little, and the army soon began to straggle. Fortunately Portugal offered no resistance, and three Spanish columns joined in the invasion along the Douro, south of the Tagus and in the Algarve. On October 22 the regent made an agreement with the English authorizing them to occupy Madeira and arranging for the transport of the royal family to Brazil. The vast contents of the British depots were shipped to safety; Siniavine's fleet, which had put in to Lisbon, was escorted to England; and on November 29 the Portuguese court sailed overseas. On the 30th Junot entered Lisbon. He imposed on the country an indemnity of 100 million francs, and despatched to France the remnants of the Portuguese army, some 8,000 to 9,000 men. The peculiarly risky situation occupied by Junot had given Napoleon an excuse for his progressive occupation of Spain. On October 12 he had ordered a new corps to be formed, and in November Dupont brought it along to occupy Old Castile. In January, it was followed by another under Moncey at Burgos, and eventually by a third, organized by Mouton.

At this point a second solution of the Spanish question had become possible. At the end of October, Godoy had discovered and denounced Ferdinand's intrigue, and had put him in prison. The prince complained to Napoleon, who swore vociferously and barefacedly denied all complicity. Charles IV and Godoy were appalled, and hastened to withdraw. They released Ferdinand, his friends being acquitted and sent into exile; but from that point onwards the Emperor seems to have admitted that the heir presumptive might be declared incapable of coming to the throne. On December 2 he spoke to Joseph at Venice, and though he asked Lucien to send his daughter Charlotte to Paris, there is nothing to prove that it was to marry her to Ferdinand. On January 12 he ordered some leaflets to be drawn up on the subject of the Escurial plot and the indignity suffered by Ferdinand, but they were never distributed. Meanwhile the French troops were steadily advancing. In February they seized Pampeluna and San Sebastian. Duhesme was now bringing up a corps from the eastern Pyrenees to enter Catalonia and take possession of Barcelona and Figuères. At the beginning of March Bessières came and took command at Burgos, and Murat, now put in command of the army of Spain, proceeded to march upon Madrid, which he entered on the 23rd.

It would seem that in March Napoleon was again inclining towards the first solution. But once more events in Spain cut short the debate. Godoy was uneasy, and had recalled to Andalusia the corps operating in Portugal south of the Tagus. There was widespread alarm at the progress of the French armies, and it was suggested that the king's favourite meant to escape to Cadiz with the royal family and there embark with them to America. In the night of March 17, 1808, an insurrection broke out at Aranjuez. The troops deserted; Godoy was thrown into prison; and on the 19th the king abdicated. Napoleon learnt of the rising on the 26th and decided at once to leave for Bayonne. On the 27th he heard that Charles IV had abdicated, and he mentally saw the throne as good as vacant. That same day he offered it to Louis, which is the first positive indication we have about his views. He left Paris on April 2 and reached Bayonne by the 15th.

Charles IV, however, had complained to Murat of the violence done to him, and Napoleon had invited him to come and see him. He also gave directions that Ferdinand should be sent to him, and the latter did not dare resist. On May 2 Madrid, stirred up by these departures, rose against the French. Murat suppressed the rebellion harshly, and Napoleon paid no heed to this ominous sign for the future. 'The Spaniards are just like the other nations,' he said, 'they will be only too pleased to accept the imperial constitutions.'

Charles IV claimed the throne for his son, and then on May 5 handed it over to the Emperor. The Prince of Asturias was thoroughly frightened, and capitulated; and the whole royal family were sent to Talleyrand's chateau at Valençay. When Louis and Jerome refused the offer of this crown, Napoleon conferred it authoritatively on Joseph, whilst the Kingdom of Naples went to Murat, who was thoroughly disappointed. He had passed on to the Emperor the desire expressed by some liberals for a constitution, but it seems that Napoleon showed no interest, being preoccupied particularly with administrative reforms; all the same, he complied with the request. A junta elected by three groups of electors sorted into three classes sat at Bayonne from June 15 to July 7—though only 91 members out of 150 had responded to the appeal. Spain was given a constitution like that of the vassal states, except that all attempts to secularize the state were abandoned. Roman Catholicism remained the only lawful faith, and the Inquisition was not abolished. In deference to the susceptibilities of public opinion, there was nothing to indicate that Spain was becoming a vassal state, and her financial contributions were not increased. On July 20, Joseph made his solemn entry into Madrid. But he only resided there for eleven days, for his kingdom was already in revolt.

THE SPANISH INSURRECTION (1808)

Certain elements of the Neapolitan insurrection crop up again in the affairs of Spain. Yet the subjects of Charles IV had a more dynamic loyalty to the dynasty, and although the particularist spirit had a different kind of strength from its counterpart in France, there was no lack of a strong national spirit as well. Among the common people, however, there was as yet nothing to distinguish it from hatred of the foreigner and religious fanaticism, which had such strong roots in the struggle against the Moors. This spirit was encouraged by the physical nature of the country and by the backwardness of its economy, and was deliberately fostered by the clergy who had prevented the minds of Spaniards from making contact with European thought. Hatred of foreigners was at this time particularly directed against the heretical English and against the French—so long enemies and now oppressive allies—denounced ever since 1789 as instruments of the devil. But in order to provide a popular incentive to insurrection, foreigners must be sufficiently numerous to be an obvious menace to everyone; and it is clearly in this sense that the French invasion proved decisive. Yet the revolt began more especially in the provinces untouched by French influence—Asturias, Galicia, and Andalusia. There was thus a need to explain to the people what was happening elsewhere, and call them to arms; and this was done, not by the authorities, who generally adopted a submissive or hesitant attitude, but by the nobles and the clergy.

The nobles displayed a more refined and passionate national sentiment than the common people. As a class, they were cut off from power, and despised Godoy as a mannerless parvenu. They were therefore only too delighted to seize the chance of resuming authority. Distrustful of any reforms the French might suggest, some of them dreamt of a monarchy after the English pattern, while others had no intention of renouncing their social supremacy. If the middle classes had been powerful and imbued with the new ideas, the movement might perhaps have been opposed, for except in Cadiz it had little strength and was ill informed. Apart from the maritime provinces and Catalonia, where the economic and social structure was democratic, Spain remained a country of large properties where the great ones had only to lift a finger in order to call out the peasants who were in bondage to them. Moreover, the Spanish ascribed all their country's misfortunes to Godoy. This was the reason for Ferdinand's brief moment of popularity, and if only Napoleon had used him as a screen in order to get rid of the favourite, he would have met with little resistance. But when it was possible to represent the invader as in league with the hated minister, it was not difficult to carry the common folk in the towns along with the peasants. It is only surprising that the revolt should have been directed in the first place against the representatives of the central power, several of whom were massacred.

In Napoleon's eyes, the clergy was responsible for playing a leading part in the uprising—'an insurrection of monks', he called it. This verdict has been disputed because a certain number of bishops and priests figured among the junta at Bayonne, men like the Cardinal de Bourbon, Archbishop of Toledo. Yet a few exceptions among the higher clergy prove nothing: for there were 60,000 secular and 100,000 regular clergy in Spain, and it was they, in close touch with the people, and not their leaders, who instilled the spirit of revolt. As in la Vendée and elsewhere, preaching and the confessional served to produce a mood of overwrought fanaticism which showed itself in miracles; and it is not hard to understand the exasperation of the clergy at the thought of a secularized state and at Napoleon's rupture with the Pope. There are however certain indications that some at least of the leaders directed the propaganda and were not slow to work out a plan of organized resistance. Cardinal Desping y Dasseto, formerly Archbishop of Seville, wrote from Rome on June 30, 1808, to the Archbishop of Granada: 'You must be well aware that we cannot recognize as our king someone who is a freemason, a heretic, and a Lutheran, as are all the Bonapartes and all the French nation.' Foreseeing that he might be forced to leave the Holy City, he added: 'I shall try to come to Spain, so as to carry out our plan.' What was this plan? We can get some inkling of it when we see the same Archbishop of Granada, the Assistant Bishop of Seville and the Bishop of Santander taking a leading part in the insurrectionary juntas, and when we note that circulars were sent to the bishops with a request to distribute them as widely as possible. Some of them were intercepted, such as the following:

> Once they have mastered our country, they will introduce all kinds of strange cults and abolish the true one. . . . They will force you all to become soldiers in order to carry out their plan of conquering Europe and the whole world. . . . To arms, then! Go forward in the name of God, his Immaculate Mother, and Saint Joseph her blessed spouse, and you will certainly win the victory.

The insurrection did not break out at once: there was almost a month between the departure of Charles IV and the first rising. It began at Oviedo, where the Asturias Estates, urged on by the Marquis of Santa Cruz, declared war against Napoleon.

On June 6 the Seville junta did likewise. The movement then spread like a train of gunpowder. Often enough the risings were accompanied by murder and pillage. At Valencia, for example, Canon Calvo directed the massacre of 338 French subjects. Soon there were seventeen revolutionary juntas in existence, principally in the north-west, the south, and Aragon. These were completely inexperienced committees, consumed by personal rivalries, and jealous of their independence. The bands of men were without any military value, and in the provinces possessing militias—such as Asturias and Catalonia—there was nothing like unanimous response to the appeal or willingness to fight a regular war. But the insurrection was none the less formidable on two particular counts. First, because Spain, unlike Portugal, had an army of some importance, concentrated more especially in Galicia and Andalusia, so that these two provinces naturally took the lead. The Galician junta assumed command over its counterparts in the Asturias, and more still in Leon and Old Castille; the Seville junta claimed central power as 'the supreme junta of Spain and the Indies' and as early as June 15 laid hands upon the French fleet in Cadiz. In the second place, Canning avoided the mistake made by Pitt in la Vendée. By May 30 the Asturian representatives were in London, and by June 12 he had promised them help. True, he gave a less warm welcome to the other juntas who immediately flocked to see him, because he was mistrustful of their sectional interests and wanted to unite them into one single authority. He knew that the Spanish would not welcome an English army, but, having a free hand in Portugal, and knowing that Junot was cut off from France by the insurrection, he decided to make the most of these advantages. An expedition was sent to Spain, and there was nothing to stop them in the last resort from marching on Madrid. It was then that the command of the seas secured by the English victory at Trafalgar showed its full worth. England accordingly decided to take advantage of it and carry the struggle on to the Continent, where it would eventually have to be decided.

On June 1, 1808, the French army numbered 117,000 men, and it took in a further 44,000 up till August 14. This was too small a force for the conquest of Spain. Besides, it was far from being the equal of the Grande Armée, which had remained in

Germany, seeing that it had been improvised with the help of 'temporary regiments', conscripts, together with miscellaneous elements such as seamen, Paris National Guards, and more especially foreigners—Hanoverians and other Germans, Swiss, Italians, and Poles, who for the first time constituted an important part of the effective strength. The command was also distinctly second-rate, and material preparations—as always—more or less non-existent, and that in a country incapable of providing the resources usually presumed to be available on the spot. The geographical conditions, moreover, were once again unfavourable to Napoleon's methods. Nevertheless, this army was conveniently massed and had nothing to fear in set battle. It was the Emperor who brought disaster upon it by despising the rebels and so dispersing it in order to occupy all the provinces at the same time.

In the north-west, the French took possession of Santander, Valladolid, and Bilbao. The Galician army, commanded by Blake, 30,000 strong, advanced against them, but was routed by Bessières on July 14 at Medina del Rio Seco. In Aragon, Palafox, who was famous as a leader but in fact very second-rate, was hurled back beyond Tudela, and Verdier besieged Saragossa, carrying part of it by assault at the beginning of August. But in Catalonia Duhesme had to raise the siege of Gerona and found himself hemmed into Barcelona, whilst Moncey, reaching Valencia without any siege equipment, had to retire towards the Tagus. The war at once assumed a fearful character, the Spanish torturing or massacring their prisoners; the French, wild with rage and hunger, burning the villages by way of reprisal and putting the inhabitants to the sword. But these were minor difficulties compared with the terrible reverses which began to show up the hazards of the whole adventure.

Dupont had been told to move to Toledo, and on the Emperor's order left it on May 24 with a single division to go and occupy Cadiz. Arriving in Andalusia, he forced the passage of the Guadalquivir at Alcolea on June 7 and took Cordova, which was plundered and sacked. He soon found out, however, that Castaños had 30,000 regulars lined up against him, reinforced by at least 10,000 insurgents, so he withdrew on the 19th to Andujar to wait for reinforcements. Vedel's division debouched from the Despeña-Perros pass and covered it by taking up a position at Baylen, and then—after being replaced by Gobert's division—joined up with Dupont. Andujar—some seventeen miles from Baylen—was a bad defensive position, and there was a risk of Dupont's being attacked and surrounded; but his only thought was to resume the offensive. He probably despised his adversary, and was longing to bring off a great success that would earn him the marshal's baton he had deserved at Friedland, but which had gone instead to Victor.

Castaños carried out a clever manœuvre. He pinned down Dupont by a feigned attack and despatched Reding against Mengibar. Gobert was killed, and his division fell back towards the pass. Nevertheless Reding, considering his position too risky, recrossed the river and Vedel, leaving Dupont, came and reoccupied Baylen on July 17. So far nothing had proved disastrous; but then Vedel also fell back upon the pass, and Dupont, who was to have followed him closely, delayed his departure till the evening of the 18th. Reding and Coupigny were able to re-enter Baylen with 18,000 men, so that when Dupont attempted to force the passage with not many more than 9,000 soldiers on the morning of the 19th, he was unsuccessful and being wounded, began to sue for terms. Meanwhile Vedel, who had retraced his steps at the sound of gunfire, was on the point of taking the enemy in the rear; but his commander-in-chief having once given his word, refused to renew the fight, and ordered Vedel to cease fire. On the 22nd Dupont signed an agreement which included Vedel, who was weak enough to come and surrender his forces, though he had in fact managed to withdraw them. There was no question of capitulation: the Andalusian army was to be repatriated by sea, and Dupont's decision was in itself no more blameworthy than the one taken by Junot shortly afterwards, without ever incurring any reproaches from Napoleon. But the Seville junta refused to recognize the agreement, and the unfortunate prisoners were interned in the small island of Cabrera, where they were deliberately allowed to die of hunger. The Emperor dealt very hardly with their commander. He overwhelmed him with insults, as he did Villeneuve, cashiered him, and kept him in prison till 1814. Attempts have sometimes been made to minimize Dupont's responsibility to an excessive degree. Undoubtedly, he made mistakes; yet it remains true that the disaster was primarily due to Napoleon's rashness. The hard treatment meted out to the defeated general would be bound to call forth sympathy if he had pleaded his cause with dignity, instead of seeking revenge by violently espousing the cause of the Bourbons in 1814.

Meanwhile, Junot was confronted with a rising of the Portuguese, who followed their neighbour's example. The Spanish division at Porto rallied the forces of Galicia, and the French were obliged to concentrate in the neighbourhood of Lisbon. Nevertheless, they retained Almeida and Elvas, and the guerilla bands proved no match for them. And then suddenly, on August 1, Wellesley, the brother of the marquis and the future Lord Wellington, landed at the mouth of the Mondego with more than 13,000 men, who were then joined by 7,000 Portuguese. As Delaborde had not succeeded in stopping him at Roliça, Junot decided to attack at Vimeiro on August 21 with no more than 9,500 men. He too was unsuccessful, and on August 30 he signed the Convention of Cintra with Sir Hew Dalrymple, who had just taken command of the allied army. It was agreed that the French army in Portugal—more than 25,000 men—should be transported back to France, together with the Portuguese who had become involved on its side. This arrangement has been defended from the English point of view, for it surrendered Lisbon without a blow and opened the way for a march on Madrid; but it was severely criticized at the time, for Junot's corps returned and took part in the 1808 campaign.

The Cintra affair made less commotion than Baylen because it was said that the victory in the former case had been won by a regular army. On the other hand, the disaster to Dupont caused a sensation in Europe. It was seen as proof that the French were not invincible, and came as an encouragement to all their enemies. Forgetting that the victors had also been regular troops, people celebrated the event as a triumph for the popular movement of insurrection. On June 15 Sheridan, speaking in the name of the Whigs who had long been supporters of the French Revolution, greeted the Spanish revolt as a movement inspired by the genuine principles of the French Revolution, principles which they had later violated in order to give themselves over to oppression, but which they now saw being used against themselves. But the aristocracy of Europe was not fooled: no doubt, the Spanish insurrection was popular, and as such even filled the nobles with a secret distrust; but it had in fact been instigated and managed by them and the clergy, and was actually defending the Old Regime along with the nation, showing how the ruling classes can use popular patriotism to further their own private interests. Since they had not so far succeeded in achieving victory for their own cause, the aristocrats of every country took good care not to point out the ambiguity, but were delighted to welcome this heaven-sent help.

Napoleon felt the shock, and to make good the damage and re-establish his own prestige, he decided to take the Grande Armée to Spain. But from now onwards, who would there be to hold back Prussia and Austria? Under the arrangements made at Tilsit, the task fell upon the Czar; and this was going to be his testing-time.

THE BEGINNINGS OF THE FRANCO-RUSSIAN ALLIANCE AND THE INTERVIEW AT ERFURT (1808)

When he returned to St. Petersburg, Alexander had found the aristocracy solidly opposed to the French alliance. Savary had been appointed ambassador, and the part he had played in the affair of the Duke of Enghien was used as a pretext to bar all doors against him. The nobility did not wish to rub shoulders with the Revolution, and were afraid of the blockade, which well might leave them with corn and timber on their hands. Caulaincourt, who succeeded Savary in December, mollified them somewhat by his luxury, but did nothing to disarm their suspicions. The Russian ambassadors were of the same opinion. In Vienna, Razumovski was entirely Austrian in sympathy; Alopeus had been altogether on the Prussian side in Berlin, and was all for England in London. Count Tolstoi, who had been sent to Paris, was among the sworn enemies of France, and set about organizing treason and espionage. He joined forces with Metternich, finding his worldly connections and love-affairs with Pauline and the Duchess of Abrantes highly useful as sources of secret information. But Alexander appeared to be quite unmoved. He was affable to Savary and more than affable to Caulaincourt; his internal policy became liberal once again—in speech, at any rate—as though French influence were bringing him back to the plans he had announced in former years. Since 1805, the 'committee of friends' had dispersed, but Spéranski was clearly gaining influence with the Czar and putting one plan after another before him. Nevertheless, if he seemed well disposed towards the French alliance, it was only because he hoped to reap advantages from it. In Paris, Tolstoi was relentlessly demanding the evacuation of Russia in order to deprive France of a military base against his country. Rumiantsov at St. Petersburg, though he was well disposed to Napoleon, was none the less insistent on retaining the Principalities. Not without some regret did Alexander feel himself to be in the same shoes as Prussia, and wished that he had not weakened his position in the East by giving up the Adriatic. He let his agents go their own way, each one pursuing his particular personal policy.

The evacuation of Prussia had been fixed in principle for October 1, 1808, and on July 22 Napoleon, being in need of money, commissioned Daru to arrange for the payment of the indemnity as soon as possible. First of all a reckoning had to be made of the sums paid by the different provinces, as well as of the requisitions. It was agreed to deduct 44 million and pay a balance in cash of 154 million. In actual fact, the Prussians had provided for more—50 million was their claim. But Napoleon would only take into account the regular requisitions carried out through the stewards and refused to allow the king to count the mortgage credits he had arranged for him in Poland, some 4 million *Taler* or more. How was Prussia to manage payment? Her budget showed a deficit; her paper money had lost 20 per cent in value and was left to take its course, being no longer exchangeable except at a market rate; and Niebuhr had negotiated an unsuccessful loan in Holland. The simplest course seemed to sell the royal lands in the territories left to Frederick William, which were said to bring in about 3⅓ million *Taler*. In spite of Daru's objections, Napoleon appeared disposed to accept the property; but that would have amounted to creating a kind of French state within the kingdom of Prussia, which the king could not make up his mind to allow. When October 1 arrived, the Emperor declared that in the meanwhile he would continue to take the proceeds of taxation, and Daru gave notice on November 7 that Prussia would have to pay over 100 million as the first year's instalment. Then the affair proceeded to drag on because Russia was still occupying the Danube principalities, and Napoleon from this time onwards preferred to hold on to Prussia as a kind of security. Prince William, the king's brother, came to Paris in January 1808 to offer an alliance in return for a reduction in the indemnity and immediate evacuation of Prussia, and Alexander and Tolstoi hastened to give him their support. But their intervention was declined on the ground that they had not signed the convention of July 12, 1807, and were not in a position to take over Prussia's debts. In August 1808 the question still awaited a solution.

The Eastern question was thornier still. As Frederick's memory grew gradually blurred, Alexander became increasingly convinced that he had given far more than he had received in return; and since he had broken with England he thought he had a right to some compensation. After rejecting the armistice of Slobodzeia, he asked on November 18 to be allowed to keep the Principalities. But he little knew Napoleon if he imagined that this was how he viewed their alliance, more especially as the Emperor's case was legally speaking quite unassailable. According to the terms of Tilsit, the Czar was bound to evacuate the Principalities unconditionally; but it was a question of 'the old familiar tune'. Napoleon was not unwilling to let Alexander have what he wanted on a give-and-take basis; in that case, he would help himself to Silesia. But for Alexander a fresh dismemberment of Prussia was out of the question, and he felt thoroughly disappointed. The Emperor sensed the danger, and it was to gain time that he wrote him the famous letter of February 2, 1808, suggesting the possibility of dividing up the Ottoman Empire and sending an expedition to India by way of Persia and Afghanistan. Alexander once again came under the spell of Tilsit, and from March 2 to March 12 Rumiantzov and Caulaincourt discussed the dismemberment of Turkey. Russia would advance as far as the Balkans; Austria would take Serbia and Bosnia, and France Egypt and Syria. But when they came to discuss Constantinople and the Straits, they could not agree. If Russia took the Bosphorus, Caulaincourt claimed the Dardanelles, to which Rumiantzov replied that that would be giving with one hand and taking away with the other. In the end, they sent all the papers to Napoleon, and on May 31 he proposed to the Czar that they should meet in order to settle the whole question. Alexander accepted, but the meeting had to wait till Napoleon came back from Bayonne.

Meanwhile the Russians, having occupied Finland, were not at all satisfied with the French attitude in that direction. Bernadotte, La Romana, and the Danes could easily have brought Sweden to heel by landing in Scania, yet they made no move. The Swedes resumed the offensive, repulsed their enemies, and reoccupied Gotland and the Aaland Islands. To crown all, Alopeus transmitted to Paris, on behalf of Canning, an offer to negotiate under the Czar's mediation on the basis of *uti possidetis*. Napoleon did not refuse, and this attempt, although it was not followed up, no doubt produced the effect Canning had intended: Alexander suspected his ally of possible desertion, and took offence.

Thus by July 1808 Napoleon had extracted from the alliance all the advantages he had counted on, and had given nothing in exchange, though he had not asked for anything beyond the terms of the treaty. But Napoleon now needed Alexander to restrain the German powers in the absence of the Grande Armée, and therefore grew more demanding. Almost overnight he granted what he had hitherto been obstinately refusing, and announced to the Czar that he was going to evacuate Prussia and leave him the Principalities. Alexander agreed to an interview at Erfurt on September 27, but he did not come to it as one seeking favours, for the Grande Armée could not depart for Spain without leaving Prussia. He was well aware that he was in a position where he could dictate his own terms. The concessions being now granted to him were ones he had already claimed as his due: they could neither dispel the bitterness of the past nor justify new obligations. Besides, the evacuation of Prussia came about in a manner quite different from what he had hoped for. Napoleon kept the taxes levied since October 1 and fixed a lump sum of 140 million. Needing liquid assets for his Spanish expedition, he accepted the bills drawn up by Prussian merchants and the *Pfandbriefe*, bonds secured on the royal lands and endorsed by the mortgage-banks of the different provinces, hoping to be able to discount both of them.

Though he recalled his army, he kept three fortresses on the Oder and subjected Prussia to new humiliations. She had to agree to limit her effective forces to 42,000 men and enter into an alliance against Austria. Champagny only succeeded in getting the agreement signed on September 8 by showing some intercepted letters indicating that Stein, who had become the head of the Prussian government, was preparing to attack France.

Napoleon was the first to arrive at Erfurt on September 27. He had brought all his court with him, and assembled all his vassals. Alexander was received with great magnificence, and there was a performance of *Talma* before 'an audience of kings'. His guest was perhaps less flattered than envious at seeing so much splendour; at all events, he did not allow himself to be dazzled. If we are to believe Metternich, Talleyrand boasted that he had put Alexander on his guard, suggesting to him that Russia had no interest in supporting Napoleon against Austria and in helping him to increase his power. Russia should, on the contrary, seek to restrain him, and this would pay France, as well as the rest of Europe: 'France is civilized, but her sovereign is not.' When the Emperor sounded his ally as to the possibility of a marriage with his sister, the Grand Duchess Anne, Talleyrand advised Alexander to steer clear of such a course. Moreover, he persuaded his friend Caulaincourt to represent himself to Alexander as a kind of mediator between the two sovereigns, which could only harm his own sovereign's cause. Talleyrand's perfidy is beyond doubt, and he was not long in reaping his reward, thanks to the good offices of Caulaincourt, in the shape of a marriage between his nephew and the Duchess of Dino, a daughter of the Duchess of Courland. But if he did actually use the language attributed to him by Metternich, he exaggerated her merits in order to raise her in Austrian esteem. Alexander, pressed by Caulaincourt to intervene with Vienna and persuade Stadion to suspend his rearmament, had already declared that he would restrict himself to giving advice. Napoleon was not only prepared to allow Alexander to annex the Principalities: he offered as a further concession to evacuate the Grand Duchy of Warsaw. But the Czar still refused to threaten Austria; in fact Metternich, acting on Talleyrand's information, became convinced that Russia was no longer capable of being turned against her.

Once again, we must not jump to the conclusion that Napoleon had allowed himself to be duped. Erfurt, like Tilsit, was only a means to an end. It was a matter of gaining enough time to crush the Spaniards and bring the Grande Armée back on to the Danube. He might reasonably believe that the agreement on October 12 would assure peace till the following summer, and that was all he asked. That same day the Grande Armée was brought back behind the Elbe and for the moment dissolved. Davout remained alone in Germany with two corps constituting the new Rhine army. On November 1 Prussia, whose debt had been reduced at the Czar's instance to 120 million, paid off 50 of this in the form of commercial bills payable at the rate of 4 million a month, and covered the rest by state bonds until such time as those of the mortgage banks should be issued. In accordance with the recent Franco-Russian agreement, Rumiantzov went to Paris to try and renew the discussion with England. This effort was bound to fail. Canning could not possibly admit that on the basis of *uti possidetis* Portugal and Spain should belong to Napoleon. It would at least be necessary for him to have conquered them!

NAPOLEON IN SPAIN (NOVEMBER 1808–JANUARY 1809)

In spite of his brother's orders to hold on firmly to Burgos and Tudela, Joseph had fallen back behind the Ebro. Moreover he had scattered the 65,000 men he possessed (apart from those in Catalonia) from the Bay of Biscay to Aragon. It had not taken him long to see himself as another Charles V or Philip II. He signed himself 'I, the King', and refused to award Bessières the Order of the Golden Fleece. 'He considers himself every inch a king,' said Napoleon when he came to see him. When Jourdan had been sent to assist him on August 22, he began to work out strategic schemes. 'The army', Napoleon wrote to him, 'looks as though it was being run by post-office inspectors.'

But the Spaniards failed to take advantage of these favourable circumstances. They did not reach Madrid from Valencia till August 13, and Castaños not till the 23rd, and then only with a single division. This was because the juntas, who were thoroughly ineffective and commanded little obedience, were primarily interested in their own provinces and wrangled among themselves. Galicia watched Asturias reasserting its independence and Cuesta, the general in command of Old Castile, defying their authority. In Seville, Count de Tilly proposed that the army should not leave Andalusia, and others that the junta of Granada should be forcibly subjugated. Pretenders to the regency were plentiful. From Sicily there came a son of Ferdinand IV, accompanied by the Duke of Orleans, who had made it up with the legitimate princes; but the English refused to let him land. At the suggestion of the junta of Murcia, whose leading spirit was Florida Blanca, a central junta was in the end set up, composed of thirty-five delegates from the provincial juntas, mostly nobles and priests. They met at Aranjuez on September 25 but were soon lost in discussions about protocol or constitutional matters. A majority gathered round Jovellanos showed sympathy for the English system, whilst Florida Blanca remained faithful to an enlightened despotism. A ministry was formed, but in order not to offend the generals, no commander-in-chief was appointed, and as they were only a ministry of war whose hands were tied by a council, they did very much what they pleased. Recruiting was not given much attention, and the regions directly administered by the central junta, Leon and Old Castile, raised the smallest number of men —less than 12,000 by October. England had sent 120,000 rifles, cargoes of equipment and five million in coin; but a large part of these supplies were left unused in the ports. In Lisbon, Dalrymple had re-established the regency nominated by Prince John, but it was almost completely inactive. The regular troops were recalled to the colours; yet out of 32,000, only 13,000 had rifles by the end of November and none of them saw fighting before 1809. The *ordinanza* (general levée) was only armed with pikes and did not do anything but spread disorder. The only organized force was the English army of 20,000 men commanded by Sir John Moore. But it only got under way in October, and it was not till the end of this month that Baird landed another body of 13,000 men at Corunna.

When Napoleon reached Vittoria on November 5 he found himself confronted by two chief Spanish forces spread out from the Bay of Biscay to Saragossa. These were the army of Galicia, under Blake, near the sources of the Ebro, and the army of the centre, under Castaños, towards Tudela. Between them,

Galuzzo was approaching from Estramadura and making for the Douro with some 12,000 men. Moore's army was advancing in two widely separated columns, and was only just reaching the frontier; Baird had scarcely got under way at all. Confronted with Napoleon's army of infinitely superior quality, the allies seemed doomed to disaster. All the same, the Emperor had to manœuvre with caution, since he only had 120,000 men at hand, Mortier's and Junot's corps being well in the rear. In the centre, Soult overthrew Galuzzo and took Burgos and Valladolid, from which points Napoleon counted on being able to sweep down on the two wings one after the other. But before he arrived Lefebvre and Victor had become prematurely engaged with Blake and had driven him back far enough to put him out of reach. Yet through failure to keep in touch with one another—owing to their mutual jealousy—they only partially checked him at Espinosa on November 10 and 11. Operations were therefore directed against Castaños, who was beaten by Lannes coming down the Ebro—at Tudela on the 29th, whilst Ney worked his way up the Douro in order to cut off his retreat. But these movements were badly synchronized, Ney being unable to arrive in time to fit in with Lannes' premature attack. Castaños' very experienced army succeeded in escaping towards Caenca by way of Catalayud. Napoleon marched on Madrid, and on the 30th, at the Somosierra pass, an enemy division, under fire from sharp-shooters and charged by a mere squadron of Polish light horse, fled in panic. The capital was occupied on December 4 and its approaches cleared. Lefebvre thrust Galazzo back beyond the Tagus and Victor routed the central army at Uclès. Taking up his quarters at Chamartin, on the outskirts of Madrid, Napoleon issued a whole series of decrees for the reorganization of Spain without consulting Joseph. He abolished the Inquisition, reduced the number of convents, and seized their property.

Meanwhile, however, Sir John Moore was completing his concentration north of Salamanca and joining up with La Romana, who had escaped from Denmark, come back to Asturias, and taken over command. Suddenly adopting a very bold policy, the English general was marching towards Soult, who was covering Burgos, in order to cut the French communications. Napoleon was late in getting information of this move, but despatched Ney's corps towards Salamanca and Astorga on December 20 through the snow-storms of the Sierra de Guadarrama to take him in the rear. On the 24th, Moore hurriedly began to retreat, and managed to escape because he was so feebly pursued by Soult. On January 3, 1809, at Astorga, Napoleon relinquished command. Soult gave battle at Lugo on the 7th, then at Corunna on the 15th and 16th, but not incisively enough to prevent the English from re-embarking. Lannes meanwhile had gone to join Moncey in front of Saragossa, which was heroically defended by Palafox. It took a whole month to break through the fortifications and another month to take the houses by assault. When the struggle came to an end in February 1809, 108,000 Spaniards had lost their lives, 48,000 of them from disease.

In a country where the distances, the winter, and the difficulty of communications all told against him, and where the inhabitants only gave information to his enemies, Napoleon was very far from having disposed of them. If only he had succeeded in destroying Sir John Moore's army, the English government would have had considerable difficulty in getting Parliamentary support for another one; and in any case it would have taken a long time to get a fresh force ready. Moore, being mortally wounded himself, had to blow up his magazines and sacrifice a great many men, but the bulk of the army escaped, and was soon to be back in Portugal. Nevertheless if Napoleon had been able to stay longer in Spain he would soon have reached Lisbon and Cadiz. But on January 17, 1809, he left Valladolid for Paris. It was now certain that Austria would attack in the spring.

So Spain still remained to be conquered, and Napoleon never ceased to feel the load of this task which he had so unnecessarily assumed in a spirit of pure display. After bringing about an English intervention it produced the same result in Austria and led to the rupture of the Franco-Russian alliance. From now onwards, Napoleon needed two armies. The proportion of recruits rose, and spoilt the army's cohesion. Not daring to ask France for an adequate number of conscripts, he fell back upon an increasing proportion of foreigners, and the quality of both armies began to suffer.

CHAPTER TWO

The War of 1809

THE WAR OF 1809 was the natural result of the rising in Spain. The departure of the Grande Armée awakened new hopes in Austria, and spurred her on to new adventures. The example of Spain roused the Germans to a state of romantic excitement which hastened the crisis. Napoleon was taken by surprise and was compelled to raise a new army that won its victories with difficulty. The victory of Wagram seemed for the moment to restore the Continental System; but the Franco-Russian alliance, proving unequal to this new attack on the Empire, stood inexorably condemned.

THE AWAKENING OF GERMANY

Since the early years of the century, German thought had been more and more given over to a romantic mysticism. Goethe, serene and impassive as ever, remained true to himself, although Schiller's death in 1805 had left him cruelly isolated. With the Jena and Berlin friends scattered, and Novalis dead, Heidelberg now became the centre where Grenzer, the expounder of mythologies, gathered round him the chief leaders of the second generation in the Romantic movement—men like Clemens Brentano, the son of a Rhineland merchant of Italian origin, Achim von Arnim, a Prussian junker, and Bettina, sister of the former and wife of the latter, together with La Motte-Fouqué, who was descended from French refugees. After teaching at Coblenz, Görres finally joined them, and they were in touch with Tieck, with the brothers Boisserée, who were trying to revive the study of medieval art in Cologne, and with Jacob and William Grimm, librarians at Cassel. The vogue of this school was of advantage to Schelling, who was increasingly absorbed in a mystical symbolism against which Fichte was having some difficulty in defending his reputation. Not till 1806 did Hegel approach the completion of his *Phenomenology of Mind.*

The Romantics were rapidly being impelled by a return to the past—and sometimes by their own interests—towards the traditional religions and the counter-revolution. Schleiermacher had taken up his duties as a pastor once again; Adam Müller and Frederick Schlegel became Catholics, in 1805 and 1808 respectively. There was general praise of the good old days—which they painted in quite imaginary colours—when the people lived happy lives under the fatherly authority of the aristocracy. Even Fichte, whom they despised for his intellectualism, and who had broken off relations with them, did not escape their influence. As early as 1804, in the third edition of the *Doctrine de la Science*, he brought back, above the level of the ego, an absolute demanding effort, and withdrew the unconditional autonomy of the self. In his *Traits essentiels de l'époque présente*, he distinguished certain periods in human history which he called, in sermon-like fashion, the 'age of innocence', 'the beginning of sin' and 'the age of total sinfulness'—this last characterizing man's present condition, given over to an unrestrained individualism from which it was necessary to rescue him in order to secure his 'salvation'. True, he was still a democrat and a republican; but having studied Machiavelli, he was temperamentally inclined to admire the heroic and conquering state and turn away in distaste from the merely utilitarian ideals of the *Aufklärung*. With an increasingly pessimistic and authoritarian outlook, he was more and more looking to the State to compel men—who were decidedly evil by nature—to conform to Reason and to the *Doctrine de la Science*.

In itself, German Romanticism as defined by Augustus Schlegel in his Berlin lectures from 1801 to 1804, gave a powerful stimulus to a cultural patriotism. He denounced classical art as the apotheosis of the artificial, whilst Romanticism, the natural expression of the Germanic genius, was entirely spontaneous; from which he drew the conclusion that German civilization led the world. But the Heidelberg Romantics, making a concrete study of their country's past literary history, exercised a far more rapid influence. Poets as they were, they cared little for strict method, but applied themselves to an enthusiastic and inquisitive examination of legends and popular tales which they translated and adapted. Tieck had led the way in 1803; and in 1805 and 1808, Brentano and Arnim published their famous collection, *Des Knabes Wunderhorn*. Görres followed in their footsteps, and in 1807 collected a certain number of tales taken from the *Teutschen Volksbücher*. The *Minnesinger* was rescued from oblivion, the *Niebelungenlied* was translated, and *Sigard* was discovered by La Motte-Fouqué. It was in this sense that Stein could write: 'It was Heidelberg that chiefly kindled the German flame which later swept the French out of our country.'

At this deeper level, national feeling thus remained cultural rather than political; but there was more than one latent sign of a hidden development at work. The re-establishment of despotism in France filled the liberals with irritation and despair. Posselt committed suicide not long after Moreau's condemnation; Schlabrendorf and Reichardt began to write against Napoleon, and Beethoven removed the name of Bonaparte from the score of the *Heroica* Symphony. All these men had a grudge against France for having, as they thought, disavowed the principles of 1789, and they declared the French nation to be vicious and frivolous. In 1804 Herder's cosmopolitan outlook was for the moment obscured by a fit of nationalism, causing him to dedicate an ode to 'Germania'. Nor were the Prussians alone in being stirred by the Austrian defeats and the disappearance of the Holy Roman Empire. In 1805 Arndt, in the first part of his *Geist der Zeit*, adopted a tone of undisguised hostility to France. The State, which had so far been distasteful to German thinkers as an organ of restraint, now began to take on a certain value in their eyes as a protector of the community and an educator of the individual. In 1802, in another of his books—*Germanien und Europa*—Arndt had declared that natural frontiers and access to the sea were necessary for the free development of a people; and as early as

1800, Fichte, describing a socialist society which would assure freedom and equality to all, thought this would only be possible in 'a closed State' that was self-supporting—a State to which he consequently gave the right to a sufficiently large and varied extent of territory to provide for all its needs. In 1805, he was also inclined to look to the State to rescue man from a condition of sin.

Nevertheless it needed the catastrophe of 1806 and the French occupation to precipitate and generalize this development. Not that this was any sudden or universal movement: after Jena, as well as before it, there were still admirers of Napoleon, like Buchholtz in Berlin. John de Müller became Jerome's minister; the University of Leipzig named a constellation after the victor; Goethe had an interview with him at the same time as the Erfurt conversations; Hegel, who had caught a glimpse of him at Jena, called him 'the soul of the world', and even in 1809, when he was professor at Nuremberg, he advised the Bavarians to adopt the Civil Code. None the less, it is clear that certain of the intellectual leaders in the German nation began to change their tone as from 1807, either in aggressive praise of the superiority of German culture, or in proclaiming their loyalty to local rulers; and there were certain symptoms to show that among the mass of the people, particularly in Prussia, apathy was being succeeded by irritation and hostility. Some of these manifestations are well known, such as Schleiermacher's sermons at Halle and Berlin, which ended by rousing distrust of the French authorities, or the publication by Arnim of *Einsiedler Zeitung* in 1808; and above all, the *Discours à la nation allemande* given by Fichte in Berlin in the year 1807. It was natural enough for Prussia's misfortunes to find a special echo in the outlook of men who were specially linked to it by birth or career. Simultaneously, however, Germans in the north, in Dresden and in Vienna, began implanting a romanticism and a national pride that were fast becoming inseparable. In the spring of 1806 Adam Müller, who was Prussian in origin, a convert to Catholicism and a friend of Gentz, who had successfully managed to find him a place in the Austrian administration, began a series of lectures on the principles that ensure the life and the continuity of States. Together with Kleist, he published in 1807 a revue entitled *Phoebus*, intended to 'foster

German art and science'; and in Vienna, Augustus Schlegel, after a long spell at Coppet as the tutor of Mme de Staël's son, followed her in her wanderings through Germany, and was authorized to begin a course in literature in which he took an even more incisive line than in Berlin. Soon Romanticism found a home in Caroline Pichler's salon, and a centre from which it could spread.

Everywhere these literary figures now began to enter into close relations with the champions of warlike action. Obliged as they were to tread delicately where foreigners were concerned and beware of governmental suspicions, they could not exactly summon their audience to take up arms, but had to go on stressing more particularly the original characteristics and the superiority of Germanic culture. Fichte more especially took up and developed Schlegel's theme—that each people shows its inner soul through an art that is its own particular and specific expression; but that of all nations, the Germans were privileged to possess a language which had developed by a continuous progress from its earliest beginnings, an *Ursprache*, which had never undergone any serious contamination. Thus its essential character and the forms expressing it constituted an harmonious whole. The Romance languages, on the other hand, were the mere debris of a dead language, and English nothing but a hybrid dialect, whilst the genres and the rules of classical French literature had been borrowed from antiquity. The Latin and Anglo-Saxon peoples, Fichte maintained, not having created their means of expression, therefore had to translate their thought by artificial methods which stifled its life and spontaneity; whereas German literature, being the only truly original one, was supreme in the spiritual realm, and its culture was a message from God to the human race. The pretensions of the Holy Roman Empire to universal dominion and more especially the oppression suffered by millions among the Baltic and Slavonic peoples were already making Germans look upon themselves as a master race; and Fichte's *Discours*, with the mystical justification of national pride which had intoxicated their spirits since the time of Luther, were to become part of the gospel of pan-Germanism. As far as the conception of the state was concerned, Adam Müller, though less emotional, was perhaps more novel in outlook. For Fichte still considered the

State as a fitting instrument for ensuring individual progress. Once the French were expelled, his nation would have the same right to bring about a democratic and republican revolution. Müller, on the other hand, as a true Romantic, regarded the State as a being in its own right, pursuing specific ends to which the individual destiny must be subordinated. Speaking to an aristocratic audience, he would defend both the independence of Germany and feudal society over against any new-fangled ideas.

Expressed by word of mouth these doctrines must, to start with, have exercised a fairly limited influence; and even in print, their spread can only have been gradual. Yet it is possible that they proved a stimulus to masonic lodges and secret societies, and so spread more rapidly than might have been expected at first sight. In any case their immediate importance has been exaggerated through a failure to take sufficient account of the economic and social consequences of the French conquest which imbued all classes with a direct hatred of the foreigner, without there being necessarily any assistance of an ideological kind. Among writers themselves, there was still the steady fear of seeing French supplant German once again as the language of literature and so reducing the field of professional activity. 'Who knows', wrote Kleist, 'whether in a hundred years' time there will still be anyone in the country who speaks German?'

Except in Eastern Prussia, the war damage had not been very great; but the contributions and requisitionings seemed a crushing load, and military occupation, with all its excesses, abuses, and manifold burdens—such as billeting, transport, and work on fortifications—was an even greater source of annoyance. In this respect, Napoleon's methods of warfare had unexpected repercussions from the moment when hostilities seemed in danger of lasting for ever, as in 1807. All the same, his financial policy and the political upheavals were probably even more important in their consequences. In the countries under his authority he levied war contributions just as he did in enemy countries, and neither Jerome nor Murat was spared. In order to put them in a position to provide troops he restored their finances by cutting down debt, suspending the payment of dividends and pensions, and dismissing a number of officials and officers without any compensation. Prussia, face to face with bankruptcy, had to do likewise, and at any rate in her case, with the army being reduced and so many provinces taken away from her, there seemed to be little prospect for the future. The wretched state of the people was partly the reason for the rising in Hesse in December 1806 and for the sporadic attacks on French troops in Pomerania and Prussia. But more widespread causes were to be found in the impoverishment of the nobles and the middle classes, the exasperation felt by officers and officials who had lost their posts, and the unrest among the youth of the universities who were seeking employment. All these sufferings and passionate feelings became focused in a national sentiment that seemed both to justify and to ennoble them. These then were the social elements most likely to provide leaders for resistance, and it was among them that the *Tugenbund*, for instance, came into being. Founded at Königsberg in April 1808, it had twenty-five *chambres* by 1809 and more than 700 members. Its authority was not confined to Prussia, for we know that Karl Müller made contact with the patriots in Leipzig. It was in fact a 'society for the promotion of civic virtues', and aimed at keeping a watch upon the agents of the state and its citizens, and at punishing any who should co-operate with the enemy. Despite the approval given to it by the king, his ministers looked upon it as a rival authority, and Stein deplored the reappearance of a 'Sainte Vehme'.

There is every reason to believe that this society was eventually destined to become the nucleus of a popular uprising against Napoleon. The idea of a mass insurrection had its roots in the ferment of Romanticism; in the literary idealization of the primitive German warrior under the command of Hermann in the middle of primeval forests, defying the Roman legions who were the instruments of despotism; and in the revolt of William Tell and the German Swiss, which Schiller's masterpiece had added to the national heritage in 1805. It drew sustenance too from the recent history of France, recalling on the one hand the example of La Vendée, and on the other the volunteers of the Committee of Public Safety. But it was the revolt in Spain that was principally responsible for raising excitement to fever pitch. From July 1808 onwards newspapers, pamphlets, and speeches vied with one another in its praise, with the tacit approval of the various governments. Its complex origins enabled it to win the approval of all parties: the aristocrats saw the Spaniards as faithful subjects, the democrats as free men rising up against their oppressors, and the statesmen as good citizens who had hastened to the assistance of the regular army.

Nevertheless, a mass uprising was inevitably associated with the ideas spread by the Revolution. In appealing to the people to take part in public life, it was also an inducement to claim in return for their military services to their country the civil and political rights that properly belonged to them. It seemed to be the symbol of the new power that would be acquired by the State if it abolished privilege and set free the energies of the individual man. It borrowed from Napoleon, the revolutionary leader, some of his own weapons and used them back against him. This was why in the end the aristocracy and the governments of the Old Regime refused to make an open appeal to the masses. And so in the history of the German national movement, Austria and Prussia would once again be found in opposing camps. From the very beginning, patriots turned to one or to the other, according to their origin, their career and their religion, but also according to their political leanings. Austria, with its Catholic tradition, stifled all intellectual life, and obscurantism stood in the way of any hopes of reform or popular movement. Prussia, on the other hand, had always prided herself on allowing a certain freedom of thought and had recently raised to power a certain number of men drawn from all parts of Germany who were open to Western influences and determined to modernize both government and society. Yet it was Austria that provided the Romantic ferment with its man of action in the person of Stadion, whilst in Prussia the leaders of the patriotic party were in the end disowned by the king. The eminently dramatic crisis of 1809 is thus a proof of the demoralizing effect of this dual and contradictory strain in the German outlook.

PRUSSIA

The old Prussia was led by a bureaucracy, and its army by the nobility. In any other country, the catastrophe of 1806, which was thought to be impossible in Prussia, might have produced a revolution. True, Napoleon would not have permitted it, for he knew the simplest way to exploit a conquered country was to preserve its traditional framework. Because they lacked a powerful middle class, the Prussians were unable to rebel. The reforming party was recruited from the higher bureaucracy itself, and had the assistance of a small number of nobles and cultivated bourgeois. But the unique feature was that these aristocrats, who were both conservative and liberal in outlook, were intelligent enough to realize the need for revitalizing the State, and had the necessary moral strength to impose their views. Although the creation of modern Prussia took a long time, extending right through the nineteenth century, these men did at least make a beginning.

Immediately after Tilsit, Frederick William III was reinstated in Königsberg. A commission was appointed to purge the army command under Scharnhorst and Gneisenau, who gradually enlisted the help of Grolman, Götzen, and Boyen. Another commission was appointed to carry out a special reorganization of Eastern Prussia in collaboration with Schrötter, its president; it included Schön, Niebuhr, and Altenstein. By July 10 Stein had been recalled on Napoleon's own advice—probably because he had been told of the good impression he had made on the French in passing through Berlin on his withdrawal to the Rhine Provinces after his dismissal. He reached Königsberg on September 30, armed with a scheme for reform drawn up by him in the course of the summer, the famous *Mémoire de Nassau*. A certain number of these reformers, such as Schön, Schrötter, Clausewitz, and Boyen, were Prussian-born, but the most famous of them came from other parts of Germany—men like Grolman, the son of a Westphalian magistrate; Cötzen, a Franconian count; Scharnhorst, a native of Hanover; Gneisenau, from Saxony; Stein, who belonged to the Rhineland *Ritterschaft*. Some of them were of humble origin. Scharnhorst's father was a non-commissioned officer and Gneisenau, though the son of an officer, had had a haphazard upbringing. Prussia, which was less set in its ways, and had been disorganized by the shocks of 1806, began to act as a focus for the national energies of Germany.

These men differed greatly in origin and in temperament, and it is not surprising that there is not complete agreement about the spirit that inspired them and their work. Some would see in them no more than men who carried on the traditions of enlightened despotism in Prussia; but their will to create a nation by associating the common people with their schemes of regeneration clearly shows that such a classification is far too narrow for them. It must not be forgotten that the *Junkers* were strongly opposed to them, and that the king himself was not at all in their favour. Others have seen them rather as the representatives of Germany's moral and religious culture, intent on linking up their reforms with the nation's past; but though they clearly betray the influence of philosophical idealism and romanticism, it is none the less true that some features of their schemes are more naturally explained by Western influences. No one, it is true, would deny the influence of England, which has already been discussed; nor can it be questioned that Stein had read Montesquieu and had probably known the physiocrats, as well as the projects of Turgot, and Dupont de Nemours. On the other hand, the influence of the Revolution is a debatable point. This at any rate must be conceded—that there were men in Prussia who were fairly familiar with it. Frey, director of police at Königsberg, who prepared the municipal regulations in 1808, had certainly studied the laws of the Constituent Assembly, and Rehdiger, the Silesian noble who submitted to Stein a scheme for a constitution, was well versed in Sieyes' writings. Gneisenau seems to have had the best grasp of the use that might be made of French experience:

> What infinite powers lie dormant at the heart of the nation, quite undeveloped and unused! Whilst an empire lies mouldering in powerless shame, there is perhaps some Caesar guiding the plough in a wretched village, and some Epaminondas who is eking out a living from the work of his hands.

It is however generally agreed that however much attention they paid to England and France, they never dreamt of borrowing the English Parliamentary system or the French spirit of equality which was the essence of the Revolution. In a modern Prussia as they conceived it, the middle classes and the peasants were to be associated with the life of the State, but power was to remain with the king. Castes were to disappear, but the social authority of the *Junkers* would remain. This was an original scheme of things, half-way between the Western countries and the monarchies of the Old Regime, though much more akin to the latter than to the former.

The task confronting the government in Königsberg was not an enviable one. While the discussions with Daru were going on concerning the indemnity, attention was being given to the restoration of the devastated villages, and the question of agrarian reform necessarily came to the fore. The cost of rebuilding the farms fell upon the *seigneurs*. It was they who had to reconstitute the livestock, provide the peasants with seed, and even supply them with food in hard times like these. The seigneurs themselves were extremely hard pressed, and it had been necessary to grant them an *indult* or moratorium on their mortgage debts. In their eyes, the simplest course was to join the devastated peasant holdings onto their own *Gut*, their own property, and reduce the holders to the state of day labourers. The law forbade eviction and demanded the abolition of the *Bauernschutz*; but it offered nothing in exchange, and left the peasant as a mere *Untertan* (subject). But the government officials did not view the matter in this light. Steeped in the lessons learnt from Smith and Young, they declared themselves —Schön in particular—in favour of large-scale cultivation, and had no objection to the abolition of the *Bauernschutz*; but it was a first principle of liberal economy to abolish the feudal system. Although the monarchy had allowed individual bourgeois to acquire land and had gone a long way to abolishing serfdom on its own crown lands, together with the transformation of tenant into owner, it had never yet dared question the *Junkers*' monopoly of the landed property, or interfere in the internal affairs of the manor.

But now it seized the opportunity—and this is the cardinal importance of the 1807 reforms. On the one hand, the government abolished *Untertänigkeit* in exchange for the suppression of *Bauernschutz*; on the other, it authorized the middle classes and the peasants to acquire land. The nobles were freed from their Caste restrictions, and allowed in return to enter professions that had hitherto been reserved for the middle classes, and also gave the peasants the same rights. A start was made in replacing the various castes by *Stände*, classes based upon wealth and profession. The East Prussian *Landtag* gave way, and the reforms were decided upon in principle in August 1807. Altenstein's advice was to extend it throughout the royal dominions, without waiting for the approval of the other *Landtage*. Napoleon reorganized society on French principles in the Grand Duchy of Warsaw and in the Kingdom of Westphalia; and this example was not without its influence, for it was likely to provoke discontent and lead to emigration.

Stein only arrived on September 30 and was thus not the initiator of the reforms. They were not even mentioned in his *Mémoire de Nassau*. He did not favour capitalism, and it should be noted that as far as the peasants were concerned, he had not set them free on his own lands. His role was to support Altenstein and make certain reservations about the outright abolition of the *Bauernschutz*, the regulation of it being postponed till later. The order was signed on October 9, 1807. Instead of a general law to regulate the *Bauernschutz*, provincial edicts were substituted. These appeared between 1808 and 1810, and represented in effect a compromise. The new holdings—that is to say, those established between 1752 and 1774 according to the respective regions—were given over to eviction; the old ones could only be joined to the *Gut* if the new units constituted farms whose total extent was equivalent to all the holdings that had disappeared, but of course much larger than any single one of them. The royal lands kept their more advanced position as compared with the private manors. On October 28, 1807, Frederick William III abolished *Untertänigkeit* in them, which was hardly of any importance except in Silesia, and on July 27, 1808, he extended to East Prussia the arrangements previously promulgated by edict in the other provinces concerning the making over of properties to tenants, in return for compensation payment and the compulsory redemption of the feudal dues. There are good grounds for believing that some 30,000 peasants in this province thus became landowners.

The order of 1807 and those which completed it produced a chorus of praise in Germany and England, some of which can be rightly discounted. The motive behind these measures were primarily fiscal and economic, and the essential results told in favour of the State and the *Junkers*. The terms of the settlement ensured the treasury a considerable gain. By conceding ownership of property to the peasants, the king got rid of his customary obligations to them and abolished their common rights on his own lands, chiefly in the forests, which profited greatly by this step. In the private manors, the concessions made to the peasants were chiefly of a legal kind. As from 1810, *Untertänigkeit* was to be abolished—though it was never really defined. Henceforward it would appear that peasants might leave the glebe, have freedom to marry and withdraw their children from the *Gesindedienst*; but a measure of uncertainty hung over many of the other obligations, which worked to their disadvantage. The feudal dues and forced labour rights continued in their entirety, and tenure remained just as precarious as before. The seigneur kept the right to administer justice, which made him the administrator of the village and gave him power over all police arrangements and the infliction of penalties, even of corporal punishment. In so far as there was real progress, it was more than offset for a good many peasants by the evictions which turned them into mere daily wage-earners. On the royal lands, the cost of redemption and the wretched conditions of those times obliged many of them to sell their land, and allow the concentration of land in the hands of big owners to go forward. No one even thought of allowing them to benefit by mortgage loans, though these were readily available to the middle classes. Apart from the monopoly in landownership, the nobles retained all their other privileges.

These reforms worked out in favour of the re-grouping of land, the disappearance of the customary rights, and so the dissolution of the rural community. Economic liberty would likewise have called for big reforms in industry and commerce. In East Prussia, Stein did carry out a few such reforms. He abolished several corporations and the lords' milling-dues, and proclaimed equality of status as between town and country, thus making it possible for peasants to buy and sell on the spot. This last reform had a very serious effect on the receipts from the excise, which was chiefly levied in the towns, and made a reform of taxation seem probable. Stein did in fact show a marked preference for taxation of income. As East Prussia had contracted a debt in order to pay a war contribution, he induced the *Landtag* to vote an income tax, the first of its kind; but it remained exceptional, and was not extended to the rest of the kingdom.

Stein's personal efforts were chiefly directed to reorganizing the bureaucracy, whose power he wished to reduce by linking representatives of the nation with it. He was authoritarian, quick, and sometimes surly in manner, and had insisted upon dismissing two favourites—Lombard and Beyme—and placing Scharnhorst at the head of the military cabinet which became part of the Ministry of War in 1809. Moreover, he planned a reorganization of the central government under five strictly specialized ministries, and the creation of a council of ministers. In fact, however, he could not get the better of the clique: the King of Prussia's civil and military cabinets still held the real power. He also planned to set up a national consultative *Landtag*. When he had to get approval in East Prussia for the *Einkommensteuer* and for mortgage-bonds on behalf of Napoleon, he changed the constitution of the *Landtag* by increasing the number of middle-class representatives, admitting representatives of the peasants elected on a property qualification basis, and introducing individual voting. His national *Landtag* would have been constituted by 'orders', with individual voting at any rate in financial matters, and there would have been popular representation, to the advantage of the rich. But in the other provinces, there was no reform of the *Landtag*, and the national *Landtag* never came into existence.

The administrative reforms were promulgated after his fall, on December 26, 1808. They did not do more than join together in the provincial subdivisions the powers of the old *Kammer* on the royal lands and the *Regierung*, which remained collegiate in structure, whilst taking away from the latter all that remained of its judicial functions. At the head of the province was the *Oberpräsident*, formerly a customary office, but now made an official appointment. In the *Regierung*, there were representatives of the nobles associated with the officials, but it was soon obvious that they would not be able to work together. Stein's purpose had been to keep the bureaucracy and at the same time imitate the English Justices of the Peace; but he met with no success. In order not to have to borrow the Napoleonic préfet, he kept the collegiate principle, without seeing that this was against his plan of giving more drive and initiative to the administration. Only in the towns did his order of November 19, 1808, produce significant and enduring results. Without excluding local features, he laid down the broad lines to be followed by all the cities. They were given an elective municipal assembly and a magistrature whose members were appointed by the latter, thus restricting—though not altogether abolishing—the supervision exercised by the State. The really new feature was to withdraw elective rights for the assembly from the corporations, and to transfer them to all householders with certain property qualifications, for Germany had never before had anything but a corporative franchise. Even in the English towns, an individual franchise was rare, and in any case the Germans were not very well acquainted with their organization. In spite of all that has been said to the contrary, it remains beyond a doubt that Stein's chief reform was inspired by French models and this was certainly due in part to his adviser Frey.

Stein was only in power a little over a year, and it is therefore not surprising that his ministry should have been more noted for its promise than for its performance. It must even be admitted that the results were not such as to arouse much enthusiasm, and that the reformers' military achievements made a much more substantial contribution to the resurrection of Prussia. These military reforms carried out by Scharnhorst and his assistants had already advanced some way in 1809. The purging and reorganization of the command had already been carried through, the independent company had disappeared, and the infantry was under new regulations which took account of French tactical methods. Yet in spite of all this, the Prussian army was not in a condition to beat Napoleon, as the reformers were well aware. Up to July 1808, they had no thought of anything but an evacuation. In January, Scharnhorst was working in concert with Stein on a scheme by which Prince William should, with this end in view, offer a Prussian alliance, or entry into the Confederation of the Rhine. Gneisenau's only objection was that 'once in the Cyclops' cave, the only favour we could hope for would be the privilege of being the last to be devoured'. But at the news of the Spanish insurrection and even before learning of the Baylen disaster, they completely changed their attitude. As early as July 23, Götzen was sent to Silesia to get secretly in touch with the Austrians. On August 6, it was decided to call up for one month the conscripts whom financial stringency would not allow them to take on a permanent footing, so that it would at any rate be possible to mobilize them in an emergency. These were the famous *Krümper*, the cavalry reinforcements. In the course of the month, further details of the plan were embodied in a number of memoranda. The idea was to call the whole German nation to arms in order to fight a war to the death. The women and children would be evacuated, the countryside laid waste, and the enemy harassed and encircled by guerilla bands. Clearly, this was a revolutionary spirit: the princes and nobles who refused to lead the national uprising would be deprived of their rights and dignities, and the king would give his people a constitution.

For the first time Germany, as she was to be in the nineteenth century, began to shape herself in men's thoughts as a political entity over against the foreigner. Austria, no doubt, figured as a possible ally, but also as a separate and distinct power: it was Prussia who would appeal to the German people and take the lead. But there was as yet no idea of Prussia's being more than an instrument, nor of the risks to which her dynasty would be exposed. Nothing shows more vividly the effects of the Spanish rising and the state of romantic exaltation it produced. As a prudent precaution, Stein consented to hoodwinking Napoleon by means of an alliance till all was in readiness for the decisive move. 'Is Napoleon the only one who should be allowed to replace law by caprice, and the truth by lies?' His secret organizations were not extensive enough to prepare for insurrection, nor did he possess, like Spain, a docile clergy largely made up of monks. Too many people had to be let into the secret, and he was not sufficiently on his guard against French espionage. Two of his letters, one of them to Wittgenstein who was taking the waters in Mecklenberg, fell into the hands of Napoleon.

The Prussian aristocracy was thoroughly indignant. Oh yes, they wanted to drive out the French, but under the leadership of the king and with the help of the regular army, in concert with the allied princes, whilst keeping the common people in their traditionally subservient position. They were jealous of the threat to their privileges, and hated the parvenu immigrants, whom they treated as Jacobins. There was a positive chorus of attacks from Vienna and Frederick William was by no means insensitive to them. He held fast to the Old Regime and to his autocratic power and made a more prudent estimate of the risks involved, so that he would take no action without the Czar. In a council held on August 23, he rejected the conspirators' proposals. Alexander, then on his way to Erfurt, had advised him to play for time, and he therefore ratified on September 29 the agreement signed in Paris on the 8th. The patriots had done all they could to dissuade him from this course, and Bayen suggested calling together a national assembly, but his decision was not communicated to them till October. After offering to resign, Stein returned to the attack. On the 28th, he outlined a new plan for insurrection, and on November 6 he put before the king a proclamation announcing sweeping reforms in order to rouse public opinion. Meanwhile a third party was forming: men who favoured the reforms, such as Hardenberg and Altenstein, but who were concerned to spare the nobility as the State's only bulwark, and who wished, in common with the king, to gain time and avoid any unfortunate adventures. As Stein was against his sovereign's proposed visit to his beloved Alexander, the queen threw him over; he was dismissed on November 24 and on December 15 declared an outlaw of the Empire by Napoleon.

Altenstein and Dohna took over the reins of power, and the movement for reform began to lose its impetus. Scharnhorst, who stayed in office, was the only one to continue the work. But work on a national scale was postponed to an indefinite future, and the *Junkers* were triumphant. On November 26 York wrote:

> There's one of those madcap's heads broken, at any rate; the rest of the vipers' brood will succumb to its own poison. The safest and wisest course is to wait quietly for the outcome of political events. It would be pure folly to provoke and attack the enemy at one's own peril. Germany will never lend itself to any Sicilian Vespers or Vendean uprising. The Prussian peasant will do nothing unless he is ordered to by his king and has the support of the big battalions. . . . Our situation begins to look distinctly better, both at home and abroad.

This optimism enraged the patriots and plunged them into despair. Götzen, when negotiating with the Austrians, had spoken angrily of the resistance they were meeting with, and announced that the national movement, when it got under way, would soon see some heads falling. Grolman had followed Stein into exile—and he was not the only one to do so. The dynasty lost prestige, and so did Prussia. For a moment, the attention of Germans was once more concentrated upon Austria, who had awoken to the world of political thought, and Kleist voiced their hopes in uttering the watchword 'Austria and Freedom'.

AUSTRIA

After Austerlitz, the Emperor Francis Joseph had changed his ministers and military staff. The Archduke Charles once again became commander-in-chief, and on February 10, 1806, resumed the presidency of the *Kriegsgerath*. The office of chancellor was taken by Philip de Stadion, a former ambassador, whose elder brother, Canon Frederick, was representing Austria at Munich. The Archdukes Charles and Régnier also urged a change in the system of government, but without success. Francis continued to want to be in control of everything. In his cabinet, Baldacci enjoyed the same ascendancy as his predecessor Colloredo. He was intelligent, hard-working and honest, though he was supposed to be the son of a Corsican mercenary, whilst others said he was a noble's bastard. Stadion, who came from the mediatized *Ritterschaft*, was authoritarian, and ambitious to play an important part in affairs. Though well educated and liberal-minded, he was too much attached to his noble birth to lay a hand on the nobles' privileges. He played the enlightened despot, setting up factories, founding schools, and constructing roads, but without making any changes in the structure of the State or society. As a charming, witty, and worldly man who enjoyed life to the full and was extravagant in his ways, he was too light-minded to conceive of great reforms—in fact another Choiseul, rather than a Stein. He did not even succeed in obtaining from Hungary the appropriate subsidies, or the military modifications required. In the 1807 Diet Nagy condemned any idea of intervention in the war and repeated the usual complaints. Acting in his customary way, the Emperor postponed any examination of them, and was satisfied with a contingent of 12,000 men and a moderate level of taxation. The only fruitful piece of work, carried out by

Archduke Charles, was hindered by a lack of resources, and the chronic deficit meant that the debt rose from 438 million *Gulden* in 1805 to 572 million in 1809, and paper money from 337 to 518 million, till the loss in face value at Augsburg rose from 26 per cent to 67. In 1806, Count Zichy tried to reduce the issue of money by a forced loan, but the 1807 armaments annulled the effect of this measure, and in August 1808 he was replaced by O'Donnell, who had come to no decision when war suddenly supervened. Inflation had warm champions among the speculators and exporters, and more especially among the partisans of war, who saw no other means of financing a campaign.

Stadion had from the start been thinking of another war as a means of building up a reputation, but the lesson of 1805 had been such a stern one that for a long time the war party was powerless. From Paris, Metternich encouraged an attitude of expectancy, and Stadion was obliged to acquiesce and let the winter of 1807 pass without intervention. The Peace of Tilsit then forced him to join the blockade and break with England. During this lull, some were inclined, under the influence of the Romantic movement which was spreading in Vienna, to point back to the past history of the monarchy and use it to justify the existence of Austria as a European state, a Christian bulwark against the infidel, and a missionary of Western civilization among the Magyars and the Slavs. The same arguments were used to support its primacy among the German-speaking peoples. A distinguished protagonist of the movement was the historian Baron Hormayr, Director of the State Archives. He had close links with Archduke John, and longed to become a man of action.

Another factor in rousing Austria from her torpor was the insurrection in Spain. Stadion kept the public well informed about the tragedy of Bayonne and sang the praises of Ferdinand's faithful subjects. This propaganda at once had an effect on the Magyar nobility. On August 28, 1808, the Diet gave an enthusiastic welcome to the new Empress Marie-Louise d'Este, Francis' third wife, who was crowned Queen of Hungary. The strength of the contingent was raised to 20,000 recruits by abolishing the right of substitution, and the king was granted in advance absolute powers for three years in case of war, which would allow him on his own authority to call for an insurrection. Hungarian authors began to attack France. Verseghy, who had formerly translated 'La Marseillaise', published in 1809 a *Fidélité magyar*, and Kisfaludy a *Discours patriotique à la noblesse magyar*. The Spanish example immediately suggested that the lost provinces—especially the Tyrol, which was discontented under Bavarian administration—might possibly form a valuable rallying-point. The departure of the Grande Armée and Talleyrand's speeches at Erfurt finally brought Stadion to a decision. Moreover Metternich himself thought that the moment had come, for he noted that Napoleon only had one army, and it had just left Germany. Stadion took Talleyrand's word for it that the Emperor's position in France was thoroughly shaken.

It did not take long to build up a war party again. It was supported by all the Archdukes except Charles, and likewise by all the imperial ambassadors. Vienna once more became the headquarters of the European aristocracy. Razumovski reappeared, along with Pozzo di Borgo, and Mme de Staël had just arrived, accompanied by Augustus Schlegel, who was joined by Frederick, now secretary to the Archduke Charles. The Emperor was urged on to war by his new wife and by his mother-in-law, who could not reconcile herself to the loss of her Duchy of Modena. He finally gave way in 1808. Charles held out for longer, but in the end had to yield. Another centre of action was growing up at Prague, where Stein had taken refuge and where there were plenty of links with the German patriots. The movement won over the middle classes, and the students and the populace in the large towns, thanks to propaganda organized on the advice of Metternich by Stadion and Hormayr according to the French model. They poured out gazettes and pamphlets, and made use of the theatres and concerts. Gleich wrote patriotic plays and Collin patriotic songs. There were also great ceremonies to celebrate the establishment of the *Landwehr*. Among the students too a certain number of volunteers came forward including Grillparzer—though he very quickly changed his tune. These appeals to the people could not be allowed to mislead as to the true nature of Stadion's policy. Though he sought to rouse men's spirits, it was strictly within the limits and for the advantage of the Austrian state of the Old Regime; and it was the *Junkers'*, and not Stein's, approval that he deserved. Nor must we be deceived by Hormayr's tactics when he received delegations from the Tyrolese, one of them led by Höfer, at the beginning of 1809, who had come to plan a peasant rising with him; it was only a question of carrying through a legitimist movement. If Austria probably reckoned that disturbances would break out in Germany, she was none the less opposed to a German nationalist movement, and made no secret of it. The patriots who had looked to her were labouring under an illusion: while she welcomed their good wishes for victory and would have willingly accepted their services, she had no intention of consulting them, reckoning that she would conquer Napoleon in her own strength and then re-establish her own sovereignty as of old in Germany and in Italy.

The Austrian army had made undeniable progress under the leadership of Archduke Charles. In the first place, it had built up some reserves by forming in each recruiting zone for the respective regiments two battalions who were obliged to put in three weeks' training every year. On June 10, 1806, the *Landwehr* had been established, composed of ex-soldiers and volunteers grouped together in battalions in each district, and commanded by retired officers and notables. At the beginning of 1809 it numbered 152,000 men in Austria and Bohemia, Galicia having been kept on a separate footing. On the other hand efforts were made to introduce the French methods. The 1807 regulations adopted a battle array with the use of skirmishers, but the infantry did not in fact use it. On September 1, 1808, it was decided to form nine divisions of Tyrolese *chasseurs* —23,000 skirmishers—who proved extremely useful. As the Austrian cavalry had a tendency to scatter its forces, Charles grouped part of them together in independent corps. He also grouped the artillery in regiments—up till then they had been divided between the infantry battalions—organized a pioneer corps, and improved the services behind the lines by setting up a medical corps, a remount corps, and an army post. He reduced by half the regimental baggage-trains and lightened the convoys by establishing on-the-spot requisitioning. Finally in July 1808 the army was in principle divided into corps and given a general headquarters.

These improvements, however, needed time and money to produce results. No army corps were created because it would have needed too costly a reconstruction of the garrisons. The troop movements remained unwieldy, because the magazine and convoy arrangements had not been completely given up. Tactics, too, were little improved, because the superior officers were too old and promotion was blocked by incompetence and corruption. But in spite of everything, the Austrians showed up much better in 1809 than in 1805, which was a warning that Napoleon would have done well to heed. Yet what they most decidedly lacked was a real war leader. Archduke Charles had great qualities, such as diligence, prudence, and coolness; but he was more effective in defence than in attack, and too much wedded to traditional strategy which treated war as, in Niebuhr's phrase, 'a game of chess', and aimed not at destroying the enemy but merely at conquering a geographical objective, as Clausewitz remarked. And worst of all, he was hesitant. These faults were a matter of temperament. Although he was only thirty-eight, his health was not good, and he therefore lacked keenness and initiative. Niebuhr observed that he went to war in a joyless manner.

But the Austrians were so confident in themselves that they were not concerned to find allies. They could in fact only count on the English, for Stadion's overtures had not borne any fruit. Even in London, there was a certain reticence. In October Metternich had promised to place 400,000 men in the line in return for £5 million, plus half as much again for the expenses of mobilization. But the English replied—though not till December 24—that this was asking too much. Then King George insisted that Austria should first of all make peace—which she could not do without breaking with Napoleon. Canning conveyed £25,000 in notes to Trieste; but on April 10, he was still demurring and quoting the cost of the war in Spain. The truth of the matter is that the English government was deeply divided. It was no longer a question of debating whether they should act on the Continent; on this point there was no objection raised by any minister. The only difficulty was to decide where. Canning wanted to concentrate all available forces in the Iberian Peninsula, whilst Castlereagh advanced the claims of Holland, and there had even been some talk of Pomerania.

These last two diversions would have had the widest possible repercussions, particularly the latter, which might well have produced an extensive rising in Germany and brought Prussia in as well. Castlereagh opted for the Low Countries, the central objective of his European policy. A well-conducted expedition, he held, might take Antwerp by surprise. Through lack of preparation it did in fact prove useless to the Austrians. But like Mack in 1805, Stadion did not in fact wait for support, and this time he could give good reasons for his decision. Napoleon was unprepared, and there were hopes of taking him by surprise. Yet there can scarcely be any doubt that the romantic excitement let loose by Stadion finally swept even him off his feet.

THE CAMPAIGN OF 1809

For Napoleon, this war, coming at a point when he had not yet finished with the Spanish campaign, was a disaster. The only man who could have prevented it with a single word was Alexander: but the word was not spoken. His experience at Erfurt had taught him that in order to extract advantages from Napoleon you must catch him at a disadvantage, and the Austrian aggression came at precisely the right moment. War was still going on in Finland, and was about to be resumed in Turkey, where Russia would be able to enjoy a free hand. Moreover, Alexander was reverting to his Polish schemes of 1805. In spite of the disgrace of Czartorski, who had retired to Palavy, there was still agitation going on from the Russian party in the Grand Duchy. In the spring of 1809, the Warsaw and Galician nobles came to the Czar to offer their support if he would promise to re-establish the kingdom. On June 27 he replied that he would never abandon the provinces that had become Russian; if circumstances allowed, he would gladly recreate a Poland by joining the Grand Duchy to Galicia. Clearly, this was to be through his agency and to his advantage, for soon afterwards he was to forbid Napoleon to carry out the same measures. Sentiment, too, may have played its part, for in January 1809 the King and Queen of Prussia had come to St. Petersburg, and that had revived old memories. Whilst advising the ambassador Schwarzenberg to play for time, Alexander is said to have added: 'The moment for vengeance will come a little later.' It must therefore be concluded that from then onwards a new war between Russia and France was only a matter of time. From Valladolid the Emperor sent him one of his officers to suggest that their respective ambassadors should send Stadion identical notes ordering diplomatic relations to be broken off unless the reply was satisfactory. Alexander accepted the notes, but would not agree to breaking off relations, insisting moreover that this step should be the object of special diplomatic missions, which postponed it *sine die*. Napoleon was no longer under any illusions. Though he proposed to the Czar that they should join in guaranteeing the integrity of Austria provided she would disarm, it was only in the vain hope of gaining time and finishing the concentration of his new army before the Archduke should take the offensive.

Returning to Paris, he had to confess that the country's morale was not good. He was not seriously troubled by the royalists; but they were not disarming. On August 23, 1806, the Bishop of Vannes had been kidnapped by Lahaie-Saint-Hilaire, who was not apprehended until 1807. The following year saw the end of the Normandy exploits of Lechevalier, an accomplice of the vicomte d'Aché. The royalist agency in Jersey kept sending agents to the West, and in 1808 Prigent and six others were shot, followed by Armand de Chateaubriand, a cousin of the vicomte, on February 20, 1809. The Jacobins were still less of a threat, for they were being relentlessly harried by the police. At the end of 1807, they arrested Didier, formerly a sworn member of the Revolutionary court; in 1808 a republican plot—the first since 1801—was denounced to Dubois, the Prefect of Police, in which Demailot, formerly an agent of the Committee of Public Safety, General Malet, the Convention members Florent, Guiot, and Ricord, and the ex-tribune Jacquemont were implicated. Fouché succeeded, with Cambacérès' agreement, in persuading the Emperor that it would be best to hush the matter up.

These various attempts had no further repercussions. What alarmed the nation was rather the policy of Napoleon himself. His triumphs never reassured anybody, for they always involved a further instalment. 'This war must be our last,' he had been careful to say on entering the struggle against Russia in 1807.

Then he had represented Tilsit as the pledge of peace; yet less than a year later there was the Spanish affair—and this time it was not possible to place the responsibility on Charles IV. 'France is sick with anxiety', wrote Fiévée to the Emperor. And there was no less uneasiness among the Emperor's servants. Fontanes, as president of the *Corps Législatif*, dared to express their feelings on the eve of the 1808 campaign: 'You have only to speak, and your hearers are overcome with nameless fears that are compounded of love and hope.' In private, Decrès used much more direct terms: 'The Emperor is mad, completely mad: he'll bring ruin upon himself and upon us all.' Since he was running so lightheartedly to perdition, some thought it prudent henceforward to betray him in order to save their own skins, dressing up their villainy as the interest of their country, which it was only right to distinguish from the tyrant's cause. Moreover, if he should be killed or meet with a disaster, a successor would have to be found; but as nothing could be done without foreign approval, the safest course was to offer the Powers certain guarantees—and this was Talleyrand's secret.

One cannot fail to see the significance of the fact that attempts were made to find a successor to Napoleon during the Spanish expedition and on the eve of the Austrian attack, as at the time of Marengo. In December 1808 Talleyrand became reconciled with Fouché, and it appears that they came to an agreement on the subject of Murat. Rumours spread abroad to this effect. Eugène was said to have intercepted a letter to the King of Naples, and a secretary of Fouché's was thought to have let the matter leak out, so that *Madame Mère* was able to warn her son. It is certain at any rate that Napoleon thought he had been betrayed. He made a terrible scene with Talleyrand and removed him from the office of Grand Chamberlain. Fouché was spared—perhaps in order not to disorganize the police at a dangerous moment, perhaps because after Tilsit he had taken the initiative in proposing a divorce, and had even spoken of it to Josephine. After such an outburst, Napoleon's tolerant attitude seems as surprising as it was ill-advised. Probably he was afraid that if he struck down one of his old accomplices he would alarm others and provoke new plots. But he had either said too much, or not enough. Talleyrand's disgrace, as Mollien says, roused 'a kind of anxiety, all the more widespread because most people did not know its origins, and so no one could therefore feel safe'. Yet surrounded as he was by the *ci-devant*, and dreaming of an alliance with a royal family, how could Napoleon have shot another prince on the score of high treason?

With Napoleon absent at the front, his enemies kept on the alert. It was quite possible that there might be an English landing on the French coast, for in April they had damaged the Rochefort squadron in the île d'Aix roadstead. In Provence there was unrest among the royalists and republicans. Barreès was in touch with Generals Guidal and Monnier, with the former corsair Charabot, and with a merchant who advanced funds. There were suggestions of arranging the escape of Charles IV and Godoy, who were then interned at Marseilles. In July, Charnbot tried to link up with Collingwood, who was cruising off the coast. Napoleon's conflict with the Pope was rousing a seething unrest in Catholic circles; and in the course of the summer, the West gave new cause for anxiety, whilst there were disturbances in the Saar and the Ourthe districts. Even the army contained some doubtful elements. We have no information about the *Philadelphes* said to have been under the orders of Colonel Oudet, who was killed at Wagram; but in Soult's army in Portugal, an officer named d'Argenton formed a conspiracy and tried to get Wellington's support. We must not exaggerate the danger, but a comparison between the public mood of 1809 and the ovations of August 1807 reveals a striking contrast. The whole Empire was built on victory, and the reverses in Spain had struck a blow at its prestige which was all the more powerful because it was the cause of a new war in Germany, which—as the nation was well aware—was starting at an awkward moment. Facing Napoleon there was an armed Austria, a Spain that had risen in revolt, Portugal invaded by the English, and Germany trembling with excitement: behind him lurked an agonizing anxiety and treason; never had he played for such tremendous stakes.

Yet he proceeded to prepare for the contest with his usual coolness and calm. He had some 90,000 men immediately available, the remnants of the Grande Armée left behind in Germany and labelled the Army of the Rhine. To this could be added 100,000 allied men—Germans, Dutch, and Polish. The 1809 class, who had been called up in January 1808, were not yet fit for service. In order to take their place in the depots, the Emperor had called up in September 1808 the 1810 class as from January 1, 1809. Almost at the same time he raised the contingent numbers from 60,000 to 80,000, to take effect retrospectively as from 1806, resulting in a total call-up of 140,000 conscripts. Existing regiments had a fourth battalion added to them, and new divisions were constituted in the Boulogne and Alsace camps, and then sent beyond the Rhine. Finally, the Guard was brought back with all speed from Spain. In March 1809, Napoleon had 300,000 fighting men at his disposal in Germany, of whom he left some 100,000 in Italy, 60,000 of them in Venetia; and Marmont kept a further 15,000 in Dalmatia. To have created this new army at all was a marvel; but there could be no illusions about its value. Almost half of it consisted of foreigners who were a great disappointment in the front line. The French effectives were more than half recruits, and their formations were incomplete and largely improvised.

The deficiencies of the material preparations—as usual, of a rather perfunctory kind—were particularly apparent to these young troops. Even the superior command had lost some of its glamour. With Ney and Soult still in Spain, three army corps had to be entrusted to Lefebvre, Vendamme, and Jerome, and the Italian army to Eugène. The 1809 army, though much inferior to that of 1805, contained more than 100,000 French who had fought the 1807 campaign, and they were enough to ensure victory; but they were a makeshift collection, a foretaste of the army of 1812. For the moment, however, the danger did not lie in its composition, but in the fact that Napoleon, for all his activity, could not create it quickly enough to get it assembled in time. At the end of March, Bernadotte was still in Saxony with 50,000 Polish and Saxon troops; Jerome was in Central Germany with the Dutch and Westphalians; Davout's corps—60,000 picked men—were in Bavaria, north of the Danube; Oudinot, the Bavarians, and other Germans on the Lech; Masséna further in the rear, and the Guard still on their way from Spain. The bulk of these forces was therefore spread over a front of 150 kilometres, within a single day's march of the enemy. The Archduke took up the offensive on April 10, and Napoleon did not arrive at Donauwörth till the 17th. If the

Austrians had made a massed attack there is no knowing what might have happened.

The allied forces were more judiciously arranged than in 1805. Archduke John only had 50,000 men available for the invasion of Venetia, and only 10,000 of them were stationed on the Tyrol side, under Chasteler, and 6,000 in Croatia. However, it was necessary to give 35,000 of the total to Archduke Ferdinand for the protection of Galicia against the Poles. In Germany, Archduke Charles had 200,000 men at his disposal. His first plan was to debouch from Bohemia in order to crush Davout and cut the French forces into two halves—a piece of strategy that would have been worthy of Napoleon. But he was uneasy at the thought of leaving Vienna undefended, and he decided to move along the right bank of the Danube and occupy the Bavarian plateau. In so doing, he lost precious time and tired out his troops; nevertheless, this revised plan would have likewise produced decisive results if only it had been carried out speedily and with all his strength. As it was, he left two corps in front of Davout; and having crossed the Inn, he advanced slowly towards the Isar, his left supported by Hiller, in numerous columns whose movements were badly co-ordinated. Davout was able to fall back southwards, and would have joined up with the other corps near Ingolstadt if Berthier, through a misinterpretation of the Emperor's orders, had not kept him at Ratisbon.

Napoleon had no sooner arrived on the 17th than he hastened to summon him to join up with him, and on the 19th the marshal set out by the right bank of the river, thus passing in front of the enemy and giving him a last chance of striking a crushing blow. But the Archduke failed to seize the opportunity, and Davout was able to resist the feeble pressure of the Austrians at Tengen. Meanwhile, Napoleon had mistaken Hiller's corps for the main body and was preparing to cut the Inn and force him back on the Danube. In the centre and under Lannes' command he massed a force that attacked the Austrian columns on the left towards Abensberg on April 20 and pushed them back on Landshut, whilst Masséna was marching on this town to take them in the rear. But he arrived too late, and on the 21st Hiller, thrust out of Landshut, was able to fall back upon the Inn. The Archduke took advantage of the delay to join up with his forces that had remained to the north of the Danube—the Ratisbon garrison having meanwhile capitulated; and on the 22nd he at last decided to launch a vigorous attack on Davout. But before his right wing had been able to come into action to cut him off from the river, Davout himself attacked his left wing at Eckmühl, and soon after, Napoleon, hastening up from Landshut, took him in the rear. He accordingly retreated, and managed to cross the Danube without difficulty; but his army had lost about 30,000 men, and was cut into two parts, though both of them were still free to move downstream towards Vienna and effect a meeting, and still comprised more than 100,000 men. On the 20th the French recaptured Ratisbon, but Hiller inflicted a reverse on Bessières. The Archduke had not suffered the same fate as Mack.

The Emperor did not pursue him into Bohemia, but marched on Vienna. Not that he was drawn aside by this political objective: it was rather in order to interpose between the main Austrian army and those in Italy and the Tyrol. While Davout—now supported by Bernadotte—was keeping an eye on the Archduke's movements, Masséna rolled back Hiller's forces, and Lannes simultaneously tried to outflank them through the mountains. Meanwhile Lefebvre, seizing Salzburg, threw Jellachich back towards the Drave and could keep a watch on the Tyrol. After a bloody affray at Ebersberg, near the crossing of the Traun, Hiller managed to get across the Danube to link up with his chief, and the French entered Vienna on May 12. But this time they found the bridges cut, and an enemy force of 115,000 on the left bank of the river. Napoleon made for the islands which divide the river into several branches below the city, set up improvised bridges, and on the night of the 20th risked a crossing, in spite of an already dangerous flood level. On the 21st, 30,000 French were attacked by the whole Austrian army; yet fortunately for them the attack was not concentrated at one point, but spread over a half-circle between Aspern and Essling, so that they were unable to effect a breach. On the 22nd Napoleon, with 60,000 men, took the offensive in order to drive in the enemy centre. He would moreover have succeeded, if the chief bridges had not been swept away, so holding up the supply of reinforcements. A halt had to be made, then he had to fall back and stand on the defensive, against a counter-attack, though short of munitions. But somehow or other they made shift to hold on, and from the 23rd to the 25th were able to evacuate the left bank of the river. Twenty thousand French and 23,000 Austrians had fallen: Lannes and a number of generals had lost their lives. The Archduke had not been able to seize his opportunity, but his opponents had also failed in their objective. The battle of Essling caused an even more profound sensation than Baylen. This time, a blow had been struck at Napoleon's personal prestige.

A dangerous situation was again beginning to develop. In the rear of the army the Tyrol had risen as one man at the news that Chasteler was entering it by way of the Pustertal on April 9. Bavaria had spread popular discontent by abolishing the *Landtag* and doing away with its independence. Nevertheless it was above all the economic situation that produced the feeling of exasperation. Taxes were considerably on the increase; trade was being ruined by the blockade and the closing of the Italian and Austrian frontiers; and everyone was being hard hit by the invalidation of Austrian paper money and the suppression of the convents, which acted as banks and benevolent institutes. Finally, conscription threatened to spark off a conflagration, and had to be suspended to stop the trouble spreading further. Besides, Montgelas' enlightened despotism was Josephist in pattern; and the Catholic clergy, seeing their ascendancy and privileges threatened, had taken up the gauntlet. As in la Vendée and in Spain, they wielded tremendous influence, particularly as the chief insurgent leader, Andreas Höfer, had for his spiritual adviser the Capuchin monk Haspinger. Hofmayr and Archduke John had had a good chance to prepare the insurrection. It was essentially peasant in origin, and did not spare the middle classes, who were pillaged and roughly handled just like the Bavarian officials. There were only 5,000 soldiers to hold down the country, and they were soon surrounded and forced to capitulate. All the same, Chasteler did not succeed in organizing the insurgents, who went back to their homes after the rising, and Höfer, although his bravery and piety inspired them with confidence, was a limited and rather undecided character. Lefebvre did not have much difficulty in advancing along the Inn and entering Innsbruck on May 19. Chasteler evacuated it, and with the revolt apparently over, it was decided to leave only Deroy's division in the Tyrol. Yet when the news of Essling became known, a fresh insurrection broke out. Napoleon, needing all his forces, recalled Deroy and left the country to itself. The peasants had no intentions of leaving it to fight a campaign. They made forays into Bavaria and in July their example was followed by Italy, where an extensive insurrection broke out in the Adige region and in the Romagna.

If only Archduke John had concentrated all his forces scattered in the south of the kingdom, he would have found most valuable support. But he took a very different course. On April 10 he had taken the offensive by way of the Natisone valley and Caporetto. Eugène's forces, still scattered over a wide area, were surprised and fell back to the Mincio, thus surrendering the whole of Venetia. But when Vienna was threatened the Archduke retreated without any attempt to concentrate the Austrian forces. He himself reached the Semmering, with Eugène in pursuit, and then withdrew behind the Raab; Giulay drew away towards Laibach, whence he went upstream again via Marburg to Gratz, hard pressed by Macdonald. Chasteler, who had come from the Tyrol, did not contrive to join him. In Croatia, Marmont had fallen back in order to concentrate his forces, but then drove them back again via Fiume, Laibach, and Gratz. In the end all the French army corps rejoined the Grande Armée, whereas Archduke John found his strength reduced to some 20,000 men. Davout proceeded to threaten Presbourg, and Eugène defeated the Archduke on the Raab on June 14. Then both of them pressed on towards Vienna to take part in the battle, and John did likewise, crossing to the left bank of the Danube, but arrived some few hours late.

The most serious consequence the defeat at Essling might have had would have been to invite intervention by the King of Prussia. Several of his officers had already taken it upon themselves to compromise the situation. Katte made an attempt against Magdeburg and on April 28 Schill made a sortie from Berlin with his hussars, but was easily overcome by General Marchand. Central Germany was also astir. On April 22 Dörnberg, an ex-colonel, marched on Cassel at the head of some hundreds of peasants; and in June another retired officer tried to produce an insurrection in Marburg, whilst there was a rising of the countryside near the Tauber. The Austrians, for their part, entered Saxony and the king fled; and the Duke of Brunswick-Oels, at the head of Hessians transferred by their Elector to Bohemia, occupied Leipzig. Finally, the English were working on Hanover and Holland and on July 8 made an attempt against Cuxhaven. If the Prussians had got under way, Jerome would have had considerable difficulty in defending his kingdom. To start with, Frederick William seemed disposed to take action; but on second thoughts he confined himself to stopping payment of the indemnity. Though he did in the end send an agent to Vienna, he did not arrive till July 21.

As things turned out, then, Napoleon was able to reassemble all his forces, and did not have much difficulty in exploiting the occupied countries or bringing up the reinforcements and supplies that were available in France—20,000 foot, 10,000 cavalry, 6,000 men for the Guard, and a large amount of artillery so as to make up for the doubtful reliability of his troops. The island of Lobau was meticulously fortified and the number of solid bridges extended. In the midst of danger the Emperor himself remained imperturbable. He even went ahead with a measure that was of all things the most likely to sow disaffection among his own subjects: on May 17 he decided to annex Rome. On hearing that Pius VII was about to excommunicate him, the Emperor gave orders that he should be taken prisoner and deported, and on July 6, the day on which the battle of Wagram was fought, the Pope was in fact removed by the gendarmerie, and a *senatus-consultum* of February 17, 1810, subsequently regularized the annexation. It was thoroughly typical of the man that he should give an order like this at such a moment of crisis. He continued with untroubled brow to play double or quits with fortune. And once again he forced destiny to take his side.

At his disposal there were now 187,000 men and 488 guns, against the enemy's 136,000—though their artillery was almost of equal strength. The crossing of the Danube began on July 4, a stormy night, downstream from Essling, and was completed by the following afternoon. By this move the Emperor reckoned to turn the Archduke's flank; but when his forces fanned out over the plain, they failed to find him. The French preparations had not escaped his notice, and realizing that he could not stop this crossing, he had fallen back a short distance, with his left behind the Russbach and parallel to the Danube, and his right perpendicular to it, the top of the angle being marked by the villages of Aderklaa and Wagram. This position, supported on the left by fortified heights, possessed distinct advantages, but it was too extended, and left the Archduke with no reserves. Napoleon, disappointed of his prey, had to improvise a manœuvre and could not attach the Russbach front till seven in the evening, and then without success, for the Saxon forces yielded ground at Aderklaa. He renewed the assault at dawn on the 6th with all his available strength: Davout turned the position and forced Rosenberg to retreat. But at Aderklaa, Carra-Saint-Cyr was overwhelmed and Bernadotte's troops from Saxony once again disintegrated. Meanwhile the Austrian right was vigorously hammering at Boudet's division, which alone stood in their way, capturing Aspern and Essling and threatening the French communications with the rear. The Emperor was forced to alter his dispositions in the midst of battle. Masséna moved down towards the river and stopped the Austrian right by a flanking manœuvre, and the gap was filled with a huge battery of 100 guns, behind which the reserves advanced in massed column under the command of Macdonald. At two o'clock, there was a resumption of the general attack on the Russbach. The enemy left wing was in the end completely overrun and the centre forced to fall back. The Archduke gave the order to retreat, but there was hardly any pursuit from the exhausted French. He had lost 50,000 men to the enemy's 34,000. Tacticians have been full of admiration for the military genius displayed by Napoleon in the course of that day; but judged by results, it cannot compare with Austerlitz or Jena. For the enemy forces—still more than 80,000 men strong—withdrew through Moravia in good order, and battle was renewed at Znaim on the 11th. Yet the Archduke was no Blücher, and he had no hope of a successful issue. He requested an armistice, and his request was granted on the 12th.

The final crisis, however, was long drawn out. Excitement in Germany remained intense, and there was an attempt to assassinate the Emperor by a student named Stabs, though order was quickly re-established. The king of Prussia adopted an attitude of increasing reserve, the Austrians evacuated Saxony, and Brunswick made a daring transit of Jerome's kingdom to reach the coast where the English were waiting to pick him up. The Tyrol, on the other hand, though attacked in July by 40,000 men coming up from Salzburg, the Vorarlberg, and the Adige, continued to hold out, exterminating a division from Saxony and again forcing Lefebvre to retreat. Not till after peace was signed did Drouet d'Erlon and Eugène succeed in breaking down their resistance. Höfer had submitted, and then taken up arms again, only to be betrayed by one of his compatriots and shot on February 20, 1810. Yet the English gave still more trouble. Their expedition at last appeared off Walcheren, and on August 13 captured Flushing. This was the largest contingent they had sent to the Continent—40,000 men escorted by 35 vessels and 23 frigates—but their commander, Lord Chatham, a great courtier but totally incompetent, kept his men doing nothing when a straight march on Antwerp would probably have captured it. As it was, his troops were rapidly laid low by epidemics, and he re-embarked on September 30 with a loss of 106 killed and 4,000 who had died from disease.

Nevertheless the expedition had meanwhile spread alarm throughout the Empire, for which Fouché had been largely responsible. On June 29 Napoleon had left him for the time being in charge of the Ministry of the Interior, since Crétet was unwell. Finding himself in charge of the two political ministries, he displayed extraordinary activity, suppressing the *congregations*, arresting Noailles, who was acting as intermediary between the Pope and the Catholics, putting down disturbances in the West and in the Rhineland, and supporting government stock by purchases on the Stock Exchange without any reference at all to Millien. On learning that the English expedition had landed, he proposed to his colleagues that the National Guards should be mobilized in the fifteen northern départments and brushed aside all objections. Bernadotte had quarrelled with Napoleon because he had gone to the defence of Saxony after Wagram, and had just returned to France. He now accepted an offer from Fouché, who put him in charge of the defence of Antwerp. The préfets were then instructed to hold themselves in readiness for a mass levy of the National Guards in view of the fear of other coastal attacks, particularly in Provence. In Paris, the National Guard was reconstituted. Fouché dealt out ranks to the citizens, who eagerly accepted them, and himself reviewed the force. The military authorities grew alarmed: were they back again in 1793? Clarke was loud in fury, and Fiévée wrote to the Emperor. There seems to be little doubt that Fouché, overjoyed at once again finding himself in a commanding position, had allowed himself to be carried away by memories of his days as representative of the people. Yet there may also have been certain other thoughts at the back of his mind, for he probably knew of the plot in Provence and was most likely in touch with the English through Montrond, an agent of Talleyrand, whom he had sent to Antwerp. One can well imagine what suspicions must have run through Napoleon's mind after all the intrigues of 1808. In August, he was supporting Fouché's first measures; but by September, with the English showing no signs of action, he was beginning to listen to the critics. He did away with the Paris National Guards, replaced Bernadotte by Bessières, and peremptorily requested Fouché to stop turning the Empire upside down in this fashion. When he returned he gave him a sharp dressing down on October 27, but did not dismiss him, because he was on Napoleon's side in the coming divorce, and had even been promoted to be Duke of Otranto on August 15.

These harassments in the rear only made the Emperor the more anxious about Alexander's attitude. At Caulaincourt's request the Czar had massed 60,000 men on the Galician frontier, but had postponed the question of hostilities. Naturally enough, he was primarily occupied with his own affairs, which had taken a favourable turn. In March, Baron Adelspare, in command on the Norwegian frontier, pronounced against Gustavus IV, and the king had to abdicate on the 29th in favour of his uncle, the venerable Duke of Sudermania, who took the name of Charles XIII. Sweden immediately entered into peace negotiations and ceded Finland on September 17. War with Turkey had begun again in April. In December 1808 Kara-Georges, who had been proclaimed hereditary prince of the Serbians, invaded Herzegovina; and in August the Ottomans entered Serbia from their side, but had to evacuate it in September, when Bagration captured Ismailia. As Galicia had been left without defending forces, Alexander could—in spite of these preoccupations—have occupied it very easily, and thus secured its possession when peace was signed. But his objections to Napoleon got the better of his own interests, and so became obvious to all. Archduke Ferdinand was therefore able to invade the Grand Duchy and occupy Warsaw. Poniatovski let him proceed without interference, but himself invaded Austrian territory, occupying Lublin, Zamosc, and even Lemberg. At this point—on June 3—Alexander made up his mind to enter Galicia in order to take the province from the Poles. Meanwhile, however, Ferdinand was hastening to the scene and succeeded in recapturing Sandomir. Galitzine refused to help Poniatovski to save this place, and entered into a secret agreement with the enemy, by which he promised not to proceed beyond the Wisloka, and the Archduke withdrew without firing a single shot. But better still, when Poniatovski approached Cracow, he called in the Russians and handed the town over to them. Alexander was showing increased feeling against the Grand Duchy, and Rumiantzov, now that he had got rid of the Swedes, could think of nothing else. On July 26 Napoleon was invited to give an assurance that he would never reconstitute Poland. 'At all costs I want to be left quietly at peace,' said Alexander to Caulaincourt on August 3. Such a declaration was intended to separate the Poles from France and at the same time imply a veto against all increase of territory for the Grand Duchy—for the name was basically irrelevant. The Czar's attitude filled Napoleon with a growing irritation. 'This is not the behaviour of an ally,' he said. He had for some time been straining at the leash, and now he was still forced to manœuvre for position.

Austria meanwhile was taking good note of the difficulties that confronted him on all sides. Francis had sought refuge in the château de Dotis, near Presburg, where he was surrounded by a war party who were loud in their protests. The Empress, Stadion, and Baldacci all reproached the Archduke for having suspended hostilities and abandoned the Tyrol and Saxony. They reduced his command to that of a single army, which led to his resignation on July 23. There was hope of support from Russia, and this was why the peace negotiations, opened between Metternich and Champagny at Altenburg in the middle of August, were allowed to drag on. These tactics suited Napoleon; for on August 12 he had offered the Czar to partition Galicia between him and the Grand Duchy, the latter to receive four-fifths. In return, he promised to start official negotiations on Poland; and while waiting for a reply he claimed the right to keep all the Austrian territory he had occupied. Finally on September 1 Chernitchev arrived to warn the Austrians that for the moment Russia would not break with France. And so the vanquished had to resign themselves to giving up whatever was required in Galicia, whilst defending inch by inch all their Western provinces. The game was only too obvious: like Napoleon they now knew that Alexander was laying claim to almost everything they might give up. Not wishing either to benefit the man who had betrayed him or to drive him to extremes, the Emperor now took the line of reducing what there was to be shared. Austria's last resistance was broken by an ultimatum, and on October 14 peace was signed at Schönbrunn. Bavaria was given the Inn district and Salzburg; Napoleon took maritime Croatia with Fiume, Istria, and Trieste, together with part of Carinthia and Carniola. The Grand Duchy of Warsaw increased its population by 1,500,000, including Lublin and Cracow; and Russia, with Tarnopol, by 400,000. Austria lost 3½ million inhabitants along with all access to the sea; and she had to pay an indemnity of 75 million.

The most outstanding characteristic of the treaty was that Napoleon had ignored Alexander's claims by maintaining the proportions fixed at the outset for the partition of Galicia. He thus reminded Russia of her vassal status. She had failed to give her master due and proper service, so her wages were reduced. Alexander expressed his dissatisfaction to Caulaincourt, but the Emperor was not alarmed. He kept making a parade of his intentions to satisfy the Czar by giving up all claim to reconstitute Poland. But the Russian demands were never more than a screen. Alexander had really hoped to be offered the Grand Duchy, not to mention Galicia, as the price of his help against Austria; but in his disappointment he had tacitly refused his aid, though he nevertheless clung to his own ambitions. As autumn went on a rupture with France seemed inevitable to him, and when Czartoryski returned to St. Petersburg he began to talk to him in covert terms about his 1805 plans, and the use that could be made of the Poles against Napoleon. The Emperor, on the other hand, refused to believe the evidence, for in his eyes the Continental System remained firmly based upon the agreement of Tilsit. The fact is that he had now made up his mind to get rid of Josephine, and had been thinking since Erfurt of replacing her by Alexander's sister. As usual, the plan of the moment held the entire field; and as the Russian alliance might help it, he refused to see that it was no longer more than a name. The unexpected turn taken in the choice of a new empress was to convert this alliance into a relationship of avowed hostility.

THE AUSTRIAN MARRIAGE

Napoleon's second marriage was destined to upset the balance of the Continental System which had not been fully restored, and hasten the outbreak of a war in which he himself would perish. It was far less inspired by external policy than by the development of Napoleon's personal power. As soon as there were certain suggestions of making him an hereditary sovereign in 1800, the possibility of divorce came into the picture because Josephine was not giving him an heir. Once the monarchy had been restored, this became a much more urgent question. It is possible, however, that Napoleon may have doubted for a time whether he could become a father. Although several illegitimate children have been attributed to him, it would seem that there was still some uncertainty in the matter until the birth of the Count of Leon on December 13, 1807. Nor is it unlikely that the separation from Josephine caused him a good deal of suffering, for the passionate love she had inspired—even though unfaithful—was one of his loveliest memories; and even after he had deserted her, he could never bear to hear that she was unhappy. 'I don't want her to cry,' he would say. When Hortense had given birth to a son he had him baptized with great ceremony, and it was thought that Napoleon might adopt him, but the child died on May 5, 1807. Up till then, moreover, Napoleon could not see any possible substitute for Josephine. Being an Emperor, he was bound to marry a princess of a reigning royal family. As his power grew more aristocratic and more despotic, the papal anointing began to seem more and more insufficient to him. It was no good his boasting, even before kings, that he had built his own fortunes, for he suffered from a constant itch for legitimacy.

Tilsit, however, had suddenly seemed to make the hope of entering into a royal family belonging to a traditional dynasty something more than an idle dream. By the end of the year, the possibility of a divorce became more definite through the efforts of Fouché; and although Napoleon disavowed his help, he nevertheless made up his mind before going to Erfurt, since he then made overtures to Alexander for the hand of his sister. Returning to Paris on November 15, 1809, his only thought was to proceed to action. On the 22nd, Caulaincourt was ordered to present an official request. Since Alexander had insisted that the promise concerning Poland should be embodied in a treaty, the ambassador was at the same time authorized to sign the document. But the Czar had reached a point where there could no longer be any question of this marriage. Nevertheless, this approach was just as much of a windfall, because it might perhaps make it possible, before saying no, to get the treaty rectified, which would then be a step towards winning Poland over to the Russian side. It is strange that Caulaincourt should have been taken in by this manœuvre. He began by negotiating the agreement, which was signed on January 4, 1810, laying down that the kingdom of Poland should never be reconstituted, and that the very name of Poland should disappear from all public documents. He waited till December 28 to come on to the subject of the marriage. Yet he knew that the Czar was likely to put the matter off, since Talleyrand had suggested a pretext for doing so at Erfurt. He would explain the necessity for consulting the dowager empress, who wanted to consult her daughter Catherine then residing at Tver. The daughter had no objection to the marriage, but her mother, while not making an outright refusal, produced objections concerning the young girl's age—she was only 16—and the difference in religion. Inwardly she was deeply opposed to this union. Yet the final decision rested with Alexander in his autocratic position of head of the family; and he took good care to delay his answer.

But the matter was urgent. On November 30, in a celebrated scene with Josephine, the Emperor told her of his will.

On December 15 she declared her consent to the divorce before an assembly of princes and high dignitaries, and it was confirmed on the 16th by a *senatus-consultum*, though this was not in accordance with the Civil Code, nor with the spirit—if not the letter—of the statute regulating the Imperial family. Josephine kept the title of Empress, and was given la Malmaison and a dowry. The annulment of the religious marriage was rather more difficult. It was not possible to approach the Pope, because he was a prisoner; moreover, in abbé Émerg's opinion, precedent did not positively indicate that his intervention would be required. Fesch accordingly held up proceedings, while the ecclesiastical officials in Paris—at diocesan and at metropolitan level—took the responsibility of declaring the marriage null. The diocesan authorities alleged that the union had been celebrated secretly, without the parish priest and witnesses. This was something that could not be authorized—according to the Gallican Church—by any dispensation, even from the Pope. The metropolitan authorities preferred the grounds put forward by the Emperor, namely that the ceremony of 1804 had been imposed by circumstances and was therefore invalid in default of a positively expressed consent.

Once this point had been settled on January 12, 1810, Napoleon waited impatiently for the Czar's reply. When he realized that it was being delayed, although the treaty of January 4 was submitted to him, he suspected a trap and held up the ratification. Alexander's refusal, which now seemed probable, was no doubt mortifying, but he could have his revenge, for Austria offered him an alternative bride.

Since the signing of peace, Metternich had been at the Chancery. There were some obvious resemblances between him and Stadion. Metternich, too, had been sobered by the French conquest. He was a worldly aristocrat, and a libertine who was capable of endless infatuations. He too had a double motive for hating France and the Revolution. Yet he possessed more experience of diplomacy and especially more cool deliberation, for there was never any trace of romantic enthusiasm about him. He was a man of the eighteenth century, a disciple and son-in-law of Kaunitz, and attached to the old idea of a European balance of power to be restored by bringing down Napoleon. Moreover, he remained faithful to enlightened despotism, and certainly felt no hostility in principle to reforms calculated to strengthen the state, provided that the social preponderance of the aristocracy was more respected than under Joseph II. Attempts have been made to attribute to him an original political philosophy inspired by Burke and characterized by an experimental rationalism. Having made a disciple of Gentz, whom he could get to justify any thesis, Metternich did in fact possess a whole arsenal of principles, but to explain his policy as the outcome of disinterested reflection gives the man too great a stature.

Delighting in the exercise of power, and determined to keep it, Metternich was a most able manager of the Hapsburg's affairs. Though the faults of the regime did not escape his notice, he took good care not to antagonize the Emperor and the nobility by making efforts to correct them. The European crusade which Gentz expected the dynasty to undertake only really interested him in so far as it could bring advantage to Austria in Italy and Germany. His unflinching realism was his greatest quality. By 1809 he had come to the conclusion that Napoleon had done all he could; and this mistaken opinion was responsible for the extreme caution with which he acted during the following years. His only thought was to survive till the moment came when he could safely join in the rush for the spoils. Already the shock to the Franco-Russian alliance was working in his favour; it was only a question of helping to turn it into positive antagonism. The safety of Austria would be better served by coming to terms with the victor, and this new Tilsit might be turned to positively good account. Napoleon's desire to take a wife was thus an unlooked-for opportunity: by marrying the Archduchess Marie-Louise he would bring about a final breach with Alexander, and would then look upon Austria as a natural ally.

No one knew better than Metternich that the Hapsburgs were bound to regard such a union as a blot on their reputation. But by suggesting that Napoleon should put forward a request and by presenting it to Francis as an ultimatum, it would be made clear to him that he must give way for reasons of state. The chancellor seems to have first alluded to the matter on November 29 in a conversation with Alexandre de Laborde, an 'auditeur' (assistant to the Conseil d'État) on a mission to Vienna; and chevalier de Floret, chargé d'affaires in Paris, talking to Sémonville in the course of an official dinner, was explicit enough to send his table-partner in haste to report to Maret. On December 16 Napoleon gave orders to make a tentative approach to the Austrian ambassador, Schwarzenberg, who was then seen by Alexandre de Laborde when he returned at the end of the month. There is no reason to believe that from now onwards Napoleon preferred an Austrian bride, but he must at all events have felt flattered. When he heard that the Czar was playing for time, the solution seemed to lie in Austria. There was a division of opinion among the imperial entourage. The smart counter-revolutionary circles were in favour of Austria, fondly imagining that the court of Vienna would demand the disgrace of the regicides, and that this would be a big step towards reaction. The revolutionaries, led by Fouché, were accordingly of the opposite opinion. The Beauharnais and Josephine herself were for Marie-Louise; the Bonapartes—headed by Murat—were for the Grand Duchess. Napoleon gave a hearing to both sides in a Privy Council on January 29, 1810, but reserved his decision. Finally on February 5 a dispatch from Caulaincourt announcing that the Czar was asking for further delay suggested to Napoleon that there would be a humiliation in store for him, and made him decide to forestall it. In the evening of the 6th, Eugène presented the official request to Schwarzenberg, requiring immediate consent to an engagement; and this was agreed to on the following day. It was the right moment, for on the 4th Alexander had just signified his refusal to Caulincourt. He was annoyed to find himself out-manœuvred but—diplomatically speaking—he came off best, for he was able to accuse Napoleon of playing a double game. Metternich had been right in his calculations: the breach between France and Russia began to widen.

Marie-Louise arrived at Strasbourg on March 22, Napoleon went to meet her, and with his usual impatience took possession of her in defiance of all etiquette; he then led her away to St. Cloud. The marriage was celebrated at the Louvre on April 2 and was followed at the end of the month by a journey to the north. On March 20, 1811, a son was born who had been given as early as February 17, 1810, the name of 'King of Rome'.

His baptism on June 9 was the last great celebration of the regime.

The Austrian marriage hastened the development that was removing Napoleon further and further from the Revolution. For her personal attendant, Marie-Louise was given Mme de Montesquieu, formerly governess to the Bourbon royal children; Fiévée became Master of Requests, and those who had come over to Napoleon took the upper hand in the Court of one who had now become by this new alliance the nephew of Marie-Antoinette and Louis XVI. Fouché, on the other hand, was dismissed on June 3 and replaced by Savary. The *ci-devant* were right in reckoning that there would be other measures to follow. A rumour went round that there was a secret article in the marriage contract stipulating that the regicides should be exiled, and that there would be a solemn rehabilitation of the memory of Louis XVI, who was constantly being whitewashed in the royalist brochures. Those who had come into possession of nationalized property also began to receive threatening letters. Institutions, too, moved further in the direction of the Old Regime. In 1810 the State prisons and arbitrary imprisonment were officially re-established and the censorship of books was openly reorganized.

Then again, Napoleon, in starting a new family, offended his own kith and kin, whom he constantly loaded with honours, but who never seemed satisfied. Their back-bitings, discords, and escapades had for some time disturbed his private life and damaged the new dynasty's prestige. Marie-Louise, with all her eighteen-year-old freshness, roused him to a second youth and to pleasures which she seems fully to have shared, for she was of a rather soft and sensual nature. But his critical sense did not desert him with respect to his son. He realized—as we know from his words—that the King of Rome would only keep the Empire if he too was a man of genius; he had a father's pride and did not despair of his son. His lively sense of the family bond, which has been attributed to the Latin tradition, but goes back more probably to Corsican custom, naturally led him from now onwards to show preference for his own posterity. When arranging the dowry for the new Empress on January 30, 1810, the apanages of his future children and the possible division of the crown possessions between them, he had made no reference at all to his brothers. Some have therefore been disposed to attribute to the Austrian marriage a deep influence on the change in the structure of the Grand Empire that begins to be evident from this time onwards. It has been said that its federative—if not Carolingian—structure tended now to become dynastic or Roman, with all conquests reserved for the King of Rome and so annexed to France. In any case they could only be distributed among his possible future brothers. In this way the Kingdom of Italy was assigned in advance to his second son, so that Eugène de Beauharnais saw his title of heir presumptive taken away, and was made instead the heir to Dalberg in the Grand Duchy of Frankfurt. Yet there has been some exaggeration of the influence which the marriage exercised in this respect, for the Emperor had long been exasperated at the refractoriness or incompetence of the vassal princes, and had long been threatening to annex their states. When Louis lost his kingdom, or when Murat and even Joseph and Jerome thought that a similar fate was in store for them, they may perhaps have accused Napoleon of sacrificing them to his new family; but the truth is that the federative Empire was evolving spontaneously towards a unified structure.

The essential consequence of the Austrian marriage lay elsewhere. In crowning the triumph of Wagram, it restored the Continental System in Napoleon's eyes, and raised his will to power to an even higher level through his feelings of personal euphoria. In entering into a closer relationship with Austria, it never occurred to him to treat her as an equal or to make a new Tilsit with her, as Metternich hoped. In Paris, the Austrian statesman had expressed his anxiety about the Russian advances in the East, and insinuated that they might agree to set limits to it. Napoleon admitted that France and Austria had common interests in this direction, and promised to intervene if Alexander claimed the right to expand south to the Danube; but he would not sign any document. Austria was still at his mercy, and imagining probably that the Hapsburg ruler would not be willing to do anything against the interests of his son-in-law, he continued to treat him as a vassal. His refusal to contest the Danube principalities with Russia in conformity with the agreement of Erfurt made him continue to delude himself for several months that the pact of Tilsit was still in existence.

Once again then, the only enemy was England. Metternich cherished the hope of re-establishing peace on the seas so as to avoid the dangerous obligation of coming out against her. In March 1810, he drew up an astonishing memoir in which Gentz solemnly proceeded to show the English that France was invincible, and that in her own interests she should leave her the whole continent, including Spain. About the same time Fouché was making efforts in the same direction. He had sent to the Marquis of Wellesley, then at the Foreign Office, a former *émigré* called Fagan whose father lived in London. Louis too considered a general reconciliation to be the only way of saving his kingdom; and it seemed likely that England would like to prevent the annexation of Holland, which remained an important outlet for her produce and so was of prime value to the bankers, Labouchère in particular. He also saw Wellesley in February 1810. Finally Ouvrard was employed by Fouché, who never ceased to protect him, no doubt in recollection of their common speculations. This financier was always involved in transactions with Labouchère, and did not forget the piastres of Mexico. This led him to suggest a political combination by which Charles IV would be transported to Mexico, England would hand Sicily over to Napoleon, who would give her Malta and help her to reconquer the United States! When set free from prison in Sainte-Pélagie, he came to an agreement with Labouchère, who let Baring into the secret. After discussing this plan with the latter and with Canning, Wellesley refused to give up Spain and Naples. At this point Louis, thinking that his brother was in the secret, spoke to him about it on April 27 when he was passing through Antwerp. Ouvrard was arrested, and a pretext found for dismissing Fouché. The talks were broken off. The Emperor had no more intention of giving way than the English.

In the course of this year he set himself to perfect the blockade. On August 5, the famous Trianon decrees were published, and on October 18 the Fontainebleau decree. In order to keep a close eye on their application, Napoleon pushed on more vigorously than ever with annexation, so much so that the blockade could now truly be said to have given a new impetus to the spirit of conquest. At the beginning of 1810, Holland had had to cede Zealand and its southern provinces as far as the Rhine; on July 2 Louis fled to Bohemia; and on the 9th his kingdom was annexed, a step legitimized by a *senatus-consultum* of December 13. In order to put a solid padlock on all the North Sea ports and the frontiers of Holstein, Napoleon called together on January 22, 1811, all the German countries lying north of a line between the Lippe and the Trave—namely the Hanseatic ports, a part of the Grand Duchy of Berg and the Kingdom of Westphalia, the principalities of Arenberg and Salm, and the Grand Duchy of Oldenburg. In order to shut off Italy definitely against Swiss contraband he took possession of the Valais and occupied the canton of the Tessin with troops.

Meanwhile, however, the Iberian peninsula was still under arms. It seemed likely then that after Wagram Napoleon would prepare a big expedition to destroy the English army or force it to re-embark, after which the surrender of the whole country would only have been a matter of time. He did to be sure send 140,000 men by way of reinforcement, but this was not enough to strike a decisive blow, nor did he supply them with the indispensable material support. Most important of all, he did not follow them in person. Absorbed in his dynastic plans, and giving himself entirely to his new wife, he let this crucial year slip by, till at the end of 1810 there could no longer be any question of his being able to go to Spain with all his available forces, because the attitude of Alexander was giving cause for anxiety. Thus his dreams of personal grandeur and his new marriage prevented him from restoring the unity of the Grande Armée and condemned him to a struggle with Russia in the absence of an important part of his fighting force.

The Austrian marriage was not the root cause of this supreme contest, but it precipitated the crisis, although Napoleon would not admit it to himself, by exciting the jealousy of the Russians, who saw the Austrians being given special favours at Napoleon's court, and more still by ensuring the failure of the Polish negotiations. At the same time that he addressed his official request to Schwarzenberg the Emperor had rejected the treaty signed by Caulaincourt. He drew up another, which he then sent to Caulaincourt already endorsed with his ratification, indicating that he would give no one any help in re-establishing Poland and would agree to removing the very name from all official documents. In return, Russia and

Saxony would agree not to take for themselves any of the Polish provinces outside the Grand Duchy, and the treaty was to remain secret. This did not suit Alexander at all. On July 13 Nesselrode refused to make any modifications in the January agreement, and Napoleon at once broke off the negotiations. He refused moreover to authorize a Russian loan. In the summer of 1810, he did not yet regard war as inevitable, yet he was well aware that Alexander, cut loose from France, might make it up with England, in which case he would have to take up arms.

At the same time events in Sweden served to irritate the Czar. Charles XIII had signed a peace treaty with France on January 6, 1810, and joined the blockade. But he did not really possess enough authority to be able to obey its requirements to the full, especially as Saumarez' fleet was in command of the Baltic. The Emperor was soon furious, and threatened to re-occupy Pomerania. Sweden promised to do all he demanded, all the more readily because she was in the throes of a crisis about the succession. The brother-in-law of Frederick VI, King of Denmark, Charles Augustus of Augustenburg, whom Charles XIII had accepted as his heir, had died on May 28, 1810. The opponents of the 1809 revolution were accused of having poisoned him, and on the day of his funeral Fersen was massacred in the course of a riot. The government wanted to replace the dead man by his brother, but Napoleon would give no explicit answer, and an intrigue—of doubtful origins—took advantage of this ambiguous situation. There was a party in Stockholm who favoured the French and would have preferred a relation or lieutenant of Napoleon's as a means of winning his protection against Russia. At the end of June Lieutenant Mörner came to sound Bernadotte in his name and won the support of Count Wrede, who had been sent to Paris on the occasion of the marriage. Bernadotte informed the Emperor, who hesitated. It was perfectly clear that Alexander would not take at all kindly to the election of a French Marshal; on the other hand if war broke out, Sweden would be a great help. Bernadotte, it is true, was not a very reliable man: Eugène would have been a better choice. But the Emperor reckoned that the French party, who wanted to reconquer Finland, would hold him to his duty. He therefore did not forbid him to accept, though he would make no official pronouncement, in order to spare the feelings of the Czar. The Swedish Diet, meeting at Orebro, seemed to be in favour of Augustenburg, until a man called Fournier came on the scene. He had been formerly consul at Götelborg, a merchant who had failed in business, and was now sent by Champagny to act as an observer, but was really Bernadotte's agent. Giving himself out to be the Emperor's official agent, he recommended the election of the marshal; whereupon one of the king's inner circle, the Count Suremain, an emigré, brought his consent and the Diet followed suit on August 21. Napoleon was surprised at such a rapid result, and was doubtful whether he should endorse it; but the thought that it would be particularly mortifying to England finally carried the day. Sweden, moreover, seemed to be confirmed in its francophile policy and on November 17 declared war against England. But there was a reverse side to the medal. Alexander was furious. Yet Napoleon did not know that Bernadotte was losing no time in reassuring the Czar by declaring to Chernikov, who was passing through Stockholm, that he would by no means be merely the Emperor's man, and would never attempt to resume possession of Finland. Thus Alexander was very soon filled with hope that the new king's disloyalty would guarantee him the neutrality, if not the positive assistance, of Sweden.

Though the Emperor was unaware of the fact, Russia's preparations were steadily taking shape. The Czar's first preoccupation was to induce Czartoryski to come forward with some offers. Then, in April 1810, he made up his mind to speak out. War would begin in nine months' time: would it not be possible to have the help of the Grand Duchy, and so be able to transport Russian troops in one move to the Oder, thus involving the Prussians? Czartoryski showed considerable reserve, for Napoleon had been very successful in hoodwinking him. Nevertheless, Alexander proceeded to steal a march on him. He appointed Alopeus and Pozzo di Borgo as ambassadors to Naples and Constantinople respectively, but sent them by way of Vienna, where they found opinion in the *salons* very favourable to their master, and still infatuated with Ragumovski and Princess Bagration. They managed to obtain an audience with Metternich's father who was holding the fort while the chancellor was away in Paris. The suggestion was that Austria might take Serbia, particularly in order to settle the eastern disagreement. But when Metternich reappeared he put an end to negotiations. Nevertheless, the Russian army began during the last months of the year to move quietly westwards. It would seem probable then that, failing Austria, Alexander was building some hopes upon Poland; perhaps Czartoryski had after all made up his mind.

By the end of the year the alliance had been officially broken by a double violation of the agreement made at Erfurt. Like all the purely agricultural countries, Russia suffered from the blockade, but without any kind of compensation. Alexander now lent an ear to the aristocracy's complaints, and came to the conclusion that the sluggishness of trade was harming the finances. Having now taken sides against Napoleon, he was inclined to make an approach to England. Though he had decided to go to war, he nevertheless wanted to put himself in the right by provoking his enemy to take the offensive. Already, he had taken good care not to adopt the edicts of Trianon and Fontainebleau; and on December 31, 1810, he went one better. Goods imported over land were now made subject to very heavy duties, whilst favoured treatment was given to seaborne trade in neutral vessels, together with the English trade, which was officially forbidden by Napoleon. Meanwhile Napoleon was annexing the Grand Duchy of Oldenburg, whose integrity had been guaranteed at Erfurt, after offering in vain to compensate the Grand Duke, Alexander's brother-in-law, in Thuringia. From that moment onwards, another war was inevitable.

CHAPTER THREE

England's Successes (1807–1811)

WHILE NAPOLEON was strengthening his Continental hegemony, England was achieving the mastery of the seas as the outcome of her quiet and dogged efforts. Up till 1808, there did not appear to be any very decisive results. Squadrons were still coming and going from the French ports, and there were still some colonies that had not succumbed. It was the Spanish insurrection that brought decisive aid to British policy, on sea no less than on land, by finalizing her command of the seas and at the same time inducing her to set foot once more on the Continent in order to give direct help to the coalitions which were the only means of defeating the conqueror.

THE COMMAND OF THE SEAS AND ITS CONSEQUENCES

After Trafalgar, the British fleet had resumed the blockade of the enemy ports. Ships kept a close watch on the ports while the squadrons out at sea stood ready to pursue any vessels that might contrive to escape. This monotonous and humdrum watch was not without its hazards. Between 1806 and 1815 the English lost eighteen vessels, without a single one of them being captured or sunk by the enemy. The convoys also required a large supply of vessels. Naval construction was therefore unceasing: the budget—which was less than £9 million in 1803—rose to more than £20 million in 1811; and by 1814 the English had 240 vessels, plus 317 frigates and 611 minor craft. Gradually all the warships that might have reinforced the French had fallen into their hands, Dutch, Danish, Neapolitan, and Portuguese. In 1808 and 1809 the Spanish and Turks also joined the English side; and after those of Siniavine, the Russian ships blockaded at Cronstadt were escorted to England in 1812.

Napoleon was also engaged in constant construction—83 vessels and 65 frigates between 1800 and 1814, at the end of which period he possessed 103 vessels and 54 frigates. But he could only have restored the balance by making himself master of the whole Continent, which would have needed years of effort. Up till 1809, however, he did not give up squadron action, but limited it to raids on the enemy lines of communication or against their colonies. There were some successful attempts to slip between the meshes of the blockade—by Leyssègues and Willaumez in 1805, Leduc and Soleil in 1806, Allemand and Gauteaume in 1808, Willaumez, Jarien, Troude, and Baudouin in 1809. But they were immediately pursued, and almost all of them suffered enormous losses or complete disaster. The English destroyed Leyssègues' squadron at St. Domingo; Willaumez lost two ships out of six; and in 1806 Linois, returning from the Île-de-France, was roughly handled in the Canaries. In 1809, Willaumez and Jurien, having effected a junction in the île d'Aix roadstead on the way to the Antilles, had fire-ships sent in among them by Gambier. Their ships foundered, and none of them would have escaped if Gambier had supported the intrepid Cochrane. Troude's squadron succeeded in reaching the Saints, only to disintegrate. Allemand and Gauteaume were allowed to get through with new supplies for Corfu, but this was due to the age of Collingwood, who died at sea in 1809. The Spanish insurrection put an end to these attempts, because the juntas took possession of the French ships in Cadiz and Le Ferrol, and the English—who had previously been forced by the alliance between Charles IV and the Directory to abandon the Mediterranean—now found the peninsular ports a most valuable help. In more distant waters, there were even more important results. The Spanish colonies ceased to serve as French bases and now became available to the other side, thus bringing about a complete reversal of conditions in the war at sea and the course of the colonial struggle.

Between 1806 and 1815 France and her allies lost 124 vessels, 157 frigates, and 288 smaller craft. In 1806, there were 36,000 French prisoners in England and 120,000 in 1815—a large part of them captured by the British sea forces. The war between squadrons came to an end, and all the French could now do was to attempt random attacks. The English suffered some damage from these, the maximum losses being 619 in 1810. Between 1803 and 1814 the total rose to 5,244, or 2½ per cent of all comings and goings. Added to the losses at sea, this meant a 5 per cent reduction in the merchant navy. Although construction had fallen from 1,402 ships drawing 135,000 tons in 1803 to 596 drawing 61,000 tons in 1809, this gap was subsequently more than filled, so that the merchant fleet rose from 22,000 ships in 1805 to 24,000 in 1810. These results were a clear proof that corsairs, unsupported by squadrons, were unable to strike an effective blow at the enemy shipping, which mostly moved in escorted convoys. The measure of safety is attested by the insurance rates. They varied a good deal according to the region, and were always higher for the Baltic; but they came down at once for more distant waters, and fell on the average from 12 per cent in 1806 to 6 per cent in 1810, whereas they had risen to 25 per cent in the Revolution and 50 per cent during the American war. Now that they commanded the seas the English were able to destroy the merchant navy of France and her allies. In 1801, France possessed 1,500 ocean-going vessels; in 1810, she still had 343; but in 1812 only 179 remained. The fishing industry had dwindled to nothing. Her naval supremacy therefore assured Great Britain control of the maritime trade and enabled her to extend it significantly, thus allowing her to cope with the Continental blockade, cover her constantly increasing expenses, and provide finance for the conditions.

This commercial exploitation of the successes achieved by her warships was what occupied her chief attention. Contrary to what might have been expected, colonial conquests only came second. In the eyes of the mercantile world, the essential thing was to prevent the neutrals from trading with enemy colonies and to monopolize this trade for Great Britain. Up to Trafalgar, moreover, the British government had to concentrate all its forces in European waters. After the seizure in 1803 of St.

Lucia, Tobago, and a part of Dutch Guyana, there was a pause till 1806 before Surinam could be captured. In 1807, Britain took possession of Curaçao, and the Danish Antilles, St. Thomas and Santa Cruz; in 1808, of Maria-Galante and La Désirade. Attention was also given to the African ports of call along the route to India. In January 1806, Popham, Baird, and Beresford landed at the Cape and forced Janssens to surrender. In 1807, Madeira was occupied, then the other Portuguese colonies; in 1808, Goré succumbed, and in 1809 St. Louis. In America, the face of things was changed by the Spanish insurrection. Up till then the English had felt obliged to go warily because the coasts of Latin America might be used as bases for hostile expeditions. Then the situation completely changed. In 1809, Guyana and Martinique were conquered; in 1810, Guadeloupe, St. Martin, St. Eustatius, and Saba.

In the Indian Ocean, the change of sides by Spain also deprived Decaen, who was in command of the Île-de-France, of the support provided by the Philippines, but the final decision was dependent in the main on the policy of the governors of India.

After Wellesley's departure, his successors—Cornwallis, Barlow, and Minto—adopted an attitude exactly the opposite of his own and came to terms with the native princes in order to re-establish peace. Sindhia was the first to treat, and he was given Rajputana; Holkar then recovered the greater part of his states; Ranjit Singh, who ruled over the Sikhs of the Punjab, and who had momentarily reoccupied it, finally sided with the English and in 1809 signed an agreement fixing the frontier at the Sutlej and giving him Jaipur. Having secured this frontier, he took possession of Multan, Peshawar, and Kashmir and entered into alliance with Afghanistan, which reoccupied Baluchistan and Sind. All this took time and opened up considerable problems for the future. Moreover, Central India, left to itself, soon relapsed into anarchy. Roving bands of ex-soldiers and brigands, known as the Pindaris, committed appalling ravages in these parts. Nor were the fortunes of the missions without their hazards. The London Missionary Society opened work in India in 1804; and the Baptists entered Burma in 1807 and Ceylon in 1812. In 1813, India had its first bishop. There was however an element of frenzied fanaticism in the revolt of the Sepoys at Vellore in 1807. At any rate the abandonment of Warren Hastings's and Wellesley's aggressive schemes had the advantage of allowing Lord Minto to pursue a vigorous external policy.

In the Mascarenhas, Decaen had succeeded in imposing Napoleon's views. He suppressed the colonial assemblies, reintroduced centralization and reorganized the old militias under the name of National Guards. The colonists missed the autonomy they had in fact enjoyed during the Revolution, but gave in to authority because slavery was reintroduced. To supply the slave-trade, Decaen entered into contact with Madagascar and created a trading-centre at Tamatave. But his thoughts were never far from India, and in 1804 he asked for reinforcements to support the Mahrattas. After Tilsit, he proposed a maritime diversion to support the projected Franco-Russian expedition. In January 1808, his brother came and spoke about it to the Emperor, who promised a squadron and 15,000 men. Although the English never had real cause for alarm, they hated this 'nest of pirates', for Surcouf had given them a hard time. In 1810, Lord Minto resolved to have done with it. In July he seized the Île Bonaparte (formerly the Île Bourbon or Réunion). In August, Duperré and Bouvet destroyed a squadron of four frigates in the Port-Louis roadstead; but at the end of November 16,000 men landed in the north of the Île-de-France, and Decaen, who only had 1,846 men, was defeated. He surrendered on December 3. The following year the English occupied Tamatave. The Seychelles had entered into an agreement of neutrality from the start. Then Lord Minto turned his attention to the Dutch Indies, where Java and the Moluccas fell into his hands.

The French and Dutch colonial empires counted very little, however, in comparison with the Spanish. As soon as the Spaniards had declared war in 1804, Windham and Grenville sponsored the schemes of Popham and Miranda. After offering his services to Napoleon, who had had him extradited in 1801, when he was immersed in his negotiations with Spain and well aware that he was in the pay of the English, Miranda had returned to London. In October 1804, he proposed—with Popham's agreement—to attack simultaneously Caracas, Buenos Aires, and Valparaiso. Grenville wanted to get at

Mexico, by way of the Gulf on the one hand and the Pacific on the other. At the same time there was to be an expedition from India which would land at Acapulco, having taken Manila on the way. But Pitt, busy with negotiations for the third coalition, confined himself to sending Miranda to the United States to attack Florida. Jefferson, however, refused permission, and only allowed him to organize a small expedition against Venezuela, which came to grief in February 1806. Cochrane, who was cruising off the Antilles, assembled a new squadron which left Granada in July, but was no more successful than the first. In 1807, Miranda came back to England.

Thanks to Popham, the matter had now a more serious complexion. Acting on his own responsibility, he took Beresford's troops from the Cape and landed them south of Buenos Aires in June 1806, where the viceroy was defeated and lost possession of the city. A French *émigré*, Jacques Liniers by name, who had a district command, hastened to Montevideo and collected a small body of men who forced Beresford to capitulate on August 12. But the English government had not been able to resist the temptation to hold on to this acquisition, and Auchmunty's expedition was already on the way. But finding Buenos Aires in Liniers' hands, they took possession of Montevideo on February 3, 1807. They were followed by Craufurd, who had originally been meant for Valparaiso, and then by Whitelocke, who took over the command. On July 5, he gained a footing in Buenos Aires, but was surrounded after some street-fighting, and on the next day signed an evacuation agreement. In recognition of his services Liniers was made a count and a grandee of Spain, and appointed viceroy.

Once more Spain provided the means of revenge for England. In May 1808, Napoleon had the idea of using Liniers to procure recognition for Joseph—Liniers having written to him as to the ally of Charles IV—and sent him the Marquis of Sassenay, whilst he sent another noble to Caracas. But the result was deplorable. At Montevideo, Sassenay found a Spaniard called Elio who was jealous of Liniers and passed on the word to warn his fellow countrymen in Buenos Aires. When Sassenay arrived, they forced Liniers to send him back to Montevideo, where there was a rising that forced the governor to expel the French ship, which was then captured by the English. Everywhere

Ferdinand VII was proclaimed king, and Spanish America slipped from Napoleon's hands. But Spain too was in danger of losing it, for the half-castes, knowing that Spain was powerless to intervene, and regarding a captive king as a ruler only in name, intended to take advantage of this chance of securing their independence. At Buenos Aires, they were satisfied merely to support Liniers against the Spaniards who attempted to overthrow him, but at Caracas Bolivar and his friends seized power in July 1808, and did the same the following year at Quito, Charcas, and La Paz. But it was a premature effort, for the Seville junta sent out fresh officials who generally speaking asserted their authority without much difficulty. Emparan reestablished the Old Regime at Caracas, and Cisneros took Liniers' place. The troops from Lima subjugated Quito and the towns of high Peru. Now that they were in alliance with Spain, the English did not dare to support the rebels; nevertheless, they reaped the expected benefits from these events. As early as 1807 Popham had addressed a circular to British merchants, inviting them to send all the cargoes they could to Buenos Aires, which had resulted in an amazing rush. The half-castes then began to trade freely with the defenders of their sovereign; and on November 6, 1809, the government of Buenos Aires officially allowed England to trade with the colony. In 1810, customs produced more than 2½ million piastres as compared with less than 1 million before the war. Brazil too had opened her ports to the English. At a time when Europe was threatening to close its doors to British exports, the acquisition of such valuable markets elsewhere aroused much enthusiasm in England. But the fresh half-caste rebellions and the resulting civil war were soon to prove an impediment to the progress of British trade.

The European advantages of the command of the seas in the commercial world soon became equally evident. The process of tightening the blockade of the Empire, and the bases incidentally utilized, served to develop contraband and outwit the Continental blockade. In the North Sea, Heligoland became an English depot, and a number of islands along the French coast were put to the same use—Saint-Marcouf, les Chausey, les Molènes, les Glenans, Houat and Hoëdic, l'île Verte opposite la Ciotat, and the islands off Hyères; and the English anchored buoys in Quiberon roads and in Douarnenez Bay. Furthermore, the English fleet remained in command of the Sound and the Baltic. Progress, however, was particularly remarkable in the Mediterranean and the Levant, with the result that the chain of alliances contrived by Napoleon in order to extend his influence as far as Persia began to recoil against him. With Gibraltar and Malta in her possession, England could close the western Mediterranean. She had been in command of Sicily since 1798, and in 1806 she occupied its north-east tip. The alliance signed on March 30, 1808, granted Ferdinand IV a subsidy of £300,000, later raised to £400,000 expressly earmarked for armaments, so that the government in London could insist on accounts being rendered, and before long on the right to inspect the Neapolitan troops. In spite of this, there were always some lingering doubts about the intentions of the Court, Marie-Caroline in particular. The English supervision seemed oppressive and the subsidy meagre. In 1810, having failed to induce the assembled Estates to vote new taxes, the king authorized them himself and broke all resistance by arresting and deporting five of the most recalcitrant barons on July 19, 1811.

On the 24th, Lord Bentinck landed in Sicily, invested both with diplomatic powers and with the rank of Commander-in-Chief. He had formerly been governor of Madras, and was a colonial of the authoritarian and peremptory type. Moreover, he was a convinced Whig, to whom the introduction of the British constitutional system in foreign parts seemed to be a matter of conscience and essential for the welfare of the human race. Besides, in supporting the opposition he reckoned that he would have a means of making the Court see reason. But as they would not listen to him, he re-embarked on August 27, and went back to London to seek full powers and the suspension of the subsidy. On his return he concentrated his forces round Palermo, demanded the control of the Sicilian army, the recall of those who had been banished, and the dismissal of the existing ministers. The king saved face by delegating his powers—at least nominally—to his son as Vicar-General on January 14, 1812. Bentinck subsequently forced the queen to leave Palermo; and in March the prince was obliged to hand over the reins of government to those who had been banished, and Bentinck made them call Parliament to approve a constitution worked out by himself. At this juncture the western Mediterranean—thanks to the Spanish insurrection which had brought about the surrender of the Balearic Islands—had become something very like an English lake. Even the Berbers, while not giving up piracy, adjusted themselves to the new situation and the Sultan of Morocco kept on good terms with the rulers of the sea. Malta and Sicily provided an easy gateway into the Adriatic, and in 1809 the British cruisers succeeded in finally gaining control of the Ionian Islands—all except Corfu. They then proceeded to attack the Dalmatian Islands and occupied several, winning a naval victory at Liasa in March 1811. Control over the Adriatic gave them the upper hand in Albania and Epirus; and Ali-Tebelen once more changed his allegiance.

In the eastern Mediterranean action was likewise taken in 1807 from Malta and Sicily against Constantinople and Egypt. Although it was not successful, the Turkish coasts were nevertheless soon at the mercy of the English, and the Sultan, alarmed and exasperated by the Franco-Russian alliance, made peace and undertook once more to close the Straits to foreign warships. From now on the British agents—and in particular Stratford Canning, a cousin of the minister, who began a famous career at Constantinople in 1809—worked to bring about a reconciliation between the Turks and the Russians. England monopolized the markets of the Levant, which soon developed tremendously. Persia too changed sides, whilst in spite of Gardane's efforts, war broke out again in Armenia. After a victory at Nakhitchevan, the Russians besieged Erivan. The English, however, having made peace with the Turks, entered the Persian Gulf from India, and in May 1808 Malcolm landed at Bender-Abbas. The Shah, who was not obtaining any benefits from France, decided to receive the British envoy, Sir Harford Jones, whereupon Gardane left Teheran on February 1, 1809. By a treaty signed on March 12 the country was closed to the French; and in 1814 a further treaty aimed at guaranteeing its integrity against Russia. In 1809, a mission to the Emir of Afghanistan obtained an assurance that he would not assist any expedition directed against India.

The independence of the pashas in Egypt, Syria, and Bagdad was another constant source of concern. The English therefore entered into relations with the Wahabites, who were hostile to all of them. Saoud, the son of Abdul-Aziz, having captured Medina in 1804, threatened Damascus and Aleppo, and in 1808 and 1811, attacked the Pasha of Baghdad. When the latter was being attacked in the north by the Pasha of Suleimania and by the Kurds, he saw the English effecting a landing at Bassorah and decided to make friends with them. Saoud performed the further service of defeating the Imam of Muscat and harassing the French throughout Arabia. As for Mehemet-Ali, he was engaged for a long while and subjugated the last of the mamelukes, who had taken up arms again in 1808. On March 1, 1811, however, he got the better of them by means of a trap. He invited them all to a meal in the course of which he had them massacred. He then undertook to subdue the Wahabites, and after an unfortunate attempt in 1811 his son Tussun reconquered the holy cities in 1812. Mehemet's campaign in the following year was unsuccessful; but in 1814 Tussan seized Taïf, and in 1815, after Saound's death, Mehemet was able to take Rass, the capital of the Nedjd, and sign a treaty of peace. These arduous undertakings did not allow him to cross swords with the English. Thus the whole of the East eluded the clutches of Napoleon and from Gibraltar to India, by sea and by land, the English had succeeded in isolating the Empire.

WELLINGTON'S CAMPAIGNS

The Napoleonic Empire had the appearance of an island from which there was no means of escape, whilst its enemies could enjoy free movement all around and anywhere they liked in the world. But it was also a fortress which could neither be reduced by famine nor taken by assault as long as the French army was intact. All the British fleet could do was to land troops at suitable spots to help the Continental allies. But this threat, though useful in itself, because it forced Napoleon to guard every coast and kept the inhabitants' nerves on edge, was not enough to be decisive. England's allies were well aware of this, and though very ready to pocket English money, were not satisfied with this alone. As long as English ships did not bring redcoats, they were reproached with the suggestion that the command of the seas was exercised solely for England's benefit.

Yet most English ministers and the vast majority of their fellow-citizens were none the less averse to fighting on the Continent. Their insular feelings—strongly reinforced by the experiences of 1793 and 1799 and then by the threatened landings in Great Britain—were increased by the fact that manpower was not overabundant. Though the English were willing to enlist in defence of their own country, the army was only reconciled by dint of offering bonuses among the poorer classes, and even then there was a dearth of recruits. Her overseas possessions were continually extending, and it was not practicable to denude England entirely of troops, let alone Ireland, which was still under martial law. There were thus very few troops available, and there was all the greater reluctance to risk an expeditionary force, seeing that it would be extremely difficult to replace.

It was also necessary to take expenses and monetary difficulties into account. The English troops were accustomed to pay for what they took from the country, even in Portugal and Spain, and in France in 1814, and they consequently needed coin or means of exchange. And lastly, there was the difficulty in Parliament, where any Continental undertaking provided the opposition with a means of stirring up strong feeling. They had no hesitation in declaring that Napoleon was invincible on land, which was an indirect argument for peace. For all these reasons, Fox and his successors refrained from any interventions on the Continent—apart from the reinforcements sent to the Swedes in Pomerania; and this was an attitude that contributed not a little to the alienation of Russia. Canning and Castlereagh were in favour of an exactly opposite policy; but Tilsit had dissolved the coalition, and it was not till Copenhagen that Canning was able to show his abilities.

Here too the Spanish insurrection was of capital importance. Canning did not hesitate to promise the juntas his support and, not content merely to promise them money and supplies, he arranged for the reconquest of Portugal, which up till then had been denied any military aid, and despatched Baird to Galicia. His path was smoothed by the initial support of the Whigs, who first of all greeted the insurrection with enthusiasm. But after the Emperor's campaign they changed their tune. The opposition came to life again and proceeded to criticize the Convention of Cintra, and to maintain that Portugal was not defensible. Sir John Moore had also been of this opinion, and the government began to wonder whether they should recall Craddock, who had remained in Lisbon with 10,000 men, or transfer to Portugal the army that had returned from Galicia in a deplorable state. This time, it was Castlereagh who made the decision. After consulting Arthur Wellesley, he made up his mind on April 2, 1809, to despatch this army to Portugal, acting on the assurance that 30,000 men would be enough to save the country. At this juncture, however, Austria was just entering the war, and Castlereagh, like a good disciple of Pitt, keeping his eyes firmly fixed upon the Netherlands, could not resist the temptation to send an expedition to Holland under the pretext that it would help Austria. And so England, having neglected to take action between 1805 and 1807, now intervened simultaneously in two places, but the reinforcements sent to Portugal hardly raised the strength to more than 26,000 men. On the other hand, in the spring of 1809, if England had sent all available forces to the German coast, she might have struck a decisive blow. But the Walcheren expedition was a failure, and from this time onwards England's activities abroad were to be confined to the Spanish peninsula.

Even then, English policy was not pursued without considerable hesitation and debate. In 1809, the Portland Cabinet was disintegrating, for Canning and Castlereagh were so different in background and character that they found it hard to work together. The former aspired to becoming the head of the government and to direct the war effort as well as diplomacy, and in April he called upon his colleagues to choose between his rival and himself. They put off making a decision until the end of the war, but the Walderen expedition was followed by a crisis. Canning resigned, and was wounded in a duel by Castlereagh on September 21. And then Portland died, enabling Perceval, who had remained at the Exchequer, to reconstitute his government and call Richard Wellesley to the Foreign Office. He had formerly been governor of India, and did his best to provide reinforcements for his brother's army. Nevertheless, this continued to be a weak government. The defeat of Austria and Napoleon's marriage had produced a division in public opinion. Grenville, Grey, and Ponsonby were strongly in favour of evacuating Spain, they criticized the general and were unwilling to admit his successes. The government had been obliged to hold an enquiry into the Zealand expedition, and the throne came in for a good deal of mud-slinging because of the scandal involving the Duke of York's mistress, who was convicted of having sold officers' commissions. To crown everything, the king once again went out of his mind. The Prince of Wales had a bad reputation because of his quarrels with Caroline of Brunswick, whom he publicly accused of adultery; but he nevertheless found himself being made Regent, under the same conditions as in 1788, up till February 1, 1812. As he had always enjoyed intimate relations with the Whigs, it was to be expected that he would call them to office now that he was invested with full power. Finally, in 1811, the country was hit by a severe economic crisis which upset the finances and produced a number of disturbances. It is thus not surprising that the Perceval government showed some reserve in their attitude to Arthur Wellesley, who had meanwhile become Viscount Wellington. It was made clear to him that if he were to meet with a serious reverse, evacuation would be bound to follow. When Massena's offensive was announced in 1810, Wellington was warned that he would be excused if he withdrew his forces earlier rather than later. There was extreme parsimony in the supply of reinforcements, and the general was left to grapple with the most harassing financial difficulties.

But Massena's retreat brought a renewal of confidence. Reinforcements were notably increased, and made the victorious campaign of 1812 possible. For three years, however, Wellington had only himself to rely on: he had not only to fight a war but also to raise the morale of the government. This fact explains the cautiousness of his strategy up to well on in 1812, and the care with which he reorganized the Portuguese army. One of his outstanding qualities was his ability to persist in spite of all difficulties in carrying on the war within the framework of the general British policy, which he understood to perfection. He showed that the Spanish undertaking as such possessed immense possibilities and lent a real effectiveness to the command of the seas. It was thanks to him, as well as to Canning and Castlereagh, that England was able to come to close grips with the Napoleonic giant.

In 1809, Arthur Wellesley, Viscount Wellington, was forty

years old, the same age as Napoleon. He had served under his brother for a long period in India—from 1798 to 1805—and was only just beginning his European career. He was a sober character and blessed with an iron constitution. Like the Emperor, he could work long hours and do with little sleep. He had a clear and precise mind of a positive cast, with good organizing ability. He was a man of cool and tenacious will-power, though this did not exclude an ability to take bold and calculated risks. As a young man, he had shown himself very independent, but when he came to command he proved extremely authoritarian, never allowing his officers—who were incidentally of rather mediocre calibre—any initiative what-soever. His expression was marked by an aristocratic pride, hardened still further by his long years among the Indians. He treated his officers with a haughty disdain, and had an unlimited contempt for the common people, and for his own soldiers who were of the people, calling them 'the scum of the earth', 'a pack of rascals', 'a crowd who only enlist for drink, and can only be managed with the whip'. At any rate his pride of country bound him closely to his own social caste and to the land of which they were, in his view, the lawful owners, and his only thought was to serve them. With a hard and dry character in which imagination and affection were equally wanting, he was at any rate preserved from the romantic in-dividualism that was the ruin of Napoleon, but his talent lacked the unending fascination exercised by the genius of the Emperor.

Wellington's mind and character were perfectly suited to the life he was leading as a warrior in command of a professional army of only moderate effectiveness, slowly and monotonously campaigning with defensive battles whose object was to wear out the enemy. Considered from the technical point of view, he was essentially an infantry leader, hardly making use of the cavalry, and very rarely pursuing the enemy. His artillery, whether mounted or unmounted, was excellent but not very plentiful. There were no sappers, engineers, or siege equipment: his foot soldiers had to suffice for all tasks, and suffered enor-mous losses in taking fortified places by assault. Yet of all the Emperor's enemies he was the one who enjoyed the pre-eminent advantage of having given mature thought to the tactics to be adopted in his encounters with the French. He preserved the line formation, while giving greater elasticity to the method of combat. For defence against sharp-shooters, he would shelter his lines behind hedges, ruins, or houses with loopholes, or conceal them on a counter-slope, and did not despise dispersed fire or individual random fire. Each battalion had a company strung out ahead of it, and from 1809 onwards he used a regiment of 'rifles' and foreign troops deployed in the same way. He did not fail to realize that the enemy, whose triumphs had turned their heads, tended to cut short the sharp-shooting preparation for battle and advance more and more promptly with their battalions in deep column. At Maida, they had attacked without preliminary firing. Wellington concealed his troops, reckoning that the French were incapable of appreciating the results of fire, or would be impatient at the slow progress made by their skirmishers, and that they would then be all the more eager to charge with the bayonet. In that case, troops who were arranged in shallow order, were cool-headed, and almost intact, would be at a great advantage. The professional English foot-soldier was well drilled in firing volleys, and his weapon fired heavier bullets than the French. Furthermore, Wellington adopted a line two-deep instead of three-deep, so that a battalion of 800 men could fire 800 rounds in one salvo. The French battalion, however, was arranged in column by companies, 40 wide and 18 deep, or in double companies, 80 wide and 9 deep, so that the first two ranks could only reply with 80 or 160 rounds. If they attempted to deploy, they would lose a good many men in the process, and as a rule got out of formation, so bringing the attack to a halt. When he had proved the effectiveness of these tactics, the English general did not hesitate to use them now and again—as at Salamanca—to attack in the same order, the line advancing at walking pace, and stopping deliberately every so often to fire. But Wellington's tactics were above all marvellously effective in a defensive battle, and so fitted with the conditions generally prevailing in his campaigns. They demanded, moreover, a professional army, implacably disciplined to an automatic obedience by the use of corporal punishment, like the army of Frederick II. Napoleon's lieutenants failed to learn their lesson through the reverses that Wellington inflicted upon them; and because he never came to observe these tactics in action, Napoleon was only able to appreciate their value on the field of Waterloo.

Yet for all his talent, Wellington would probably not have succeeded in maintaining his forces in the peninsula without having Portugal at his disposal. He used it as a base that could be freely replenished by the British fleet, and reorganized a national Portuguese army which provided him with important contingents. The regency was never able to treat with England on level terms, and in 1810 it co-opted the assistance of Charles Stuart, who became the head of the administration. But Wellington never ceased to complain of the nepotism and ineffectiveness of the aristocracy, and their obstinacy in maintaining their own fiscal privileges. He wanted the subsidy—£1½ million and then £2 million—to be put at his disposal for feeding the army, but London would never agree, in deference to the feelings of the Portuguese. As the country subsisted solely on goods imported from the United States, and was selling half as much wine as before the war, the regency could only make both ends meet by feeding the soldiers on requisitions paid for by a depreciated paper money, with the result that they were badly fed, and fell ill or deserted in large numbers. In February 1809, the regency asked the English to appoint a commander-in-chief. They chose Beresford, who was not outstanding as a general, but was a good organizer. He introduced a certain number of British officers and instructors into the Portuguese regiments, and, with two exceptions, the generals were also British. In September 1809, there were 42,000 men available, and by 1810 they had more or less reached an effective strength of 56,000, which was the target. All the same, there were great difficulties in providing them with weapons, and the cavalry was always short of mounts. The militia was also used for garrison duties, reconnaissance and guerilla warfare, and in 1810 they had to fall back upon the *ordenanza* or *levée en masse*.

The Spaniards did not procure the same degree of help. They had no intention of letting themselves be governed, and up to 1812 refused to put their forces under the command of the English. The central junta, however, had only a limited authority. It had to flee to Seville in December 1808, and then took refuge in Cadiz in January 1810, where it abdicated in favour of a council of regency. In September, the Cortes met and set up an executive council which was replaced in 1812 by a new regency. All these governments showed indecision, and were suspected of nepotism and corruption. The old council of Castile and the former junta of Seville disputed one another's powers, and certain persons—such as the Count of Montijo, the Duke of Infadato, the brother of Palafox, conspired to overthrow them. The provincial juntas too were unstable, generally moving from one town to another, and only obeying orders when they felt inclined. Co-operation between the juntas and the military leaders was always precarious, and the guerillas were a law to themselves. Moreover, though the population hated the invaders, it by no means followed that most of the men were disposed to fight; and in any case they disliked the conscription that was imposed by the central junta in 1811. Although the aim had been an army of 800,000 men, the regulars never in fact rose to 100,000 men. There were difficulties too in organizing them and supplying them, in spite of the funds sent from America, which rose to nearly three million in the first year. Conscription was followed by an insurrection, which was a customary institution in several of the northern provinces, and was made general by the central junta on April 17, 1809; but here again the results were disappointing. In Asturias, for example, the peasants were successfully mobilized in 1809, but in 1810 they stayed at home. Moreover, as they could be provided neither with officers nor arms, they could hardly be used for anything but auxiliary services.

Guerilla warfare was what suited the Spaniards best of all, because in it the soldier could remain his own master. The central junta legalized partisan warfare on December 28, 1808, and there was an abundance of guerilla bands, some of which became famous, such as those of the Castile farm-hand l'Empecinado, and the two Minas in Navarre. They embarrassed the French by attacking forage-parties, convoys, and isolated posts, and wore down their strength by small daily losses, or by forcing them to detach a significant number of fighting men to guard their communications, whilst in the north the Emperor had to increase the number of gendarmerie squadrons. But the effectiveness of these bands has been exaggerated: whenever the French could occupy a province in sufficient strength, the guerillas, far from being able to prevent them, were not even able to be a serious threat to their security. This was so in Asturias under Bonnet's command, though the country was ideal for guerilla warfare. Besides, these bands were a motley collection, and not always clearly to be distinguished from highwaymen. Even when they consisted of peasants loyally serving the cause of religion, they were none the less a terror to the rich by reason of their extortionate demands and their plundering, so that sympathies sometimes lay with the French. Bonnet was able to organize a counter-guerilla force, and in Andalusia Soult succeeded in creating companies of *escoperelas*, a genuine national guard consisting of *afrancesados*. With their resistance decisively broken in this open country, the *guerilleros* would soon have disappeared. Now without the English help, the regulars would never have been able to hold on. Nevertheless the central junta was highly mistrustful, and refused to allow them into Cadiz; and in spite of the efforts of Wellesley—the future Lord Cowley—they would not consent to recognize Wellington as commander-in-chief, even after the battle of Talavera, and the Spanish commanders only co-operated with him in a grudging manner. The disturbances in South America and the opening up of the Spanish colonies to British trade merely made the misunderstandings worse.

If Napoleon had come back to Spain after the battle of Wagram, there would have been no doubt about the triumph of the French forces. This might even have been ensured if he had left someone like Davout in command, armed with full powers. But Joseph, even with Jourdan by his side, was incapable of managing a war like this. He did not even wield civil authority, though he had behind him Urquijo, Azanza, Cabarrus, Canon Llorente, and others—enough to form a court, a ministry, and a council of state. But there was a lack of money, and the king only subsisted with difficulty on municipal tolls, forced loans, and paper money backed merely by the doubtful security of a possible sale of clerical property. Napoleon reserved for himself the confiscated property of the rebels. In the provinces the generals were left to their own resources, and did not even receive their pay. They laid their hands on anything that was available, and acquired the habit of thinking only of their own sector. When Napoleon gave supreme authority to a particular marshal, the others ruined all the plans by ill-will or negligence. Ney went so far as positively to refuse obedience to Massena. This anarchy was made worse by Napoleon's habit of sending direct orders to the army chiefs, quite apart from the fact that he was often imperfectly informed or unable to judge properly at such a distance, so that he sometimes sent out instructions which were impossible to carry out or out of date. Though Wellington had reason to complain of the Spanish generals, the enemy operations were equally disjointed, and he was usually able to beat them or hold them up one at a time.

As regards the physical and economic conditions in which the war was fought—the mountainous nature of the country, the climate, the absence of roads, the scantiness of foodstuffs—it has usually been said, and rightly enough, that they were greatly to the disadvantage of the French. But it should be added that their enemies also suffered a good deal from the same conditions. The English were decimated by disease, and they had great difficulties over transport. One is particularly struck by the central importance of food supplies, which was equally vital and difficult for all the combatants. The Spanish and Portuguese were no doubt used to living on very little; but the English found themselves badly in need of supplies. The cavalry had more than once to be partly dismounted through shortage of fodder. The regulars were thus reduced, one way or another, to the habit of living like the guerillas, so that the peninsula might well seem to have reverted to the days of the *grandes compagnies*. The inhabitants were despoiled by friend and foe alike, and marauding encouraged desertion. As there were many foreigners in the English ranks, and as Napoleon sent a number of regiments to Spain from vassal or allied countries, deserters commonly passed from one camp to the other, or fraternized among themselves, and bands were formed operating solely on their own behalf. The French, who were used to making shift with living on the country, ended up by becoming demoralized in this country where one was perpetually hungry and where nothing was to be had but by stealth and force of arms. Too often their commanders set them a bad example of extortion—for example, Sébastiani, Kellermann, Soult, Duhesme in Barcelona, and Goudinot, who, when his conduct was subject to an official enquiry, committed suicide in 1812. The English compensated for their sufferings by appalling orgies of drunkenness, and by the systematic plunder of all towns taken by assault. From the strategic point of view, Wellington's unwillingness to stray too far from his base and to return to it after each campaign is clearly to be explained by the scarcity of provisions and the difficulties of transport. Hence also his justifiable confidence in face of the French offensives. He reckoned he would be able to hold them up by laying waste the intervening countryside, calculating that if they had achieved the impossible in the way of supplies, mules, and wagons would certainly be lacking. Things would have been very different if Napoleon had come over in person to prepare the campaign with the same care that he displayed in Russia. Since he decided not to do so, the advantage—taken all round—lay with Wellington. As he paid cash, the peasants —who were on the whole friendly—brought him what they could. Thanks to the British fleet, he received outside help and built up stores, while the French were sent no supplies by their own country. When Wellington opened his winter campaign of 1812, he took the enemy by surprise, for they were barely in a position to begin operations before harvest-time.

These general conditions gave the fighting in Spain a character that was entirely different from the other Napoleonic campaigns. A considerable part of the Spanish and Portuguese forces remained in scattered units, who engaged in a whole series of random engagements, without having the means to impose a decisive result, so that they alternately advanced and retreated with monotonous regularity. When he left the peninsula, Napoleon little imagined that things would turn out like this. In January 1809, there only remained Craddock with 10,000 English at Lisbon, and it looked as though they would have to withdraw, after which the Spaniards could not hold out for long. Wellington's arrival completely upset the Emperor's plans. Of the 193,000 men he left in Spain, slightly over one-third were in the west. Ney was keeping watch over Galicia, whilst Soult, leaving this province with 23,000 men, was marching on Lisbon, where he would link up with Victor, who was coming down the Tagus with a force of 22,000. Lapine, who had set out from Salamanca, was to be responsible for liaison. With considerable difficulty Soult reached Oporto, and took it on March 29, 1809. Once there, he refused to move. He had dreams of becoming King of Portugal, and spent his time organizing petitions in his favour. The army, moreover, did not take at all kindly to the prospect of a King Nicholas —for that was Soult's Christian name—and the discontent grew to such proportions that it culminated in a plot and Argenton got into touch with the English. Meanwhile Victor was driving back Cuesta beyond the Guadiuna. Having beaten him on March 28 at Medellin, though without destroying his forces, he called for reinforcements from Lapisse; but they allowed the Alcantara bridge to be cut—the only one available for crossing the Tagus and entering Portugal. Wellington was therefore able to land unmolested on April 22, concentrate 25,000 men at Coïmbra, and attack the two French armies one at a time.

In the first place he turned his attention to Soult, who was off his guard and lost Oporto on May 12. As Beresford had crossed the Douro upstream, Soult could only escape via the mountains, which means abandoning his artillery. Instead of planning joint operations to save, at least, Galicia, Ney and Soult procceded to go their separate ways, and finally evacuated the province and retired on Leon and Zamorra respectively. Wellington had turned back on Victor, but having experienced a great deal of difficulty in getting ready and coming to an agreement with Cuesta, he did not resume action till June 27. Victor fell back towards Madrid so as to link up with Sébastiani. They were also counting on help from Mortier; but Napoleon had placed him, together with Ney, under Soult's orders, with instructions to cut off Wellington's line of retreat by crossing the Sierra de Gredos. Nevertheless Victor and Sébastiani—nominally under Joseph's command—took the offensive and on July 28 attacked the allies, who had slightly superior numbers and held a strong position at Talavera. But they were thrown back. Wellington, under threat from Soult, recrossed the Tagus and withdrew towards Badajoz; nevertheless, his victory made a great stir and he was raised to the peerage as Lord Wellington. Although there were five French corps grouped together and the road to Lisbon lay open, no one dared take the initiative and boldly seize this chance: the armies simply went their several ways, and Sébastiani hastened to repulse Venagas' army at Almonacid, which had come from the direction of the Channel.

Wellington, however, was not at all satisfied with this Spanish commander nor with Cuesta, nor with the junta's refusal to make him commander-in-chief; from now on he therefore went his own way. He had a feeling, moreover, that after his defeat of Austria Napoleon would launch a great effort against him in Spain, and thought it wise to reserve his strength and organize a fortified base in Portugal. The junta disregarded this plan and ordered a general offensive. Arizaga advanced towards the Tagus at the head of the Andalusian army and was routed by Soult at Ocaña on November 29. Del Parque made a momentary entry into Salamanca; but Kellermann came on the scene and on November 28 overwhelmed the Estramadure army, led by Albuquerque, at Alba de Tormès. Joseph and Soult then suggested the conquest of Andalusia and Napoleon gave way, lured on by the prospect of the resources to be found there. The French occupied Seville on February 1, 1810, and Malaga on the 5th, hardly meeting with any resistance. However, they made the mistake of not marching straight upon Cadiz where the junta had taken refuge, so that Albuquerque arrived in time to shut himself in there on February 3, and the French had to undertake a siege which proved unsuccessful. Three army corps were thus immobilized in Andalusia.

This was all the more vexatious because Napoleon, as Wellington had foreseen, was preparing a new expedition to Portugal. In 1811 he had more than 360,000 men in the peninsula. In theory, Massena's army should have numbered 130,000. But as he had had to commission Bonset to reoccupy Asturias and make solid provision for Navarre, Biscay, and Old Castile, he in fact had only 60,000 men left—an altogether insufficient fighting force. He did not set up any powder magazines, or transport depots; and he waited till the end of harvest to take Cuidad Rodrigo and Almeida. Not till September was he ready to move. He found the countryside more or less empty after the summoning of the *ordenanza*, which involved the evacuation of the inhabitants and the destruction of all food that could not be carried away. Wellington only offered battle at the gates of Coïmbra. Entrenched on the heights of Busaco, he was able to throw back Massena on September 27; but as the French general was manœuvring to turn the position, Wellington withdrew. In the course of pursuit, Massena soon came up against the lines of Torres-Vedras, three of them, one behind the other. The first, 40 kilometres long, contained 126 fortifications armed with 247 guns. Wellington had 33,000 English, 30,000 Portuguese, and 6,000 Spaniards, not to mention the partisans; and there was no question of being able to reduce the position by famine, since its supplies were replenished by sea. Massena had no siege equipment, and only 35,000 men. In spite of urgent requests, Drouet only brought him 10,000. There was an appalling dearth of food. On March 5, 1811, he gave orders to retreat, and did not halt till Salamanca was reached. Wellington followed in pursuit and at once laid siege to Almeida. In order to free it, Massena came in to attack on May 5 at Fuentes de Onoro, on the Coa, and was driven back. Just at this moment, Napoleon was beginning preparations for the war against Russia; and for the time being, at any rate, this reverse could not be remedied. Only Soult had received orders to support Massena. He did not dare refuse, but only went so far as to capture Badajoz on March 11. Wellington thought his own position strong enough to send out Beresford against him, who forced him back, besieged Badajoz once again, and repulsed the attacks on Albuera on May 16. Wellington, who was now rid of Massena, then joined up with him; but Marmont, who had taken command at Salamanca, likewise went and joined forces with Soult. Here was one last chance to fight a major battle in favourable conditions against the Anglo-Portuguese forces. But this does not appear to have occurred to the two marshals; they separated, and went their several ways. Wellington made for Cuidad-Rodrigo; but as Marmont was approaching, he did not persist, and instead retired to Portugal.

This, however, was only a short breathing-space. When he had been reinforced he knew that—contrary to the Emperor's belief—he was now stronger than Marmont, who had a bare 34,000 men; besides, he was reckoning on the surprise value of a winter campaign. This time he acted with a boldness that proved completely successful. Setting out on January 7, 1812, he took Cuidad-Rodrigo by assault on the 19th and straight away marched on Badajoz, which he captured on April 6. Soult had been slow to move, and Marmont did not dare to undertake any major diversion. Wellington gave orders, moreover, to multiply attacks on every hand so as to give no chance of coming to their assistance. The Galicians besieged Astorga; Popham appeared on the Biscay coast and kept Caffarelli busy, whilst Bentinck sent Maitland to the coast of Valencia to look after Suchet. Since Napoleon had recalled 25,000 men to send to Russia, Joseph besought Soult to evacuate Andalusia, but in vain. On June 14 Wellington resumed the offensive and Marmont was forced to withdraw behind the Douro. Recalling Bonnet from Asturias, he made a clever crossing of the river and turned the enemy's flank, so that they fell back towards Salamanca. On July 22 he crossed the Tormes and attacked the Arapiles position, but so clumsily that he was set upon in mid-manœuvre and routed. The French lost 14,000 men and Clausel was only able with great difficulty to get them back to Burgos. Wellington marched on Madrid, Joseph evacuating it in order to join up with Suchet. Soult finally left Andalusia, linked forces with them, and retook the capital in October. Wellington, on his way to occupy Burgos, now fell back upon the Tormes, and Soult seemed in no hurry to attack him, but withdrew to Portugal, having taken 20,000 prisoners, captured or destroyed 3,000 guns, and freed Andalusia.

In the east of Spain, operations pursued an independent course. In Catalonia, Rosas fell in 1808 and Gerona in 1809. Figueras was lost and recaptured in 1811, and it seemed impossible to bring peace to this province. In Aragon, Suchet at first withstood Blake, who was threatening Saragossa; but when he had been reinforced he took Lerida and Mequinenza in 1810, and in 1811 Tortosa and Tarragona. After he had been proclaimed Marshal he discomforted Blake outside the fortress of Sagonto, then before Valencia, which he entered on January 9, 1812. As part of his troops had been taken away from him, he did not venture further forward, and Maitland was able to occupy Alicante.

Wellington had thus more than lived up to his promises. Not only had he saved Portugal, but he was holding down a considerable French force in the peninsula. It should be noted, however, that England's Continental diversion had not up till then been decisive, for it had neither prevented the defeat of

Austria nor the invasion of Russia. If Russia had been defeated, Wellington would have stood no chance of maintaining his footing, even in Portugal. Not till 1813, when the old army of Spain had ensured Napoleon's victory in Germany, was he able to give decisive help to the Coalition—and even then, not until winter had destroyed the *Grande Armée.*

CHAPTER FOUR

The Continental Blockade

ALTHOUGH ENGLAND commanded the seas, she could not—in spite of the Spanish diversion—wrest the Continent from the French army. On the other hand Napoleon, by concentrating on a federated Europe under his own control, was depriving himself—at any rate for a considerable period—of the ability to attack his enemy at home. This is why the economic war played such an important part after the peace of Tilsit. The British blockade was more or less of a purely mercantile character. Far from attempting to starve out her adversary and to disrupt her manufacturing war potential—which the state of the Continental economy would have made useless—England's effort was bent upon selling her, through neutral channels, all the goods she could possibly desire. The maritime blockade aimed at enriching England herself, and not at destroying the military power of France—a goal that would in any case have been beyond her capacity.

During his early years Napoleon had followed a similar policy. But subsequently he had returned by way of the Berlin and Milan decrees to the policy of the Convention and the Directory, with the avowed intention of hermetically sealing the Continent against English goods, thus condemning her to live as an enclosed economy purely on her own resources. Such a decisive resolve, involving so many risks, could only be based upon a relentless determination to transform the

Continental blockade into a weapon of war. As long as he did not possess the command of the seas, he had no illusions about the possibility of starving England out and depriving her of raw materials. While not appreciating to the full the solid basis of England's capitalism or its up-to-date structure, he realized that it depended on credit and export, and was therefore vulnerable. He thought that if he could severely shake this edifice, he could bring about bankruptcy, mass unemployment, possibly even a revolution: at all events, force England to give in. But was this a realistic threat? This has been generally denied by the economists, and others have been disposed to follow their verdict; yet it remains an open question. Moreover, did Napoleon ever put the policy into force with maximum rigour? And did he ever completely free himself from the mercantile and fiscal considerations which were bound to weaken its impact? This is a subsidiary question which is also worth examining.

ENGLISH COMMERCE DURING THE EARLY YEARS OF THE BLOCKADE

Up to the time of the Berlin and Milan decrees, England had the advantage of attack in the economic war. Once she had eliminated enemy shipping and obtained complete control over the neutrals, she could interfere with French exports and deprive her of markets, while continuing to sell to her and even buy from her when convenient. But the Napoleonic conquests and the Continental blockade reversed the positions. Now, the French intention was to prevent her from supplying the Continent—much her best customer. She was now reduced to the defensive, and it was up to her to make the enemy take her goods.

In order to get the better of these awkward circumstances, she had no need to modify her policies, and in fact she did not make any change at all in them. It was rather the opposite: her economic pragmatism was if anything intensified. In April 1808, the government even obtained Parliamentary powers to grant licences as it liked, in violation of the principles recently laid down by itself in the regulations of 1807. It thus gave permission for the import and export of forbidden goods, for sailing to ports that were effectively blockaded, for proceeding in ballast-trim from one enemy port to another, and even allowed the French flag to appear on suffrance in its own harbours. Though as a result of the Franco-Austrian war licences for ships proceeding to the Empire were abruptly discontinued on April 26, 1809, they continued to be issued for Germany and the Baltic, and in fact soon began to be granted for Holland and Italy. With the harvest giving cause for anxiety, the government even went so far on September 28 as to authorize ships to ply between any ports from Holland to Bayonne, in ballast-trim, which was quite unprecedented. This toleration was withdrawn in November, re-established in May 1810, suspended in October, and then reinstituted once again, according to the prevalent view as to the state of supplies. In 1811, trade with the enemy was once again prohibited; but it was re-opened in 1812, even with the United States, who had already declared war. From 1807 to 1812, 44,346 licences were granted, nearly 26,000 of them in 1809 and 1810. The neutrals received their share, and it would seem that there was a traffic in these documents even on the Continent. This was in fact the channel through which all the maritime commerce flowed, and even when the government did not insist on licences, they were nevertheless in request because the war-fleet hardly made any distinctions in practice between friend and foe. The distribution of licences came in the end to be regulated not by any real rules, but solely by judging each case on its merits. This encouraged arbitrary dealings, corruption, slow procedure, and mistakes; and protests were raised against a regime that perpetuated the suspension of the navigation acts and for practical purposes abolished the regulations of 1807. Nevertheless, this system helped England to defend herself, for in most cases, the licences only allowed imports with a view to re-export. It could when convenient be used to exert diplomatic pressure; and as the licences cost £13 or £14, they were a not inconsiderable source of revenue.

In Europe, success depended primarily on the effective strength of the Continental System. In 1807 and 1808, after the Peace of Tilsit, it was for a while extensive enough to make a perceptible reduction in imports coming from Great Britain. But its strength soon diminished. Spain and Portugal were lost to Napoleon, and in 1809 Turkey made peace with England

and threw the Levant open to her; Austria was once more accessible; the requirements of war drew the French forces away from the German coasts, and trade again became very nearly free there. This was what they called the second Tönning period in Holstein. Moreover, there was a more or less open government connivance among Napoleon's allies or vassal states. Up to 1810 Holland continued to be an important market for Britain. Louis had promulgated the Berlin decree, but did not manage to secure respect for it; and from 1806 onwards, he too began to allow licences, and exports to England went steadily ahead, involving, of course, return journeys and cargoes. More than 237,000 quarters of grain arrived from the Low Countries in 1807. In addition, ships became accustomed to providing themselves with two sorts of papers, one to show to the English and the other to the French; and a Liverpool house sent out circulars offering to provide such documents. Finally, the English made full use of the dealers in contraband. In order to encourage the blockade-runner, the French methods of packing and labelling were adopted. All kinds of subterfuges came into play, such as lowering nets full of goods at agreed spots, which would then be picked up at night by fishermen. Most important of all were the depots set up as close as possible to the Empire coasts. In 1808, Heligoland was chosen as a North Sea base. Extensive works were carried out there, and 200 merchants took up permanent residence there—among them one of the Parish brothers of Hamburg—so much so that it became known as 'Little London'. Between August and November 1808, 120 ships called in there, and arrivals were valued at 8 million a year. From this point goods went on to Holstein for Hamburg via Altona, or were landed by night with the help of coastal fishermen; after which there were all sorts of devices for despatching them to Frankfurt, Leipzig, Basle, and Strasburg. In the Baltic, Göteborg became the principal centre. By 1808 this port was already exporting 1,300,000 pounds of coffee and nearly 3,000,000 pounds of sugar, and these figures rose respectively to 4½ and 7½ million in 1809, and doubled the following year. These consignments found their way via Pomerania and Prussia partly to Leipzig, and also to Poland and Russia. In the Mediterranean the requisite bases were provided by Gibraltar, Sardinia, and Sicily, Malta, the Balearic islands (after 1808), and the Dalmatian and Ionian islands after 1809, Malta being undoubtedly the essential depot above all others. There was access to Austria via Trieste and Vienna, and thence by another route to Leipzig. When the English gained a footing in Turkey a new route was opened up from Salonica and Constantinople to Belgrade and Hungary, all the profits from which went to Vienna.

According to the English statistics, exports to Northern Europe, including France, were only perceptibly diminished in 1808; they recovered in 1809, and by 1810 had risen to a level very close to the value of 1805. Taking the latter as 100, then the index figure for 1808 would have been 20·9 for goods of English origin and 51·6 for re-exports, essentially colonial produce. In 1809, they rose to 55·2 and 140 respectively; in 1810, to 74·6 and 97·3. For the total of exports to the same region, the index figures in comparison with 1805 were 32·6 in 1808, 87·5 in 1809, and 83·2 in 1810, the 1809 rise being due to the Austrian war, and the 1810 fall to the first effects of tightening up the Continental System and the Trianon and Fontainebleau decrees. In 1810, British exports to Northern Europe and France were thus not notably diminished; but the devastating drop in 1808 proves that the continental blockade was in itself effective, though it all depended on the length of time and the completeness with which it was applied, that is to say, on the power of the French armies.

All the same, even if the Napoleonic blockade had been extended over the whole of Europe, and even if it had been perfectly observed, British exports would not have been killed, for the Continent only took three-quarters of them as far as colonial produce was concerned, whilst the proportion of goods coming directly from England was not more than one-third—37 per cent in 1805, 25 per cent in 1808, and 34 per cent in 1810. The Emperor could therefore only have been certain of attaining his goal by conquering the East as well, and if oversea countries, or at any rate the United States, whether they were in concert with him or no, had adopted the same policy. In fact, the real difficulties encountered by England were due to the American rebellion against the ordinances of 1807, in which respect they reacted differently from the Swedes and Norwegians, the Creeks and the Berbers. To be sure, the Americans did not like the Napoleonic decrees either, but they had other grievances as well against the English, leaving the question of the 'press-gangs' and the nationality of crews for the time being in suspense. On May 27, 1807, the English captured a ship of theirs and took several of its crew to London. Those who had taken these steps were reprimanded, but England refused to give way on the basic issue, and a breach between the two countries took place. On December 22, Jefferson declared an embargo, closing his ports to belligerents who had taken measures against neutrals, and forbidding his own ships to leave these ports. Only the English stood to suffer by this ruling. In actual fact, the embargo was not scrupulously enforced, in spite of the passing of an Enforcement Act in 1808. All the same, the import of grain that year from the United States was only a twentieth of the amount imported in 1807, and Liverpool only received 23,000 sacks of cotton instead of 143,000. The price of bread rose, and there was a manufacturing crisis, whilst a fall in wages led to a general strike in Manchester and a series of disturbances. On the other hand on the Continent, though colonial imports fell off considerably, this was due only to the withdrawal of the American ships. According to Gogel, the Dutch Minister of Finance, Holland received from America in 1807 nearly 30 million pounds of coffee and 41 million pounds of sugar; in 1808, she only obtained a million pounds of coffee and four million of sugar. These goods came of course mostly from the English colonies. And lastly, the sale of English goods to the United States fell by more than half, though in the ordinary way they formed a third of her exports.

But thanks to the acquisition of new markets, England was able to guard against this situation, which was becoming serious. Portugal and Spain were only a moderate help. Though the amount of goods sent to them rose greatly, the increase was chiefly devoted to feeding Wellington's troops. On the other hand, the Levant markets proved a most valuable acquisition. The total figure for peninsular exports and Mediterranean exports rose from £4 million in 1805 to more than £16 million in 1811. But the really crucial event was the opening up of markets in Brazil and the Spanish colonies. We have no exact information about their trade; yet this development is the most likely explanation of the sudden rise of English sales in America—excluding the United States—which increased from £8 million in 1805 to £11 million in 1806 and 1807, and to nearly £20 million in 1808 and 1809. One of the permanent results of the crisis was therefore to reduce the importance of the Continental market in British eyes and to turn attention to outlets overseas. Apart from the Levant, Asia and Africa did not for the moment play any part in this development. If anything, British exports to those parts fell off during this period. The importance of Napoleon's Spanish adventure stands out all the more clearly against the facts that have just been reviewed.

Thus renewed in strength, England could afford to wait till the United States came to a better mind, which they were not long in doing. They could not live without exporting their corn, wood, cotton, and tobacco: on this point New England and the South were agreed. Moreover, there had been protests from the shipowners, and the agitation soon threatened to lead to civil war. At all events, the embargo provided an excellent platform for the Federalists, who accused Jefferson of siding with the French. Nevertheless, Madison was elected in 1808; but it had been agreed that the embargo should be withdrawn. On March 4, 1809, a Non-intercourse Act was substituted, forbidding all trade with the belligerents; but it did not apply to Spain or Portugal, Denmark or Sweden, and once on the way, American ships contrived to go where they liked, particularly to Holland and to England. Girard, for example, was arranging food supplies for Portugal, and from there his ships went on with wine for England, from which they returned with fresh cargoes. Moreover, the English ambassador promised that the Orders in Council would soon be repealed, and although the government issued a disclaimer, Madison had meanwhile been elected, the Non-intercourse Act had been repealed, and there was an enormous rush for Europe. In 1809, English exports to the United States rose to nearly £7½ million, and the American fleet was once more put at the disposal of the British. In 1809, the percentage of ships leaving British ports under foreign flags rose from 45 to 70.

Making allowance for the variations in price, and so in profit, and for the hazards of payment, which were apt to be very much a matter of chance in these new countries—as was soon to be discovered—the result of the English entry into Latin America and the Levant was that Napoleon's designs were effectively foiled. To be sure, the export index went down a little in 1808 to 91; but thanks to the shock administered to the Continental System, and to the reconciliation with the United States, it was remarkably buoyant in 1809, when it rose to 125, and even to more than 126 in 1810. These customs figures are confirmed by estimates of imports by weight in the cotton industry. From 1801 to 1805, England imported on the average 56·5 million pounds of cotton bales; from 1807 to 1812, the figures were 79·7 million, or an increase of 40·7 per cent. The sale of cotton goods rose from £8,600,000 in 1805 to £12,500,000 in 1808 and £14·4 million in 1809. There was an equal growth in the production of coal and iron, and continued technical progress. The population rose from 10,943,000 in 1801 to 12,597,000 in 1811. All this evidence goes to prove that Britain's economic structure during the early years of the century emerged victorious from the tests it had undergone. Success was primarily due to its unrivalled use of machinery and the monopoly of goods from the colonies. And so the publicists employed by the government were able to snap their fingers at Napoleon, in particular Ivernois, whose book *Les effets du blocus continental* came out in July 1809:

Votre blocus ne bloque point
Et grâce à notre heureuse adresse
Ceux que vous affamez sans cesse
Ne périront que d'embonpoint.*

Yet it was too early to imagine that the day was won. After the defeat of Austria, there was a tightening up of the Continental System, and there seemed to be nothing to prevent Napoleon from making an end of Spain. It looked as though with Alexander's support—or when he had been defeated—Napoleon would contrive to expel England from the Levant. Besides, the Continental blockade could well go hand in hand with closing the American market. Just then Latin America was proving a disappointment in the matter of payments, and

* Your blockade doesn't block,
And thanks to our nautical skill
The folk you think you're starving
Can more than eat their fill.

by plunging into civil war was narrowing down the markets; and it was not long before there was a renewal of the conflict with the United States. Even during the years of prosperity, certain imports gave cause for grave anxiety. It was no good Saumarez commanding the Baltic, because as its ports were gradually sealed, it became increasingly difficult to export the wood, grain, hemp, and flax that had previously come from those parts—and these were goods that did not lend themselves to contraband dealings. For textiles, England now turned to Ireland. But wood supplies were a very different matter. In 1808, the consumption rose to 60,000 loads, each load being roughly equivalent to a cubic metre and a tenth. Although the British forests were denuded and a great deal of wood was imported from Canada from 1804 onwards, England had in that year to buy 20,000 loads abroad. The House of Solly always managed to send some from Danzig; but from now on, the supply dwindled—not more than 3,319 poles and 2,500 loads in 1811, whilst Canada sent 23,000 poles and 24,000 loads of oak and 145,000 of pine. Previously, more had come from Sweden, and especially from the United States; but in 1810 there was nothing at all from this quarter. There was a search for new sources of supply; but the wood-trade was not organized anywhere else as it was in the Baltic, and freights often proved prohibitive. There was particular difficulty in obtaining supplies for the Malta docks, in spite of the treaties signed with Adamitsch of Fiume and after 1809 with Ali-Tebelen. Once again it proved necessary to infringe the Navigation Acts by arranging for the construction of ships—even warships—at Halifax and in India. The merchant navy suffered in consequence. Instead of the 95,000 tons delivered in 1804, it only received 54,000 in 1810. The year 1810 was a very hard one, and only 47,000 loads were used in construction, 10,000 of them coming from abroad.

Grain supplies required even more careful consideration. High prices had led to a large increase in home production. Something like 750,000 acres were cleared for cultivation at this time, chiefly in the common lands. Ireland also provided important supplies. In her struggle with Napoleon England's trump card was the progress made by the capitalist system, which gave her industry an invincible superiority, though not to the extent of making home-grown foodstuffs superfluous. Nevertheless according to Young's estimate imported food supplied a sixth of the total consumption. Although prices never reached the 1801 level, corn remained more expensive than on the Continent. A quarter rose to 100 shillings in 1805, then fell to 66 in 1807, and rose again to 94 in 1808–9. For these two reasons, opinion was always nervous about anything that might hold up consignments. Three-quarters of the imported corn came from the Baltic, the other quarter from the United States and Canada. Now the Baltic ports were in Napoleon's hands, and in spite of contraband, England only managed to get 65,000 quarters from the Continent in 1808 as against 514,000 in 1807. On the other hand the United States only contributed 6 per cent to grain imports in 1808, instead of the 14 per cent of the previous year. Since the harvest was not a bad one, no great harm was done; but in a poor season the result would have been very different. Besides, there were Portugal and Spain to feed; and here America came to the rescue and so indirectly gave help to England. But supposing they were to declare war? Finally, there were the Antilles to consider. In 1808, the home country had to be responsible for feeding them too. If the Baltic and the United States had failed simultaneously, there would have been at least a two months' deficit, and even more in a bad harvest season. It has been said that England could have managed by introducing rationing, by raising the extraction rate for milling and so on. None the less, the psychological effect would have been tremendous.

In 1809 then, prospects for the Napoleonic blockade were uncertain; but there was a tendency to be too complacent and to minimize its chances of success. By itself, it would not have brought England to her knees. Nevertheless, if applied rigorously and to the whole of Europe, it might have so weakened her that at some moment or other she would have felt unable to endure such stress, quite independently of Napoleon's specific endeavours, but decisively enough to give him certain victory. Thus the essential point for him was to extend his domination of the Continent and at the same time maintain an unrelenting blockade. But he did just the opposite—he relaxed its rigours.

THE DEVELOPMENT OF THE CONTINENTAL BLOCKADE

If strictly applied, the Continental blockade, representing the Mercantile Theory at its extreme, would have required Europe to live entirely on its own resources. But as the vast majority of Europeans were still engaged in agriculture, there was no need to be uneasy about food supplies. For the same reason she was self-sufficient in fatty products and in textiles, apart from cotton; nor was it impossible for her to supply her own needs in fuel and mining products. On the other hand she was very hard hit by the disappearance of colonial goods. Attempts were made to find substitutes—chicory for coffee, honey and grape-syrup for sugar, 2,000 tons of which were manufactured in France about 1811. More important still—at least for the future—was the attention now paid to beet-sugar, which was isolated by Margraf in 1757 and had been produced commercially in Silesia by a German called Achard since the beginning of the century. For lack of indigo and cochineal, recourse was had to woad and madder. Attempts were also made to cultivate salt-wort—in the Papal States, for instance, and the chemical industry quickly popularized the product Nicholas Leblanc had produced by breaking down sea salt. There were efforts also to acclimatize cotton round Naples and Malaga, and they proved quite successful, since France ended by obtaining a sixth of her whole consumption from these sources, and managed to gain access to cotton from the Levant by way of Illyria. Nevertheless, this remained a permanent difficulty where cotton supplies were concerned, and but for contraband imports, the looms would have had to shut down, especially in Switzerland and Saxony. Napoleon's attitude to this industry shows most clearly of all his desire to reduce the Continent to a position of economic self-sufficiency. He had never liked the cotton industry just because it was dependent on supplies from abroad, and quite early on he gave protection to Douglas in setting up in France the manufacture of machinery for spinning wool. Moreover, he agreed to grant loans to cotton manufacturers wishing to change over their machinery to a different raw material, and offered a prize of a million francs to anyone who could invent a machine for spinning flax. In 1811, all cotton materials were barred from the imperial palaces.

Even if Europe had been well supplied with raw materials, her troubles would not have been at an end, for her manufacturing capacity was very much smaller than her needs. It could only be hoped that as the blockade became a more perfect instrument for establishing protection, production would achieve the requisite advances. But time would be needed, for up till then both machinery and skilled mechanics had come from England. Moreover, there was nowhere an adequate amount of capital, and the situation was not such as to attract it. Industrial centres being few and the seas closed to commerce, self-sufficiency required amongst other things a general rearrangement of distribution and methods of transport. And so the blockade upset people's habits, interfered with the usual routines, and damaged an untold number of interests. The shipowners, merchants, and industrialists in the seaports knew that their interests were disregarded out of hand. Consumers—that is to say, everybody, alas!—felt that they were expected to stand the racket. They did not like chicory and grape-syrup, and woollens and linens were much dearer than cottons. In a general way, leading industrialists and even Napoleon himself were concerned to supply the market without much concern for costs. The ideal of self-sufficiency clashed at too many points with the producer's and the consumer's independence, which was founded on individual liberty and free employment, everywhere proclaimed by Napoleon to be one of the cardinal principles of the new society. A conspiracy was bound to develop of its own accord against the blockade, and nothing but the controls and pressures exercised by a military and police state would have succeeded in enforcing obedience to the system.

The allied countries prevented by the blockade from exporting their agricultural produce often lacked the industries that would have compensated for this loss. Others again—like the Hanseatic towns—were nearly killed by the veto on all sea trade, but they more or less openly contrived to get round the regulations in proportion as they still enjoyed some measure of independence. All they had to do was not to apply the measures relating to neutrals. And so the blockade relaxed or tightened up according as Napoleon's military ascendancy decreased or increased. It had started by being a symbol of the Grand Empire, but in the end became a reason for its extension, and had an effect upon its structure, for the vassal states scarely behaved any more obediently than the allies of Napoleon.

Holland provides the most instructive example. In response to threats from his brother, Louis closed the Dutch ports on September 4, 1807. But as early as 1808 La Rochefoucault, the French ambassador, pointing out the importance of contraband, particularly in East Frisia, which had recently been annexed, and in Walcheren, which gave access to Antwerp, was advising the annexation of the country at least as far as the Meuse. A royal decree authorized the export of butter and cheese; but Napoleon decided to close his frontier to the Dutch on September 16. Then on October 23 Louis forbade all exports, and closed his ports to all ships. In French eyes, such excessive measures showed the absurdity of the blockade; besides, these regulations had no sooner been made than they were undermined by a series of exceptions. In June 1809, Louis once more opened his ports to American vessels on condition that they should consign their cargoes to the state warehouses until peace was signed—from which place it was mere child's play to remove them. On July 18, Napoleon replied by setting up a customs cordon from the Rhine to the Trave, and Louis had once again to give way. A dogged repetition of these efforts finally provoked Napoleon into annexing his kingdom in 1810.

Murat was already pursuing the same tactics. Sovereigns like the King of Saxony and the Grand Duke of Frankfurt, who had no contact with the sea, were in an even better position to ignore vetoes on contraband. Since Western Germany had been at peace, Frankfurt had recovered its prosperity by acting as a clearing-house on the French frontier, and in 1810 the Prussian representative stated that there had never been so many colonial goods in transit. Leipzig continued to be a big English market providing goods for Central and Eastern Europe. At the Michaelmas fair of 1810 there were more than 65½ million thalers-worth of colonial goods on sale; and Switzerland was a regular buyer of all the yarn she needed—190,000 pounds in 1807–1808, 430,000 in 1808–1809, 950,000 in 1809–1810; and it was through her territory that British exports reached Italy. The blockade thus became one of the factors pointing to the superiority of an Empire organized on a unitary, rather than on a federative, basis.

Even where Napoleon was in sole command, it was not easy to get the better of contraband traffic. At no period had it been so flourishing, thanks to the enormous profits reaped from it and the universal connivance at the system. In 1810, the Emperor himself gave some idea of the excellence of his arrangements in detailing his various agents, such as the *entrepreneurs*, the *assureurs*, the *intéressés*, the *chefs de bande*, the *porteurs*. For goods intended for France, Basle, and Strasburg were the busiest centres, and fortunes were made there by this trade. Customs officials were not sufficient for keeping watch over such an extent of coastline and more particularly of land-frontiers; military occupation alone could be effective. When Napoleon needed to withdraw troops, as in 1809, there were breaches in the system everywhere. In 1811, he had to exclude Dalmatia and Croatia from the imperial customs domain because he could not keep an adequate watch on them. Nor could the Emperor rely completely upon his officials. Consuls became corrupt—like Bourrienne at Hamburg and Clérembaut at Königsberg: Massena had put up licences for sale in Italy. Customs officials could be bribed too, including their chiefs, as wc learn from what took place at Strasburg. These disadvantages would have been best overcome by reducing the size of the sectors controlled from each centre; from which it seemed obvious—as always—that the whole of Europe should be annexed to the Empire—an argument that was by no means displeasing to Napoleon.

There would thus have been no inducement to modify his policy if the blockade had not involved consequences that seemed to be dangerous to him personally. Decrès was not long in complaining that the navy could not get its vital supplies, which usually came from the Baltic. The cotton manufacturers, who had at first rejoiced in the exclusion of English cotton goods and had extended their factories, began to change their tune because raw material was running short: if this was to be the result of the blockade, then they had no use for it. However impatient the Emperor might be at their complaints, he was forced to take note of them because there was nothing he so much dreaded as unemployment. Moreover, the Empire's exports were going down. In spite of the war, they had steadily risen up to 1806, when they were valued at 456 million francs;

in 1807, they dropped to 376 million; in 1808 and 1809, they were hardly more than 330 million. Certain industries showed a decline, particularly silk manufacture, and in the West, textiles, so that there was a further threat of unemployment from this direction too. The salt refiners on the coasts, the vine-growers, and the peasants in the provinces adjacent to the Channel and the North Sea were equally loud in complaint. There were difficulties in disposing of butter and cheese, fruit and vegetables, and—what was more important—wines and brandy. When there was a glut in the corn-market the situation grew even worse. Under the Consulate, corn had been dear, which had had no small part in making Bonaparte popular with the landowners and large-scale farmers. In Year X and Year XI, the average price had been more than 24 francs a hectolitre. Since 1804, a series of good harvests had brought the price down below 20 francs; in 1809, it even went as low as 15 francs, and in the Paris basin and in Brittany it really fell to 11 or 12 francs, and in la Vendée to less than 10. Napoleon became disturbed: though he did not want bread to be dear, neither did he wish slumps to spread discontent among the growers and make it difficult to collect the tax. In such cases he would give previous authorization for corn export on a provisional basis, as was the custon under the *Ancien Régime*. On November 23, 1808, a trader in Havre had asked for permission to export, and England would have been delighted to be able once more to buy from France.

Again, the question of export had more general implications, for it also affected the balance of trade. Napoleon would have made a distinction between this and the balance of account which Colbert would hardly have allowed, for though France in his time did not possess the resources derived from freightage and tourism, her capitalists did at least conduct certain speculative operations in the conquered countries, and war provided significant quantities of specie. Nevertheless, his ideas were too traditional not to insist at all costs on giving the precedence to export. Up to 1808, he did not succeed, although the deficit fell from 83 million francs in 1803 to 17 million in 1807. Among its other advantages, the Continental blockade seemed to Napoleon to have the merit of redressing this whole situation. Imports went down from 477 million francs in 1806 to 289 million in 1809. From 1808 onwards, there was a favourable balance of trade, leaving a cash balance of 43 million francs in 1809. In the Emperor's eyes, this was the essential thing; but the result would have been even more satisfactory if exports, instead of going down, had also maintained their level. Since the war-blockade as he saw it was aimed at England's currency, it did not contradict his mercantile theories: the essential point was to go on selling to the English, while not buying from them, so as to rob them of their coin. When he heard in 1808 that Louis was issuing export licences for Great Britain, he forgave him on condition that nothing should be bought from her in exchange: 'they must pay in cash, but never in goods—never, do you understand?'

For him, however, there was no relaxing the rigorous attitude to neutrals. When he heard of Jefferson's embargo, he announced in the Bayonne decree of April 17, 1808, that it must now be assumed in principle that American navigation had ceased to exist, and that any vessels claiming United States allegiance must be deemed fraudulent, and might therefore be taken as lawful prize. Napoleon had them sequestrated, and by the Rambouillet decree of March 23, 1810, ordered them to be sold together with their cargoes. When neutral vessels were excluded, French exporters ran short of shipping, and there was bound to be a fall in the quantity of goods despatched. It is possible that to begin with, Napoleon may not have noticed this contradictory state of affairs, seeing that his gaze was fixed above all on France, and that he was quite indifferent to the fate of the agricultural countries' export trade—the Baltic States, for example. Even if he had conquered the whole of Europe, France would nevertheless have remained the essential port of the Empire, the centre to which money must flow. Since the blockade gave her the Continental market (he argued), she had only to seize it to maintain, and even to increase, her sales. But were French resources really sufficient to replace the goods from England? And could overland porterage and canal traffic be so greatly increased that transport by sea would become unnecessary? Events were to prove that these hopes could not be realized, and even if they had been, there would still have been the problem of what to do with the superfluous corn.

Most of the men who served Napoleon did not really approve

of the new character he was giving to the blockade and wanted to return to the system in force before 1806. Chaptal made no secret of his opinion; Crétet and Montalivet at the Ministry of the Interior were in touch with the cotton manufacturers and seaport traders, and would have liked to meet their interests. They could not go so far as to ask that the Berlin and Milan decrees should be repealed, but they insinuated that it would be profitable to follow the English example and issue export licences, and that it would be as well to allow the neutrals to have them too, though without giving them back complete freedom. In order to meet the needs of the army and navy, certain goods would be delivered in return; all other outgoings would be only against payment in money, which would ensure a comfortable cash balance. Did not Coquebert de Montbret recommend in 1802 that there should be exchanges on a compensatory basis? And in 1807, did not Napoleon himself consider at a certain point issuing import licences on condition that an equivalent amount of goods was exported to keep the balance? Contrary to what he relates in his memoirs, Mollien opposed this plan, pointing out that exporters, even if refused authority to exact payment in kind, would nevertheless not fail to take on a return cargo—even if fraudulently—and that they would moreover be compelled by the English to do so; and in this way, Mollien reckoned, the exchange with Britain would be equalized. Coquebert de Montbret likewise pointed out that if corn was sent to the English, this would spoil the chance of starving them out. These results could not be reconciled with the theory of an offensive blockade.

They were right: but another argument advanced by Gaudin and Collin de Sussy, the head of the customs, won Napoleon over. By reducing imports, they argued, he would curtail the customs revenue, which went down from 60 million francs in 1808 to 11½ million in 1809. On the eve of the campaign against Austria, it was important to restore the level of receipts; moreover the export of corn would enable the peasants to pay the land-tax. In March 1809, Napoleon did in fact dictate a plan for licensing. A confidential circular from Crétet announced on April 14 that it was a question of an exceptional and temporary expedient which would not be publicized. These licences—later called 'the old-type licences'—would allow the export of wines and brandies, fruit and vegetables, grain and salt against the import of wood, hemp, iron, and cinchona or against payment in coin, plus the customs-dues and a tax of from 30 to 40 louis for each licence. Crétet issued 40 of these; but Fouché, who succeeded him as the intermediate authority, was much more generous, for by October 5 he had issued 200. However, Gaudin and Montalivet insisted on the needs of industry being also considered, and so a second type of licence was brought out on December 4, 1809, incorporated subsequently in a decree of February 14, 1810. This measure reserved three-quarters of each cargo exported for agricultural produce—to which were now added oils and textile raw materials; the rest of the cargo could be taken up by manufactured products.

As was to be expected, the conditions governing reimport and payment in coin clashed with the English requirements, and there was not as great a demand for licences as might be imagined. In June 1810, it was reported to the Emperor that 351 had been issued, exports being valued at 10 million francs against 6 million of imports. Nevertheless, the export of grain is still shrouded in obscurity. According to the English figures, the Empire and its allies sent Great Britain in 1809 and 1810 nearly 1,500,000 quarters, and this was said to have been paid for in gold, involving a transfer of £1,400,000 sterling. The value of English imports did in fact rise in 1809 to £75·5 million, and in 1810 to £89·7 million, whereas the famine of 1801 had only made the figure go up to £73·7. It therefore seems likely that corn was exported not only under imperial licence. Since the end of September 1809, England had been issuing licences to go and fetch corn from the Continent, even as ballast; and it looks as though Napoleon closed his eyes and allowed the enemy ships to load as freely as they liked, until it came to the poor harvest of 1810, when he stopped exports at the end of the summer. The glut in corn had been cleared; but the vine-growers, the industrialists, and the treasury had little cause for satisfaction. During the first half of 1810 the Emperor became convinced that this first attempt was not enough. In the course of his northern journey, the manufacturers' grievances were more and more loudly voiced, and on January 12 he gave permission for selling prize goods, in spite of the veto against them—except for certain cottons—subject to a duty of 40 per cent. These were called products 'of permitted origin'. In other words, he authorized certain imports. Where exports were concerned, he organized official relationships with the English smugglers at Dunkirk, and in 1811 their base was moved to Gravelines. On June 6, a traders' and manufacturers' council was set up, and at the end of the month the Emperor began to work out with them a general rearrangement of the blockade.

A new motive was also urging him in that direction. On May 1, 1810, the American Congress authorized the president in the Macon Bill to forbid imports by belligerents who had not repealed the measures directed against the neutrals before March 3, 1811. If England persisted in maintaining them, Napoleon would, while giving the United States favoured treatment, urge them to break off relations with her. By the decree of Milan, neutrals who stood up for their rights would be exempt from these provisions. Through a diplomatic device it was arranged to advance the date of their coming into force, an event of considerable importance, since it would reinforce the effectiveness of the blockade.

On July 3, 1810, the decree of St. Cloud made licences an official institution. They were subsequently granted to Italy, and the Hanseatic cities; and to Danzig out of consideration for the Poles. By a further decree of July 25 the French Empire's maritime trade was put under state control. It was now forbidden to enter or leave Empire ports without a licence signed by the Emperor in person. These licences were called 'normal licences', and were only issued to French subjects. Thus Napoleon had in effect promulgated a navigation act, like the one passed by the Convention. But as his ships could not sail, it was inoperative. And so an exception studied by the Trade Council in an important session on June 25 was made in favour of the Americans. On July 5, they were granted by decree permission to import, provided that they re-exported the equivalent. But as Madison had forbidden his countrymen to ask for licences, which in his view implied an authorization contrary to the freedom of the seas and his country's sovereignty, his veto was evaded by calling them 'permits' when they applied to seamen of the United States. The truth was that France could not do without them; but—diplomatically—this concession was much publicized, and on August 6 Champagny gave notice that the Emperor would repeal the Berlin and Milan decrees in November, if the English on their side would revoke the Orders in Council. Montalivet at once proposed that these permits should be granted to all allied or neutral vessels; but the Emperor refused, and even impounded some Danish ships. It must therefore be realized that he had most adroitly turned his absolute need for neutral vessels into a diplomatic manœuvre likely to put the United States at loggerheads with Great Britain.

The decree of July 25 stipulated that all imports must be balanced by an equivalent export of certain designated goods, which varied from port to port, but always contained from a third to a half in silks. If the general prohibitions and those relating to English manufactures had been observed, imports ought only to have consisted of foodstuffs and raw materials from the United States or the Continent; but in actual fact, colonial goods were once more admitted, although known to be of enemy origin. Thus the method put forward by Coquebert de Montbret in 1802 had in effect been adopted—state regulation of all maritime trade, and a compulsory minimum export to balance the imports. Napoleon gave up demanding that the former must be paid for in money in order to revive the export trade and especially to provide industry with the necessary raw materials, and consumers with their sugar and coffee. He had had the same inspiration as the Committee of Public Safety; yet in Year II France, though obliged to import at all costs, agreed if need be to pay in coin. Now, in Napoleon's time, the position was reversed, and France expected the foreigner to pay her in cash. None the less, it was clear that the Emperor, by consenting to purchases which would partly be to the enemy's advantage, was in fact diminishing the rigour of the Continental blockade.

The treasury also took its share, for each licence cost a thousand francs. The customs tariff had been revised, and on August 1 the Trianon decree was published, increasing the tax on colonial goods to a formidable degree. The American colonist, who had paid one franc per quintal in 1804 and 60 francs since 1806, would in future have to pay 800. The duty on indigo was raised from 15 to 900, and on coffee from 150 to 400. There seemed to be a flat contradiction between the policy of obtaining raw materials for the manufacturers, and the imposition of this overwhelming level of duty. But in thus striking a blow at cotton Napoleon was aiming at giving an advantage to the national textile industry; he also imagined that the English would lower their prices to make up for the duty and thus no longer show a profit, whilst the regular imports would discourage buyers from turning to contraband sources. But he was over-optimistic. The English ruled the market and could hold to their prices; and exorbitant taxation was not likely either to discourage fraudulent dealing. And so there was soon a tightening up of repressive measures. By the Fontainebleau decree of October 18 the contrabandist could be sentenced to ten years' penal servitude, not to mention branding, and put under the jurisdiction of a new court, the *cours douanières*, which followed the same procedure as a special court. In 1812, the Hamburg court pronounced 127 sentences in a fortnight, several of them death-sentences in view of aggravating circumstances. Contraband colonial goods were to be confiscated and sold, and manufactured products destroyed. But there remained the goods that had already been brought in despite the blockade in order to improve the market and bring in some money. To deal with this situation, the Trianon decree set a huge police operation on foot. Throughout the Empire, house-to-house searches were the order of the day; and as the vassal states showed some reluctance to comply, Napoleon decided to make an example of Frankfurt. In the night of October 17, the city was surrounded by a division and occupied the next day, and 234 merchants—including Bethmann and Rothschild—had everything confiscated that they had not managed to hide. The princes of the Rhine Confederation, Prussia, and Switzerland, were threatened with invasion, and had their German frontiers closed—after which they decided to obey the Emperor's orders.

The decrees of 1810 did not however yield all the results that had been hoped for, and constantly involved serious drawbacks. The new licences were not much more popular than the old had been. According to the report produced by Montalivet, the Emperor had signed 1,153 by November 25, 1811, but only

494 were issued. They covered exports estimated at 45 million francs and imports of nearly 28 million. The Americans had only taken out some hundred permits, brought in rather less than 3 million in goods, and purchased about 3½ million's worth. This favourable balance appeared in Napoleon's eyes to justify the experiment. In actual fact, it is doubtful whether there was any gain. In the Ministry's figures, the estimated value of exports was increased by 50 per cent to allow for the French merchants' profits, and imports were reduced by one quarter; moreover, the English refused to purchase, and in Illyria the Emperor had to make an exception because when re-exports were demanded they simply refused to deliver any salt. The result was that the exports were often artificial, their only purpose being to justify the corresponding imports. The customs were cheated by arranging for consignments of cheap goods which were subsequently thrown overboard. In any case, though industry experienced a certain relief, it was not enough to disarm the hostility of the business community. Savary has passed on to us Lafitte's strictures; and the chamber of commerce at Geneva, through the pen of its secretary Sismondi, was loud in its criticisms of the blockade, to the consternation of government departments. As soon as Napoleon was not willing to grant licences with the same degree of opportunism that was shown by the English—which would not have been consistent with the Berlin and Milan decrees—he might as well not have issued any at all.

Moreover there was still a long way to go in cleaning up the market. People succeeded in hiding a great deal of the illicit goods, or in declaring them legal, by bribing the French agents or obtaining the connivance of the local authorities. For colonial goods, the Emperor was willing to make a variety of concessions. He authorized the payment of dues in kind, allowed the Dutch seizures to come into the Empire at a reduction of 50 per cent, permitted the Danes extra time to import the stocks for Holstein at Hamburg, and subsequently accepted the sequestrations in Prussia by way of payment to be deducted from the war indemnity. All that was already in circulation was remitted so that it again became impossible to exercise any kind of check on it. Moreover, this whole procedure had produced the most violent reactions. The destruction of the confiscated manufactured goods brought their holders face to face with bankruptcy, for it required an enormous sum of money to enter into possession of the colonial goods—more than nine million at Frankfurt—which many were quite unable to advance. Each state claimed the right to apply the Trianon decree to its own advantage, with the result that the whole movement of goods came to a standstill until it was agreed only to require the dues to be paid once; and even then, because Prussia accepted payment in its own depreciated paper money, its certificates ended by being refused. This shock led to the great economic crisis of 1811; and so the customs extortion and red tape only served to aggravate the evils which the licences had been intended to cure.

Nor was the effect on morale at all healthy. The licences and the Trianon decree confused public opinion by suggesting that the Emperor had seen his mistake and was now going to give up the Continental blockade; and in August, after the assurances given to the United States, even Montalivet was for a while under the same illusion. The Fontainebleau decree and the ruthless manner in which it was applied were a bitter disappointment to the peoples concerned, who considered they had been more hardly treated than the English, and thought it a scandal that the produce they so badly needed should be burnt in the public squares or thrown into the rivers. It was possible at a pinch to persuade the French that this procedure was in the national interest, but not so the other nations. The American envoy at St. Petersburg had called it 'a policy of vandalism', and this was the generally voiced opinion. And then again, by reserving licences for the French, Napoleon justified the view of those who proclaimed the blockade to be solely in the interests of the dominant nation; and by making an exception for the Americans, he called forth the indignation of the allied and vassal states. From the end of 1809 onwards, Murat was in league with Fouché, Ouvrard, and Labouchère to issue licences himself; and Russia, seeing corn going out of the Empire, began to demand an explanation. She did not apply the Trianon decrees, nor did Austria. Finally, Alexander resumed his freedom of action. Since France was trafficking with the enemy and admitting American ships to her ports, he decided to reopen his to the neutrals on December 31, 1810.

The new arrangements therefore compromised the blockade and at the same time shook the Continental System. The break with Russia had other underlying causes as well; but it would have been possible to avoid giving it a further pretext if—in keeping with the spirit of the Continental federation—licences had been issued to the vassal states and allies, as well as to the French, for trade with Empire ports; and this would likewise have been profitable to the Americans. The Navigation Act of 1810 was in such circumstances completely useless. It was a most untimely and dangerous demonstration of the obstinacy of Napoleon's mercantilist outlook.

Apart from this mistake, contemporary recriminations do not conceal the plain fact that his policy was remarkably astute. Not for one moment did he intend to give up the Continental blockade, and his reorganization of it still gave only a secondary place to the difficulties of industry. The purpose had been essentially fiscal: the Emperor needed money for the war against Austria, and by allowing the peasants to sell their corn he could pocket the tax—a point that did not escape the English. In 1810, he foresaw that he would need still more money to get ready to fight against Russia; and at the end of 1810, the Trianon and Fontainebleau decrees brought him in an estimated 150 million, not to mention the proceeds from the sale of confiscated goods. As always, he bent his policy to meet present needs, and he got what he wanted. At the same time he combined this financial policy with a diplomatic move calculated to win over the United States, and was equally successful in this as well. Taking the Emperor's promises seriously, Madison re-established free trade with the Empire on November 2, 1810, whereas English imports were still forbidden.

The Berlin and Milan decrees, however, remained in full force, and there is no doubt that if licences had seemed to Napoleon likely to impair their effectiveness, he would have brought the system to an end; for as in 1809, licences were only a temporary expedient. Nor would he have continued the American permits unless the United States had been destined (in his view) to declare war against England. There was a peremptory note about his announcement of March 24, 1811, to the merchants of Paris:

I regard the neutral flags as a territorial extension. But the power that allows them to be violated cannot be looked upon as neutral. The fate of American trade will soon be decided. I will give it my help if the United States obey these decrees. If not, their ships will be turned away from my imperial ports. The continent will be closed to all imports from England. I shall be prepared to use armed force, if need be, to carry out my decrees.

To be sure, in 1811 England was back in the bad days of 1808. Sweden had just joined the blockade, and the English fleet had no port left in the Baltic to which they could have free access. But in September 1810 they encountered a severe reverse. When 600 ships who had had to shelter from gales in the straits tried to make land on the southern coasts, 140 of them were seized, with an estimated cargo of a million and a half sterling; and Sweden herself had to put up with the confiscation of a further hundred, worth half a million. Holland and the German North Sea coast were now annexed and the *Grande Armée* poured over Germany on its way to Russia, and made the watch more strict. Never before had English exports been so seriously affected. In 1810, they were still rising, and reached £7,700,000 for Northern Europe inclusive of France, plus £9,160,000 for re-exports. In 1811, these figures fell respectively to £1,500,000 and £1,960,000: in other words, to only 14·5 per cent and 32·2 per cent of the 1805 values. That same year England only sold the United States £1,870,000 worth of goods, instead of the £11,300,000 of 1810. At the same time the disturbances that had begun in Spanish America brought down the figure for exports to the New World—excluding the United States—to less than 13 million, against more than 17½ million in 1810. The total of British exports fell to £39½ million in 1811, or 82 per cent as compared to 1805, and 65 per cent as compared with 1810.

It may perhaps be alleged that in 1811 England was suffering from a severe industrial crisis; but this was responsible for a startling drop in prices and the building up of enormous stocks of goods. Though England sold less, it was only because no one would buy her wares, and not because there was any shortage of them. Thus the blockade was working satisfactorily: certain factors outside Napoleon's control, which had previously worked against him, were now running in his favour; and as was shown by the 1811 crisis, there were other favourable factors as well. It is therefore easy to understand his confidence: 'I know that my measures have been severely censured,' he was still saying on March 24, 1811; 'those however who have recently come from England and have seen the effects now beginning to be felt in the interruption of their trade with the continent cannot but say that the Emperor may possibly be right, and that his plans will very likely succeed.'

He had failed, however, to take advantage of some of the favourable factors. It annoyed him to see England continuing to sell on the Continent and pocketing the returns in cash or passing them on to her allies in the form of subsidies; but he ought to have laid the blame at his own door. For he continued to respect the international banking framework which acted as a support for the British trade and managed the transfer of specie, which played an important part in payment, as well as the circulation of commercial paper money—a vital necessity for exchange, at least in Western Europe. As the Dutch minister Valckenaer wrote to King Louis on January 25, 1808:

> Of all the English manufactured goods circulating on the continent, none is more profitable or more important to the English than bank paper money. . . . Its magic power sustains the vast fabric of English trade in the four quarters of the world. . . . Such is the powerful effect of the system of bills and letters of exchange drawn either directly on England, or indirectly on English accounts, in all the commercial centres of the European continent.

Again, the banks served as intermediaries for the Elector of Hesse and Dutch capitalists to subscribe to the English loans, and for Nathan Rothschild to send funds to Wellington by procuring French bills! The key centres were Amsterdam, Hamburg, and Frankfurt. The Houses of Hope-Labouchère and Paris kept in touch with them, as well as with the Baring Bank and the financial Houses of Paris. The Continental Rothschilds kept in touch with their brother Nathan in London, and in 1811 three of them—James, Charles, and Solomon—came to do business in Paris, where James remained to found the French branch of the family. The big banks on the Continent were under the Emperor's control. However, if the export of coin was still forbidden in the Empire, this was not so elsewhere; it does not even seem to have ceased in Holland after the annexation. Again, commercial discounting went on uninterruptedly everywhere, though the *Moniteur* had stopped quoting the London exchange rate in 1807. No one had failed to realize that this was in fact the Gordian knot. Commercial paper credit, according to Valckenaer, was the only kind of merchandise that was not forbidden, and, he said, 'that is where we must strike'. He therefore proposed to reckon as high treason any creation, acceptance, endorsement, discount, despatch or payment of any bill to the benefit or credit or account of any English subject. No doubt Louis took good care not to let this suggestion come to his brother's notice; but the cleavage in policy could not escape Mollien or Napoleon, and in 1811 he fulminated against 'the discounters of English commerce'. Nevertheless, he did not take measures against them—an omission that can only be explained by his mercantilist outlook. Although he wished to stop the English from selling, he did not give up exporting to them and drawing on their coin. Holland, too, continued to obtain important revenue from her investments abroad, and the Emperor had no intention of giving these up: to have taken steps against the international bank would have been a blow to his own interests. The warlike ardour which had inspired the Berlin and Milan decrees did not contain any such mitigations; and so he was prepared to curb it—though perhaps without quite admitting to himself that he was doing so.

The lure of gold and certain fiscal considerations also made him turn down the chance of starving England out and led him to deliver her the corn she badly needed. It would seem that in the first flush of warlike ardour he had argued otherwise, for the export of foodstuffs had come to a complete halt in France in 1807, had been forbidden in Holland, and had ceased in Germany in 1808. But in 1809 he authorized it again, in spite of Coquebert de Montbret's observations, and it was by this means that his new policy showed a substantial profit. Out of the total imports of 1,567,000 quarters in 1810, Great Britain received 1,306,000 from the Empire and its allies. As Napoleon had hoped, her rate of exchange went down and her gold left the country; but she kept some reserves, which is proved by the fact that in spite of the disastrous famine of 1810, she only imported in 1811 336,130 quarters of corn, a third of which still came from Prussia; and that nevertheless the quarter, which averaged 103s. in 1810 (about 44 fr. a hectolitre), went down to 92s. (33 fr. 50 a hectolitre). There is no doubt that without French help England would have gone short over several weeks; and even if she had managed to come through by one expedient or another, prices would certainly have soared. Now at this particular juncture England was going through an unprecedented economic crisis; and by tying his hands in advance Napoleon missed what was perhaps a unique opportunity of achieving his purposes.

THE CRISIS OF 1811

An important part in this crisis was played by the Trianon and Fontainebleau decrees, but they were not an indispensable element in bringing it about. Here, too, it must be realized that Napoleon was helped by circumstances that were not under his control. Capitalist production is by its nature subject to periodical disturbances, and the war and blockade simply created unhealthy conditions which precipitated the crisis. They did not altogether spare the Continent; yet the English economy, just because of its more advanced development, suffered infinitely more serious damage.

Prices since 1807 had been artificially inflated. In England, for example, supplies from the Baltic, silks and cotton had more than doubled by 1808. Freights from Canada were twice as much, from Riga, three times or more. In 1810, it was calculated that the voyage of a 100-ton vessel from Calais to London and back cost £50,000, and from Bordeaux to London and back, £80,000, with the result that there was more and more capital locked up in maritime trade. At the same time risks were on the increase, not only because of captures and confiscations, but also in proportion to the exorbitant and unforeseeable variations in prices. Thus in Paris Pernambuc cotton was worth 7 fr. a pound in 1806, 15 in 1807, and 24 in 1808; and in 1810 the price stayed between 12 and 14. At Hamburg, a sack was quoted at 75 gulden at the beginning of 1808, 260 in the middle of the year, and 175 at the end. In London, the fluctuations were smaller, though large enough to provide huge possibilities for speculation. In Hamburg, the father of the Parish family was already deploring in 1800 that short-term speculation was getting such a grip on the business world. And in the end it became a ruling passion. In England, there was gambling on every kind of goods and societies were even formed with this one and only purpose.

On the Continent, the chief interest was in the colonial products, and opportunities for speculation were found in the larger towns. All the same, there were not such constant arrivals of shipping, and the activity was much greater in Amsterdam and in the Hanseatic cities, where French banks invested large sums, either on their own account, or for their clients. In 1810, for example, there was mention of the tenant of the du Caveau Café as a strong investor in colonial goods at Antwerp. The Bulls took the lead, and there was plenty of scheming, especially by circulating false rumours. In April 1807, in order to force the price of cotton up, the news was spread abroad that the English were blockading Lisbon. In Holland, the big firms bought up stocks in the warehouse, so as to control the market. In England, where government borrowing was continuous, there was also much interest shown in stocks and shares. In this department, the Bears were in control of the situation. The brokers were all the more insistent on bringing down the Consolidated Funds because the bankers, with one exception, would not lend on forward dealings; they themselves advanced it at the rate of 5 per cent (the legal maximum), by borrowing on much more favourable terms, whilst the Bank of England countered their operations through the Goldsmith Bank. In Paris, speculation on stocks and shares did not become nearly as important, though it was by no means neglected. The uncertain political situation made it a very unstable business. As long as Talleyrand was at the Foreign Office, he took advantage of the information reaching him in his official capacity to make highly profitable deals on the Stock Exchange. Mollien kept up the price of government stock to the best of his ability; but the Bears never ceased to justify the invectives launched by Napoleon. The spirit of speculation spread into business and industry. There were two big booms in England—one in 1807 and 1808, when Popham announced the capture of Buenos Aires, and when the news came through that the Spanish possessions had proclaimed Ferdinand VII and would henceforward look upon the English as their allies; and the other in 1810, when the last French colonies had fallen and when the Americans reappeared in Europe. In order to cope with all the orders, factories were extended, and the artisans working in their homes were given better equipment in the shape of looms, either on hire or sold to them on credit. In France, Saxony, and Switzerland, the veto on English cotton goods had similar effects. Considerable capital sums were likewise invested, the service of which was a heavy burden on these firms, and put them at the mercy of any crisis.

Although circumstances provide an explanation for this feverish excitement, it would not have been able to develop in this way without the existence of inflation, both in money and in credit. In this respect England's position was very different from that of France. After freeing the banknote from gold, the British government had bent its efforts to maintaining a healthy financial state of affairs in order to avoid having to fall back on paper money. In general, their efforts had been successful, no doubt thanks to the increase in taxation, for from 1804 to 1811 taxation nearly always covered more than half the national expenditure; but also thanks to the plentiful supply of capital and the confidence they were at pains to maintain by supporting the Consols through the sinking fund and by intervention on the Stock Exchange, so that they were always able to borrow both on a short and on a long term basis. In spite of all these efforts, however, the government had to compel the Bank of England to keep a considerable quantity of exchequer bills on hand—more than 40 millions worth from 1808 onwards—with a resulting increase in the money circulation. The actual rate of increase is not known; but it rose from 17 million in 1805 to 23½ in 1811. In that year a committee of enquiry gave the assurance that there had recently been issued to the public £2 million in banknotes. In addition to this, local banks—of which there were now 800—were thought to have issued some 4 or 5 millions worth of notes. And lastly, banking methods were steadily improving. Forty banking firms were affiliated to the clearing-house, and the result was a more rapid circulation of money. The rise in prices, moreover, was continuous: in relation to 1790, the index figure was 176 in 1809. The rise was gradual, and as wages always lagged behind, whilst the plentiful supply of money lowered the rate for borrowing, there can be little doubt that inflation was a contributory factor in encouraging the spirit of enterprise. Nevertheless, some of the contemporary critics were positive that the private banks—if not the Bank of England—gave excessive credit, and we can well believe them. And lastly, merchants themselves offered long credit for payments in order to attract customers—often twelve to fifteen months—and in Latin America and the Levant, it was credit without adequate guarantees.

On the Continent, most of the states also issued paper money; but as the economies were not usually very advanced, production does not seem to have been much stimulated by it. Napoleon, on the other hand, had ruled out paper money once and for all; but he was none the less keen to increase the stock of metallic money by all possible means, and war provided him with substantial indemnities, a good part of which came back into the Empire, and the money in circulation was therefore correspondingly increased. All the same it is clear that credit was chiefly inflated by unsound procedures, as happened under the Consulate. Since banks were still rather rare, especially in the provinces, traders, industrialists, and speculators continued to obtain money by mortgaging their real estate or by accommodation bills. In spite of the reforms in the Bank of France, it is not certain that these did not go on being accepted; for we know that Martin's son, a Genevan who was one of the Bank's auditors, went bankrupt in 1811 as a result of speculation and having been involved in some contraband business.

It did not require the decrees of 1810, then, to produce a crisis, and in England at any rate the crisis preceded the decrees. Although there was greater activity than ever, the economy began to show signs of weakness from 1809 onwards through a sagging of the money market. The price of gold and silver had not increased since 1806; but the Bank of England's cash reserves, which were more than £6 million in 1808, suddenly fell to £4 million. The pound, which had been worth 23 francs in Paris and 35 shillings in Hamburg the previous year, suddenly dropped to 20 francs and 28 shillings respectively. By August 1809, Ricardo was sounding a note of alarm, thus opening up a controversy which has remained famous in the history of monetary theories. He blamed inflation for the crisis, and laid the responsibility at the door of the Bank of England. At this point Huskisson intervened to defend the Bank; and in February 1810 the Commons appointed a committee of enquiry which reported in 1811 in favour of Ricardo. Even today, the debate is by no means closed. The premium on precious metals must have encouraged a certain degree of hoarding, but capital did not leave the country because there was easy government borrowing: besides, where else could the capital have gone? The fall in the rate of exchange and the disappearance of gold must therefore have been due to external payments by the State, and not to internal inflation. These payments had been considerably increased by the Peninsular War, by subsidies to the Portuguese, the Spaniards, and the Austrians, and finally by grain purchases, which were responsible for almost an additional £6 million in 1809. In short, England paid out an annual average of about 3 million on the Continent in the years between 1805 and 1807. The total was more than 6½ million in 1808, 8 in 1809, and 14 in 1810. It should be added that she was always having to pay out sums in other parts of the world for the upkeep of her garrisons, her ships, and her agencies, as well as find the interest on the funds invested by foreigners in Great Britain. On this last account, Holland by herself took 32 million florins from London. Finally, the commercial balance showed a deficit of 15·5 million sterling in 1809, 8·9 million in 1810, and 11·1 million in 1811.

Even if we admit that the budget was balanced, it is none the less certain that the ministry found itself compelled to send large quantities of specie abroad, part of which they sought from the Bank of England. The prime reason for this drain on money was the carelessness and incompetence of the Treasury. Nathan Rothschild has related that one day, learning that the East India Company wished to dispose of a large sum of silver, he quickly acquired it and sold it again at once to the Paymaster, who could not manage to find any ready money. He then undertook to send it to Wellington, and dispatched it with this end in view to France, where he bought bills drawn on Sicily, Malta, and even Spain. All the same, the accounts could not be balanced in the ordinary way, for the conditions imposed on trade by warfare, the blockade, and the opening up of new and distant markets made payments from abroad slow and irregular, whilst the government could not delay paying its own debts without serious trouble. For the same reasons, credit transfers were often not possible: Wellington could not be satisfied, for instance, by paper credits drawn on Germany. Advances and the transfer of precious metals were therefore unavoidable. It was not only the exchange rate that suffered, for it was not possible to insure that these transfers were scrupulously carried out. At the end of April 1812, Wellington found that he was short of 5 million piastres. By striking at exports from England, Napoleon was thus also able to make things difficult for him in the military sphere.

If Ricardo's view had won the day, the Emperor's success would have been greater, for his solution was to go back to the gold standard. If this had happened, the Bank of England would not have been able to advance cash any longer, and it would have been difficult to maintain Wellington in the Spanish Peninsula. Moreover, there would have been a deflationary crisis which would have restricted productivity and restricted the market for capital. It would then have become difficult for the Treasury to obtain funds, and so to finance the war. It is strange that the Bank's opponents did not envisage any of these consequences. No doubt there were private interests lurking behind the theoretical arguments, for the re-establishment of the gold standard would have prevented the Bank from supporting consols, in which case the Bears would have triumphed. It is probable, too, that Ricardo's supporters had a shrewd insight into the situation, and realized that his scheme would be bound to force the country to make peace. The government denounced this dangerous course. 'I am bound to regard the proposed measure (wrote Perceval) as a declaration by Parliament that we must submit to no matter what conditions of peace rather than continue the war.' And so a return to the gold standard was rejected on May 10, 1811, and depreciation continued. In 1811, the cash reserves fell to 3 million, and the gold premium was only a quarter. The French franc was at 39 per cent and the Hamburg shilling 44 per cent. Inside the country those living on investments began at last to protest, and Lord King claimed from his tenants a bonus equal to the loss in the value of the banknotes. As a result, Parliament had to decide to make the note legal tender at its nominal value, and

England found herself firmly saddled with an artificial exchange rate, which meant—as it always does—considerable hardship for those on fixed incomes.

But neither the monetary crisis nor the blockade seriously worried the industrialists and merchants during the first six months of 1810. It was rather the reverse, for the fall in the pound was an advantage for exports. But when they had exhausted their credit or completely immobilized their liquid pounds, the shortage of money coming in from abroad finally brought them hard up against reality. Latin America was generally held to be the villain of the piece. At the beginning of August 1810, five Manchester firms went bankrupt, with liabilities amounting to £2 million, and a veritable cyclone was unleased. The banks, hit by bankruptcies, restricted credit and by so doing brought about further bankruptcies, or forced manufacturers to slow down production and finally come to a halt. There was a landslide in prices: the 1811 index figure was 158 instead of the 176 of 1810. Colonial goods fell in value by 50 per cent, and coffee by nearly two-thirds. Napoleon could not have chosen a better moment for tightening up the blockade. His Draconian measures, the Baltic seizures, the staggering fall in British exports which resulted—all these aggravated the crisis and made it last longer. The year 1811 was marked by a profound stagnation in the business world, accompanied by a fall in prices in manufactured articles, a slowing down of production, and widespread unemployment. The index figure for business activity as a whole in Great Britain was 64, as compared with 74·8 in 1810. In the big exporting industries, the slowing down was no doubt even more marked, and seems to have been something like only 25 per cent of the 1809–1810 level. Production would have fallen off still further and brought even severer unemployment if the firms working for the American market had not continued to produce, gambling on a rapid repeal of the Orders in Council, and the re-opening of the United States market. The depression went on into 1812, up to June 23, when the Orders in Council were repealed. This step enabled the exporting industries to clear their stocks, which were despatched with all speed to the United States. There was an undoubted recovery, but it was short-lived. At the news that America had declared war stagnation once again descended upon industry, and lasted till the news of the Russian disaster. For the year as a whole, the index figure of general business activity was scarcely higher than for 1811—65·3 as against 64. It would no doubt be an exaggeration to say that British industry was paralysed by the blockade and Madison's policy combined; but it is quite clear that the effects were most serious.

There were violent social repercussions. In May 1811, the cotton mills were only working three days a week, and at Bolton the weekly wage was down to 5s. Two-thirds of the looms were out of action. As the workers had long considered their wretched condition to be due to the introduction of machinery, it was the machines that they attacked. The trouble started in March in the Nottingham district, and had become extremely serious by November; by 1812, it had spread to the Yorkshire, Derbyshire, and Leicestershire counties. Lancashire and Cheshire also rose in revolt, and in these parts there were not only attacks on machinery but also market riots, for bread was still dear. These 1812 disturbances were the longest, most widespread, and most serious that had taken place in England since the seventeenth century. For several weeks certain districts were practically in the hands of the rebels, and 12,000 regular troops were needed to put down the disturbances. This outbreak showed up in glaring fashion the faults, not to say vices, of the social and economic system in Great Britain, and the inadequacy of its antiquated system of local government.

Clearly, this was where Napoleon made his mistake in delivering corn to England. No one can say what the turn of events might have been if famine had come in to make the crisis still worse. Grave though the crisis was, it did not produce panic. In spite of their misgivings, neither the aristocracy nor the middle classes lost their heads. The finances, too, stood up to the squall; in spite of the rise in the country's expenditure from 128 million in 1810 to 147 million in 1812, and a slight fall in revenue, where there was a two million drop in 1811 and 1812 from a falling off in customs. The government had borrowed 22½ million in 1809; in 1810, it had to be content with a million less, but managed to collect 23½ million in 1811, and in 1812 nearly 35 million. But as that was not enough, the government also borrowed an additional 37 million on short term in 1810, 41 million in 1811, and 45 million in 1812. A longer ordeal would have been needed to exhaust Great Britain's reserves.

Although the Emperor's confidence was increased by these difficulties in England, he did not escape the counter-effects of the measures he had adopted in 1810. In March of that year, some misgivings had been produced in Paris by the bankruptcies in Brittany; but it was definitely the Trianon decree that let loose the Continental crisis. It began in the Hanseatic cities and in Holland, where speculation in colonial goods had been rasher than elsewhere, so that the effects of the decree were more damaging. In September the House of Rodda of Lübeck went bankrupt to the extent of 2½ million marks; and a little later on, the Desmedt Bank at Amsterdam stopped all payments. Since the Paris banks were closely linked to both of them, businessmen expressed their fears in no uncertain terms in November at a trade council meeting; and the following month the Fould Bank collapsed, as well as the Simons, whose chief was the husband of Mlle Lange, and thirty-seven other firms. This was the signal for the spread of panic, and Talleyrand even went so far as to recommend a moratorium. In January 1811, Bidermann, who had been a constant speculator ever since the end of the *Ancien Régime*, went bankrupt along with sixty others. Little by little all districts were affected, and manufacturers were hard hit, with consequent severe unemployment. Since Napoleon had cleared out all stocks of corn, the average price of corn again rose above 20 francs in 1810, and a poorish harvest added to the rise, which continued in the following year. There were not any disturbances like the English ones; but it is well known how nervous Napoleon was of such outbreaks in similar circumstances.

Neither in London nor in Paris was there any liking for government interference. The British cabinet and Parliament showed a growing inclination to adopt a *laissez-faire* policy. Though Napoleon was inclined to pursue an opposite course, he had no tender feelings towards industrialists, and towards bankers and merchants more particularly, but rather reproached them bitterly for having run into these troubles through their own wild speculations. But both countries were forced to seek a remedy for the unemployment. Parliament provided a credit of 2 million for loans on the security of goods, as in 1793. In France, the Emperor at first tried to get more commercial discount by buying up a certain number of shares from the Bank of France, and by compelling it to open branches in the provinces. He also considered forming a loan fund on the security of goods; but in the end he did not do more than give local or individual help, as in 1807. The Amiens chamber of commerce obtained an advance for setting up an emergency loan fund, and others were granted to large banks like Tourton-Ravel or the House of Doyen in Rouen, as well as to important manufacturers like Richard-Lenoir in Paris and Gros-Davillier in Alsace. Mollien estimated these at a total of 12 or 13 million. Besides this help, the state greatly increased its purchases. Napoleon bought two million worth of silks and six of other goods, which he put in the hands of the exporters in return for the necessary licences. Without advertising his own hand in the affair, he arranged a two million credit with the Hottinger Bank in various places, especially at Rouen, for the financing of orders.

The crisis was a severe test of both the belligerents, and its most curious result was to make them more accommodating to one another, and lead them to harmonize their respective licensing system so as to make exchanges easier. In England, business people could make their voices heard, and put vigorous pressure on the Board of Trade. But it would appear that they received offers or encouragement from the Continent—probably from Holland—in the course of negotiations with Fouché, Ouvrard, and Labouchère, and also from Belgium, for Van Acken, a merchant and adviser to the *préfecture* at Ghent, passed on to Montalivet letters that had been sent to him from England relating to these efforts. In 1810, the Board of Trade showed a readiness to accept goods that Napoleon had agreed to export under licence, on condition that he would take British products and colonial goods in exchange; but in November he went back on his promise. As the crisis was growing worse, the merchants returned to the attack. For example, on April 14, 1811, the Glasgow Chamber of Commerce demanded that there should be an agreement with the enemy. On November 15, the English newspapers announced that trade with France would once more be allowed on a reciprocal basis; and a circular of April 14 had in fact admitted wines to England,

In February 1812, Mollien announced that England was going to allow them warehouse facilities: 'such an event seemed a miracle at the time'.

The Board of Trade did not go as far as that; but it granted facilities to French ships, lifted the embargo on cinchona and baled cotton, allowed enemy subjects to take up quarters in England to organize trading under licence, and expressed its view that insurers could safely quote on cargoes intended for France. Napoleon seems to have been surprised, but Montalivet kept things moving by advising on November 25 that the licences should be adapted to comply with the English conditions. The proposed exchange was between wine and silks on the one side and sugar on the other. Montalivet would appear to have won the day, for in December numerous licences were issued to this effect. On the 31st, it was decided also to accept coffee, dyestuffs, skins, and medicaments; and on January 13, 1812, Napoleon spoke in council of importing 450,000 quintals of sugar. Up till February, he was still signing licences; from March to July these became few and far between; but as Mollien's records were lost in the retreat from Russia, it is difficult to know exactly what happened. In any case, from July to October 299 licences were issued, more particularly for bringing cotton to Rouen. Napoleon is thought to have signed in all 799 in the course of 1812. The English were more and more conciliatory, and as from March 25, 1812, they issued licences along the same lines as the French.

This unspoken agreement was a great help to international finance, which alone was in a position to make adjustments between the two regimes. It was in this context that the Rothschilds took up their abode in Paris and succeeded in rendering the services to the British Treasury which have been referred to above. According to a report by Montalivet on January 6, 1813, the Empire exported 58 millions worth and imported to the value of 22 million. It was recognized in England that the balance was in favour of France; but the vital task was to sell at all costs. There is no need, moreover, to exaggerate the importance of this deal. If English exports rose in 1812, this was more particularly due to the reopening of the Russian and Swedish markets, and to the resumption of contraband traffic after the *Grande Armée* had cleared out of Germany. The

Empire, which had been much less badly affected, seems to have recovered fairly quickly. At Ghent during the last three months of 1812, there were about as many spindles and rather more looms in action than in 1810; and in the Kingdom of Italy, the export of silk and silk-stuffs was greater than in 1809, and the total trade almost equal to that of 1810. Production also started up again in Lyons and Rouen. During the winter a pronounced shortage made itself felt, but Napoleon looked upon this as merely a passing trouble. Come what might, he was confident that the Continental economy would stand up to the inevitable inconveniences produced by the blockade. He was less than ever inclined to give it up: the licences issued in 1812 were of the same kind as before, and were viewed by him as a temporary expedient which harmed the English rather than France, since the balance of trade was unfavourable to them. Because he had given way in the matter of corn exports, he had not made all the capital he could have out of the crisis; but if he had come back victorious from Russia he would surely have applied his decrees with new vigour and new effectiveness, seeing that his dominion would have been even more far-reaching than before.

But for the French economy, circumstances would not have been so favourable. Since the crisis had produced a healthier market and kept down prices, business was beginning to revive. The number of bankruptcies was diminishing, though the figures were still as high as for 1810; and exports to Britain rose to 50 million, an increase of 28 per cent over the 1811 value, though 17 per cent below the figure for 1810. Although imports generally were recovering, coffee and sugar had dropped again, showing that the market for colonial goods was still suffering from the glut. In the same way baled cotton sank to 63,000 pounds against 91,000 in 1811 and 132,000 in 1810—a sign of weakness, suggesting that exports were drawing more particularly on liquidated stocks at rock-bottom prices. The Bank's gold continued to drain away, and there was no significant improvement in the exchange-rate. Corn kept going up in price, reaching 154s. in 1812. Disturbances among the working classes broke out more violently than ever. On the other hand if the Emperor had been victorious, he would no doubt have closed the Levant to English trade; and the American market was already lost. On February 2, 1811, Madison, relying on Napoleon's promises, had called on England to repeal the Orders in Council. Under the pressure of public opinion the cabinet in London agreed to do so on April 21, 1812, provided it could be shown that the Emperor had repealed his decrees. Maret then took a decision in line with this policy, antedating it for April 28, 1811, and the English—quite taken aback—complied on June 23. But it was too late: on June 19, Madison, maintaining that the question of the press-gangs had still not been settled, decided to declare war.

A blockade can always be used for several purposes. In the eighteenth century, the English had used it more particularly as a source of enrichment; but nowadays its main aim is to destroy the military power of the enemy. The Napoleonic blockade was a kind of half-way stage. It was forward-looking, in the sense that it sought to break down England's resistance. But it was also tied to the past, in that it aimed at reaching its goal by a roundabout and thoroughly mercantilist route designed to rob the enemy of his gold, but not to starve him out. In this watered-down form, its effects could not be rapid; moreover, the British fleet had command of the seas, and the blockade, to be successful, needed the help of circumstances more or less outside Napoleon's control. Nevertheless, the experiment had been worthwhile, though in the ultimate analysis its success depended on the *Grande Armée*, whose ruin in so short a space of time no one could have prophesied. It was not the natural laws of a liberal economy, but the Russian winter, that saved England.

CHAPTER FIVE

The Preliminaries of the Russian Campaign (1811–1812)

ALEXANDER HAD been well aware that his attitude since Tilsit, and especially since the 1809 campaign, was bound sooner or later to provoke a conflict with Napoleon. He was itching to cross swords with his rival, to determine which of them should be master of the Continent, or at any rate of the East. It took some time for the Emperor to become convinced that anyone was actually bold enough to defy him; but after the ukaz of December 31, 1810, he decided to make an end of this presumption. The Czar should be reduced to the rank of vassal; and if he resisted, he should be hurled back into Asia, and the fairest of his European provinces incorporated in the *Grand Empire*.

Napoleon has been blamed for having compromised the real national interests of France by indulging in such an adventure; but since 1803 at least, these interests had ceased to count: the only thing that mattered to him was to rule the Continent and the world. The Continental System could contain allies, but without allowing them real independence or tolerating any rebellions. Once Rome had been conquered, the Emperor's dreams turned inevitably to Constantinople; and to take possession of this, the power of the Czar must first be broken. The blockade provided a concrete justification for the new undertaking; and Alexander's infringement of it made this fresh enterprise seem absolutely necessary, for his defeat would then enable Napoleon to recapture the Levant market from England. Napoleon did not in any way conceal from himself the fact that this was the most dangerous campaign he had ever conceived. He could hardly fail to remember that Charles XII had taken this risk and that it had been his undoing. It is said that he spent three sleepless months before finally making up his mind. Yet as there was no other court of appeal but his own will, he could hardly draw back. He expressed the matter very simply when he left Paris, saying that he owed it to himself to 'finish what he had begun'.

THE SCARE OF 1811

For several months Napoleon's attention was absorbed by the difficulties involved in transferring half a million men to the Russian frontier, a task which involved immense transport facilities, huge supplies, and proportionately vast expense. The 1811 class had been called up and was already in the depots, and from the end of January he began to reinforce the troops in Germany, doubling the units one by one, forming new corps, bringing up arms and munitions and laying down supplies and depots. But in spite of the precautions he took, these measures did not escape the notice of Chermitchev and Nesselrode through their espionage service. By getting in the first blow, Alexander might surprise the Emperor in the midst of his preparations and by carrying the war into Germany give Russia a protective cover. But would he dare to do so?

At the beginning of 1811 this was what he intended to do. But his finances were in a pitiful state, with a deficit running up to 100 million roubles and paper money losing up to five-sixths of its value. Russia under the Czars, however, had never been deterred by difficulties of this kind. There were 240,000 Russians grouped in two armies, who confronted on the other side of the border 56,000 men from Warsaw and 46,000 Frenchmen, though the latter were at some distance, and widely scattered. In March, five divisions out of nine were recalled from the army on the Danube, and everywhere the troops went steadily marching on day by day towards the Grand Duchy frontier. Yet although Poniatovski was giving Napoleon time to move his forces forward, Alexander did not feel sure of his ground. Accordingly, on January 8, he returned to the charge with Czartoryski, the need for money finally brought home to him, cap in hand, proposing that he should win over the support of Poland, so that her army, by moving in as far as the Oder without striking a blow, would induce the Prussians to enter the lists. Once again the prince observed that in order to gain his country's support it would at least be necessary for the Czar to enter into a formal engagement to reconstitute the Kingdom of Poland, fix its boundaries, and accept the constitution of 1791. Alexander promised to hand over his Polish provinces, and Galicia if possible; as to internal government, he conceded that there should be autonomy, but said nothing about a constitution.

Meanwhile, he did not inform Rumiantzov of his plans, for he was always against war and disposed to come to terms with Napoleon; but he put out secret diplomatic feelers in the direction of Sweden, Prussia and more particularly Austria, and on February 13, Metternich was offered the Danubian principalities. But these tentative approaches met with no success. Czartoryski had to admit that the Poles were not willing to betray the Emperor, and Metternich refused to accept the proffered gift. Frederick William, who had bought a faked memorandum from Champagny, composed by Esmiénard, which announced the intention to eliminate Prussia, became so worked up that in May, Hardenberg proposed an alliance with France. Bernadotte, who had become regent and was looking out for subsidies, hoped to get some from his motherland. He offered Alquier, the new French ambassador, a contingent of 50,000 men against Russia, provided he was allowed to take over Norway. The offensive policy continued to have its partisans, notably Armfelt; yet among the Czar's cosmopolitan entourage, where there were beginning to be many enemies of the Emperor, it also had its opponents. A Prussian named Phull proposed that they entered themselves between the Duma and the Dnieper in order to make a flank attack on the *Grand Armée* as it marched on Moscow. Alexander was not yet resigned to a policy of methodical retreat; but an offensive policy was definitely rejected, and the troops were brought to a halt.

Caulaincourt remained quite unaware of what was happening. The Poles, on the other hand, became alarmed. Poniatovski sent an aide-de-camp to Napoleon; and then, on his way to be present at the baptism of the King of Rome, he put the government at Dresden on the alert. Davout, who was at first incredulous, became convinced by the evidence. During the month of April, the Emperor remained constantly on the alert, and from the 15th to the 17th, in the midst of the festivities following the birth of the King of Rome, he redoubled his military preparations. The Poles, when mobilized, were to evacuate the Duchy at the first signal and move to join up with Davout and the Saxon contingent on the Oder. Champagny, who was probably blamed for not having been aware of what was afoot, was replaced by Maret, and Napoleon gave orders for negotiations with Prussia, Sweden, and Turkey, whilst he himself spoke to Schwarzenberg of a possible alliance. In May, there was more reassuring news. Rumiantzov had in fact managed to arrange for negotiations to be opened for compensating the Duke of Oldenburg, hoping that part of the Duchy of Warsaw could be made over to him. Neither he nor his master said so in explicit terms; but the Emperor understood, and refused point blank. The discussions went on, however, the Duke receiving another offer of Erfurt, and Russia an offer of the treaty proposed the previous year relating to Poland; but the Czar replied with various complaints, though without advancing his claims. Caulaincourt, who had returned to Paris on June 5, was at once received by Napoleon and vouched for Alexander's loyalty. He asked for reasonable proposals to be put before the Czar. Lauriston, who succeeded him, assured the Emperor that the Russian sovereign was still peaceful in his intentions. Caulaincourt, however, made it clear that in case of attack Alexander would decide to retreat and lure the *Grande Armée* on into the unending plains, where winter would bring destruction. 'One good battle will get the better of your friend Alexander,' was Napoleon's reply. The two protagonists seemed at one in playing for time, the Emperor in order to complete his preparations, the Czar to contrive the alliances which at present seemed to elude him; but each was equally determined to force his rival to give in. Napoleon did not exclude the possibility of a bloodless surrender, but he was growing impatient. On August 15 there was a scene with Kurakine; and shortly afterwards, he decided to go to war in June 1812.

Alexander was better informed. Nesselrode and Chernitchev had long ago corrupted various employees in the Ministry of War, and Talleyrand—who was constantly asking Alexander for payment—was lavish in advice. He it was who had suggested the offer of the Principalities to Austria; and he continually insisted on the necessity of peace with Turkey and an accommodation with Bernadotte. Caulaincourt himself was disposed to listen to him, and Nesselrode wrote that his behaviour was 'in keeping with the confidence that Louise (that is, Alexander) has in him'. Talleyrand also advised the Russians to remain on the defensive and to refrain from carrying the war into Germany, so that he could pose as the defender of an oppressed Europe. Alexander's duplicity was perfectly suited to such a part; and Napoleon—whether out of infatuation or negligence—let him win several hands in the diplomatic game.

THE DIPLOMATIC CAMPAIGN AND THE MARCH OF THE 'GRAND ARMÉE'

To start with, Russia had considerable hopes of Prussia. Since Napoleon had not responded to his offer, the king decided on July 16 to seek the support of the Czar, and sent him Scharnhorst, who signed a military convention with him on October 17. The army, meanwhile, was being organized as best they could, and the war party began to look up. Gneisenau, who was temporarily head of the General Staff, was writing a memorandum to advocate a new national rising. In Prague, Stein and Grüner, a former Berlin prefect of police, were in touch with representatives of the *Tugenbund*, which had nevertheless been dissolved by the king. In Berlin, they also worked through the agency of Ompteda and other representatives of Count Münster and Baron Hardenberg, a relation of the Prussian minister in English service at Vienna as the representative of Hanover.

Once again, however, the king disappointed them. The agreement brought back by Scharnhorst stipulated that the Prussians would retreat before the French if they invaded their kingdom, and would link up with the Russians on the Vistula or shut themselves up in their strongholds. But Alexander would not even allow his generals to enter East Prussia if plainly requested by Berlin to do so. Frederick William decided that the risk involved would be too great; but by way of consolation he allowed Scharnhorst to go and try his hand in Vienna. As was to be expected, Metternich roundly rejected his approaches on December 26. From this moment onwards, there was no other course open but to submit to Napoleon. He, too, was kept very badly informed in this quarter by the Ambassador, Saint-Marsan, who was Piedmontese by birth. In Prussia, at any rate, his police gave him due warning, and on September 4, he ordered Hardenberg to disarm. As he was just then awaiting a reply from the Czar, the minister made promises that he failed to keep, and in October he had to submit to French inspection. At last, on December 29, he was forced to obey orders and resign himself to declaring that he was prepared for an alliance. The Emperor was in no hurry; but finally on February 23, the Prussian ambassador Krusemark was suddenly called upon to sign, and complied immediately. It was just as well he did, for all preparations had been made to occupy his country; and on March 2, Gudin crossed the frontier while the king was still unaware that a treaty had been signed. On the 5th he ratified it. Prussia thereby agreed to let the *Grand Armée* take up quarters in Prussia, promised to supply it with provisions of every sort, to be set against the war indemnity, which was still far from being paid off, and to send to Russia a contingent of 20,000 men. In the end, Victor, commander of the 9th corps, assumed complete control of Berlin and compelled the Prussian forces to evacuate it. This was a terrible blow for Stein's friends, and it seemed likely that the prestige of the dynasty would not survive it. Scharnhorst was sent on leave; Gneisenau went on a mission to London; Boyen, Clausewitz and many others emigrated to Russia; and in May Stein accepted an invitation from Alexander and left Prague.

Meanwhile, Austria was also siding with France, and without much hesitation, though Metternich was prodigal of advice to the Czar to avoid a war which he feared would lead to disaster, whichever way it went, for it would put him at the mercy of the victor. On December 17, Schwarzenberg was summoned to decide, and the two parties promptly came to an agreement. Napoleon would exchange the Illyrian provinces for Galicia, and would guarantee the integrity of Turkey; Austria on her side promised to contribute an army of 30,000 men. The treaty was signed on March 14, 1812. Nevertheless the war-party was taking shape again in Vienna, and Gentz, Metternich's friend and secretary, dismissed by England since he had come down on the side of peace in September 1809, was trying his best to reopen negotiations with the British Treasury by drawing up memoranda against the Continental blockade, one of them intended for the Czar in person. But the Chancellor did not intend to have his hand forced. He even took advantage of the circumstances to complete the rout of the Prussian National Party, whom he looked upon as the harbinger of revolution. Although Hardenberg was being lenient towards his enemies, he gave him support when he saw him in Dresden at the end of May; in August, Grüner was arrested at Prague.

Alexander, then, could not congratulate himself upon his efforts with the Germans. But as he had himself at times bowed to necessity not long before, he did not bear them any grudge. He knew, moreover, that they would desert Napoleon at the first opportunity. Besides, Metternich, who was the most suspect in Alexander's eyes, was certain that the Principalities would not remain Russian, and lost no time in recovering his self-assurance; for in the army of the Danube, Chitchagov was talking of an alliance with the Turks and the possibility of taking Austria in the rear by engineering a rising of the Slavs and Hungarians. The Comte de Saint-Julien came and warned the Czar that they would only fight him as a matter of form and that their contingent would not be reinforced; and a secret agreement was signed on June 2. Behind the screen of a dynastic alliance, Metternich was playing a double game that would at any rate guarantee the safety of Austria, while waiting for better days.

With the Swedes and the Ottomans, Alexander was more successful through Napoleon's own fault. The Emperor seems to have believed that both of them could not fail to come to him of their own accord. Perhaps he was also unwilling to treat with them until the last possible moment, as he had with Prussia and Austria, in order not to drive the Russians into taking the offensive; but his opponents outpaced him. In 1811 his relations with Bernadotte had become strained, and the ambassador Alquier had something to do with this. Knowing that the blockade was being openly violated in spite of his protests, he decided to break off diplomatic relations, and there was a violent scene between him and the regent on August 25. The Emperor recalled him, but made no effort to win over Bernadotte, who from now onwards swung decidedly towards Russia. In January 1812, Davout was ordered to occupy Swedish Pomerania in order to seal it off from English trade, and this was the finishing touch. On February 18, Count Loewenhielm came to St. Petersburg to propose an alliance. Bernadotte offered to disembark troops in Germany in the rear of Napoleon, on condition that Russian troops should first help him to conquer Norway. Alexander accepted, but stipulated that he must first make an agreement with Frederick VI, King of Denmark, who might be indemnified—say by the Duchy of Oldenburg. He sent Suchtelen to Stockholm, and the details were discussed in both capitals, each of the plenipotentiaries making it a point of honour to steal a march on his opposite number. They signed at almost the same time, on April 5 and 9 respectively.

With the Sultan, Alexander had been negotiating since 1811. After Bagration's successes in 1809, the war had dragged on. The Turks evacuated Serbia, which had for a moment shown French leanings, but returned to the Russian alliance after Kara-Georges' coup d'état eliminating the influence of Austria, as well as his rival Miloch Obrenovitch. In 1810 Kaminski conducted a successful campaign to bring about the surrender of the Danubian strongholds, and advanced in the direction of Chumla. In the Caucasus, Imeretia and Mingrelia both fell, and Sukhum-Kale and Akkalkalaki were conquered. Finally in 1811, Kutusov won a decisive victory. When the Turkish army had crossed the Danube in the direction of Rustchuk, he cut it in two, surrounded 36,000 of the enemy, and only allowed an armistice on condition that peace should be negotiated on the basis of annexing Bessarabia as far as Sereth. The talks opened at Giurgin on October 25, but produced no agreement, the Turks being unwilling to concede more than the line of the Pruth, and refusing to give Serbia her independence.

Another attempt was made on January 12, 1812, at Bucharest, Stratford Canning doing his best to persuade Mahmud to treat, but in vain. Finally, just as the French invasion was about to begin, Alexander ordered his representative to give in, and peace was signed on May 28. Chitchagov, Kutusov's successor, could set out for the north, whilst the troops in Asia could turn their attention to Persia. Since the summer of 1811, Napoleon's forces had taken possession of Germany, and by the beginning of 1812 it only remained to concentrate them and move on the Niemen. Danzig was transformed into a base stocked with an abundance of supplies and guarded by Rupp with 25,000 men. Poniatovski covered the Vistula with 60,000 more; and Davout was in command of 100,000 on the Oder and had pushed forward beyond it with vanguards; while Oudinot was crossing Westphalia and entering Berlin on March 28. Ney was just reaching Mainz with troops from the camp at Boulogne; the Germans were working their way towards the Elbe; and the Guards, who had been in cantonments in the east of France, were getting ready to follow. There was still the difficulty of managing to get the army in Italy back across the Alps. Napoleon gave final orders at the beginning of February, and on the 23rd Eugène got under way and the whole army began to move at the same time. In order to foil the Russian espionage, Savory managed to harass Chernitchev so thoroughly that he secured his departure on February 26; and the police discovered in his apartment a note that enabled them to shoot a certain traitor in the Ministry of War and to compromise the Russians in the eyes of the French public.

The army could not be assembled on the Niemen before the end of May. Now on April 8, Alexander, who knew that he could safely count on Bernadotte, finally decided to put forward his demands. In the first place Napoleon would have to evacuate Prussia and Swedish Pomerania and bring his troops back behind the Elbe. Then a commercial treaty would be negotiated, along with the indemnity promised to the Duke of Oldenburg; but in any case neutral trade was to remain free. Meanwhile, Napoleon kept Kurakine on a string until May 7, trying meanwhile to wind up affairs in Spain, and proposing to Canning on April 18 that peace should be signed on a basis of *uti possidetis*; except for Portugal, which would go back to its ruling house. Sicily would remain Ferdinand's, and Spain continue to belong to Joseph. All three countries would be evacuated by France and England. But England refused to leave Joseph in Madrid. When Kurakine finally demanded an answer, the Emperor left Saint-Cloud on May 9 without a word and the next day Maret followed, also without giving any answer. Narbonne had already left in order to negotiate with Alexander. He found him at Vilna, and was dismissed without a chance to enter into discussion. On May 25 the Emperor reached Dresden where he received the Emperor of Austria, the King of Prussia, and a number of vassal princes. On the 28th he set out for the Niemen.

The great adventure had begun. Napoleon could only return from it master of the whole of Europe, or fallen from glory. Once again he was playing double or quits.

II

THE WORLD IN 1812

CHAPTER SIX

Imperial France

In 1812, the French Empire covered about 750,000 square kilometres. It had, in all probability, 44 million inhabitants, and was divided into 130 *départements*. Gradually Napoleon had added to his legacy of 102 *départements* bounded by natural frontiers, lands which constituted two antennae pointing towards the north-east and south-east. One of these was made up of Holland with its nine *départements* together with the German territories bordering the North Sea, which constituted four others—here, in fact, the Empire, with the Bouches-de-la-Trave, whose capital was Lübeck, reached as far as the Baltic. The other was made up of the Valais, Piedmont, Liguria, Parma, Tuscany, and the western part of the Papal States, fifteen *départements* in all. The majority of these recent annexations was by no means completely assimilated. They were more in the nature of vassal states. So it was that Holland had a Governor General, as had Tuscany. The German *départements*, forming the 22nd military division, remained subject to the orders of a special commission, while Illyria, although annexed to the Empire, had always had a separate administration and its territorial divisions were not counted among the 130 *départements*. In short, the Napoleonic system of government functioned normally only within the framework of the natural frontiers—if we except Piedmont and Liguria, reunited quite early on.

This system was never absolutely rigid. From 1804 to 1811 Napoleon was constantly remoulding his institutions. From the experiments he continued to make in the vassal states, we may conclude that the era of perfecting was not yet ended; and in particular the social order in France had not yet assumed the form he desired. None the less, though his work remained unfinished, it was sufficiently advanced in 1812 for its spirit to be discernible.

AUTHORITARIAN GOVERNMENT

Success had, little by little, transformed the person and way of life of the Emperor. After Tilsit, it is hardly possible to recognize the man of Brumaire, angular, sombre, the absolutely Roman cast of the countenance. The complexion had become softer, serenity had made the features less rigid. His activity was no less intense, but was more subject to order. At eight o'clock at the latest he started to work at his desk, and only broke off for lunch which he normally took alone and, once or twice a week, he would go for a walk or go hunting. At six, he dined with his family and, after a few minutes' conversation, returned to his work and went to bed between nine and ten. Sunday was a day of ceremony. After Mass and the parade, he reviewed his court which waited in silence in the salons, drawn up in precise order of rank and elaborately attired in accordance with the strictest etiquette. In the evening there was a great family dinner, after which the sovereigns provided a concert or play and held a reception.

Round about 1810, slight signs of ageing began to show. His face grew fat, his complexion dulled, his body slumped and thickened; there were indications that the Empire, with its vast extent, overtaxed his energies. 'Did I not give such and such an order?' he would write. This however was not so important; to the end his mind remained astonishingly vigorous and lucid. What is more evident is the effect of omnipotence on his moral attitude: 'My people of Italy know me well enough to stop them ever forgetting that I know more in my little finger than they do in all their heads put together.' Pessimism made him brutal: 'I have always observed that the respectable are good for nothing.' The worship of force and success became cynical:

'There is only one secret of managing the world and that is to be strong, because in strength there is no error or illusion; that's the naked truth.' 'You have to succeed; I only judge men by the results of their actions.' As a natural consequence, he felt himself more and more solitary; he showed himself increasingly disillusioned about the permanence of his work. 'Both within and without,' he said to Chaptal, 'I only reign by the fear I inspire'; and, later, to Mollien, 'They joined up with me to enjoy security; they would abandon me tomorrow if disorder returned.' How would men feel when his end came?—'All they would say is "*Ouf!*" '

The fewer obstacles he met, the more jealous and irritable he became. Like Frederick II, he continually emphasized the personal character of his government. Judging by the constitutions he gave to the realms of Naples and Westphalia, his intention was to eliminate finally the elective principle. However, neither the electorate nor the assembly did anything to hinder him. The district assemblies, embodying universal suffrage, were not consulted until 1813 and then only in certain *départements*. The choices of the colleges were settled in advance by personal relationships and few members took part. In 1810 in the Cote d'Or the list of candidates for the general council could not be completed and the *sous-préfet* of Châtillon-sur-Seine himself proceeded to designate the council of the *arrondissement*. For legislative functions all proposals favoured officials and soldiers, except one position which fell to Berlier's father-in-law. Little by little the assemblies became dominated by these people. The *Tribunat* disappeared in 1807 and the sessions of the *Corps Législatif* became gradually shorter. Napoleon legislating either by *senatus-consulta*, for such things as conscription levies and annexations, or by decree, as for the re-establishment of the tobacco monopoly. As long as the Codes were still unfinished, the *Conseil d'État* was still to some extent active; after their completion, it was hardly left with anything but legal points, whereas the administrative councils, dealing only with the technique of execution, preserved their importance.

The part played by ministers became more and more reduced, and their powers continued to be whittled down. The *Grande Armée* and the foreign territories had their supervisors, conscription and the commissariat, two directors. One after the other the regime's great administrators saw themselves thrust aside—first Chaptal, then Talleyrand, and finally Fouché. The Emperor preferred to have in their stead second-rate men whom he treated as clerks, like Crétet, Champagny, Bigot de Préameneu, Savary and Maret. A growing share of the places fell to survivors from the *Ancien Régime*. Napoleon believed that they had a prior loyalty to the new legitimate line, and thought they would be easy to manipulate: 'It is only people like that who know how to be servants'. Many of them were lacking in ability or experience, and so those he noticed received rapid promotion. Molé, for example, *maître des requêtes* in 1806, became *préfet* in 1807, Councillor of State and director of roads and highways in 1809, and a minister in 1813; and this accounts for the holding together of a number of posts. In 1806, in order to set up a reserve of officials distinguished by birth and fortune (and so very poorly paid), but shaped by himself, Napoleon reintroduced the *maîtres des requêtes* in the *Conseil d'État*, appointing in all 72, and multiplied the assistants in the councils and in the administration, in the provinces no less than in Paris. In 1811, there were 360 of them in the ordinary service. As far as the *Conseil d'État* was concerned, he cannot be said to have made any radical changes in the nature of its composition; though it is true that in 1813, he appointed once more the ex-convention member Zangiacomé—not indeed a regicide—and the brother of Coffinhal. He only got rid of a dozen councillors, and only carried out two dismissals—incidentally, for reasons that had nothing to do with the work of the Council. None the less, one can clearly see the direction in which things were moving; and there is no doubt what the outcome would have been if the Empire had lasted. Moreover, the men of Brumaire were beginning to feel at home: they were awarded the Legion of Honour, and took their place among the new nobility; some of them even set up entails.

The recruitment of *préfets* underwent a much more perceptible change. The Côte d'Or, previously in the hands of a former member of the Constituent Assembly, then in those of a tribune, subsequently passed to Molé, and finally in 1812 to the Duke of Cossé-Brissac. The remaining survivors of the Revolution were few and far between—such men as Jeanbon, who continued to be loyal to the past. In Marseilles, Thibaudeau, influenced by his wife and out of prudence and vanity, set about engineering a reaction. These *préfets* followed their master's example. To begin with, the *Conseils Généraux* contested a particular item of expenditure, cut down the accounts, and expressed their wishes; but they lost heart when they found that the credits they had refused were officially reinstated, no supporting documents produced, and their wishes scornfully disregarded. The purges took place as vacancies occurred. In 1809, in the Bouches-du-Rhône, six out of seven nobles or officials were got rid of in one sweep; in the Pas-de-Calais, you can see the Artois nobility beginning to get an entry. The same procedure took place for the councillors in the *préfectures* and *sous-préfectures*. The evidence from the Côtes-du-Nord suggests that the revolutionaries put up a better resistance in the west, where the *chouans* offered stubborn opposition. As for the municipalities, there continued to be the problem of finding capable men to fill the places. It often proved impossible to complete the councils or ensure their meeting; but a mayor at least was necessary, and for this the *préfets* fell back upon the big proprietors, even if they were hostile to the regime. The difficulty was greater still for the minor offices, such as secretaries and rural police; and the same was true in all administrative departments. The people could not yet provide the material for a lower middle class from which could be drawn officials well enough educated to have a sense of professional integrity. Some *préfets* attempted to govern directly through itinerant secretaries or inspectors—for example in the Bas-Rhin, Pas-de-Calais, and Meurthe; but they were obliged to extract their salaries from the already heavily indebted *communes*. There can thus be no illusions about the imperfections of local administration, which only time could improve. But such as it was, it gave Napoleon what he wanted—money, men, and the preservation of order.

It is not easy to say how far centralization was in practice carried out. From Year XI onwards, the *préfets* were regretting that they were not allowed more initiative, and pointing out that the necessity of corresponding with each of the ministers meant that they often received contradictory orders; and those they governed complained that constant reference to Paris delayed decisive action. Some of them, all the same, made free use of their authority, including summary arrests. For example, in the Doubs in 1805, de Bry put through a forced loan. The Emperor accused them of playing the despot—a rather amusing touch—and the ministers sometimes expressed dissatisfaction with them. 'In general,' wrote Montalivet in 1812, 'the *préfets* say what they like to me; but I see more clearly than ever that we do not know anything about what is really going on.' When Napoleon really wanted to know where he stood or wished to 'repair the machinery', as the Committee of Public Safety had tried to do, he would send down special commissioners, as he did in 1812. Moreover, in the *départements* the central power was in collision with the covert power of the important civil and military figures, whether they were natives of the district or no; especially the bishop, who contrived—without defying the central power—to intervene in the choice of persons and the details of administration. Taken as a whole, centralization may be said to have been more thoroughgoing than before 1789; but the slowness of communications tended to safeguard the *préfets*' independence, so that it varied in accordance with the distance, the circumstances, and the character of the men concerned. In proportion as the Consulate *préfets* disappeared and the country grew more peaceful, centralization progressed.

The reorganization of justice was doggedly pursued. There were soon complaints of the people who had been chosen somewhat at random in Year VIII. Napoleon took steps to improve the methods of recruiting. In Year XII, he established the law schools, and in 1808, judges who would hear cases in a consultative capacity. From 1807 onwards, he thought it possible to undertake a purge, which was handed over by a *senatus-consultum* to a special commission. Of the 194 magistrates denounced, 170 were proposed for dismissal; and in actual fact, the decree of March 24, 1808, deprived 68 of office and accepted the resignation of 94. At the same time the codification of the law was nearing completion. The code for civil procedure was finished in 1806; the commercial code in 1807; the criminal code in 1808; the penal code in 1810. The rural code, which had also been drawn up, was not promulgated. The spirit of 1789 did not altogether disappear from it. The *Conseil d'État* preserved unimpaired the social work of the Revolution. It was at pains to separate the administrative from the judicial machinery, took care to assure the judge's independence, and obstinately defended the jury system. But, in parallel with these provisions, the property and authority of the middle classes could reckon on its support provided they did not trespass on the authority of the State, which was regarded as in the general public interest. Whether revolutionaries or men of the *Ancien Régime*, all its members would unhesitatingly sacrifice their principles out of class interest or political opportunism. Necessity knows no law, said Portalis; there is no theory that must not give way to necessity, Berlier confirmed. These traits were already apparent in the Civil Code; and subsequent codes were to mark the reaction even more clearly.

The first two are very close to Colbert's ordinances. The second in particular did not prove well adapted to the conditions of economic progress, for example as regards insurance and companies; at least, although continuing to subordinate the limited liability company to the extent of authorizing only those under a collective name or in limited partnership, it made the concession that the responsibility of the shareholders should be restricted to their holdings. Previously, the law had been doubtful on this point, some judgments obliging them to support the company with the whole of their possessions. But there was nothing as striking as the discussion relating to promissory notes. Well aware that the expansion of the economy depended on that of credit, and so on the trustworthiness of the banks, some were in favour of treating the single private individual, in any case of protest, like the businessman, and so making him liable to bodily constraint. But Molé spoke up loudly for the opposing view, pointing out that such conduct was a departure from common law, entailing the sacrifice of personal liberty in favour of business interests and bankers, who were a selfish minority—as had happened in England. France, he maintained, should no doubt foster trade, but above all remain essentially agricultural. The opposition party went on to point out that if the methods of trade and finance were to be adopted, citizens would be inclined to entrust their savings to these agencies and invest them in life interests, giving pride of place to personal estate, which is always unstable. It would mean the end of the great families and classes, and would undermine the monarchy—considerations that were well calculated to appeal to Napoleon, particularly at that period. But his broad intelligence won the day, and he came down in favour of a compromise: it was decided that the private person should be treated as a businessman if he had subscribed his share as a result of commercial transactions.

The last two codes in particular marked an important date. They came into force in 1810, when the law of April 28 once more re-fashioned the judiciary organization, giving it the form that it still preserves, though it gave the mayor—except in the cantonal capital—powers of simple police which he has since then lost. This law regulated the manner and conditions for nominating judges, as well as their discipline; and the occasion served as an opportunity to carry out a fresh purge: the Paris court of appeal lost 8 councillors out of 31. These changes do not seem to have been inspired by political motives; but none the less, the composition of the staff moved in the same direction as in the other cases. At Besançon, for example, two presidents and five councillors from the former Parliament became members of the court. All the same, the revolutionaries kept their power more successfully here because—apart from the purges—they were appointed to their posts for life.

But now there was a further increase of repression. The standing magistrate (*parquet*) was at this time given its definitive organization. Instruction was made a matter of complete secrecy. The *magistrat de Sûreté* disappeared, and the business of accusation became centralized in the hands of public prosecutors, advocates general, and examining magistrates. The *préfet* regained the power to appoint juries to try cases; and when the Grand Jury was suppressed, its functions passed to one of the courts of appeal. The special tribunals were retained under the title of 'ordinary special courts', but they were now manned entirely by soldiers. Provision was also made for 'extraordinary special courts' where the jury had been suspended, or for combating certain crimes; and the same year saw the appearance of the 'special customs courts'. Moreover, the Senate could by virtue of the constitution quash a jury's verdict as detrimental to the safety of the State. For example in 1813 it brought the mayor of Antwerp before a special court on the charge of indulging in contraband, a charge of which he had been acquitted in the assize court. As for the penal code, while not restoring torture, it re-established branding, the iron collar, the loss of a hand for parricide, and the loss of all civil rights.

In spite of the strengthening of penal justice, the Empire did not rely solely upon this, any more than the Consulate had done: it placed more reliance upon administrative repression, that is to say, on the police. Under the minister—first Fouché, then in 1810 Savary—there were councillors of State in charge of the *arrondissements*; then, from 1808 onwards, directors-general in Turin, Florence, Rome, and Amsterdam. Centralization was not pushed to an extreme: the *préfets*, who were not solely dependent on Fouché, kept their own powers. Councillors and directors corresponded direct with the Emperor, and so did Dubois, the prefect of police, who was replaced by Pasquier in 1811.

The *gendarmerie* had its own chiefs, and was in competition with them. They claimed, as the *préfet* of the Loire-Inférieure observed in 1808, 'to be armed magistrates, with the duty of keeping an eye on all civilian officials'. In the Emperor's view, the ideal system would have been to keep an up-to-date file of all persons who had any influence whatsoever. Fouché had already compiled a comprehensive list of the *chouans*; Napoleon wanted to draw up 'personal and moral statistics' for the whole Empire. His knowledge was extensive, but did not cover everything; and the *préfets*, who would have been in the best position to give him information about people's private lives, usually preserved their discretion. Secret informers and Lavalette's postal censorship remained the chief means of information.

The police were all the more feared because they themselves sanctioned enquiry by means of arbitrary detention, for which mental asylums were used in addition to the prisons. The poet Desorgues, who had taken the liberty of perpetrating a famous epigram in 1804 ('Yes—Napoleon is great—a great chameleon'), and Faure, a medical student of Saint-Louis, who had cried out on December 5, 1804, when the eagles were distributed, 'Death or freedom!' were both confined as lunatics. Nobody felt safe; and the provision merchant Lassalle, whose deals had been interfered with by the Emperor, was in addition imprisoned without trial. And even release did not end the matter: a large number of individuals were told where they must live and kept under supervision. Finally on March 3, 1810, a decree reintroduced the State prisons, in which interment could be decreed *in camera* by the *Grand Juge*, the Minister of Justice and the Minister of Police, though in practice he was rarely consulted. In Napoleon's eyes, administrative detention was not only calculated to stifle opposition, but also to eliminate offences under common law where the jury allowed themselves to be intimidated, or legal proof was lacking. It was, however, convenient to use the expression 'prisoners of State' so as to present the public with 'a terrifying image', while not being under any illusions about the abuses deriving from a police who were under no control. The *gendarmes* were held in such fear that 'it would be difficult to collect evidence against them', as the *préfet* of the Loire-Inférieure remarked, although he accused them of fraud, extortion, and even assassination. Even the *préfets* were swayed by the importunities of influential persons. In 1808, for example, the Camp-Commandant Despinoy de Saint-Luc was arrested in the Somme district, on the verbal order of the mayor, who owed him money. The decree of 1810 therefore directed that prisons should be annually inspected. But they were not all examined, and the Emperor only looked at some of the reports. In 1811, he released 145 individuals out of the 810 mentioned; in 1812, 29 out of 314. By 1814, it was estimated that there were 2,500 of these prisoners. As for the senatorial commission entrusted with the protection of individual freedom, it did not even ask for a list of those in detention, and only intervened when petitioned. In 1804, it managed to get 44 people set free out of the 116 petitioners; but Fouché's passive resistance soon discouraged its efforts. In short, France from 1800 to 1814 lived under a regime where the law could condemn on suspicion; but Napoleon took good care not to apply the system too rigorously, realizing that a reign of terror would only be tolerated if it was confined to a small number of victims, and that this would in no way detract from its success.

Speakers and writers were particularly liable to attract attention. The Institute, which had relied so much upon

Napoleon, did not escape his scrutiny either. As early as 1803, the classes in moral and political science had disappeared; in 1805 when Lalande had suppressed Maréchal's *Dictionnaire des athées*, the Emperor denounced him as 'in his second childhood' and forbade him to publish anything at all. Again, when annoyed by the speech of welcome which Chateaubriand found he was not allowed to deliver, Napoleon threatened to suppress the class in language and literature, formerly belonging to the French Academy, calling it 'an undesirable club'. There were police informers in every *salon*, one of whom was the academician Esménard. As far as the lawyers were concerned, Napoleon positively hated them. 'They stir up trouble and are the authors of crime and treason. . . . I should like to cut out the tongues of barristers who use them against the government.' In 1804, he had obliged them to apply to the courts for registration in the list of authorized barristers, and he did not give them back the right to a president and a disciplinary commission until December 14, 1810; and even then, they were only allowed to bring candidates before the public prosecutor, the court itself retaining the right to inflict penalties on them.

His hatred of 'the printed word' was almost as vehement, by the very fact that 'it appeals to public opinion instead of to authority'. 'You must print very little,' he wrote to Eugène, 'the less, the better.' From 1805 onwards, newspapers had to submit their accounts to the police and hand over up to a third of their profits to pay those who were given authority to keep an eye on them. In 1807, an article of Chateaubriand caused the *Mercure* to be suppressed; in 1810, it was decided that each *département* should only have one paper, and more than a hundred disappeared; in October, Savary reduced the Paris press to four gazettes, the *Moniteur officiel* being one of them. In February 1811, a paper formerly called *les Débats* and now renamed the *Journal de l'Empire*, was taken out of the hands of the brothers Bertin, who were suspected of having relations with the English, and split up into shares, a third going to the police; and in September the *Journal de Paris* and the *Gazette de France* suffered the same fate. In order to control the publication of books, new restrictions had been placed upon the printers in 1805, compelling them to have a personal licence that could be revoked, and to take an oath of loyalty; and the police would seize their productions whenever they thought fit. Fouché added to his Press Office a consultative office comprising Lemontey, Lacretelle, and Esmenard.

An official censorship would have been better than arbitrary police action; and on February 10, 1810, the Emperor finally made up his mind to establish it. He created a directorship of the press, entrusting it in the first place to Portalis' son, then to the former *préfet* Pommereul, as well as 'imperial censors', one of whom was a theologian; but in the provinces, power remained in the hands of the *préfets*. At the same time, 97 out of the 157 Paris printing presses were shut down; and in the end booksellers also had to be licensed and take the oath. As might have been foreseen, the censorship used its authority to cover its tracks, and abused its powers at its own sweet will. Not only did it prove absurdly gallican, anglophobe, and suspicious, but extremely prudish and hostile to *genres* such as the historical novel. In December 1811, Napoleon showed his displeasure: the censorship was to confine his efforts to suppressing libels and 'on other subjects allow freedom of expression'. The lesson went home: in 1811, nearly 12 per cent of manuscripts had been refused publication; in 1812, the proportion sank to less than 4 per cent. Here too he showed more liberality than his agents, which indeed was not difficult, and up to a certain point he remained faithful to the best traditions of enlightened despotism. But the administration remained none the less hostile to reading-rooms and lending libraries, and especially to pedlars. It realized the importance of almanacs and popular coloured prints, and even school primers were not forgotten. The Senate also possessed a commission for the protection of freedom, but it achieved nothing. As for the theatres, where political parties easily clashed, they too were not spared. In 1805, Napoleon asked Fouché's opinion about Mozart's *Don Juan* 'from the point of view of the public morale'; and Brifaut, who had written a play entitled *Don Sanche*, had to transform it into *Ninus d'Assyrie* on account of the Spanish war.

To sum up, it may be said that the imperial administration perfected the work of the Consulate, and accentuated its arbitrary features. Nothing remained of liberty but freedom of conscience, because intolerance at this point would have been harmful to the State by depriving it of good servants. Even so, it was not permissible to attack the recognized religions, to profess atheism or adhere to the schismatic *petite Église*. Frenchmen were not much surprised by the Napoleonic despotism, just emerging as they were from the *Ancien Régime* and the turmoil of revolution; moreover, they knew that other countries were very much in the same boat. The original feature of Napoleon's despotism was its simplicity, and the nice adjustment of its machinery; and this it owed to the Revolution, which by its destruction of the chaotic institutions and privileges of the *Ancien Régime* had made it possible to build anew.

FINANCES AND THE NATIONAL ECONOMY

Money provides the very sinews of war, and the example of Louis XVI had proved that a crisis in the national finances can be fatal to authority. Frederick II, who served as a model for enlightened despots, had always been very careful about finance. He had given preference to indirect taxation as easier to collect, providing a more regular yield, and more popular with the ruling classes. And Napoleon followed suit. From 1804 to 1812, he reduced taxation on land and personal estate, which had the advantage of making the consent of the *Corps Législatif* a pure formality. Moreover, he carried out a rational reassessment of the former class of property, and finally in 1807 undertook a register of landed property, thus meeting one of the essential requests made in the *cahiers* of 1789. He spent 55 million francs on it, but never succeeded in completing it in more than 5,000 to 6,000 communes.

From the very start, Gaudin had suggested the re-establishment of the duties on consumption; but they were so unpopular that Napoleon did not dare take the risk before 1804. On Ventôse 5, Year XII (February 25, 1804), there came into force the 'combined duties', which were put under the management of Français de Nantes. The first tax to be instituted was one on drinks, at a low rate, but nevertheless requiring inventories. Under the authority of the State, the 'cellar-rats' of the former excise department once more came into action. The method of collection was modified and the rate raised in 1806 and 1808. In 1806, an additional tax was imposed on salt in compensation for the abolition of the transit duty on the roads. After an increase on the tax on tobacco, a monopoly was finally re-established in 1810. In that year, the yield of the 'combined duties' seems to have been considerably greater than that of the direct taxes, not to mention the customs. There was active public discontent, and more than one disturbance. Property owners, for their part, noted that the relief in direct taxation was no more than apparent, for a share of State expenses had been transferred to local finance—for example, a proportion of the Church expenses, the property register, canals, and casual wards; and in 1810, half the *préfets*' salaries. When the extra centimes were taken into account, the Côtes-du-Nord, which had paid out 2,489,000 francs in Year IX, paid 3,423,000 in 1813. Moreover, in order to make existence possible for the municipalities, the local tolls had to be increased in number. Besides, there was much coming and going of troops, who had to be billeted, and more than one of the *préfets*—Molé, for example—reinstituted forced labour on the roads. Although Napoleon was very economical, the situation—taken all round—was that he increased the financial load on the French nation. Civil expenses did not figure largely in this increase. In the *départements*, the various services were so poorly provided with money that there was little progress in the roads, schools, and public assistance. In the Côtes-du-Nord, much paper-work was necessary in order to restrict the various plans, through shortage of funds. From 1807 onwards, some 37 million were allotted to public works; but not many regions benefited. The increase came chiefly from the civil list, Church dues, the national debt, and above all the war, which still absorbed 50 to 60 per cent of all receipts, if not more, in spite of the large contribution made by the enemy.

If the Treasury escaped the foregoing risks thanks to the reforms of 1806, it was none the less never in a comfortable position through lack of borrowing-powers. This constituted the essential difference between English and French finance, even more than before 1789. The sinking fund was the only department to succeed in issuing some millions of bonds. Although it managed to find the interest, and although Napoleon bought some on behalf of the Legion of Honour, senatorships, and inalienable endowments that he dispensed—

to such an extent that in 1809 only 33 out of the 58 million were in private hands, and that the market was becoming more and more restricted—the market-rate remained low and the position weak. And so various expedients were tried: there was an increase in premiums; a little money was minted; and in 1807 and 1810, the war fund provided 84, and subsequently 45 million. But the favourite method continued to be to assign the payment of contractors to particular funds, and to make them wait for their proceeds to be realized, an old *Ancien Régime* device that led to speculative interest rates and misappropriation; or to postpone auditing on the pretext of checking the figures. From time to time part of the arrears would be liquidated by distributing sinking-fund bonds or interest-bearing securities—a disguised form of forced loan. Thus in 1813, there was a million franc issue to cover the balances dating from 1801 to 1808. By the end of the reign, the permanent debt had risen to 63 million and the floating debt, arising particularly from ecclesiastical pensions, had reached 57 million. In spite of all this, contractors continued to hold great power because their advances were indispensable.

In the circumstances, Napoleon's finances seem to have been as successful as could have been expected; but to all appearances, they were never in balance. What harmed them particularly in the eyes of the public was that no one knew (or ever will know) the true position, for the indefinite postponement of payments due is the negation of a genuine budget. Moreover, the public audit department, which had been re-established in 1807, was not given the right to examine the legality of expenditure. If the Emperor was unable to borrow, it was because investors remained distrustful after so many bankruptcies, and because his policies did not inspire confidence in anyone that his regime would last; but it was also because his financial operations remained mysterious. Rather than put himself under the control of the middle classes, Napoleon preferred to do without their help.

Besides, there was a better way open to him. Like Frederick II, who had earmarked for himself the revenues from Silesia, and had reconstituted the *roi-sergent's* war fund, Napoleon possessed cash resources under his sole management, namely the civil list, the crown lands and his private estates. He aimed at making certain of a freely disposable fund of at least 100 million, saying that with such resources a sovereign could be prepared for all eventualities. Moreover, to avoid exhausting the peoples of the Empire or stirring up unrest, he needed financial machinery in the conquered territories as well if he were to avoid financing warfare from the pockets of the Empire alone; and of such machinery he became the sole master. On October 28, 1805, he set up the army fund, which levied war contributions from Austria and Prussia. We learn from his receiver, La Bouillerie, that it was supposed to have produced 743 million between 1805 and 1810, 311 million of which were used to supply his forces. On January 30, 1810, the Emperor instituted the *domaine extraordinaire*, and put it under the management of Defermon; and to him was handed over any surplus from the army fund, as well as the lands and revenues the Emperor had reserved for himself in the vassal States, then estimated at 2,000 million, with an income between 30 and 40 million. Napoleon used it to control the circulation of money by buying investments or shares in the Bank of France and other large undertakings, and to make advances to industry in 1811, and above all to reward his servants or give them pensions. Warfare therefore provided him with large resources. On the eve of the Russian campaign he is reported to have said: 'It will help my finances too; for haven't I rehabilitated them by warfare? And wasn't this how Rome acquired the whole world's wealth?'

For the nation, however, the advantage was more doubtful. A certain number of individuals enriched themselves from these spoils; the stock of metal was usefully augmented; and the budget was momentarily eased. But the war fell no less heavily upon the tax-payer. Although Spain was said to have contributed 350 million, it was still necessary to despatch just as many supplies to it, apart from 24 to 30 million monthly instalment and the pensions for the fallen princes, all at French expense, for the army treasury and the foreign estates did not contribute a half-penny. And finally it must be noted that if Napoleon increased his personal authority in these ways, his liquid reserves never rose to the figure he had set himself, for he had to spend a large part of the revenue from his domains under the pressure of circumstance.

Whatever profit he made from war, it accordingly remained essential to develop the country's contributory capacity. To this end the enlightened despots had encouraged production by obeying the principles of the Mercantile Theory; and Napoleon did the same. Regimentation was natural to an authoritarian government; and on various sides pleas were made for a return to guilds and to trade-marks. The upper middle classes remained in a general way faithful to freedom of employment; and Napoleon showed more respect for them than he has usually been credited with. At Lyons, he confined himself to imposing on the home-workers a certificate of book-keeping. Trade-marks were re-established for brocades and velvets in the Year XII; in 1807, for cloths for the Levant; in 1810, for Louviers cloth; in 1811 for soaps; in 1812 for the whole cloth trade, though they remained optional. The monopoly in weapons of war, powder, minting, and tobacco can be explained for reasons of public order or fiscal considerations. The same is true of the laws governing expropriation for reasons of public utility, those relating to unhealthy premises, and to the mines. Here, the law of 1810 attributed ownership of such property to the State, but allowed it to be exploited by private individuals, with the exception of the Saar mines. The same also applies to the control of the baking and butchery trades, where the return to the *Ancien Régime* was most marked of all. The corporative constitution of the bakers, which had been re-established under the Consulate, was extended to several provincial towns; and in 1811, the syndical savings bank of the Paris butchers became once again the *caisse de Poissy*, its duty being to advance on behalf of the town the necessary sums for paying the graziers. At the request of the wine merchants, their numbers in the capital were limited and they had to be authorized by the police; the professions of wine-dealer and wine-taster were made into official posts under government nomination.

As far as agriculture was concerned, it was more or less left to itself. The forests were once more put under guards, but nothing was done to disrupt the collective customs, nor were the land registers used so as to favour or compel regrouping—a process which nearly all the peasants would have opposed. The blockade simply made the Emperor insist that certain crops should be grown, in particular that 32,000 and then 100,000 hectares should be allotted to sugar-beet. Concern for public order obliged him to do as the *Ancien Régime* had done, and act to some extent as arbiter in fixing the price of corn as between peasant and consumer, either by raising it by authorizing its export, or by imposing a maximum price—as he did in 1812.

But it was the working classes who particularly felt the hand of the law. This was no novelty, for the law of 1791 had re-enacted the prohibition of strikes and workers' associations, and the law of Year XI and the penal code did no more than confirm it. But apprenticeship was also re-established, and the expression 'master and workman' was reintroduced. Certain administrators went further still. For example in Paris, in 1806, the *préfet* of police fixed the hours of work for the building trade, and in the Yonne, the *préfet* regrouped the craftsmen and fixed a tariff for them. But the Council of State rejected schemes for apprenticeship and the regulation of workshops; and the minister refused to intervene to sanction disciplinary action against the Maine-et-Loire slaters, the paper-makers in the Paris region, and the Bauwens spinning-mills in Ghent. The setting up of 'conciliation boards' on March 18, 1806, for settling differences between employers and workmen, without any representation for the latter, was solely due to the technical incompetence of the ordinary judges. With certain reservations, the nascent forces of capitalism were a law to themselves, quite independently of the regime. They maintained the various regulations against the workers and prevented all attempts to act in combination, which would have been contrary to their own freedom of action.

Thus of the two principles of the Mercantile System, protection occupied the foremost place. Yet war and the blockade were much more powerful than any specific measures in closing down national markets and handing over allied or vassal countries to the power of France. This hardly produced any advantage for agriculture, since Napoleon insisted on controlling the price of corn. On the contrary, it proved more difficult to sell its wines and brandies. Industry was what Napoleon—like Colbert—chiefly encouraged, using exhibitions, special orders, honours for inventors, and sometimes even concessions in the form of buildings or advances. But he gave no privileges, and, taking good care of the pence, was only willing to grant loans in times of crisis, and then rather in order to avoid unemployment than to benefit the industries concerned. In his opinion, the greatest service he could render them was to lower the money rate by increasing the Bank of France's discount. He was less interested in profits than in the amounts produced; but because machinery was giving England an advantage, he did much for technical progress, helping Douglas to set up a factory in Paris to produce machinery for the woollen industry, and invited open competition for several inventions, such as a light steam-engine in 1807 and a flax-spinning loom in 1810. He added a school of arts and crafts at Angers to the one at Châlons, opened mining schools, resurrected the Gobelins dyeing-school, added a practical course to the *Conservatoire des arts et métiers*, and recommended new procedures and tools by means of official propaganda, as the Committee of Public Safety had also done. Roads and canals would have been of great service in knitting together the national markets and linking them to the vassal countries. Napoleon accordingly set work in train on the Burgundy, Rhone and Rhine, Ille et Rance, and Nantes to Brest canals, finished the Central canal and Saint-Quentin canal, repaired a big proportion of the *routes nationales*, and opened the alpine routes, which were vital for trade with Italy and the Levant. He would have done more still if there had been the time and the money.

All the same in the plans for these various works the economy was of less importance than military considerations and questions of prestige, the first predominating for the alpine routes, those to the Rhine and the West, the extension of the Cherbourg dike, and the Antwerp undertakings; and the second in the attractions and improvements carried out in Paris, where he lengthened the quays, constructed new bridges, cleared the surroundings of Notre-Dame, the place du Châtelet, and le Carrousel, opened up the Rue de Rivoli, Rue de la Paix, Rue de Castiglione, built the Bourse and the Vendome column, undertook the construction of the Arc de Triomphe, and planned a *Temple de la Gloire*. In connection with the provisioning of the capital, there was the Commarket and the Grande Halle, the Grand Reserve, the slaughter-houses, and the Ourcq canal. Great builder that the Emperor was, his motive was partly to give employment; for one of the essentials in the policy of all Caesars has always been to provide the people with work and cheap bread.

In agriculture, progress followed the same lines as under the Directory, but was extremely slow. There was far more perceptible advance in industry. The production of luxury goods was resumed, especially in the silk trade; and the blockade gave an impetus to metallurgy, ironmongery, cutlery, and the manufacture of machines and tools, sheet-iron, tin and brass, pins and needles. It was also favourable to chemical products and textiles; cotton-spinning and printed materials continued to show the greatest activity and the newest improvements, so much so that in 1812 the former had a million spindles in action and produced 10 million kilogrammes of thread. At the end of the Empire, there was a flourishing new industry with a great future, for in the year 1811, the factories at Lille and Auby produced the first lumps of sugar from sugar-beet. Allart at Chaillot and Delessert in Paris set up refineries, and Napoleon established four technical schools and a sugar-works on his own property at Rambouillet. By 1813, the estimated production was 3½ million kilogrammes in 334 factories; the amount actually realized seems to have been about a third of this figure.

But there was another and tragic side to these beneficial effects of the blockade, namely the total ruin of the maritime ports. In 1807, Marseilles still had 330 ocean-going ships, but by 1811 only nine were left; and the product of her manufactures fell from 50 million in 1789 to 12 million, while her population fell in the same period from 120,000 to 90,000. Bordeaux, which was reckoned to have the same number in 1789, only had 70,000; with the result that these two towns became the citadels of royalism. On the other hand Strasburg and Lyons, taking advantage of their rivals' misfortunes to acquire the monopoly of the German and Italian trade, were bitterly to regret the fall of Napoleon. It is not surprising that in spite of the annexations external trade remained below the figure reached in 1789, seeing that France had lost her colonies. It goes without saying that peace and a commercial treaty with England would have been of more benefit to the national production than the blockade. Napoleon's policy being what it was, it is none the less true that the Empire succeeded in keeping alive, and even enjoyed a certain measure of prosperity.

To sum up, it might be said that the Emperor behaved much less despotically over the control of things than he did over persons; his state despotism in the economic sphere has been exaggerated. On the other hand, although he did not introduce many innovations in this department, he was successful in conciliating a wide variety of motives and interests. Finally, he maintained sufficient activity in his various States to enable them to support the war; and it must not be forgotten that as far as he was concerned, this was the cardinal point.

THE CONTROL OF MEN'S MINDS

His system did not consist simply and solely in prohibiting all criticism and placating as many interests as possible. Although Napoleon usually affected to despise ideas, he would sometimes admit their influence. 'There are only two powers in the world,' he said, 'the sword and the spirit; and in the long run, the sword is always conquered by the spirit.' What was needed then was to rally the spirit to the dominance of the sword, so that there might be willing obedience, and as far as possible, joyful and devoted obedience. It was in order to make the Churches teach this along with morality that the enlightened despots had gained control over the Churches; and when the *Concordat* had been concluded, this was one of the advantages Bonaparte derived from it. He filled the ranks of the Catholic clergy with a view to holding their allegiance out of self-interest and getting them to produce loyal subjects. Fearful of priests who were not his own officials, he introduced his own supporters everywhere, especially in the State schools; and this he did as a precaution, and to avoid worse possibilities. There were always covert struggles going on around him between the friends and enemies of the Roman Church; of the former Portalis and Fontanes finally won the victory over Fouché, and Cardinal Fesch, who had a good deal to be forgiven, showed himself full of zeal. The Emperor more than once rebuffed him, ascribing his fears to 'a delirious imagination' and advising him 'to take cold baths'; but it suited his ends to give way to him on many occasions.

The first requisite was to make certain of the clergy stipends and the conduct of worship, for the pressure that had been put upon the municipalities to stimulate their generosity was only a moderate success. 'The peasants', wrote one priest, 'are well disposed to their religion and their priests, provided they do not cost them anything.' Napoleon decided to take a part of the expense upon himself. From 1803, he granted stipends to the canons; then in 1804, as the plebiscite and the coronation drew near, 500 francs a year to 24,000 officials, raising the number in 1807 to 30,000. In 1804, he had handed over a monopoly in funerals to the Church councils, and had guaranteed to support a large seminary in each diocese, allotting 600,000 francs in 1807 for the provision of scholarships. The rest of the expenses fell on the local finances—such as the salaries of those officiants who were not paid by the State (December 26, 1804), the parochial clergy's board and lodging and the expenses of worship (February 2, 1805). In order to manage the Church services subsidy, an 'external' council was set up in 1807. In 1809, the administration of parish funds was all handed over to the parochial Church councils, who were now appointed for the first time by the *préfet*, then added to by co-optation, and who had to elect a body of churchwardens. The *préfets* continued to require them to vote supplementary stipends and to support the curates. Finally, the law of February 14, 1810, definitely settled the charges falling on the commune. The curates' salaries, and the upkeep and repair of buildings, also became a compulsory charge in cases where the Church councils had insufficient resources; but the supplementary payments remained optional. This organization of Church finances continued in being for nearly a century. In 1811, it cost the communes of the Bouche-du-Rhône 100,000 francs; and the State spent 16 million, over and above the 31 million for pensions.

The Church was very much aware of the respect shown to it, which gave it good standing in the eyes of the people, and of the favours which helped recruitment to the ministry and the extension of its influence. The members of seminaries were exempted from military service; Church dignitaries were favourably placed in the decree of Year XII fixing the order of precedence; processions were revived almost everywhere;

'home missions' were subsidized, and Cardinal Fesch set up a society to organize them. Some *préfets* closed the taverns on Sundays during the hours of divine service; and Portalis gave them his approval, and even an assurance that the *Conseil d'État* would be responsible for punishing those who remained standing, or kept their hats on, while processions were passing by. As early as 1803, the lycées and colleges had acquired almoners, and religious observance had become compulsory. Portalis expected the bishops to keep him informed about their staff. When the Bishop of Versailles, in 1805, claimed the right to appoint the schoolmasters, he signified his agreement; and in 1807, they were authorized by decree to take charge of religious instruction in the schools. In 1809, a circular from Fontanes advised them to get the curates to supervise the masters, promising to replace with their own nominees any on whom there should be an unfavourable report. Besides this, the bishops organized confessional teaching, being authorized to found smaller seminaries as preparatory for the main ones; and these became the equivalent of colleges. The clergy were also admitted to the commission for hospices and the office for charitable aid; and the sisters reoccupied the hospitals. And lastly, the unity of the Church was defended in face of the 'little Church', and its discipline supported in at least one point, the marriage of priests being forbidden by administrative action. It was due to Napoleon that the secularizing of the State did not run into further difficulties, for he refused to give way to Portalis over the observance of Sunday, the respect to be shown for processions, and the nomination of schoolmasters. He blamed Fontanes for having handed over control of the latter to the bishops.

It was owing to him moreover that the progress of the regular Orders was kept within bounds. In principle, he disapproved of masculine Orders. 'There are to be no monks', he said, 'for monastic discipline destroys all virtue, energy and initiative.' But under the Consulate, he had allowed the re-establishment of some Orders, notably the *Pères de la Foi* or *Paccanaristes*, whom the police quite rightly held to be the heirs of the Society of Jesus. In the end, Fouché won the day, and the decree of 3 Messidor, Year XII (June 22, 1804), made the existence of the regular Orders subject to authorization. The Lazarists, the

Fathers of the Holy Spirit and those of foreign missions, although in principle amalgamated, continued nevertheless to exist because of the services they were able to render to French influence in the outside world. The *Frères de la doctrine chrétienne* and those of Saint-Sulpice were treated with equal favour; and toleration was extended to certain Trappist houses because they looked after the Alpine hospices. The other Orders were suppressed, including the *Pères de la Foi*, their superior, Paccanari, being a foreigner. But this Order, claiming that they had been given back their autonomy, nevertheless managed to be left in peace, Fesch even putting them in charge of the Largentière seminary; and they were not definitely condemned till December 15, 1807. Nuns received better treatment from Napoleon, because he reckoned that it paid to put them in charge of the hospitals. He authorized a number of communities and tolerated the existence of others as well. To keep a more effective eye upon them, he would have liked to group them together, and would gladly have united them. At any rate in 1807 he called together 'a chapter general of the hospital sisterhoods and the daughters of charity', presided over by Madame Mère, who had been made their protectress; and in 1808 a decree gave them a certain status. In fact, these hospital sisters often ran a school, like the new Order, the Sisters of Mercy of the Reverend Mother Postel, or the Ladies of the Sacred Heart of the Reverend Mother Barat, who were by profession contemplatives. There was moreover no lack of teaching Orders. The enquiry in 1808 noted a total of more than 2,000 houses and 10,000 nuns. As for the non-conventual groups and communities, Portalis decided that Year XII decree did not refer to them. The Penitants, for instance, reappeared everywhere in the south; the *Congrégation de la Vierge* grew in numbers in Paris, and added branches in the provinces; and the same thing happened at Bordeaux and Lyons, where Ampère became an enthusiastic proselyte.

Taken as a whole, the bishops showed their gratitude. In 1806, they even resigned themselves to accepting the catechism drawn up by Bernier and the Abbot of Astros, Portalis' secretary, in which Napoleon himself had a hand. It contained a long chapter detailing amongst a Christian's duties obedience to the Emperor, payment of taxes, and the acceptance of conscription. Some of them—Bernier, for example—were zealous to the point of becoming auxiliaries of the police when Fouché wrote to them: 'There are a number of links between your functions and my own.' Others, however, such as the brother of Cambacérès at Rouen and Caffarelli at Saint-Brieuc, made themselves intolerable by their demands. But most of them reaped an advantage from their prudent compliance and increased their influence. Knowing that in the end they would be sacrificed, the *préfets* gave up the struggle: in Marseilles, Thibaudeau consulted Champion de Cicé before choosing his officials. The power of the bishops, protected by the official Gallicaniom against the Papacy, also put them into a position of strength over against the lower clergy, since the latter had been unreservedly subordinated to them by the Concordat, with the sole exception of the parish priests as such. All the same, the position was far from being one of moral unity, and the conforming bishops remained in bad odour. At Besançon, Archbishop Le Coz was constantly at odds with his priests and seminarists, who were egged on by rebellious spirits from revolutionary days. Nor did the parish priests resign themselves at the outset to lay control, and there were numerous incidents; but in the end the majority of the clergy remained attached to royalty, as the sequel clearly showed. As for their influence on the people, this must not be measured by the material progress of the Church. In many regions, there remained a large measure of indifference, and in the towns, there was always a public ready to applaud a performance of the *Oedipus* or *Tartuffe*. Moreover, there is reason to believe that Napoleon was not anxious for a complete re-Christianizing of France; he was content with an arrangement which gave him control of those whose first loyalty was to their priests; and this was all he needed.

But the conflict with the Papacy prevented this policy from being entirely successful. It was not religious in origin; and although Pius VII reproached the Emperor with the Organic Articles, and much more so with his policy towards the clergy in the kingdom of Italy, there would never have been a rupture if Napoleon had not been a temporal sovereign. But this rupture led Napoleon to revive the claims of the Roman Emperor to rule over the clergy, and to treat the Bishop of Rome as his vassal. As it was, the *senatus-consultum* of February 7, 1810, made the declaration of the four articles into an imperial law; and in the Council of State Napoleon declared that he was about to 're-establish the right, always possessed by the emperors, of confirming the papal nomination' and demanding that 'before his enthronement, the Pope should swear by the hands of the Emperor of the French, that he submits to the four articles'. Popes can no longer make the monstrous claims which in former times were so calamitous to the nations, and so shameful to the Church; yet fundamentally, they have renounced none of their pretensions, and even today they look upon themselves as masters of the world.

Pius VII was a prisoner at Savona. The cardinals had been taken to Paris, and when 13 out of 27 had refused to be present at the Emperor's marriage, he exiled the 'black-leg' cardinals. It then became impossible to implement the Concordat. From 1808 onwards, the papal bulls granting investiture to the bishops had departed from the formula laid down by the Concordat to such an extent that the *Conseil d'État* refused to accept them. It then became impossible to fill the vacancies: the Emperor directed the nominated bishops to take up the administration of their dioceses, and Cardinal Maury accepted the see of Paris, and d'Osmond that of Florence. But this could only be a temporary expedient. In 1809, an ecclesiastical committee gave the opinion that if for temporal reasons the Pope delayed a bishop's investiture, the metropolitan could make provision; but it refused to come to a decision, and advised the convening of a national council. In 1811, a second committee tendered the same advice. The only man to stand up for the authority of the Holy See—and that with great boldness, in the very presence of the Emperor—was Abbé Émery, whose gallicanism grew less and less pronounced as the temporal power became more and more burdensome to the clergy. But he died before the opening of the national council, which had been fixed for June 17, 1811. Up till now the bishops had been cowed into silence, and were too frightened to utter a word. As in the days of Louis XIV and the Constituent Assembly, they felt that the Church of France, hard pressed on the one side by the head of the nation and on the other by the head of the Catholic Church, was in danger of having to bear the whole brunt of the dispute. Napoleon was obliged to get round them one at a time in order to press them to agree to his plan; but even then, they would only agree subject to the Pope's approval. If after six months the Pope had not conferred investiture, it was agreed that it could be given by the metropolitan or the senior suffragan; and this amounted to a return to the civil constitution of the clergy. Pius VII consented, provided that the investiture was conferred 'expressly in the name of the sovereign pontiff', which allowed him to forbid it if he thought fit. On February 23, 1812, Napoleon declared that this brief was unacceptable, and that he regarded the Concordat as annulled.

This rupture with the Pope changed the clergy's feelings with regard to the regime. A section of the priests gradually went back into open opposition. The bishops were forced to resign, or sent into exile; priests had their stipends or pensions suspended; refractory seminarists lost their scholarships and had to join the army; the men's Orders were disbanded. The *Pères de la Foi* came under the decree in 1807; the Lazarists, the Fathers of the Holy Spirit and of foreign missions were suppressed and their superior, Hanon by name, arrested; and in 1810 it was the turn of Saint-Sulpice. The *Congrégation de la Vierge* were struck down as early as 1809, but their members spread the bull of excommunication throughout France and kept up a secret correspondence with Pius VII. Next came a number of brotherhoods; and finally the reform of the University in 1811 involved the closure of most of the episcopal schools or minor seminaries. The *Concordat* had robbed the royalist cause and the counter-revolution of the clergy's support: the breach with the Pope meant that this support was regained; it also revived hostility to France in the countries that had been annexed. Nevertheless the years gained by Napoleon bore their fruit. Most churchmen hesitated to press their opposition once again to an extreme and thus lose the benefit of the advantages already won. As long as worship was not suspended or parish priests removed from office, the people were not inclined to protest overmuch. The conflict revived royalist hopes and helped their intrigues; but it was not in itself enough to shake the regime.

The Protestants did not cause him any difficulty; but it was a very different matter with the Jews. If it had been a purely religious question, there would have been no difficulties, for the Rabbis themselves asked for comprehensive articles of agreement. The difficulty was to know whether they thought the law of Moses compatible with the civil law and the duties of a French citizen. The Sefardim in the south and in Italy were thought to have long been well adapted to the customs of the country, whilst the Askenazim of the east were reckoned to be attached to ritualism; and in 1805 Bonald threw doubts upon the possibility of assimilating the Jews. And finally, certain Jews in Alsace and Lorraine had aroused fierce hatred by lending at high rates of interest, which often led to peasant expropriation. The Emperor had a prejudice against usury and on May 30, 1806, in spite of the *Council d'État*, he granted their debtors a moratorium. There was thus a three-fold problem. An assembly of Jews, the 70 members being appointed by the *préfets*, met in Paris on July 20, 1806, and came to an agreement with the imperial commissioners. It was then decided to resurrect in theatrical fashion the Great Sanhedrin, consisting of 26 laymen and 45 Rabbis, which addressed a proclamation to all European Jews, and on February 9, 1807, admitted the abolition of polygamy, allowed civil marriage and military service without the right to send a substitute, and such economic measures as might seem necessary. The Emperor's decision was not made known till March 18, 1808. Worship was organized in synagogues, with not more than one consistorial synagogue in each *département* and a central consistory in Paris, supported by compulsory subscriptions from the faithful. By another decree, valid for ten years only, which excluded the Gironde and in fact only applied to Alsace and Lorraine, the debts of minors, women, and soldiers, were cancelled. The Jewish creditor had to prove that he had provided the whole of the capital, unless the debtor was a businessman; and the courts were authorized to reduce or cancel interest in arrears and to grant a moratorium for payment. A special licence was imposed on the Jews, and their pawnbroking was regulated. They were forbidden to settle in Alsace, and made subject elsewhere to the purchase of a property in the country. Finally in 1810 they were compelled to choose a family name. One can well understand Napoleon's anxiety to put an end to extortionate interest, which might give rise to disturbances and force peasants to emigrate; but it is doubtful whether his measures were conducive to assimilation, and the free choice of a patronimic actually worked against it. In spite of everything, his contemporaries did not think his policy unfavourable to the Jews. It had repercussions in Europe, by comparison with which it earned him the favour of Jewish communities and the abuse of their enemies.

The Emperor also laid hands upon freemasonry, which had been revived under the Directory and more particularly the *Consulat*. In 1805, Joseph became grand master of the Grand Lodge of France; and when the Scottish branch, organized in 1804, finally seceded, Kellerman and Cambacérès undertook its management. The Emperor's protection worked in favour of unity and the hierarchical principle in freemasonry, and led to the multiplication of lodges. The Grand Lodge, under the effective management of Roëttiers de Montaleau, had control over 300 lodges in 1804 and a thousand in 1814. There were many freemasons among high-ranking civilians and soldiers, and the order proved thoroughly loyal. But its ideas remained those of the eighteenth century, and some of the *préfets* finally came to the opinion that the lodges were a bad influence. 'It is always a question of equality, *our brothers*, philosophy and republican notions,' wrote Capelle in the *département* of Léman. But Napoleon never took offence at these views.

The shaping of youth proved a more anxious task. Although wishing to give religion a place, he had no intention of simply handing it over to the Churches: his aim was to produce good subjects rather than good Christians, men of the age and not theologians. All the enlightened despots had aimed at this. The spirit of the regime tended towards a State monopoly; and as State education would have cost a great deal of money, Napoleon's scholastic policy was dominated by the question of finance. First and foremost he provided for the recruitment of officers, officials, jurists, and health officers by setting up *lycées*, national scholarships, a military academy in Year XI, and schools of law and medicine in Year XII. Even so, he had to leave the recognized secondary schools to the municipalities, and admit the existence of numerous private institutions, as well as confessional teaching in the minor seminaries. Yet the *lycées* were slow in opening, owing to the lack of funds: by 1808, only 37 of the 45 planned had come into being. Nor did they flourish as Napoleon had hoped; for he had reckoned that with their fee-paying pupils they ought to cost him nothing at all. The order of Year XI had introduced military discipline, which the middle classes did not like; and the clergy saw the *lycées* as sinks of iniquity, since their staff included ex-priests and independents. Lastly, there was the objection that the independent schools gave their education on the cheap. There were thus two possible courses: to close the *lycées* and so cut down costs, or to suppress the private establishments. This latter solution would doubtless have been preferred by Fourcroy as head of the educational department, and by the party of the philosophers; but Portalis was against it, upholding the parents' right to freedom of choice—an argument that benefited the Church. The Emperor ended by adopting a compromise solution, for he had neither the money nor the staff to set up a State monopoly. The law of May 10, 1806, announced that a corporation would be formed called *Université*, with the sole right of teaching; nevertheless private institutions could continue to exist under its supervision, subject to the payment of a tax which would relieve the budget and limit the competition. The organization, though adopted on July 4, was postponed because of the war, and did not come into force until September 17, 1808. In the meanwhile, thanks to Fesch and Fontanes, the Church consolidated her position; and the decree—and more especially the way it was applied—were regarded as a defeat for the party of the philosophers. Fourcroy, who expected to be made head of the *Université*, was superseded by Fontanes.

Fontanes was now given the title of Grand Master, and though not ranking as a minister, he was in direct correspondence with the Emperor, and was given the help of a chancellor, a treasurer, a council of thirty members, and a body of inspectors general. The Empire was divided up into academies under the control of rectors assisted by inspectors and academic councils. Education was split up into three grades, primary, secondary, and higher. For the first time the State took control of the primary school. The municipal council, which had up till then appointed the schoolmaster, now had to rest content with proposing its own candidate; and the Grand Master awarded teaching certificates. The *lycées* remained as before, but the secondary schools were now called colleges. It was at last decided to organize science and arts faculties—the masters, however, remaining attached to the *lycées*; and theological faculties were also added. The *Collège de France* and the great revolutionary institutions continued as they were and did not become part of the *Université*. The staff were all appointed by the Emperor or the Grand Master. The teaching staff in the *lycées* and faculties came under regulations which laid down their grades, titles, dress, and salary, with deductions for retirement pensions, and disciplinary measures. The masters in the *lycées* were the only ones allowed to marry.

The private schools could only open with the authorization of the *Université* (which could always be withdrawn), and had to be staffed by persons holding its degrees, as well as coming under its inspectors and disciplinary control. Thus there was no absolute monopoly for public education: private and competing establishments continued and even increased in number. Moreover, the sovereignty of the *Université* was only nominal, for its degrees were not to become compulsory until 1815, and freelance masters with ten years' service could be exempted; nor were there enough inspectors to exercise effective control. And finally the seminaries were simply exempted from these measures of authority. On the other hand, the Catholic Church was given a share of influence in the State schools. Her doctrine was made one of the express bases of the teaching given, and Fontanes' loyalty to the Church was such that he wrote to his friend Gaillard: 'I advise you to send your son to Juilly' (the famous Oratorian college). A bishop was appointed chancellor of the *Université*; and Abbé Émery, as well as Bonald and Amboise Rendu—both keen Catholics—were members of the council. Joubert, and the Protestant Cuvier, who played an important part in reorganizing public bodies, were both inspectors who approved of religious instruction. Abbé Frayssinous, a member of the *Congrégation de la Vierge*, became an inspector in the Paris academy. Priests were headmasters of *lycées* and colleges, or members of the teaching staff. None the less, it was the Emperor who had undertaken to organize public education on these definite lines, which was why the Church could not forgive this self-styled monopoly exercised by the *Université*, for she had counted on setting up her own.

For the moment, moreover, the grievances of the private boarding schools, whether secular or Church schools, were of a more matter-of-fact kind, since the decree controlling their organization compelled their heads to take out a certificate for a consideration and for each of their pupils—even day-boys—to pay over a twentieth of the whole boarding fee. But this was a system which proved difficult to check. It was not possible to exact complete payment of this deduction; moreover, the seminaries were exempt. Savary was accordingly told to hold an enquiry in 1810, especially as Napoleon, having fallen out with the Pope, now viewed the seminaries with suspicion. On November 15, 1811, the monopoly was strengthened by a new decree. The new measures prescribed that in every town possessing a *lycée* or college, the pupils of private schools must now join their classes, and permission was only given for one minor seminary or episcopal school in each *département*. The result was clear enough: by 1813 the *lycées* and colleges with 38,000 pupils in 1810 had risen in numbers to 44,000; and since 1811, the private schools had lost 5,000. Nevertheless the application of the decree remained incomplete, and the mitigations contrived by Fontanes and his colleague contributed towards easing its harshness. In 1814, when talking to Louis XVIII, the Grand Master boasted that he had been able to 'prevent a certain amount of harm'.

The Emperor achieved his immediate aim of drawing from the secondary schools and high schools a succession of capable administrators. The curriculum of the central schools was considerably pruned in favour of Latin and Greek, and philosophy was reduced to the study of logic; history, modern languages, and the experimental sciences were neglected. But the national literature and mathematics kept the importance given to them by the Revolution; and in higher education, the original character it had imparted to French science was maintained, and scholars continued to concern themselves with research as well as teaching. Yet Napoleon's dream of a complete control over the moulding of French youth was far from being realized. He cared little for the common people, and did nothing for primary education, which he was content to leave in the hands of the municipalities. Apart from a few regions such as Alsace, the smaller schools showed no improvement; at the most, they were restored to their condition at the end of the *Ancien Régime.* Still less was Napoleon interested in the education of women. But it was important that he should mould the sons of the middle classes; and here he was hardly successful, for a large number of them were educated outside his schools, and at the University he did not manage to put before the rising generation any fitting ideal that would have won them over to his support.

The same may be said of his intellectual and artistic activities. He wanted to play the part of a Maecenas, for it was universally agreed that no sovereign was truly great unless he had had his *siècle.* In 1804, he established the decennial prizes which were to be awarded for the first time in 1810. He claimed to control literary production through the censorship, the academies, and the French Academy in Rome. He exercised a strange form of control over the theatres, forcing them to take Rémusat as their superintendent. In 1807, he limited their number to four big and four secondary ones in Paris. Five other towns were authorized to form two companies, and fourteen were only allowed a single one. The rest of the Empire comprised twenty-five districts, each with one or two travelling companies. In Paris, each theatre was given a particular style of play to perform, and all of them had to pay a contribution to the Opéra. The decree establishing the Théâtre Français was signed at Moscow in 1812. Napoleon felt particularly at ease in protecting the arts, more especially architecture, since he himself was a great buyer and builder.* It would be an exaggeration to say that he left his mark upon works of art, for the Empire style is not derived from him; but he managed to gather great artists round him. In literature, on the other hand, he was completely unsuccessful: only the second-rate rallied to his side, the first-class writers all giving him a wide berth. He does not seem to have had the same idea as the Committee of Public Safety, namely to use writers and artists to mould the public mind; at the most, he thought of having the history of his campaigns taught in the schools, using the *Bulletins de la Grande Armée*, and the articles in the *Moniteur* to build up the Napoleonic legend, and commissioning the painter David to execute

* See page 177.

some topical pictures. To be sure, he had neither the financial resources nor the technical means of subsequent dictatorships for organizing propaganda. Moreover, claiming as he did to be the founder of a universal empire and dynasty, he had no particular message for his compatriots as such. Those who followed him to the end, with utter loyalty and no thought of self, were defending in his person both the nation and the Revolution; but others could not seriously accept the legitimacy of this Vendémiaire general, even though he had been anointed by the Pope. Though he managed to lull and constrain the public mind and spirit, he did not succeed in becoming its master: the two poles of thought remained Tradition and the Revolution.

SOCIAL DEVELOPMENT AND PUBLIC OPINION

Napoleon was well aware that the mind of the nation would never be fully brought under control. He therefore continued to work as he had done under the *Consulat* for the re-establishment of a social hierarchy. His aim was to win over, either out of personal advantage or vanity, all who wielded authority, and strengthen this authority in order to subject it to himself. He continued to bring influential people into his orbit, those who controlled an immense number of farmers and smallholders, of workmen and contractors, by drawing them into the circle of Councils and administration, ministerial office and public institutions. In multiplying officials, he was not only extending the powers of the State; he did so because he saw the advantages of building up a social group whose dignities and livelihood depended on him, and who would therefore be set on maintaining the established order, not to mention the additional influence exercised by their family relationships and their personal connections. Moreover his wars, with the resulting increase in offices, also provided him with a large number of devoted servants.

He kept up between these two groups a corporate and personal rivalry which divided them, made them assiduous in their duties, and caused them to look to him as the source of money and distinctions. This was why he attached great importance to decorations, for which he realized there was a keen desire.

In 1805, he had completely transformed the Legion of Honour, so that the whole value now lay in the insignia. In the kingdom of Italy, he created the *Ordre de la Couronne de fer*, which was received by many Frenchmen. In 1809, he created the *Trois toisons d'or*, and in 1811 the Réunion. There was an endless distribution of rewards, pension, gifts in the form of income or land. The army received the lion's share; but true to his promise, he did not refuse to decorate civilians, and even gave Talma the Legion of Honour, though more than nine-tenths of the crosses went to soldiers. Frenchmen fell in with this policy, to which they had been accustomed in the *Ancien Régime*, because these distinctions, carrying no privileges, being open to all, and not being hereditary, did not seem contrary to a civil equality which reserved reward for merit. It remained possible to rise in the social scale, along lines sanctioned by the Revolution; war and promotion were in favour of it; and the extension of public functions and scholarships gradually built up from among the people a lower middle class.

With his dreams of establishing a legitimate dynasty and his desire to complete the attachment of the ancient aristocracy, whose titles he was none the less unwilling to recognize, Napoleon took a further step and recreated a nobility. It was to be one of office, held directly from himself, but hereditary and linked to a degree of wealth that would allow the holder to preserve his rank. The organization of the imperial court, and the creation of the vassal States and the great fiefs, served as a prelude. A *senatas-consultum* of August 14, 1806, authorized Napoleon to extend the system of great hereditary fiefs over the whole Empire, with entail to the eldest son. Finally, on March 1, 1808, the imperial *noblesse* came into being. It belonged as of right to great dignitaries who had been made princes, to ministers, senators, archbishops, councillors of State for life, and the president of the legislative body, who became counts. Other officials, such as the mayors of the large towns, were made barons, and the members of the Legion of Honour, knights. The Emperor could also confer nobility by commission. The title became hereditary, provided that it constituted an entail for the benefit of the heir, to which Napoleon often made a contribution. In parallel with this development, the numbers at court constantly increased, and after the

Austrian marriage it once more became an institution, as it had been under the *Ancien Régime*. In 1812, there were sixteen Equerries and eighty-five Chamberlains. Precedence had been re-established in 1811, and was marked by the chair, the stool, and the number of carriage-horses, court dress, and presentation at court. At this point, the return to the old ways was even more marked. M. de Ségur was master of ceremonies: the ladies in waiting and the chamberlains came for the most part from the old nobility. The Revolution seemed no more than a bad dream. Napoleon was soon to say to Molé: 'The doctrines that are called the principles of 1789 will always remain a threatening weapon in the hands of the malcontents, the ambitious and the ideologues of every age.' He also spoke of the knitting-women who hated the new Empress. His violent dislike for any opposition to his authority grew so great that he no longer made any distinction between these *sans-culottes* women and the royalist citizens who had risen against the Convention:

> As long as I am here, these dregs of society shall never again be given a chance to stir, because they saw what stuff I am made of on 13 Vendémiaire; and they know that I shall always be ready to crush them if I find them up to any tricks.

And his supporters joined in the chorus: Réal, the former deputy to Chaumette, was to exclaim in 1812: 'The common people have never been properly put in their place!'

If Napoleon had been given the time, he would perhaps have gone still further. There are certain indications suggesting that he would have liked to group his subjects in social categories, in such a way that the constitution of the vassal States would have carried a corporate suffrage, seats being distributed between landed proprietors, businessmen, and the liberal professions, for they all were clearly property-holders. In this respect, it was tempting for him to reconstitute the corporations. If recreated under State control, equipped with auxiliary institutions and technical instructors, and forbidden to strike or enter into combinations, they would have provided a framework for subjecting the workers to the patriarchal authority of the leaders in industry and commerce. The Emperor was also in favour of granting perpetual leaseholds as a suitable means of setting up patronage for the landed proprietors.

Of all his schemes, the ones aiming at a reconstruction of society were the most uncertain. The fact is that they were contrary to the course of evolution, which swept away the few that were realized, leaving no permanent effect on the national life. In the first place, Chaptal was wrong in imagining that the Revolution had been forgotten. Even at court, there was only a superficial fusion between the old and the new aristocracies; and the imperial setting often did no more than produce a surface impression. 'Another chamber-pot on the head of these nobles'—as Pommereul was heard to mutter at each new chamberlain's nomination, although he himself belonged to the *Ancien Régime*. 'Have you seen Sieyes?' said Doulcet de Pontécoulant after the ceremony for the Order of the *Réunion* in which Sieyes, like the others, had appeared in robes covered with gold and spangled with stars; 'Have you seen Sieyes? What is the third estate?'

Deep down, Napoleon himself did not feel at ease in the midst of the nobles of the *Ancien Régime* who were in a position to make so many comparisons, and for whom he never ceased to express contempt. 'I opened my antechambers to them,' he said, 'and they rushed in.' Witness again the evidence of this footnote in a letter to the Prince-Bishop of Bâle, in 1805, who was concerned about his financial interests: 'Oh! you cowardly nobles: what would your ancestors say if they saw you—your ancestors, who were so proud of their virtues!'* But things were very different in the country. The people of privilege under the *Ancien Régime* never ceased bemoaning what they had lost; and the imperial nobility, like the middle classes, remained determined not to give any of it back to them. Those who had accepted the new regime put up with conditions as they were. Those who were irreconcilable dreamed of the *Ancien Régime*, some of them even attempting to form groups to prepare for possible action in favour of the legitimate monarchy. For this purpose Ferdinand de Bertier and Mathieu de Montmorency, both members of the *Congrégation de la Vierge* that was to become famous under the Restoration, organized a secret society of the

* *Fürstenbriefe an Napoléon I*, published by F. Kircheisen (Stuttgart and Berlin, 1929), vol. II, 336.

Knights of the Faith, which seems to have revived in Bordeaux memories of the Philosophical Institute that had been so active under the Directory. The rest of the nobility, as they waited for better days, rebuilt their fortunes and resumed their rank as far as that was possible. The returning *émigrés* bought back their land on good terms (half of it situated in the Côtes-du-Nord) or had it given back to them. They remained in secret agreement with a large section of the clergy; and once again they had friends in all the administrative bodies and in the law-courts. They were in no way grateful to Bonaparte, but were waiting for his downfall. If only he had taken over the national possessions to hand them back to themselves! For their part, the new owners began to grow uneasy. In 1807, the estates department had undertaken, for a very small profit, to revise the deductions allowed; it also went into the question of the nationalized revenues, and sought to demand proof from debtors of their feudal status. Some courts—at Dijon, for example—claimed the power to restore the feudal revenues themselves when the creditor could prove that they corresponded to a concession in land; and the General Council of the Côte d'Or expressed the same desire. Nothing could fill the gulf created by the social revolution: the old and the new nobilities were long to remain at enmity, and in spite of anything that Napoleon could say or do, democracy would take advantage of their discords to gain a further triumph.

On the other hand Napoleon had only become the most powerful of the enlightened despots because when he rose to fame the French aristocracy had been annihilated. Any real re-establishment of it was something of a contradiction. Firmly based upon big landed properties and supported by a body of tenants in perpetuity, the nobility would have recovered an independent power which he—or at any rate his successors—would, like Louis XV and Louis XVI before them, soon have confronted as a rising force ranged against themselves. The nobility that he had created and intended to keep under control only amounted to a clique of courtiers and officials who gave him no support; and once he had gone, they melted away. Finally, it was just as contradictory to pose as the representative of a revolution carried out in the name of equality and yet to wish to restore an aristocracy worthy of the name. At the time, a personal nobility may well have seemed generally acceptable. It was just a decoration, much the same as any other; and the common people were quite disposed to have their dukes and counts after they had set up kings. It was a new way of humiliating the *ci-devant*. But to revive the rights of primogeniture was going too far; and in immobilizing a part of property by the principle of entail, Napoleon came into conflict with one of the essential principles of the capitalist economy.

The action of Napoleon upon society was only really effective to the extent that it strengthened and increased the predominance of the *bourgeoisie*, because at this point it was in line with the national evolution. By giving the nobles an essential part in the regime he unconsciously prepared the way for their assumption of political power. But he also greatly increased their influence, their prestige, and their wealth by reconstituting the administrative posts and making them virtually an invitation to corrupt practices through the misappropriation of securities; by re-establishing in the financial system treasurers and receivers personally interested in the manipulation of funds by their right to a percentage on them; and by multiplying public offices of every description. The Bank of France, the formation of certain large societies, and the restoration of investment in stocks began to develop moneyed estate. Industrial expansion and the prosperity of various big business chiefs were a sign of a developing capitalism, though the middle classes continued to draw their wealth from the traditional sources, namely the purchase of land and the supply of the sinews of war. And lastly, the imperial legislation kept the workers in a state of subjection. Nevertheless, the more power the middle classes acquired, the more they turned away from the Napoleonic regime.

True, the government under Napoleon was far from meeting his interests at every point. It is hardly possible to approve of his financial management, his arbitrary control over the contractors, the adventurer's attitude to war, and the excesses of the blockade. But none of this was perhaps the heart of the matter. The middle classes had only helped him on that day in Brumaire in order to install themselves in power under his wing; but he seized the whole power and deprived the middle classes of all freedom. Thus constitutional monarchy came to be regarded with nostalgic longings, and the English parliamentary system came back into fashion. Royer-Collard even went as far as to blame those who accepted the new regime, although he ended by accepting a chair at the Sorbonne. In the *Corps Législatif*, Laîné waited for an opportunity of posing as an opponent; and Guizot, who had been appointed to the Sorbonne, refused to slip into his first lesson a passage in praise of the tyrant. There was talk in the salons, particularly in Mme Récamier's circle; in the theatres, there was applause for any passages that could be taken as topical allusions; books and articles passed in all innocence by the censorship were eagerly devoured; pamphlets were circulated in manuscript, and people let themselves go—not without some risk—in personal correspondence. The more startling incidents were connected especially with the history of literature. In 1807, Chateaubriand, who had only just come back from his travels in the East, was ordered to leave Paris because of an article in the *Mercure*; and although he was elected to the Academy in 1811, he was unable to deliver his inaugural speech. Mme de Staël was even worse treated. Returning to France after the publication of *Delphine*, in which she gave a picture of 'silent France', she was asked to leave the country again; and in 1806 she was not allowed to come within twenty miles of Paris. At Coppet, she gathered a circle of admirers around her—Benjamin Constant (though he was now a married man), Sismondi, Bonstetten, the Barantes, and Augustus Schlegel—a court that rivalled the official court. From 1808 onwards, it was hardly possible to risk being seen there without the chance of official disfavour or worse; and in 1810, the impression made by her *L'Allemagne* was the last straw Barante, who was *préfet* of the *Léman département*, was dismissed and Mme Récamier exiled. The heroine herself fled on May 23, 1812, and made for St. Petersburg.

But these events were only of episodic importance, concerning no one but so-called 'society' or 'the fashionable world', that is to say, an infinitesimal number of people. It is more important to note the hundred and one less well-known signs that everyone was living in a state of doubt and expectancy; for who could consider the Empire as finally consolidated when each new campaign threw it into the melting pot? The Lyons chamber of commerce boldly expressed in a memorandum what everyone was thinking: 'France cannot stand up to the all-out effort required by an indefinitely prolonged state of war. The extreme tension resulting from this effort exhausts the energies of the whole of society.' The stock exchanges unwearingly reflected the universal pessimism by steadily remaining at the lowest level. It was this uncertainty that continually fanned the current fears and discontent.

Yet neither of these was reflected among the lower classes. They were scarcely affected by the Napoleonic despotism. Only taxation, conscription, and poverty would have stirred them to action. Up to 1812, military service did not provoke as much resistance as has been supposed. The privations and high prices due to the blockade scarcely affected the poor, as long as bread was not too expensive and unemployment not too bad. The combined duties were very unpopular, but they were not nearly as oppressive as before 1789. As long as he remained victorious, Napoleon's demands do not seem to have been greater than the people could bear provided they had their daily bread, which was as far as possible the case from 1803 to 1811, thanks to good harvests and the Emperor's measures to ensure the supply of work.

The condition of the rural population was tending to become more settled. During the whole of the Empire, the nationalized lands continued to be sold, but not much of them remained, apart from the forests, which the State kept under its own control. The lands mostly went to the middle classes, and the peasants who bought them were already fairly well off. In Year XII, the sharing out of the common lands had been confirmed, provided the legal requirements had been respected; but as this was not often the case, many transfers were annulled. On the other hand, though the law of June 10 1793 was not revoked, it ceased to be applied.

Nevertheless, it seems that peasant property-owning continued to spread because the marked drop in the price of land was in favour of private purchase. Moreover, the laws of succession ensured that it quickly became subdivided. The working units seem likewise to have become smaller and more numerous. The 1814 enquiry noted that in the Mantes district and in the Seine-Inférieure, large farms had been split up, and that small-scale cultivation was on the increase in Alsace in the Ille-et-Vilaine, in the Doubs, and in the Tarn. All the same, although the original features of the country's social structure were growing fainter in this process, they remained easily recognizable. The great majority of peasant proprietors still owned too little land; the cost of farming was on the increase, and the expenses of those who paid rent-in-kind were rising. There was a rapidly growing population, and the daily wage proletariat had hardly gone down in number. The rural community only managed to subsist by virtue of the customary rights, such as free access and pasture on the commons, gleaning, and common lands, so that the closing of the forests was often a cause of suffering to them. As under the *Ancien Régime*, they sought to add to their livelihood by means of industry, by temporary migrations, and by begging. In Alsace, Lorraine, and the Rhinelands the peasants, making poverty the ostensible reason, emigrated to Russia in fairly large numbers, especially in 1808 and 1809; and severe measures had to be taken to put a stop to this movement.

There was still less change in the situation of the workers. Not till 1813 did Napoleon intervene—and then solely on behalf of the miners—to prevent accidents, forbid the employment underground of children less than ten years of age, and approve the formation of an optional provident society in the coalmines of the Ourthe *département*. He announced his intention—which had been expressed so often before—of abolishing all mendicancy, but his efforts were no more successful than those of his predecessors, although in 1808 he seriously undertook to set up institutions for interning beggars. But with the exception of a few towns, public assistance made little progress: the machinery set up by the Directory was kept going, but there was a lack of funds. Only by private initiative were a few improvements obtained. In Paris, La Rochefoucauld-Liancourt and his friends had in the Year IX revived the Philanthropic Society, which opened the first dispensaries, and others were founded in the provinces. They supported the Savings Banks and Mutual Assistance Societies, of which there were more than a hundred in 1815; the *Société maternelle* was also revived. The essential point was that wages remained steady or increased, both in town and country. In Paris about 1811, they rose from 2 fr. 50 to 4 fr. 20; but as prices were rising to an equal degree, people were not much better off, though with bread not too dear, life was just possible. The rapid increase in the population proves that this was so. Early marriages were more than ever a contributory factor, because this was a possible way of avoiding conscription. In 1812, there were 220,000 marriages, and 387,000 in 1813, resulting in 122,000 more births in 1814 than in 1813. From 1801 to 1810, the birth-rate exceeded 32 per thousand, and the nation never showed greater vitality. Some administrative efforts were made to reduce the death-rate, especially by extending the use of vaccine. In the Bas-Rhin, Lezay-Marnésia organized a free medical service. From 1801 to 1810, this venerable France, in spite of her wars, added 1,700,000 souls to her population. Many there were who deplored the fact, believing that it would only lead to an increase in poverty and begging.

The industrial crisis of 1811 interrupted the succession of good years; but there was a rapid recovery in 1812, which was fortunate, for there had been a bad harvest in 1811, and as export had meant the disappearance of all old stocks, the dearth of that winter was as severe as in Year X. The crisis came in the spring of 1812, when the average price of a hectolitre rose from 15 francs in 1809 to 33 francs, and bread in certain regions from 2 sous to 12 a pound. The usual disturbances recurred. Beggars multiplied and formed bands, farms were raided and set on fire, grain supplies were seized, and there were market riots, such as those at Caen at the beginning of March. The formidable repressive machinery of the regime went into pitiless action. Caen was occupied by a detachment of the Imperial Guard and a military commission ordered six executions. At the same time efforts were made to import grain. As early as August 28, 1811, Napoleon set up a food council, and the director of supplies undertook considerable purchases. As always, Paris was the chief consideration, the State selling 450,000 sacks of grain there, at a loss of 14½ million, in order to keep the price of bread at 4½ sous a pound. On the eve of his departure for Russia, the Emperor nevertheless felt overloaded with stocks, and had no compunction in following the example of the Convention. By a law passed on May 4 it was made compulsory to sell in the markets; their regulation was authorized, and the grain merchants were compelled to declare their stocks. On May 8, a maximum price was again fixed. Corn was fixed at 33 francs in the Paris district, and the *préfets* were ordered to fix prices in each *département*. The results were the same as those that followed the law of May 4, 1793, because the authorities did not go as far as to requisition supplies: the open markets were deserted, and a secret 'black-market' trade grew up. As soon as the harvest began the maximum price was abandoned. In spite of these trials, the Empire does not seem to have gone down in popular esteem. The reports issued by Las Casas, one of the commissioners who was sent on a tour of enquiry, do not anywhere leave the impressions that Napoleon had lost popularity; in any case, it did not even cross the minds of peasants and workers that he could be replaced by a Bourbon.

In the countries annexed before 1804—Belgium, the Rhineland, Geneva, Piedmont, and Liguria—the revolutionary changes had been thoroughly carried through and the Napoleonic system was in regular operation. The inhabitants appreciated its merits, particularly the zeal and firmness of *préfets* like Jeanbon in Mont-Tounerre and Lezay-Marnésia in Rhin-et-Moselle. Moreover, there were signs of economic progress. This was when large-scale industry began in Belgium, thanks to the opening of the French market, and capital and orders from Paris. The same was true of the Rhineland plain between Aix-la-Chapelle and Cologne, and of the Saar region. Belgian and Piedmontese agriculture do not seem to have shown great improvement; but a great deal of fallow land was brought under cultivation in the Rhineland. Although Belgium (apart from Antwerp) could not show any large public works, Piedmont took full advantage of the great Alpine roads. The Rhineland saw the opening of a road along its river, the Moselle, and another from Paris to Hamburg via Wesel; and the Saar was linked up with Lorraine by canal. Circumstances prevented all interests from being satisfied: Genoa, Antwerp, and the Rhineland ports were condemned to stagnation; and the Palatinate failed to find in the Empire the agricultural market it had lost east of the Rhine. As in France, there seemed to be heavy burdens. Taxation was better spread, but it more than made up for the dues that had been abolished; the consumer suffered under the blockade; and conscription was even more unpopular. Nevertheless, the population increased everywhere; and although there was not much advance in the standard of living, the inhabitants were certainly not weighed down by poverty.

In all regions it was the middle classes who reaped the greatest gains from the regime and were most solidly attached to it. The sale of the national lands, together with industry and public enterprise, led to the appearance of *nouveaux riches* and a lower middle class who stood to lose everything by a return to the *Ancien Régime*. But the *Concordat* had also allayed the fears of the Catholic clergy; and even the aristocracy were partly won round when they saw Napoleon getting rid of the Jacobins and the patriots. The Piedmontese Saint-Marsan became an ambassador; the duc de Mérode-Westerloo and the duc d'Ursel were mayors of Brussels. What the notables especially complained of to the Emperor was his failure to show them enough confidence. The *préfets*, bishops and principal heads of the services were French; a few only from the annexed countries obtained similar posts in the rest of the Empire; in their homelands they became *préfets'* councillors, judges, mayors, professors, not to mention various more humble posts. There could be no question of giving them a monopoly of employment in their home countries; and seeing that they had only been recently united with France, the Emperor may be considered to have given them a fair share. The essential difference between the old and the new *départements* was that in the latter the inhabitants did not reap nearly as much benefit from the laws of the Revolution. The abolition of feudal rights had not caused much of a sensation in Belgium and the north of Italy, where not many of them existed, it would seem, when the French regime was set up. But it was a different matter in the Rhineland, though the popularity of the measure was compromised for a long time by the claim to make those who owed rent prove their feudal status. The suppression of tithe had a great effect everywhere; yet the peasants only reaped the full benefit if they were owners of the land. Now in Belgium the alienation of the national lands had only begun at the end of the Directory; in the Rhineland and in Piedmont, the religious orders were not suppressed till 1802 and 1803, and the land was not sold till 1804. By this time the laws of 1793 were no more than a memory, and as in France, the methods operated against the poor and in favour of the middle classes, in spite of the *préfets'* opinion that the surest way of winning over the country people would be to divide the lots before putting them up for sale. 'The people are greedy for land,' said one of them in Year XI. Jeanbon prided himself on having carried out this division, so creating 10,000 proprietors. The property-dealers split up their purchases in order to resell them. Nevertheless, it cannot be denied that the operation disappointed the peasants of the annexed countries even more than in France.

It is equally clear that the break with the Pope made more impression in these territories than in France, especially in Belgium and the Rhineland, which had never been national States and so were strongly ultramontane. At Mainz, for example, Bishop Colmar was training a generation of priests for Alsace and Germany who were devoted to Rome. French influence was also cancelled out to a large extent in Piedmont by the memories of its own dynasty, in Genoa by the ruin of the port, and at Geneva by the regrets of the local aristocracy, who could not forgive their loss of power. But in spite of all the reservations that can be made, it remains true that no one in the occupied countries raised a finger against Napoleon's sovereign sway.

CHAPTER SEVEN

The Continental System

GREAT AS IT HAD now become, the French Empire was only the kernel of the *Grand Empire*, which had come into being in 1806, and was completed by the vassal States allotted by Napoleon to his relations or servants, or taken under his protection, as was the case for Switzerland and most members of the Rhine Confederation. After the Peace of Tilsit, this *Grand Empire* became in itself the predominant element in the Continental System, in which still independent States ranged themselves as friends or allies. This system never became as stable as the *Grand Empire*. At the beginning of 1808, only Sweden was lacking; but it soon began to disintegrate, and from then onwards the history of Napoleon is the story of a perpetual effort to piece it together again. Portugal and Spain were the first to escape from it, the former never rejoining, and the latter only being nominally reintegrated. Austria left it in her turn, only to seek readmission almost immediately. In 1810, Sweden submitted; soon after, Russia broke free and took her neighbour along with her. Besides, these States remained unequal and variable in their dependence. Up to 1808, Spain remained France's benevolent ally; Russia and Denmark were forced by circumstances into apparently willing acceptance of the same position. Without being admitted as equals, Prussia in 1807, Austria in 1808 and again in 1809, Sweden in 1810, were all obliged to join the system, and the first two were transformed into allies by an authoritative edict in 1812. And lastly Turkey, coming in in 1807 and 1808, was never more than a friend.

This European federation, which was in a perpetual state of formation, had as its immediate and avowed aim to fight against England. In this sense, the reverses of the war at sea and the plans for invasion were its logical antecedents; but historically speaking, it was only after the war of 1805 that the idea took shape in the form of the *Grand Empire* and the blockade, and only at Tilsit that it expanded into the Continental System. Circumstances thus helped in its birth, whilst being heavily loaded against its realization, and imposing France both as its manager and its model. All the same, arising themselves from Napoleon's policy, these circumstances only had the effect of multiplying tenfold the impetus behind this policy from the time of Lunéville onwards, the first sign of which was the foundation of the Cisalpine League in 1796. There was no need to have broken the Peace of Amiens; and even if one takes the opposite point of view, there were other possible methods of carrying on the battle against England. Napoleon deliberately assumed the title of Emperor; he made constant reference to Charlemagne and the Roman Empire; he chose Rome as his second capital; he refused along with Constantinople to allow Alexander 'the empire of the world': in all these ways Napoleon showed the profound unity given to his work by his energetic temperament and the thirst for power which is its psychological expression, an energy which spontaneously tended to refashion the Western World as a political unity and at the same time to renew its civilization. This was abundantly proved by his systematic efforts to instil new life into the administrative and social structure of the Continent: there was no positive necessity for the imposition of the Civil Code in order to defeat England. Beneath the flux of events there lay concealed a plan which gradually became conscious—the intention to restore an *orbis romanus*.

THE POLITICAL ORGANIZATION OF THE SYSTEM

We must not, however, allow ourselves to be misled by this reference to the Roman Empire: the constitution of the *Grand Empire* was not based upon an historical memory or on any abstract conception. Geographically, it comprised three domains corresponding to the possible directions of French conquest. The Italian domain deserves the first place, by virtue of its seniority, the advances made in concentration of territory, and the perfection of its institutions; and within it was included the extension to Illyria and the Ionian islands. It was grouped round four great centres of unity: French Italy, the kingdom of Italy, the Illyrian provinces, and the Kingdom of Naples, the first three in the hands of the Emperor, the fourth handed over to a protégé. The peninsula provided a base against England, for possible landings in Sicily and threats to Malta, and then for launching an expedition to the East. Meanwhile, it was less important than Northern Italy and Illyria, which would make it possible to take Austria in the rear and break into the plains of Hungary. The same route would lead to Salonica and Constantinople; and on this side economic relationships with the Levant had already been established. The Confederation of the Rhine constituted an even more valuable domain covering the most exposed of the French frontiers, holding Austria and Prussia to ransom, and serving as a parade-ground from which to attack the heart of Russia. The possession of Germany closed Central Europe to English trade and opened the chief continental market to the trade of France. The third domain was the Spanish Peninsula, mastery over which would have opened up interesting prospects for taking up the struggle again in the Mediterranean and in the Atlantic Ocean, and would have been of even wider scope if it had brought with it the submission of the Spanish and Portuguese colonies; but in actual fact it turned out to be nothing but a very serious burden.

The influence of circumstances is very perceptible too in the organization of the *Grand Empire*. It was important for Napoleon to group his territories in huge units, both in order to raise strong auxiliary forces from the conquered lands and to hasten the unification of their social and administrative services. In Italy, this work was reasonably far advanced; in Germany—bearing in mind its fragmentary character—there had also been a tremendous advance in concentration; but as long as Prussia and Austria continued to exist, and Russia was still independent, the loyal princes had to be humoured, and the work of unification remained incomplete.

Moreover, it was necessary to conciliate the peoples who were accustomed to autonomy or who possessed a strong national tradition. As a prepartion for the unity of France the Capetian kings, instead of at once uniting newly acquired provinces to their kingdom, had made them into appanages for the benefit of their relatives. In the Girondin idea of surrounding France by a girdle of protected States Napoleon saw an analogous method of compromise; besides, his strong attachment to his own family and his desire to reward faithful servants made it convenient to multiply the number of vassal countries. Hence he first of all envisaged the *Grand Empire* as a federative system. Whilst remaining sovereign over the kingdom of Italy, he gave it an independent status under his viceroy Prince Eugène. Later on, countries annexed to the French Empire enjoyed an apparent autonomy under governor-generals, Borghese in Piedmont and Liguria, Elisa in Tuscany, Marmont in Illyria, Lebrun in Holland. Outside the Empire, certain territories such as Hanover, Bayreuth, Fulda and Hanau were for several years under the rule of imperial administrators; and Erfurt never had any other status. An apparently more real sovereignty was enjoyed under a hereditary title by the Emperor's brothers and brother-in-law, Joseph—first in Naples and then in Spain, Louis in Holland, Murat in the Grand Duchy of Berg and then at Naples, and Jerome in Westphalia; but although they were members of the family and dignitaries of the Empire, they remained subject to the authority of their head. If the Pope had been willing, he would have constituted a unique and special category among these vassal princes. Along with them, but on a lower level, were Elisa at Piombino, Bacciochi at Lucca, and Berthier at Neuchâtel, all of them hereditary sovereigns, but only able to transmit their heritage subject to a fresh investiture. Next came Talleyrand, prince of Benevento, and Bernadotte, prince of Ponte Corvo, who were invested with a purely administrative authority. And finally, within the sphere of sovereignty, Napoleon left his direct mark by distributing a number of useful fiefs, such as the Italian duchies, and various gifts of land.

Among the federated princes, Napoleon met with the same difficulties and dangers as the Capetian kings had done with the holders of appanages, or the German emperors in the Middle Ages with the ducal dynasties. To start with, he was under an illusion about their talents, and imagined they would be as active and able in administration as himself. In practice, they proved very mediocre; and he would have been still more out of reckoning if he had not shouldered part of the work himself —in Westphalia, for example—or provided them with able administrators, as he did at Naples. He at least had a right to hope they would remain his loyal lieutenants. 'Never give up being French,' was his advice to Louis. 'Remember,' he said to Murat, 'I've only made you king to further my system'; and Berthier passed this on to the King of Naples in equally expressive terms: 'Do as king what you did as a soldier.' And to Caroline he wrote: 'Above all, my wish is that people should do what suits France; for I have only conquered kingdoms in order that France should reap the benefits.' It was not for his protégés to reason why—and some of them were well aware of this. Prince Eugène always remained loyal: so did Elisa, who was not without ambition, but was fairly talented, and in whom Napoleon—rather grudgingly—saw something of himself. Jerome, too, did his best, though, truth to tell, this was nothing very great. On the other hand, some of them proved refractory. True, they had no easy task: they had to remodel institutions, create an army, apply the blockade and find money at a time when Napoleon burdened their budgets with various gifts and war contributions, and reserved for himself a part of their domains. In his attitude to them, Napoleon proved touchy and impossible. 'If you were to ask His Majesty for orders or advice in altering the ceiling of your room,' said Duroc to Eugène, 'you would have to wait till they arrived; and if Milan were on fire and you asked for the wherewithal to put the fire out, you would have to let Milan go up in flames and await his orders.' And it was not advisable to go ahead without asking for orders. And to his son-in-law he wrote: 'On no pretext whatsoever, even if the moon threatened to fall on Milan, are you to do anything that falls outside your authority.'

Nevertheless, the root of the trouble went deeper. As nearly always happens in such cases, the Emperor's puppet rulers considered themselves the owners of their fiefs and founders of independent dynasties. 'I have not been made a king in order to obey!' exclaimed Murat. They instinctively tried to take on their subjects' nationality in order to get their support against France. 'If they want me to govern Spain for the sole benefit of

France,' said Joseph, 'well—they needn't expect me to oblige!' They showed the naïve and comic vanity of the *parvenu*, surrounding themselves with favourites, living in exaggerated luxury, creating court duties and marshals, and instituting decorations. Furthermore, they shared their mother's uncertainty about Napoleon's future, and attributed his success to chance. They did not intend to be dragged down in his fall, and so tried to make themselves popular. Caroline noted this fact when she wrote to her husband with an unconscious frankness:

The whole of Europe is bowed down beneath the yoke of France. What is your aim? It is to contrive to stay where we are and keep our kingdoms. We are therefore bound to do what he [Napoleon] wants and not cross him when he makes a request, for he is stronger, and you can do nothing against him. And if in the end you are reduced to leaving the kingdom, let it only be when you cannot hold out any longer, and your children will then have nothing to reproach you with.

That was also Talleyrand's outlook: and it was to lead Murat to commit treason. In the end, his family's rivalries were equally upsetting to the Emperor. His sisters had lovers, and Pauline's escapades in particular were notorious. Louis and Hortense were an ill-assorted couple, he quite incurable and suffering from megalomania even more than his brothers, and with persecution on the brain; she, orthodox and steeped in improving advice, yet laying herself open to suspicion. They had separated after the birth of their second son, and only came together again for a short while in 1807. The future Napoleon III was born at Paris in 1808, but Louis never believed himself the father of his youngest son, nor of the one before him. In 1811, Hortense gave birth secretly to a child, the son of the comte de Flahaut, and the future duc de Morny. Napoleon sided with his daughter-in-law rather than his brother. When in 1809 he handed over the duchy of Berg to their son Charles, he took guardianship of the child himself, and then immediately handed it over to Hortense. There were also strained relations between Murat and Caroline. The treaty that had given them Naples offended Murat, for the present was in fact meant for Caroline. She was to survive her husband and wear the crown to the detriment of her eldest son, though she lived quite apart from public life and in semi-seclusion. As for

Lucien, he ended by embarking for the United States on August 7, 1810, but was captured and taken to England. Napoleon's mother took the part of her other children against Napoleon. He waited till she disavowed Jerome's first marriage and then gave her an official title, with the style 'S.A.I. Madame, mère de l'empereur'; but she was not satisfied and clamoured in vain for a dowry and 'some political status'.

Thus from 1806 to 1810 we see the Emperor growing more and more annoyed with his vassals and threatening to annex their States. In this way the evolution of the federated Empire, destined for final unity by the introduction of Napoleonic institutions, was given more rapid development. The Austrian marriage, the desire to increase the heritage of the King of Rome, and the prospect of having to find places for the future younger sons of the family, made the Bonaparte's position more and more precarious, though they had known long before that it was already compromised. The annexation of Holland is almost contemporary with the marriage. It seemed to be imminent as early as 1809; but early in 1810 Louis delayed it by ceding Zeeland and the southern provinces as far as the Rhine and on July 2, 1810, he fled and succeeded in reaching Austria. In April, Murat in Paris was equally certain that his cause was lost; but Caroline, having accepted the position of chaperon to Marie-Louise, patched up a reconciliation which only lasted for a very brief space. The Emperor forbade the king to appoint ambassadors. Murat was surrounding himself with suspect Italians, such as Gallo and Maghella, whom he appointed Minister of Police. This man was in touch with the secret anti-French societies, and may have been one of the first to conceive the idea of a united Italy under his master's rule. Caroline was once again sent into retirement and threatened with divorce. Murat took various customs measures against France, dismissed several high French officials, and finally made those who continued to live there take an oath of loyalty. Then matters came to a head. On July 2, 1811, Napoleon forbade his subjects to take the oath, and a rumour went round that he was going to annex the kingdom of Naples. But tempers were cooled by the threat from Russia. Murat was present at the baptism and left for Russia with the *Grande Armée*. But no one believed that matters would rest there. At the same moment, Jerome saw a part of Hanover taken away from him and was afraid it would be made over to Poland; and Joseph complained that he was no more than a nominal king. And finally, since Murat's departure for Naples, the Grand Duchy of Berg had been administered by the Emperor.

In contradistinction to the vassal States, the protected federations, who were linked to the Empire by a permanent alliance, continued to exist as before. There was no reason for Napoleon to alter the Act of Mediation which he had drawn up. Switzerland, now encircled by territories subject to Napoleon, was no longer of any immediate strategical importance; and there was no need to occupy it in order to reduce it to obedience. Swiss neutrality was only violated by the use of the bridge at Bâle in 1809 and by the occupation of le Tessin. On the other hand, the Confederation of the Rhine demanded reorganization, for its territory still remained too fragmentary. There was no equality even in the legal status of its members. The Grand Duke of Berg and the King of Westphalia were vassal princes, whilst the Grand Duke of Frankfurt, a puppet of Napoleon's, did not belong either to the family of the French Empire, nor to its great dignitaries, as long as Eugène did not take the place of Dalberg. The existence of the Grand Duchy of Wurzburg was guaranteed by the treaty of 1809 with Austria, who secretly considered herself invested with the right of being next in succession that she had possessed over Ferdinand's former domains, Tuscany and Salzburg. The other sovereign's rights were based upon legitimacy, although the most important of them held their new titles under agreements signed with the Emperor. But above all the Confederation still had no constitution, and was without a central authority able to push on with unification in administrative affairs, in the Church, in social life, and even in military matters.

In its further extensions, the Continental System was completed by alliances that depended upon the ups and downs of policy, alliances that future efforts would have to convert into permanent bonds. For Prussia and Austria, resistance was impossible; and Prussia was in fact reduced to vassal status by the treaty of 1812. Only Alexander, firmly persuaded that he had negotiated as one equal with another, although he had been conquered, figured as a genuine ally. He was resolved to consult nothing but his own interests and to exact payment for his support, whenever this was required, by demanding appropriate gratuities. This perpetual blackmail was a strong inducement to undertake the campaign against Russia. As long as Alexander remained independent, the political constitution of the Continental System would remain incomplete. Once this last obstacle had been removed, Russia could be absorbed into the *Grand Empire*; and with allies transformed into vassals, the *Grand Empire* itself would in time have been absorbed into the French Empire.

Up till 1811, French supremacy was only represented legally by the status of the vassal princes. Murat's resistance led Napoleon to define the position of Frenchmen in their service. While forbidding his subjects to take an oath of allegiance to his brother-in-law, he decreed that they were legally citizens of the Kingdom of Naples. This decision was all the more remarkable in that he has done his utmost to break the links which allowed the great families under the *Ancien Régime* not to take on a particular nationality, holding possessions as they did here and there across the frontiers, as vassals of several sovereigns and serving whom they pleased, and forming a small cosmopolitan society outside the national States. The law of 21 Floréal, Year XIII (May 11, 1805), confiscated the possessions of the imperial princes in France and only restored those of the other German lords subject to alienation unless their owners opted for French sovereignty. In the vassal countries—Westphalia, for instance—he forbade the subjects of the new princes to remain in foreign service. Schulenberg could only keep his lands by leaving the king of Prussia's service; and the other members of the Confederation of the Rhine had been invited to recall those of their dependants who had made their careers in Austria. The principle laid down for the Kingdom of Naples was therefore a privilege for the French, for without losing their French nationality they were to become citizens of the States in the *Grand Empire* to which they might happen to be sent. If this system had lasted, it might have been the beginning of something like Roman citizenship. This would have worked all the more conveniently in that the *Grand Empire* was not simply a political unity, for Napoleon's intention was to give it the same institutions and social structure as those of imperial France.

THE NAPOLEONIC REFORMS

In implanting his system of government, the first idea in the Emperor's mind was to give a certain sacrosanctity to his power, for it was important that he, his vassals, and his allies should all hold undisputed sovereignty. Any intermediate bodies, privileges or feudal rights must therefore be swept away, so that all men should become directly subject to the State. It was also advisable for the laws of succession to reduce the size of the great fortunes, so making the aristocracy subordinate to the sovereign, and the priests his officials. Another primary obligation fell upon all the members of the *Grand Empire*, namely to provide money and men. The *Ancien Régime*, with its slow and chaotic administration, could not mobilize the country's resources quickly enough: a clean break had to be made, and the Napoleonic bureaucracy put in its place. In this respect the Emperor was even urged on to further conquests by the desire to prove the superiority of the methods which an ally like Charles IV seemed unable to appreciate.

These preoccupations did not prevent him from seeing that a renewal of the administration and of society would give him a chance to conciliate the peasants and the middle classes. He wrote to Jerome:

> What the peoples of Germany long for is that those who are not nobles and have some abilities should have an equal right to your consideration, and to employment. This means that all kinds of servitude, and all intermediate links between the sovereign and the lowest classes, should be entirely abolished. . . . To be quite frank with you, I place more reliance on their efforts for extending and strengthening this monarchy than on the results of the greatest victories in the field.

Civil equality, religious liberty, the abolition of tithe and feudal rights, the sale of Church property, the suppression of the corporations, the increase in officials, 'wise and liberal' administration, a constitution carrying the right to vote taxes and make laws on the part of the people who really counted—all those were intended to weave a network of interests closely bound up with maintaining French ascendancy; and the control of public opinion, as in the French Empire, would see to the rest. The Civil Code embodied the essentials of this policy, and that is why the Emperor made such vigorous efforts to introduce it everywhere. As early as 1807 he wanted to impose it on the Hanseatic towns, on Danzig, on his German protégés, and of course on Holland and Westphalia. In 1808, he was thinking of applying it to Portugal, and in 1809 to Spain.

A realist attitude could not justify the jealous passion with which he set about its propagation, for he made this an all-out effort. The cast of mind which he inherited from the eighteenth century gave him a sincere aversion to feudalism, intolerance, and the chaotic hand-to-mouth methods of the old administrations. He resumed the work of the benevolent despots, and although his task was made considerably easier by the tradition they had left behind, he surpassed them all in speed and boldness. On the other hand, his authoritarian spirit invested his work with a kind of perfection: 'If you retouch the Code Napoléon,' he said to Louis, 'it will no longer be the Code Napoléon.' And to Murat, who wanted to cut out divorce: 'I would rather have Naples in the hands of the ex-king of Sicily than emasculate the Code Napoléon in this fashion.' In the same way, the system became invested with an eternal and universal value; he saw it as the framework for a European civilization which would consolidate the Continent's political unity and be in harmony with it. The idea that the peoples might protest struck his mind as absurd: in the first place, what was good enough for the French must be suitable for everyone, for—as he wrote to Eugène—'there is very little difference between one people and another'. In any case, if particular differences existed, they must be removed. When he reproached Louis for his behaviour on May 20, 1810, and remarked that if only he had been loyal it would have meant adding north-western Germany and Hamburg to his Dutch kingdom, Napoleon added: 'This would have formed a nucleus of peoples to banish the German spirit, which is the foremost aim of my policy.' In the end, any objection was seen as rebellion against his despotic power. 'I think it is ridiculous for you to tell me that the people of Westphalia do not agree,' he informs Jerome. 'If you listen to what the people think, you won't do anything at all. If the people refuse what makes for their own welfare they are guilty of anarchism, and the first duty of the prince is to punish them.' The expansion of French institutions was one of the expressions of his love of power.

But the supreme goal of his endeavours never made him lose sight of the need for taking circumstances into account. His mania for assimilation and unity have been much criticized; yet this is what he wrote in the margin of a letter dated September 9, 1807:

> What interest can France have in her forms of administration being adopted in Holland? What is there in common between French interests and the imposition of a unified system in Holland and a hundred and one other things connected with the various views that may be held about the administration of the country?

In the vassal and allied States he did in fact put up with more than one alteration to his plans, and even more than one pruning of his codes; but in the countries where he was completely master—particularly in the Kingdom of Italy—his system reached a perfection even greater than in the French Empire. On the other hand continual warfare, the need for dealing tactfully with sovereign allies, the constant changes of frontier, the fragmentation which was allowed to continue in Italy and Germany, all these worked against the complete spread of his system, which remained very unequally applied. For example, the Grand Duchy of Berg, although governed by the Emperor after Murat's departure, was less thoroughly transformed than Jerome's kingdom. When one considers how short was the period of Napoleon's ascendancy, the results achieved were really tremendous; but they nevertheless remained uneven.

But there were even worse hindrances from a social point of view, for opportunism was often in conflict with the 'system'. Being in need of money and wishing to provide for the foreign territories, Napoleon saw in the property of the dispossessed monarchs, *émigres*, and clergy a ready source of help. Now tithes and feudal dues formed a substantial part of this wealth: should they be given up? Then he needed a government and administrative staff to raise taxes and conscripts; and for this he had to fall back not only on the middle classes but on the aristocracy, because outside France the former were insufficient. Moreover, how was he to draw upon the kings' courts without the help of the nobility? Once this was admitted, the agrarian reforms could not take the radical shape that would have been needed to win over the peasants to the Revolution, as they had in France. Besides, Napoleon was everywhere getting rid of the Jacobins who would have warmly approved of this course; in France, he was courting the old nobility and looking for a dynastic alliance; in the Empire, the Revolution was an accomplished fact for which he could decline responsibility; but in the *Grand Empire*, the responsibility was his, and this contradiction crept into the very heart of the system. In the end, the peasants were sacrificed: the personal dues and sometimes even the tithes were declared redeemable, and this constituted a stumbling-block both for French influence and for the Napoleonic reforms.

But it is not enough to analyse the components of Napoleon's European work and direct attention to his imaginative picture of a unified Europe. More than this is needed in order to set the part he played in historical perspective, for the Continental System was never fully formed, and however inspired it may appear as a human dream, it proved to have no lasting legacy in the long run.

On the other hand the creative side of his work comes out in what he managed to infuse of the spirit of the Revolution into his conquered territories. At the head of the *Grande Armée* for which the Revolution had prepared the way, Napoleon destroyed the *Ancien Régime* which the popular uprising of 1789 had uprooted in France, replacing it by an organization which the middle classes helped him to work out more fully under the *Consulat*. Seeing that some at least of his principles—such as equality before the law and a secular State—agreed with those of the freemasons, it is not surprising that everywhere in the lodges a large number of its members made common cause with the upholders of the French regime, to such an extent that several of his opponents spoke with horror of his Masonic Empire.

To remain a soldier of the Revolution was inconsistent with the plan of reviving a legitimate dynasty and a hierarchical corporative society. But his intellectual make-up, his career, and the needs of his policy of conquest would not allow him to escape from the clutches of an evolution that was working towards the downfall of the aristocracy and the rise of the middle classes. Whatever he might say, his genius hastened on its course. One of the permanent features of his work was that wherever his arms were triumphant, his progress was marked as it were by the emancipating forces of a night of August 4.

THE MEDITERRANEAN COUNTRIES: ITALY, THE ILLYRIAN PROVINCES AND CATALONIA

Italy was the country where the system left its deepest mark, which is not surprising, seeing that the intervention of the revolutionaries and Bonaparte himself had opened the way. Piedmont, Liguria, and Parma were entirely assimilated to France by annexation. The kingdom of Italy was increased by the addition of Venetia and Guastalla in the Marches in 1808, and the Trentino in 1810. He could use it as a field for experiment, not having to take account—as in France—of the traditions of monarchy and the memories of the Revolution. He paid no attention to the constitutional statute of 1805. When the *Corps Législatif* took upon itself to discuss and even reject certain of his plans, he wrote to Eugène: 'I shall not convene it any more,' and proceeded to legislate by decree. He continued methodically with centralization. As from 1806, justice was organized on the French model. Public Works and Education, hitherto left to the local authorities, were now taken over by the State; so was the Public Health Department, and then in 1807 Public Assistance.

Having extended his powers, Napoleon proceeded to increase the number of officials. In 1805 he had created a General Superintendent of Police; the Bridges and Highways Department was set up in 1806; the magistrates in charge of dikes and canals were put under the authority of the *préfecture* councils. Central and departmental councils were established for Public Health, a superintendent and departmental committees for Assistance, and a managing body for Education under the Ministry for the Interior. *Lycées* were opened, and at Milan a Girls' College, which had no equivalent in France; a school for the Highways Department, a veterinary school, a musical *conservatoire*, and three academies for the Fine Arts; and the theatres were put under the control of a general director. In 1806, one of the brothers Caffarelli replaced Pino at the head of the army, which steadily improved and added to its effective strength. Prima, the Minister for Finance, met his growing commitments by a special war-tax, imposed in 1806 and then continued as a personal tax, by extending indirect taxation, and by introducing registration. He was a remarkable administrator, both assiduous and inventive; but his zeal aroused formidable hatred, and he lost his life in a riot in 1814. The kingdom was systematically encircled by a ring of customs-barriers and put closely under the control of the French economy by the opening of the Alpine roads; but it reaped certain advantages from some other public works.

The statute of 1805 envisaged the introduction of the Civil Code on January 1, 1806, but it had first to be translated and printed; and in spite of work at high pressure, the date for the adoption of the Code in civil procedure had to be postponed till April 1. The creation of facilities for mortgages and the organization of civil status then followed in due course. This was in fact no more than a crowning of the work of the Republic, which had abolished privilege and the feudal system. The effort of the Code was none the less sensational because it set up civil status, introduced divorce, and made revolutionary changes in the customary habits of succession. Nor were the clergy at all pleased with the reforms that had followed the *Concordat*. On June 8, 1805, the parishes had been reduced in number, the establishments of the seminaries strictly limited, and the convents suppressed, except for a few in which they grouped those religious who wished to continue a monastic life; and in 1807 the brotherhoods were also dissolved. Yet the secular clergy were more favourably treated than in the Empire, for the bishoprics were given an endowment in land or State funds, and so were the chapters and seminaries; and the clergy's property had not been nationalized. Moreover, by the terms of the *Concordat* the priests came under the authority of Napoleon, and on the whole they showed themselves compliant. The imperial catechism was imposed on them in 1807, and the pulpit used to preach submission to the payment of taxes and to conscription. It proved much more difficult to win over the landed aristocracy, though the Emperor saw this as an essential. A few nobles succumbed to the allurements of Eugène's luxurious court, or accepted sinecures and gifts because they were in need; but the majority boycotted all public office, and their sons could not be attracted either into the *lycées* or the armed forces. Only the middle classes—including the officials who came from them—showed a certain attachment to the regime. The 'Royal Italian Freemasons', which was organized on uniform lines by the Grand Orient of Milan, played an important part in bringing all Napoleon's supporters together under the leadership of its high officials. As in France, Napoleon made the maximum use of decorations; giving the kingdom its own particular award—the *Ordre de la Couronne de fer*. But he attached supreme importance to the guards of honour which became one of the most characteristic institutions of the country, though he had hesitated to organize them in the Empire.

He needed officers, and was intent upon choosing them from among the aristocracy and the middle classes, to some extent as hostages, but still more because he considered the army to be a school for developing the civic and dynastic feeling that had so far been completely unknown among Italians. The coronation gave an opportunity for mounting some guards of honour; then on June 20, 1805, a decree ordered the formation of four companies of cavalry mounted for service at the palace. They were to be recruited on a voluntary basis from the midst of the families whose heads figured among the electoral colleges or the most heavily taxed citizens. As the right of finding a substitute was suspended in those *départements* that had not furnished contingents for guards of honour, the voluntary basis was purely nominal. The relatives had to pay a sum of 1,200 lire, and the young man could become a lieutenant at the end of two years. For the lower middle classes, a dozen companies of light-armed troops were formed, who paid only 200 lire and provided the non-commissioned officers. But recruitment for the guards proved not at all easy: although the obligation had been imposed in 1810, by 1811 there were only 367 of the required 551. They saw service for the first time in Russia. The light-armed troops were easier to find. Though Napoleon's expectations were not completely realized, he cannot be said to have completely failed. The influence of conscription could not but penetrate down to the people, although they had the least to congratulate themselves upon in the imperial regime. Neither the abolition of feudalism nor the sale of the national lands seems to have changed the condition of the peasants, at any rate in the plains, which continued to be a land of large properties cultivated by smallholders and day-labourers in wretched conditions. For the small proprietors, the weight of taxation must have made up for the disappearance of the tithe and the dues which the Republic had admittedly abolished without compensation. A comparison between the land registers of fifteen communes in the plains of Bologna drawn up respectively in 1789, 1804, and 1835, shows that the property belonging to the nobles had been reduced from 80 per cent to 67 per cent, and then to 51 per cent, whilst the property in bourgeois possession rose between these same dates from 17 per cent to 30 per cent, and then to 48 per cent. The figures show, however, that the large landed estates had held their ground; they still accounted for 72·01 per cent of the total area in 1835, as compared with 72·77 per cent in 1789.

At the other end of Italy, the French impress on the Kingdom of Naples was also very marked. Reforms began as soon as Joseph came to the throne, and were carried out by a group of Frenchmen and Italians whom he had selected—Saliceti, Miot, Dumas, the son of Roederer, and the lawyer Ricciardi. They first reorganized the ministries, creating two new ones, a Ministry of the Interior and a Secretary of State; then there was the Council of State and the *Sommaria*, or Court of Accounts. The provinces continued as such, but were divided into districts, whilst the parishes were grouped into municipal administrative bodies, on the pattern of the municipalities in the French constitution of Year III. The *préfet* and *sous-préfet* crop up again, but under different names, being now styled *intendant* and *sous-intendant*, and the *conseil de préfecture* the *conseil d'intendance*. The province and the district both had their councils, and the communal group came under a *décurionat*. But no electoral colleges were set up: the king nominated the *décurions* put forward by the *sous-intendants* and chose the members of councils from among the candidates proposed by the *décurions*. The law-courts and police were remodelled on the French pattern, and no time was lost in setting up an armed police force. The Minister of Finance was faced with a particularly tough task. He replaced the countless taxes of the *Ancien Régime* by a land-tax and a tax on industry. Privileges were all abolished. The State resumed control of indirect taxation, which had been farmed out. Steps were taken to liquidate the debt by means of I.O.U.s or *cédules* recorded in the Great Book of the Public Debt; and as these changed hands at a loss, they were quickly extinguished by redemption at the market price. By 1808, the debt had been reduced from 100 million ducats to 59 million. An important part of the revenue came from the royal domain, which took over the funds of the Jesuits, vacant bishoprics, and a good many convents that had been closed. This summary can give only a faint idea of the enormous task of unifying, simplifying, and cleaning up the administration undertaken throughout the country by the new order. The suppression of sinecures and corruption, the separation of justice from administration, the creation of public accountancy, the formation of a disciplined body of officials with a respect for the law—all these were much more of a novelty than in Piedmont or Lombardy.

The abolition of the feudal system—here much more oppressive than in Northern Italy—was decreed as from August 2, 1806. The barons kept their titles and their own land; but they lost their right to administer justice, and became subject to the common law, both for their lands and in their personal status. The question of feudal rights and dues was settled according to the principles laid down by the Constituent Assembly. Personal rights, the money-payments that represented them, and the seignorial rights were simply suppressed; real property rights were declared redeemable; and a feudal commission including Cuoco among its members was appointed to carry out the law. Furthermore, agricultural reforms were set in train by a decree of 1807. In this region, *maquis* and wasteland turned over to common use and seasonal pasture, covered enormous tracts; and it was decided to divide them up among the communities in proportion to their respective populations. Moreover, it was agreed to split up the cultivable common lands among the inhabitants, giving preference to those who had occupied some part of them, provided they had cultivated and enclosed them, on condition that they paid a reasonable rent. The State itself undertook to tax the Apulian Plain, which had been farmed out each year up till then; and the same was done with the property of pious foundations.

Just as Joseph was about to hand over his kingdom to Murat, Napoleon made an arrangement intended to tie the hands of his successor. Joseph, acting by his orders, promulgated at Bayonne on June 20, 1808, a constitutional statute modelled on the Kingdom of Italy, but reducing the part played by election and allowing the clergy and the nobility a special representation—a sign that the Emperor's political ideas had undergone some development. The Parliament was composed of a hundred members, divided into five benches, the first two—clergy and nobles—being the king's choice. Colleges—likewise set up by him—elected representatives for the owners of property; whilst the king chose representatives for the businessmen and *dotti* from among the list of candidates put forward by the colleges or bodies of officials. Only Neapolitans were eligible for public employment. Two days later, it was announced that the Civil Code would be introduced the following year.

Although Joseph's work had been by no means negligible, it remained incomplete, and to a large extent nominal; above all, he had hardly begun to organize the army. Murat's reign was accordingly a time of great progress. His Minister of Finance, Agar, Count of Mosbourg, continued Roederer's work. He finished reforming the tax on land, introduced a licence system, set up machinery for collecting indirect taxation and for the waterways and forests department, founded a royal bank, completed the liquidation of the debt either by entries in the Great Book of the Public Debt or by giving national land in its stead, and converted the interest on it from 5 to 3 per cent. On the appointed day the Civil Code came into force, but with some important modifications. It was followed by the codes for civil and commercial procedure and the penal codes, as well as the code governing mortgages, registration of births, marriages and deaths, the official body of notaries, and the order of barristers.

In 1809, Murat also confirmed the decisions of his feudal commission and gave some attention to economic life. Corporations and internal customs were abolished, a body set up for bridges and highways, and public works undertaken with considerable vigour. If it had rested with him, the kingdom would have put up barriers against French imports; and he was very half-hearted in applying the blockade. All the same, his efforts were mainly directed towards the army, the creation of which was really his work.

In the Kingdom of Naples, the ground had not been prepared by the Revolution, and the whole transformation took place in a bare seven years; nevertheless, it was a solid piece of work. When he returned to power, King Ferdinand did not re-establish the feudal system, nor did he abrogate the Civil Code. The middle classes and the few liberal nobles who had welcomed the French in 1799 showed that their feelings had not changed, and formed themselves into lodges, as in Northern Italy. Murat, with his liking for sensation and display, exercised a certain fascination, and roused some sympathy by taking such an independent line with France. But in spite of reviving entails, he did not succeed in conciliating the majority of the nobles or the clergy, for he failed to make a new *Concordat* and to reorganize the hierarchy of the Church. The people, for their part, were too poor to redeem the dues, and the crown lands passed into the hands of companies, or the nobility, or rich middle-class citizens. The legal arrangements for sharing out the common lands took some time to complete, and had hardly got under way before Murat's fall. The hill people who lived by grazing were very little concerned with these reforms. The only attention General Manhès showed them was to subject them to merciless oppression; besides, the coastlands were continually under threat from the English. The Kingdom of Naples, moreover, was not administered—like the Kingdom of Italy—by civilians, and according to the ordinary laws of the land; it was kept in a continual state of siege, and was governed on a military basis.

In Central Italy, Napoleon's influence was slower in making itself felt. In her principality, at Lucca, Massa, and Carrara, Élisa suppressed the feudal system, adopted the Italian *concordat*, closed the convents and confiscated their property, opened schools, and undertook public works. When made responsible for the government of Tuscany, which had been annexed to the French Empire, she was obliged to introduce French institutions, the management of which fell to a junta that included Gérando and Count Balbo, a Piedmontese who was destined to become famous. The two main operations were the suppression of the convents and the liquidation of the ducal debt. In spite of inevitable upsets, this modernization of the government did not meet with resistance in a country where enlightened despotism had had some of its more advanced representatives.

But the course of things was very different in the part of the Papal States that had been taken over. Here, the *Ancien Régime* was without doubt at its most backward, and it was completely transformed by an Extraordinary State Council, which was appointed on June 9, 1809, and sat till the close of 1810. Among its members Gérando and Balbo once more took part, along with Miollis. The territory was put under two *départements*, with Roederer's son and, at Rome, the comte de Tournon—formerly *intendant* at Bayreuth—as *préfets*. The management of the police was taken over by Norvins. Feudalism and the Inquisition both disappeared; and in 1810 the chapters were dissolved and the convents closed. The Civil Code had been promulgated as early as 1809; but the institutions that were indispensable for implementing it—in particular the *état civil*—never came into being. Nevertheless, the religious liberty proclaimed by it caused a sensation. The Jews left their ghettoes, and the imperial staff, as they had done everywhere else, formed themselves into masonic lodges. The finances received particular attention from the administration. They introduced the French system of taxation, except for the combined duties, instead of which they kept the tax on milling; they unified the debt at 2 per cent by repaying the capital at the rate of five times the interest by means of a new issue payable in secularized property. The creditors lost—in theory, at any rate—up to or more than three-quarters of the capital value. The *préfets* proved extremely active. Tournon reorganized the hospitals and prisons, took an interest in culture and set up cotton manufacturing under the management of the Alsatian Bocher. Napoleon also had great ideas for his second capital. He repaired its buildings, tidied up and lit its streets, and made plans for building quays, bridges, roads, and imperial residences. A commission for ancient monuments carried out excavations, and Canova was put in charge of a museum; and finally the Pontine Marshes were tackled, a quarter of the area being put back into cultivation. But nowhere did the new regime meet with such great hostility. The people were used to indolent officials, begging and brigandage; discipline, regular taxation, public accountancy and regularity, and more particularly conscription, were altogether against the grain, and there was not enough time to overcome the opposition. In the towns—and especially in Rome—the middle classes lived largely on the clergy and pilgrims; for them the departure of the Pope and his court, and the suppression of 519 convents with their 5,852 monks and nuns, were an irreparable disaster. In addition, thousands of inefficient and useless officials had been dismissed. The chief form assumed by the opposition was a refusal to take the oath. It was led by the clergy and followed by many officials and nearly all the lawyers. The Emperor replied by dismissals, removal of pensions, imprisonment and exile. It was the nobles who proved to be the most compliant.

In spite of these reservations, the application of the system in Italy made rapid strides, and only a few more years would have been needed to achieve full administrative and juridical unity. But conditions were infinitely less favourable in the Illyrian provinces. Geographically, they were cut up into isolated units; the country was everywhere mountainous and poverty-stricken, and the inhabitants differed from one another in language, religion, and cultural level. They were in bondage to officials of the *Ancien Régime*, the nobility, and the clergy, and there was no real middle class, apart from a few strongly Italian coastal towns. From 1806 to 1809, Napoleon only had possession of the former Venetian territory, that is to say Dalmatia and a part of Istria and the islands, to which was added in 1808 the republic of Ragusa, though it was allowed a degree of autonomy. Marmont held the military command, whilst the administrative power was in the hands of Dandalo, who had the title of *provéditeur*. He was a rich pharmacist of Jewish extraction who had taken up new ideas in the Venetian States. Although a man of integrity and a hard worker, he was dictatorial and touchy, and did not get on well with the commander of the occupying forces. There was never any question of setting up an electoral system in Illyria; and the result was an enlightened despotism, with the added incubus of military interference. Dandolo gave himself the help of a general council with a membership of his own choice. In actual fact, he made all the decisions in his office at Zara. Having first divided the territory into four *départements*, subdivided into districts and rural communities, he appointed the various delegates, vice-delegates, and *anziani*. He organized the law courts and set up a police by using the *pandours* whom the peasants already provided for the Austrian and Venetian administrators. The old taxes remained in force, attention being directed principally to the management of public funds and the administration of the State lands.

The chief reforms were aimed at the clergy. In order to reduce the number of bishoprics, vacancies were not filled; some of the convents and all the brotherhoods were suppressed; and apart from the existing bishops' revenues, all Church property was sequestrated, part of the income being used to provide rather better stipends for the parish priests and the seminaries. In 1807, Dandalo also issued regulations for public education, instituted a *lycée* at Zara, and set up some colleges. The work on the roads was undertaken by Marmont. Conscription had to be suspended because of the disturbances it caused, and the authorities had to rest content with partial and more or less voluntary levies. As to the Civil Code, it was considered enough to introduce the sections dealing with the family and succession, which allowed women to inherit and abolished entail and trusts. Nothing was done, it seems, to curtail the rights of the great lords who held sway over a tenant population—in the Poglizza region for example, near Salona—but ecclesiastical tithe was abolished. In the interior of Dalmatia, the agrarian problem came up in an unusual form. In 1756, the Grimani law had reserved to the Venetian State all ownership of the land; but the inhabitants—the Morlasques—were given two-thirds of a hectare a head (women being excluded), with the right to farm out their plots and leave them to their male heirs, but without the right of alienation. The beneficiary owed military service and paid tithe to the government. Dandolo repealed this law and conferred possession on the tenant, keeping the State tithe as a land-tax. In 1807, realizing that speculators were persuading the peasants to sell their holdings, he imposed certain formalities which made alienation almost impossible. In spite of everything, this was one of the most solid land-reforms in any of the countries held by Napoleon.

Up till 1809, then, this French possession enjoyed autonomy, and assimilation to France was only carried out with substantial reservations. But after that date there was a radical change in the situation. Carniole, Upper Carinthia, Austrian Istria and Trieste and a good part of Croatia were added to the Venetian lands and the whole was then given the title of 'The Illyrian Provinces', borrowed from the Roman Empire. Separate treatment was given to that part of military Croatia which fell to Napoleon, preserving its social organization in *sadrougas* and its State economy under the military authority, keeping it outside the imperial customs-system, and letting it still provide a contingent along traditional lines. On December 25, 1809, the rest of Illyria was given a provisional organization consisting of ten *intendances*, with Laibach as capital; and soon after this Dandalo gave up his position. It was not till April 15, 1811, that the regime assumed its final shape. Power was delegated to a governor—Marmont first of all, then Bertrand and in 1813 Junot, who was succeeded by Fouché. The governor proposed and the Emperor nominated the high officials who formed his council, in particular the general supervisor of finance and the general commissioner for justice. Six provinces were created, each under an *intendant* and their delegated officials. From now onwards, Napoleon worked ceaselessly to unify the government and the legislation. The whole Civil Code and all the French laws came into force as from January 1, 1812; law courts were organized, along with registration, mortgages, and an official body of notaries, but not complete civil status, although civil marriages had become the rule. From 1810 to 1813, the French taxes were introduced, except for the tax on doors and windows. The liquidation of the debt was continued with the help of the nationalized lands; and in 1812, the liquidation of pensions was completed. Conscription too had come into force on November 27, 1810. The Bridges and Highways Department, set up in the same year, used forced labour to push ahead with the road from Karlovac to Fiume and the route Napoléon from Laibach to Ragusa.

The ecclesiastical tithes had been generally abolished, and on April 15, 1811, the feudal system had been brought to an end. With the disappearance of the nobles' special status and the fief went all the personal seignorial rights; forced labour and land dues were made redeemable, the latter being reduced by a fifth to compensate for the land-tax which fell upon those who were liable for it. This decree was widely welcomed, and the peasants at last began to show some interest in French rule, if only to press for complete freedom. They took the lead and refused to redeem their obligations, till in 1812 Bertrand called upon them to submit and send down bailiffs. Discontent had also been caused by depriving them of their customary rights in the forests. The nobles, likewise irritated by these policies, had continued to emigrate to Austria. The lower clergy, who were used to the regime of Joseph, remained neutral; but the Franciscans, who had formerly been the masters of the country, raised a furious agitation. Unfortunately, it did not prove possible to revive the export and transit trade which provided the country with vital resources and formed the sole livelihood of Trieste, with the result that the middle classes suffered greatly, on top of their previous trials connected with the elimination of Austrian paper money and the liquidation of the debt on disadvantageous terms. The regime thus only succeeded in conciliating a small minority, and its departure was not regretted. No one believed, moreover, that it would last for long; and in fact the 1812 treaty of alliance promised to cede the Illyrian provinces to Austria in return for the relinquishment of Galicia.

In Spain, war conditions did not make it possible to apply the Bayonne constitution to the full, nor to carry out effectively the reforms planned by Napoleon during his residence there in 1808. The only exception was Catalonia. In December 1811 the military government under Macdonald gave way to a civil administration, though this was still subordinate to General Decaen. A decree divided the province into four *départements*, and in view of Napoleon's decision to annex it, assimilation with France went steadily ahead. This period did not last much more than a year, for Suchet was obliged to re-cross the Ebro in June 1813, which brought the country back to military occupation. Besides, the changes only affected the part effectively occupied by the French, who could only find a small number of *afrancesadas* to help them, who did not show much enthusiasm for the new measures. These did not run to extremes: the Church's property was not sold, and the clauses in the Civil Code dealing with divorce and the prohibition of trusts were removed.

HOLLAND AND GERMANY

Holland differed from Italy in possessing a strong national tradition. The upper middle classes had long held the reins of power, so that privilege and seignorial rights had considerably diminished. The Batavian Republic had already achieved unity. Napoleon remodelled the central government by the constitutions of 1801, 1805, and 1806, and Louis carried out certain complementary reforms. Up to 1810, this was as far as the Emperor had gone. As in Switzerland, he made no attempt to destroy autonomy in the interests of perfect assimilation. Nevertheless there were still traces of the *Ancien Régime.* Although corporations had been abolished in principle in 1798, it is to be noted that in December 1806 the Amsterdam municipality were discussing a scheme for the abolition of guilds. The Jews had been granted citizenship in 1796; all the same, the special tax falling upon them was not abolished till 1809. Though feudalism had disappeared, feudal dues and tithes were still in existence. There was a covert resistance to unifying the tax-system, and more still to reducing the debt which Napoleon wanted to achieve by declaring a partial bankruptcy. But after union, there was a complete change. Holland was definitely a separate government, in the hands of Lebrun, and was outside the Empire as far as customs were concerned; but assimilation went on as unsparingly as in Illyria. The Civil Code and all the French laws came into force as from 1810. By July 9, the interest on the debt had been reduced by a third. A decree of July 15 1811, ordered that the French taxes should be levied as from 1813 at the latest. As always, it was the land-reforms that produced most resistance and least success. In the end, it was agreed to maintain the tithe under the plea that in a secularized form it could be considered a kind of ground-rent; and Louis' Council of State—which had not been dissolved—pronounced against the redemption of dues on real estate.

Unlike Italy, Holland, and Switzerland, which had been occupied and partly transformed by revolutionary governments, Germany beyond the Rhine did not lie open to reform until after the war of 1805. Even if Napoleon had been completely in possession, the obstacles would all the same have been greater than elsewhere, for this country was large and diverse. As it turned out, what remained of Austria and Prussia escaped his authority in this respect; for the need to keep on good terms with his allies meant that he had to allow them to adopt only the parts of his system that suited them. Even in the regions ruled by him, circumstances did not always permit him to round off his work.

Parts of the conquered lands were not distributed until 1810. Bayreuth went to Bavaria, Hanau and Fulda to the Duchy of Frankfurt, a part of Hanover to Westphalia, the rest being finally annexed to the Empire, which also retained Erfurt. The provisional administrations made no changes in the previous system except for the abolition of serfdom in 1808.

The Grand Duchy of Berg, formed in 1808 from a part of the Duchy of Cleves, plus Duisburg, and from the whole Duchy of Berg plus Düsseldorf, Elberfeld, and Barmen, was then increased by certain territories taken from Nassau or mediatized. To this were added in 1808 the Prussian possessions of Westphalia, la Mark and Iserlohn, Münster, Dortmund and Essen, and the counties of Tecklenburg and Langen—900,000 inhabitants in all, constituting the first Napoleonic State beyond the Rhine. Murat, to whom it was handed over, ceased to summon the local diets and took on discretionary powers. He abolished collegiate administration, divided the country into *arrondissements*, each under a councillor, and set up municipalities in the towns. Except in the matter of customs, he made no attempt to unify the various lands constituting this State: he left them their own budgets and systems of accountancy, though everywhere he introduced the land-tax and the personal tax, and brought in conscription, which the King of Prussia had not dared to introduce. When Murat became King of Naples on July 15, 1808, the Grand Duchy reverted to Napoleon; and although he had made it over to one of his sons, Louis, aged three, he still continued to administer the country himself through special commissioners—first Beugnot, then from 1810 onwards Roederer. In 1808, he unified the administration, and the taxation was progressively remodelled along French lines. In 1811 came the turn of the law courts; and Héron de Villefosse set matters in order in the imperial lands that included mines, forests, and 600,000 francs' worth of feudal rents. Finally in 1812 the Emperor promulgated a constitution containing a

Council of State elected by notable people to be chosen by the government, though this did not take place till 1813.

Assimilation was therefore slow and incomplete. Little change was made from the old regime as far as the Church was concerned. Only the chapters were secularized; there was no Concordat, and not till 1810 did the budget contain some provision for paying the clergy. A university was planned for Düsseldorf, but only on paper; the sole institution to take shape in this town was the *lycée*. Legal and social reform were equally slow in coming. On December 12, 1808, Napoleon abolished serfdom and the personal dues and obligations for forced labour, and made real property rights redeemable. On January 11, 1809, he abolished fiefs and feudal customs. Privileges were swept away, and marriages between nobles and commoners were authorized; and finally on January 1, 1811, the Civil Code was introduced. The peasants protested against the maintenance of the land dues, and refused to pay them to their lords. They were encouraged by a certain bookseller at Dortmund, Mallenkrodt by name; but the law courts found against them, and in 1811 two peasants were sent on a deputation to the Emperor, and put into prison on their return. Napoleon was told of this and ordered an enquiry; but Beugnot intimated that this matter concerned the imperial lands, and the decree of September 13 1811 confirmed the preceding ones. Feudal rights properly speaking remained in abeyance without compensation, including the *tailles*, the *banalités*, the *retrait* and the *justices*; but real property rights remained redeemable. The peasants continued their obstinate resistance: nowhere else had they shown themselves so wide awake, which is easily explained by the annexed territory of the Rhineland; and nowhere else did the Emperor show such consideration for the local aristocracy—who thought themselves hardly dealt with and had no love for him—although this tenderness on his part was clean contrary to the advancement of French interests.

Taken as a whole, his policy in the duchy was in marked contrast to the abrupt introduction of the new system in countries like Illyria or Poland, though these were in fact much less ready for it. It is hard to say whether this was absentmindedness or negligence, or uncertainty about the future of the duchy. The inhabitants had been placed within the jurisdiction of the

Supreme Court of Appeal in Paris, which seemed to be a prelude to union with France; and they several times demanded this in the expectation of opening up new markets for their products. Their competitors in Aix-la-Chapelle and München Gladbach were equally vigorous in their protests, which were partly responsible for the ill-success of their requests. It would seem, all the same, that if Napoleon had intended to absorb the duchy, he would have pressed on with assimilation.

In the Kingdom of Westphalia, he behaved quite differently. There, the system was introduced in principle from the start, and was applied with unfailing zeal, so that it became the Napoleonic model State in Germany, as Italy was in the peninsula. Yet it was made up of very diverse regions—the Duchy of Brunswick, the Electorate of Hesse-Cassel, the Prussian territories of Halberstadt and Minden, Osnabrück and Göttingen (split off from Hanover)—not to mention other secularized or mediatized lands; there were 2 million inhabitants in all. On January 14, 1810, the remainder of Hanover was joined on to it, but it lost the northern part again on December 13. Even before Joseph had taken possession, a constitution was proclaimed on November 15, 1807, which had been submitted to a deputation of notables in Paris. They had been chosen by the aristocracy, and put forward requests, several of which were thoroughly characteristic, showing that in this essentially Germanic country, as elsewhere, the social question was a major preoccupation. They made reservations about the abolition of serfdom, insisting on the payment of some compensation, at least as a set-off against the real property rights; and they asked for the introduction of the Civil Code to be delayed, and for the continuance of majorats and entail. But Napoleon, as was to be expected, did as he pleased. The principles governing the modern State were laid down uncompromisingly: the union of the executive and the administrative, centralization, the separation of the judiciary from the executive, and a division of labour between these last two; civil equality, religious liberty, and finally a constitutional system. This was to include four ministeries, a secretariat and a council of State, with departmental colleges, nominated by the king, which would be authorized to put forward candidates for local councils and for justices of the peace, and to elect a legislative assembly of a hundred members, seventy from the landowners, fifteen from the merchants and manufacturers, and fifteen from the liberal professions. The administrative and judiciary organization was to be entirely on the French model, and so was conscription; likewise the Civil Code, with its natural corollaries—the abolition of privileges, serfdom, and corporations.

The government had been entrusted to a French regency including Beugnot, Siméon, and Jollivet. General Lagrange held the Ministry of War, and Jean de Müller the office of Secretary of State. But no sooner had Jerome arrived than he disrupted these appointments to find places for the various adventurers who followed in his train. This young man had a good deal of the light-opera king about him, and ran up a debt of 10 million francs, which increased the difficulties of the financial situation. Nevertheless the new system continued to be applied with persevering firmness. The French taxes—the land-tax, personal tax, licences, indirect taxes, and stamp duty—were all brought in, though not without consultation with the Legislative assembly; the debt was unified and consolidated; and a system of public notaries and mortgages was organized. Thc majority of the inhabitants were Protestants, and Jerome therefore found himself the head of a large part of the clergy, instead of their former sovereign. He made no concordat, but he took upon himself the choice of the Catholic bishops. The Jews were declared citizens, and given a consistory; the registration of births, marriages, and deaths was brought in, but the work was left to the clergy; and in 1810 the greater part of Catholic Church property, that which belonged to the chapters and the convents, was totally abolished, sequestrated and subsequently sold. There only remained the reform of the land. The constitution had only abolished serfdom and personal services; but even so, several laws were required to define the latter. The redemption of property rights was regulated by a tariff drawn up in 1809. In these regions, forced labour constituted the most oppressive part of these rights. These services were now fixed, so that no new ones could be created, nor could they be altered or sold. Nevertheless, the peasants often refused to fulfil them, and hardly ever consented to their redemption. The obligation to do so had to be repeatedly confirmed; and while waiting for them to make up their minds, the courts seem to have done their best to maintain the indivisibility of tenure, in spite of the Civil Code, in order to guarantee the payment of the dues and compulsory services. On the other hand the *préfets* were encouraged to press on with the partition of the common lands and the abolition of the rights of free pasture, in order to hasten the disappearance of compulsory rotation of crops, which had in theory been abolished.

The nobility suffered bitterly from the loss of their caste privileges; yet they consoled themselves to a certain extent when they were offered superior rank and employment, for not many Frenchmen came to this country, and German was freely used in the government services. King Jerome employed former Prussian officials—Bülow, a cousin of Hardenberg, Malchus, Schulenburg, and Dohm; Baron Wollfradt, of Brunswick, became Minister of the Interior; Strombeck was largely responsible for the introduction of the Civil Code; and the electoral colleges and the army were filled with nobles. As for the middle classes, it is at least clear that literature kept its position or accepted new office—men like Leist, Martens, Jacob Grimm—not to mention Jean de Müller.

The annexations of December 1810 brought a third German territory under Napoleon's control, consisting of the northern part of Hanover, the Hanseatic towns, and a quarter of the Duchy of Berg, plus a few princely possessions which were enclosed within them; and Oldenburg was added on January 22, 1811. The whole was divided into three *départements* under one common commission. As he did at the same period in Illyria, Napoleon set about a rapid introduction of the French regime and promulgated the Civil Code on December 9, 1811. The fiefs with their rights of succession, serfdom, personal rights, the lords' honorific prerogatives, peonage, seignorial rights, fishing and hunting rights—all these were swept away in one fell swoop, and with no compensation, whilst in Westphalia and especially in the Duchy of Berg the process had been several times reversed. All the same, annexation was too short-lived to have any deep effect on social relationships; and the advantages seem to have been less appreciated here than elsewhere, seeing that the strict application of the blockade involved a military government that was extremely severe in the suppression of smuggling.

In the other States of the Rhine Federation, Napoleon was not in sovereign control. The princes were very jealous of their own newly acquired sovereignty, and had only accepted a permanent alliance and protectorate through fear that Napoleon would keep the lands ceded by Austria, and so install a French *préfecture* in Southern Germany, as Mongelas remarked. Napoleon, on his side, had written their sovereignty into the act of confederation, and put off the convening of a diet until a general peace should be signed. 'It is not yet time to set up institutions,' he would say. Meanwhile, he had recourse to persuasion. At Milan in 1807 and at Erfurt in 1808 he made more or less definite overtures on the adoption of the Civil Code, and told his diplomats to recommend this step. He would hardly have been likely to obtain any concessions if the traditions of enlightened despotism and circumstances had not continued to persuade the princes to adopt at least a part of his system. His ideals were shared by Mongelas in Bavaria and Reizenstein in Baden. Besides, the largest of these States, suddenly increased by additions of varying origin—Austrian territory, Church possessions, mediatized lands, former free cities—was a chaos of differing institutions, privileges, and religious confessions that were as a rule mutually exclusive. It was important to fuse them together, and nothing seemed more suitable for this than the French methods. Finally, there was a need for the men and money indispensable for the creation of a strong army. This would satisfy Napoleon, serve to fight against him if he were conquered, and provide defence against the victors if they looked like withdrawing the benefits he had conferred. This is why the new States and those who had acquired most were, as a general rule, the ones that carried through the greatest changes; and this is also why constitutional government, which remained largely theoretical in France, was hardly at all appreciated, since it was repugnant to the sovereign rulers. Finally, the liberation of the peasants was left in the background or completely ignored, for enlightened despotism had never broken the past that linked the monarchy and the aristocracy, and Joseph II had paid dearly for his attempts to infringe it. In this sense, the States of Southern Germany, although they imitated France, continued to be more like Prussia, where the reforms strengthened the State, but dealt lightly with the aristocracy.

One might at least have expected that in the two principalities created from all the separate components on the Main—the Grand Duchies of Frankfurt and Wurzburg—Napoleon's influence would have been triumphant. In the former, it was indeed considerable, but amounted to nothing in the latter, although the former Duke of Tuscany, who had now become the Grand Duke of Wurzburg, was favourable to Napoleon and enjoyed his court. There can be no clearer evidence of the carefulness with which he felt bound to handle his German allies. Ferdinand, it is true, knew that he was protected by the treaty with Austria in 1809, and that as a Hapsburg he enjoyed some additional influence with the Emperor after his second marriage. Dalberg, on the other hand, owed everything to Napoleon. As coadjutor with the Archbishop of Mainz, he was the only one of the ecclesiastical electors to receive some compensation in 1803, in the shape of Ratisbon, the principality of Aschaffenburg, and the town of Wetzlar. In 1806 he became German primate and was presented with several mediatized lands, Frankfurt being the most important. He did not abolish the autonomy of these ancient free cities, but was content to appoint a commissary and reserve for himself the right to choose their senates from among the lists of candidates drawn up by the inhabitants. In 1810, he had to cede Ratisbon to Bavaria and accept Fulda and Hanau by way of compensation. It was at this point that he became Grand Duke, with Eugène as his prospective heir. His lands contained 300,000 inhabitants and Letters Patent of August 16, 1810, gave them a unified administration and judiciary, and the same system of weights and measures. It proclaimed religious freedom, abolished privilege and serfdom, and established freedom of employment by doing away with the corporations. Dalberg was a *préfet* of the eighteenth-century type, a sincere believer in 'enlightenment', and a supporter of Joseph; and there is no doubt that these principles seemed to him in accordance with reason. As a good Catholic and loyal German, he had witnessed with some sorrow the secularizations, and finally the end, of the Holy Roman Empire; but this worldly and ingratiating person was not disposed to make sacrifices; and both his tastes and his interests dictated a policy of making himself agreeable to the Emperor. He adopted the Civil Code in 1810, and the Penal

Code in 1812. Nevertheless, whilst appreciating the system, he was not passionately attached to it, and took pains to rule his subjects with a light hand, particularly those of his own class, the nobility.

And so in matters of detail the Grand Duchy of Frankfurt remained a good deal behind the Kingdom of Westphalia, though it is true that Dalberg's term of office was still shorter than Jerome's. The central government included a ministry occupied by Albini and Beust, a Council of State, and Estates nominated by electors chosen for life by the Grand Duke, and grouped into corporative colleges, as in Italy and Westphalia. The land was divided into four *départements* and given the same institutions and names as in France. The same was true of the communes, so that Frankfurt lost its senate and the remnants of its independence. But between the *département* and the commune the *Amt* or *baillage* continued in existence, combining administrative and judicial functions. Moreover, although new taxes borrowed from France, registration, stamp duty, licences, indirect taxes, and the abolition of privileges, brought about a certain fiscal unity, it was left to each of the regions constituting the Duchy to continue with its traditional taxes, its budget, accounting system and treasury. The Grand Duke's exchequer only took over the surpluses.

In 1813, a reform of the judiciary was undertaken. A Supreme Court was set up, with two Courts of Appeal and a civil court and a court of summary jurisdiction for each *département*; but seignorial justice still continued to preside over courts of first instance and official positions still kept their jurisdiction—a peculiar proviso that is probably to be explained by Dalberg's ecclesiastical status. In spite of the Civil Code, freedom of conscience was not recognized, for marriage in Church remained compulsory, and there was no advance beyond a degree of toleration. In 1807 the Jews had been allowed to become landowners and to carry on certain industries, though they were still confined to a special quarter, liable to a special tax and deprived of any right of citizenship. At Frankfurt, where they were many and wealthy, they managed in 1811 to obtain the right to redeem the tax, and in 1812 to become citizens; and those living at Fulda and Aschaffenburg also contrived to get rid of the tax in 1813. The financial services rendered to the

Grand Duke by the Jewish banks, particularly by the Rothschilds, no doubt helped to hasten their liberation. Amschel Rothschild and Oppenheimer were appointed members of the Electoral College at Frankfurt, and Börne became secretary to the Superintendent of Police.

Social reform remained still more incomplete. In conformity with the act of federation, those who had been mediatized kept their privileges, the nobility retaining not only their judicial and honorific rights, but also their fiefs and their private rights. In the principalities of Hanau and Fulda serfdom had been abolished by the Emperor without compensation in 1808. Everywhere else, its abolition, though decreed under the constitution, remained merely nominal, for the peasants were made to redeem all the dues connected with serfdom, and only a few communities decided to do so. As far as land-taxes and tithes were concerned, redemption was permitted on the ducal estates, and the sequestrated Church property, but no steps were taken for the manors. The *Conseil d'État* and the officials entered a formal protest, as a result of which the Civil Code was given a new twist, and peasant tenure was held to be indivisible as long as it remained liable to feudal dues.

Passing from Frankfurt to Wurzburg, we are met by an equally striking contrast. From 1803 to 1805, the bishopric belonged to Bavaria, who secularized the property of the clergy and introduced toleration, but continued to use administrative methods that had as yet been very little modernized. The Grand Duke set up a ministry and a Council of State under the leadership of Seufert. This was the only change he made in the Bavarian system. Administration and justice both continued to be indiscriminately managed by colleges; the old laws remained in force and the Civil Code was not adopted. Yet Ferdinand was not hostile to enlightened despotism: his lethargy is more probably to be explained by the wish to live at peace after the shocks to which he had been exposed, and to deal gently with the court of Vienna, whose outlook grew more and more unenlightened.

On the other hand the large States of southern Germany were profoundly changed by the inspiration of reforming spirits. In Bavaria, under the influence of Montgelas, reforms had begun before the Electorate became a kingdom, and even before the annexations of 1803. From 1799 onwards the powers of the various ministries were rearranged so as to unify the services, and a Council of State was set up. In 1802, the judiciary and the administration were separated; in 1805, the bureaucracy was reorganized, corruption, reversions, and bribery being abolished. Recruitment and promotion were thrown open to competition, and discipline was regulated. The powers of the State were on the increase. In 1800 it took on responsibility for fire insurance, municipal courts were gradually reduced or abolished, and in 1804 conscription was introduced. In 1805, a Public Education Office was added to the Ministry of the Interior. In this stronghold of the ultramontane outlook, Montgelas' Josephist policy was rigorously applied and caused a considerable sensation. Protestants were allowed into the family circle in 1801, and Maximilian married as his second wife a Protestant princess from Baden. In 1803, annexation brought freedom of conscience and worship to Christians of all confessions, with admission to public employment and permission to celebrate mixed marriages. In 1804, the schools became interconfessional in principle, and the Catholic Church more and more closely subjected to the secular power. The Mendicant Orders were suppressed in 1802, then all convents in 1803, the State taking over their property. Montgelas showed interest in the spread of 'enlightenment', making education compulsory in 1802, and the following year doing away with the censorship of books. If left to himself, he would also have abolished the corporations; but he had to be content with reducing their monopoly and abolishing the hereditary character of the master craftsmanship, except in Munich.

There was then no need for Napoleon to win him over. But he conferred on him the sovereignty of enormous territories, notably the Tyrol, which was quite untouched by reform; and the very fact of Napoleon's prestige speeded the course of the new regime. Its principles were summed up in the constitution of 1808, clearly inspired by the example of Westphalia. Bavaria, up till now the patrimony of the prince, became judicially a State with a public legal system. Its territory became indivisible, the royal succession unalterable; the royal lands became distinct from the sovereign's own personal possessions, and were declared inalienable. Once the civil list had been fixed, the court's expenses became a private matter, and could not fall to the charge of the public debt. Central power was definitely concentrated in the hands of five ministers, the collegiate system being discarded. Montgelas did in fact manage everything, for he had three departments under his personal control, and the projected ministerial conference never came into action. Nevertheless, the *Geheimrat* was reorganized and commissioned to prepare laws and be responsible for administrative justice. The ancient provinces were replaced by *cercles* administered by commissaries, assisted by a Chief-Chancellor and councillors. In each *cercle*, finance was separated from administration and placed under a Director. The large towns were given a *Polizeidirektor* nominated by the king, and an elective council and the other communes were allowed to put forward their candidates for the office of burgomaster; but both groups found themselves kept in administrative leading-strings. The organization of the judiciary was completed by the creation of courts of appeal and a supreme court, and by making the judges irremovable from office.

The State also turned its attention to Public Assistance and Public Health. Vaccination was made compulsory in 1807, thus setting an example for the whole of Germany. The first teachers' training colleges were opened, and in 1808 Niethammer organized a secondary education that included *Gymnasien* and *Realschulen*. The Bavarian Academy was remodelled, and a Department of Fine Arts was added; those universities that were retained were brought up to date. The religious edict of 1809 made the churches even more dependent, so much so that the Pope refused to enter into a concordat. Bavaria also made some progress towards economic unity. Internal customs disappeared, the State took possession of the postal services and imposed a single system of weights and measures. The great difficulty was to find money, for the regime's expenses were high. Direct taxation was extended throughout the territory, along French lines; the land-tax was reformed on the basis of a new land survey. This was undertaken by a statistical board which took on the mapping of the whole country; new indirect taxes were brought in, as well as a strongly protectionist customs tariff. The army went on steadily growing. In 1812 an end was put to the system of exemptions; meanwhile in 1809 the National

Guard had been introduced; and in 1812 the gendarmerie was remodelled.

The constitution also strengthened the power of the State by proclaiming civil equality and abolishing the *Stände* or orders, as well as privileges. As early as 1807 fiscal exemptions had been swept away; and with the *Stände* went the assemblies representing them. They had already lost the power to vote taxes in 1807. The constitution did in fact guarantee individual freedom, freedom of conscience and freedom of the press; it also brought in constitutional government and national representation; but in practice, the legislative body was not summoned, and the regime remained a police State with absolute powers, such as arbitrary imprisonment, a secret cabinet, a rigorous censorship of the papers, and a complete veto upon all associations. At least there was a strengthening of religious liberty. In 1808, the last restrictions on the Protestants were removed. By the edict of 1809 they were granted an official organization, the freedom to transfer from one religion to another, and the abolition of the compulsory contribution they had so far been obliged to make to the Catholic parish priest. In 1813, the Jews were granted freedom of worship on a private basis, but did not become full citizens.

Transported to the Tyrol, this ready-made system, with its despotic and centralizing features, produced an insurrection. From the Napoleonic point of view, however, it was far from perfect. In the lower stages, justice remained linked to administration, the corporations were allowed to continue, and although the French penal code was adopted in 1813, the full Civil Code was not, and each of the regions that made up the kingdom kept its own customary law. Montgelas, afraid that the Emperor might interfere, seems to have toned down his reforming zeal from 1806 onwards. Perhaps he also gave up all hope of breaking the resistance of the aristocracy, for whom the *Code Napoléon* would have been the last straw. According to the agreement, those who had been mediatized retained their fiscal, judicial, and honorary privileges, as well as their special courts. The nobles also succeeded in preserving a part of their special status. As in France, entails were brought in by royal favour to take the place of the trusts that had been suppressed. Moreover in 1809 women were once more debarred from succeeding to property held by the nobility. A register of the nobles was compiled, and their prestige strengthened by imposing certain obligations on pain of being struck off the register. Seignorial courts were regulated, but not abolished. But little was done for the peasants. In 1808, serfdom was abolished, without compensation, and the personal obligations belonging to it. The year before, it had been decreed on principle that compulsory labour could not be altered, but could be redeemed, and likewise the feudal dues, subject to the signing of a contract with the lord, which he could however refuse. From the social point of view then, Bavaria was behind the times compared with the other Napoleonic States; for though the balance between the aristocracy and the State had been upset to the advantage of the latter, they still remained allies. Peasant property was only set free in the secularized lands, and then only with the payment of compensation and subject to a redeemable tax. There had been more marked changes in the agrarian arrangements of the *Ancien Régime*, for in 1803 the village community, and the compulsory rotation of crops, had both been abolished, the common lands were to be divided, and the *Hof* or family tenure was allowed to be split up; but these measures were slow in bearing fruit.

Wurtemberg seems to have developed in a different and even more characteristic manner. The Duke—who had become Elector in 1803—continued till 1805 to quarrel with his *Landtag*, and could not therefore undertake any reforms. He had to be content with reorganizing his ministers, and appointing Wintzingerode as one of them, taking good care not to unite his recent acquisitions to his older lands, and governing them despotically, but introducing religious toleration. The *Landtag* demanded union, complained to Paris, and made common cause with the heir apparent. Frederick replied with a *coup d'état*; but the newly-elected *Landtag* refused to vote the taxes and appealed to Vienna, who gave a verdict in their favour. Passing through Stuttgart on October 2, 1805, Napoleon advised making short work of this opposition: 'get rid of these bounders,' he said—for the *Landtag* had incurred his displeasure by refusing the money and the men that France required. On December 30 Frederick, who had now become fully sovereign, abolished the *Landtag*. From this time onwards, he was able to transform his State. Between 1808 and 1814 he never relaxed his efforts: there were in all 2,342 rescripts and ordinances. Bavaria, on the other hand, which had carried out a good part of the work during the previous period, now gradually slackened the pace.

The new king, like his neighbour, felt the need for strengthening his power. But being of an autocratic character, and furious at having been so long resisted, he was passionately intent on governing in a despotic manner. His ministers were no more than clerks, and although he set up a Council of State, he hardly ever consulted it. Unlike Montgelas, he had no love for 'enlightenment', and so no respect for intellectual freedom or social progress. He therefore retained still more exclusively those elements in the Napoleonic system that were to his personal advantage.

Wurtemberg was divided into districts administered by *Kreishauptleute*, that is, *préfets*; but the king took it upon himself to nominate and keep control of the municipalities. The higher law courts followed the French pattern, and were not responsible for any administration. A *gendarmerie* was set up, and the police force was extended to a most unusual degree. The financial framework was rebuilt, the State took on a monopoly in salt and tobacco, and the land-tax was considerably increased. The State took over the post and the management of the schools, and brought the Churches under its regulations. Frederick was careful not to set up a constitution or give his subjects the smallest rights. The criminal courts were not even empowered to pass sentence: they simply gave their opinion, and the King made the decision. Emigration was forbidden, travel needed a special permit, and all meetings were prohibited. A strict censorship prevailed; the University of Tübingen lost its independence and was given a warden. Permission was needed to apply for entry, and students were given no choice over the faculties to which they were assigned. Espionage was shamelessly encouraged, and the population were systematically disarmed. From this time onwards Wurtemberg was more oppressively governed than the French Empire; it was in fact a Metternich regime.

The only reform to find favour was a certain religious toleration. By the edict of October 15, 1806, all Christians received some benefit. Jews were now allowed to own land and carry on a trade. Where the organization of society was concerned, Frederick was also careful not to commit himself to any principles, and though he unified the legal system, he did not adopt the Civil Code. The nobles were kept under strict control and had to pay taxes. They were partly deprived of their special courts, lost their trust rights, and saw their ranks invaded by a number of upstarts. Marriage was now authorized as between themselves and the middle classes; and from now on, everyone could own land. The property of the Catholic clergy was secularized. But the feudal system did not disappear: no change was made in the tithes, the feudal dues and the forced labour, the king being content merely to abolish personal serfdom. Nor was any hand laid upon the corporations. Thus unification, centralization, and despotism advanced more notably in Wurtemberg than in Bavaria, whilst the *Ancien Régime* continued to prevail in the social sphere.

In Baden, reform was still later in beginning. After the annexations of 1803, the property of the Catholic clergy was secularized and the convents closed (with a few exceptions). The old and the new territories were fused into three provinces, though the local ministry and administration did not lose their collegiate form. No resistance was met with: the government had no difficulty in depriving the mediatized towns of nearly all their powers, and in 1806 the Estates of Brisgau were abolished. Charles Frederick enjoyed a well-deserved reputation as an enlightened despot; but he was growing old, and his advisers were deeply divided, for his second wife, the Countess of Hochberg, wanted to make certain that her children would succeed to the throne in case those of the first marriage had no heirs. In the end, Napoleon plainly showed his impatience, particularly as he was very displeased with the Grand Duke's grandson, who was getting on very badly with Stéphanie de Beauharnais. In 1807, Dalberg's nephew introduced a number of new measures. He replaced the colleges by five ministers, set up a Council of State, and began to reform the finances.

But the radical measures were the work of Reitzenstein, who was of Bavarian origin, and—like Montgelas—a supporter of 'enlightenment' and the *entente* with France. He divided the country into districts, which amalgamated the annexed principalities, and took the municipalities under the government's wing. All the same, he did not push reorganization to extremes, perhaps through lack of time, for he was dismissed in 1810. The districts remained subdivided into *bailliages*, in which administration and justice were linked together. Conscription was also adopted, and—most important of all—the Civil Code, as from January 1, 1811, although certain modifications were introduced. Religious toleration had already come to Baden, and was extended to the Jews in 1808. The country was less hardly treated than Wurtemberg, but no constitution was introduced. Civil equality—a cardinal point—existed only in theory. To begin with, those who had been mediatized kept their privileges, as they did everywhere else, including the private courts, honorary and feudal rights, armed guards, and special family status; then the officials remained personally subject only to the superior courts, and the same advantage was accorded to the nobility, who were likewise exempted from the personal tax and from conscription. They managed to preserve the right to form trusts and entails; and in addition they contrived to have the land-tax on their estates reduced by a third. In the end, moreover, nothing was done to disturb the fief and feudal rights, nor the tithe, the dues, or the forced labour. As serfdom had disappeared at the end of the eighteenth century, there was not much change in the position of the lower classes.

Among the other members of the Rhine Confederation there was one who closely imitated France—the Prince of Anhalt, who ruled over 29,000 subjects. He gave these a *préfet*, a *préfet's* council and a departmental council and a court of appeal and district courts, not to mention a Council of State. He adopted the *Code Napoléon*, abolished privilege and seignorial justice, and did not fail to introduce conscription. Without displaying this amount of zeal, certain other princes made use of their advantages and showed goodwill. The most important of these was Louis I, Grand Duke of Hesse-Darmstadt, who hastened to abolish the *Landtag* and do away with fiscal privilege, except for the mediatized lands. He also adopted the Civil Code in 1808, though making some alterations in it, fixed the limits of forced labour, and put an end to serfdom, with due compensation. The Duke of Nassau likewise did away with exemption from taxation, serfdom, and a number of strictly feudal rights. In 1810 the Prince of Salm also made all his subjects liable to the land-tax. The other princes of Anhalt in Thuringia and Mecklenburg were satisfied with a few changes in the fiscal system and the recruitment of officials, but the *Landtag* and the social system continued as of old. Saxony too belongs to this category. Senft would have liked to take the initiative, but he did not have enough character to carry the day with the Minister of the Interior, Hopfgarten, who was firmly opposed to all innovation, as indeed was the *Landtag*. The nobility continued to enjoy exemption from taxation, and Calvinists were still excluded from toleration, which was only granted to the Catholics. The main attention was given to reorganizing the army, to which was added a gendarmerie. The case of King Frederick was somewhat similar to that of the Grand Duke of Wurzburg. He too was a faithful ally of Napoleon; but he was limited and apathetic in outlook, and showed no interest in reform, though he would perhaps have yielded to imperial persuasion. Napoleon did not press matters here any more than in Bavaria or Wurtemberg, because he was afraid of losing his goodwill. Yet in the Grand Duchy of Warsaw which he had presented to the Emperor, Napoleon saw no need for the same delicate handling, but proceeded to organize it with the freedom he had shown in the kingdoms of Italy and Westphalia.

THE GRAND DUCHY OF WARSAW

On July 22, 1807, at Dresden, Napoleon had given the country constitutional status. The central power, the administration and the judiciary were all based upon the French model. The prince was to nominate six ministers and a Secretary of State, to be joined later on by superintendents of public education, waterways or forests, food supplies, war, and State lotteries. At first the Council of State was no more than a council of ministers; but in 1808 it was enlarged by councillors and then by referendaries, and became considerably more important than in France, for it combined administrative justice with the powers of a supreme court of appeal. Besides, it came to play an increasingly important part in politics, for its members were the official representatives in the Diet and in the Chamber of Nuncios, and in 1809 it began to take part in governing the country. None the less, it remained true that in Warsaw the executive continued to be in fact of the collegiate type, and lacked effective guidance. The Grand Duke lived in Dresden, and did not exercise his right to appoint a viceroy. True, there was a president of the Council of Ministers, Stanislas Potocki by name; but he did not wield the influence of a chief of State.

The territory was divided into *départements*, districts and communes. The collegiate principle was abolished, and administration put in the hands of a *préfet* assisted by a secretary general and a *préfet's* council, a *sous-préfet*, and a mayor and municipal magistrates. The Grand Duke chose the *préfet* and *sous-préfet*, whilst the senior *préfet* chose the municipal members. In each area a council was set up, also nominated by the Grand Duke from among the candidates put forward by the *diétines*, or assemblies of the nobles in a *département* or district, or by the communal assemblies. The districts were given a Justice of the Peace, chosen from those put forward by the *diétine*; and the *départements* a court of permanent judges. There was a criminal court for each two *départements*, and a single court of appeal. Commissioners of police were also appointed. The French tax system was brought in forthwith and a court of accounts set up. Education benefited from the serious attention given to it, and it was put into the hands of local committees. The Catholic Church was placed under the authority of the State, for the constitution gave the Grand Duke the right to nominate the bishops. The command of the army fell to Poniatovski, and in 1808 conscription was brought in. Thus for the first time in history, the Polish State had a centralized administration and a body of professional officials. The latter were destined to provide the material from which the middle classes of the Western States had been formed.

This was an authoritarian government, as in the other Napoleonic States. Individual freedom was guaranteed by the constitution, but the police enjoyed just as extensive discretionary powers as in France. Not a word had been said about the liberty of the press. Nevertheless, the Duchy was given a Diet, though without the power of initiating measures, and only meeting for a fortnight, at the most every other year; besides, its marshal or president was appointed by the king. At all events it met regularly in 1809 and 1811. There was also a Senate of bishops and nobles appointed for life by the Grand Duke, whose sole duty was to see that laws were in conformity with the constitution, and a chamber of *nuncios* or deputies comprising, for each district, a noble resident—a landowner or son of a landowner—elected by his peers assembled in diet, and the representatives of the communal electoral assemblies, in which the peasant proprietors, the parish priests and the curates took part, as well as merchants worth 10,000 florins, officers, and soldiers who had received decorations. This diet differed in its constitution from the Italian or Westphalian assemblies, and was more like the one in Naples, though it was still more aristocratic in character. Although some part was played by professional and property qualifications, the distinction between the two *curias* still rested mainly on the preservation of the social orders. True, the deputies each had a vote; but the nobles held three-fifths of the votes, not to mention the fact that the communal assemblies could also elect noblemen. On the other hand the electoral system was more enlightened than in Naples or Westphalia, where the members of the electoral colleges were nominated by the king, and merely elected candidates. In Poland, the electors' rights were guaranteed by the constitution, and their elections were genuine elections.

Thus Napoleon was accustomed to take local conditions into account. Since the middle classes in Lombardy and Westphalia enjoyed a certain stability, he did not give the aristocracy special representation. In Southern Italy, where the aristocracy were much stronger than in the north, the case was very different; but as the Bourbons had stripped them of all political authority, they were only given an Upper Chamber nominated by the king. In Poland, the power of the nobility as compared with the insignificance of the middle classes was too great to give them anything but a dominant position; moreover, it was not so long since they had been the real masters of the state, and it was advisable, whilst putting them under the law, to give them a genuine liberty to shape policy, and liberty from which the commoners reaped some incidental advantage. Napoleon's efforts to get the aristocracy on his side were therefore more marked in this country than anywhere else. The result was that the nobility kept its specific identity and became the real controllers of the state.

This was by no means an advantage for the peasants. Whilst maintaining the privileged position of the nobility as a political institution, the constitution had proclaimed civil liberty and abolished serfdom. The Civil Code was promulgated on August 15, 1810, freeing the peasants from the glebe and giving them the right to go to law; but the land nevertheless continued to belong to the nobles, and the decree of December 12, 1807, pronounced all tenure to be precarious in default of a contract, which put the tiller of the soil in a worse position, for when his right of possession was for the most part hereditary or for life, he could not usually call anything except custom to his assistance. Feudal rights, land dues, forced labour, and tithe all continued to exist; and so did even arbitrary forced labour. Notaries were appointed and model contracts published in order to encourage fixed tenure, dues, and labour; but very few written agreements saw the light of day. The lord could use his right of eviction to maintain the existing burdens, or even increase them; and there is reason to believe that a good number of peasants cultivating only small plots took advantage of their new freedom and left the land. But as the country had no industries, this could only lead to economic and social unrest. The property of the clergy, however, was left untouched, and what had been secularized by Prussia was kept as part of the royal lands. In 1812, Bignon, who represented France in Warsaw, recorded: 'the condition of the peasants has hardly altered at all.'

In spite of this, the aristocracy were a prey to anxiety lest Napoleon should not call a halt at this point. The great families were even more annoyed because the level of equality for all land-owning nobles established by the political constitution, and the opening of the diet to commoners, seemed to strike a mortal blow at the authority that had hitherto been theirs. They nevertheless continued to hold the major offices of state or to fill them with their own protégés. The Czartoriski in particular, although remaining in the background, kept well informed about the various ministries, for Stanislas Potocki had married a Lubomirska, a niece of Adam Czartoriski's father, and Matuszewicz, Minister of Finances, was regarded as a supporter of the latter; and Niemcewicz, the secretary of the senate, and very hostile to France, continued to be his devoted servant. Nor was the opposition of the Roman Catholic Church by any means to be ignored, for it was paramount over the peasants. It had been deeply offended by the proclamation of freedom of conscience and worship, although it had been allowed to keep its privileged position as the religion of the State and had been given the management of all civil registration, divorced persons being handed over to the secular arm. Though there was little protest from the secular clergy, the reaction of the monks was very different, especially after the break with the Pope. The Benonistes—most of whom were German—were supported in their agitation by the nuncio from Vienna, and had to be expelled. The establishment of masonic lodges—there were a dozen of them by 1810 in the Grand Orient—was a further source of grievance. The Jewish question (which was at the same time a social question) gave the clergy an excellent weapon. There were no exceptions in the constitution, and Jews were therefore given the same rights as Christians. But this caused such feeling that in 1809 their political rights were withdrawn from them for ten years, with certain individual exceptions granted by the prince to those who paid a licence-fee. In 1808, they were forbidden to acquire land without authorization, and in 1812 to lease imperial domain lands or to sell beverages; and in order to keep down their numbers, a system of authorization for marriage was imposed upon them. It must be admitted that they seemed in no hurry to become assimilated; and in 1812 they were at their own request—we are told—given exemption from military service upon payment of a contribution.

EUROPEAN CIVILIZATION

It is clear then that in the *Grand Empire*, the Napoleonic system showed a significant division. On the one hand, the State reforms went steadily ahead: on the other, social reform dwindled or proved abortive. The increasingly marked favour shown by the Emperor towards the aristocracy makes it difficult to say what would have been the future course of his liberating efforts. All the same, he was so bent upon the Civil Code that once peace had been established on the Continent, we can well believe he would have taken the necessary measures to apply it to the full in every place. Thus it may be said that everywhere he strove to add administrative and social unity to political unity, and this was to form the framework for a new European civilization. This did in fact develop after his time, in the course of the nineteenth century, in spite of the counter-revolutionary reaction; but with a slowness, and with disturbances and distortions, that Napoleon might well have avoided. For the most part, the principles were in alignment with those of 1789, and that was what stamped this civilization as essentially French.

Outside the French Empire, Napoleon did not take any steps to add an intellectual culture for which the French language would have served as the vehicle. In the Kingdoms of Italy, Naples, and Westphalia, by far the majority of the staff were locally recruited, and Italian or German remained the languages used for administration and education. But the case was different in the French Empire. Thus in Holland, the decree of October 22, 1811, made it compulsory for the heads of private schools to provide, within a period of three months, instruction in French. As the annexations increased, so would the sphere of the French language have extended. Even at this period, it had come into use at the courts of the vassal kings and in the great Napoleonic administrators' offices. Knowledge of French was becoming indispensable for all who aspired to the highest levels of employment, and teaching was obliged to take this into account. It would not be right to suspect Napoleon of deliberately wishing to uproot the other dialects, any more than he had done in old-world France. But French would have come in alongside of them as the language of Continental unity. It would have served as a medium for consolidating classical culture all the more so as no other existed in the Emperor's eyes. There is no doubt at all that he intended Paris to become the intellectual, artistic, and secular capital of the European Empire, as it already was the political capital. He was intent on making it the world's museum by bringing to it the works of art taken from the countries he had conquered. In stark opposition to this conception of a universal civilization, surviving from the eighteenth-century ideal, looking back to the traditions of Rome, and inspired by the Catholic Church, stood the Romantic idea of national cultures of spontaneous diversity, and irreducible in nature, which were a fundamental denial of the oneness of the human race.

THE CONTINENTAL ECONOMY

Locked in combat with England, the European federation had as its symbol and its weapon the Continental blockade; but the blockade reacted on its economy, because it was reduced to living on its own resources. This way would, if successful, increase its strength by creating interests which would have been damaged by an English victory; and by the same token it might well undermine the economy if there was any failure to organize the Continental market so as to provide a livelihood for each of its members.

Wherever it was applied with some rigour, the blockade's effects were similar to those in France. The maritime cities and their industries were ruined. In the Mediterranean, there was first Genoa, then Venice and Leghorn, and finally Trieste. In this last port, the figures dropped from more than 5,000 ships and 208,000 barrels in 1807 to 2,600 boats and 60,000 barrels in 1812. In the north, the Hanseatic ports were the first to feel the pinch, followed by the Baltic ports, and lastly by those of Holland.

The trade of the great German fairs, fed as they were by contraband goods, became a precarious business, which meant that the blockade provoked the hostility of the shipowners, the big business interests and the banks. But in industry it was different: although the cotton industry found it difficult to get raw materials and other branches suffered from the ban on exports, local production was rather fortunate in being delivered from English competition; and the veto on exports acted as a stimulus. As in France, cotton spinning and weaving showed the most marked progress, although this was lessened by the importance of contraband. In Saxony, although results were on the whole less good than in 1805, they showed a 25 per cent improvement in 1810, and the production of printed materials rose sharply, increasing more than 50 per cent during this period. Switzerland, the southern part of Baden and even Northern Italy likewise took advantage of these favourable circumstances. Wool prospered too, for instance in Switzerland and Denmark. In Germany, the Silesian and Westphalian mines extended their markets; so did ironmongery, weapons produced in Thuringia, straw hats and brushes in Baden, and chemical products. The processing of sugar-beet also developed, especially in the Duchy of Frankfurt and at Magdeburg, and struck root in Holland and Russia. At a time when the spirit of enterprise was everywhere being stimulated by England's example, the blockade taught (more effectively than the theory or fragmentary practice of the Mercantile Theory in the *Ancien Régime*) how much it could be helped in its early stages by protective custom-duties. And after 1815, this lesson was to be well remembered. In this sense, it was in the interest of all the members of the Continental System to maintain a common front against British industry. All the same, not every member reaped the same advantage, for as one went east and south, agriculture assumed a growing preponderance, so that the blockade was especially favourable to France, and in the second place to Germany, Switzerland, and Northern Germany. Needless to say, the consumer did not share the industrialists' satisfaction; and the states themselves, seeing their customs-revenue diminish with the cutting off of English imports, shared the anxieties felt by the Emperor.

Hence it was not enough simply to produce at all costs: it was also a question of adapting the wheels of commerce to new conditions and redistributing markets so as to provide for the consumer and find new customers for the manufacturers who had hitherto exported overseas, such as the cloth-makers of Hanover and Silesia. And this was an extremely difficult task. The English market, with its control of the seas, underwent a natural growth, by virtue of the living impetus of productive activity. On the other hand each of the Continental regions naturally turned towards its particular coast, and the European market, though in theory unified by the blockade, tended in practice to be split up as it were by a centrifugal force. The proof of this was the persistence of the cross-country trade routes which had come into being across Central Europe since

France had been cut off by war. The Frankfurt, and more particularly the Leipzig, fairs continued to be well patronized, and as late as 1809 Trieste was still getting the produce of the Levant through to Bavaria and Saxony. From then onwards, the cross-country traffic tended to stretch still further east, along caravan routes from the Baltic to Leipzig, and from Salonica to Vienna.

On the other hand the really new feature was the advance of essentially Continental routes running from west to east. It may be said that the success of the blockade and the liquidation of the Continental System depended on the routes running north and south, thus bearing witness to the vitality of the maritime traffic and the dealers in contraband. Strasburg and Lyons were the chief centres where these trade-routes crossed. The former became the French depot for goods destined for Germany, Austria, and Russia, which were subsequently sorted at Leipzig. In return, the town also received goods from Frankfurt via the Rhine, and from Vienna, which up to 1810 sent it cotton from the Levant. But the transformation of Lyons' commerce was an even greater novelty, because Napoleon was completely master of Italy and had opened the Alpine routes. His first object was political and military. To begin with he concentrated on the Simplon in order to link up with Milan, and the road was finished in 1805. But as Piedmont had just been annexed, the main effort was switched to the Mont Cenis, which was completed as early as 1806. Work also went ahead on the Genèvre, which was of purely strategic importance.

As French rule spread to Central Italy, the Corniche road came into the picture; and in 1810, Napoleon decided to build it and extend it via La Spezzia and Florence towards Ancona and Trieste, but he never had time to complete it. Up till 1810 the Simplon, which had difficult approaches and was not easily controlled by the customs, was chiefly used by troops and travellers. On the other hand the Mont Cenis at once assumed great economic importance, and the pre-eminence of Lyons was largely due to it, for nearly all the Italian traffic went that way, amounting in 1810 to almost 3,000 travellers' vehicles, 14,000 heavy wagons, and 37,000 pack-mules. As Piedmont and the Kingdom of Italy had become to some extent colonies of France, buying her manufactures and sending her agricultural and textile goods, the industries of Lyons reaped the advantage, for the Mount Cenis route was used by the silk-trade. Illyria became important in another way, for in 1810 the Emperor made it the centre for the cotton caravans arriving from the Levant. Lyons then became the gateway for cotton, since Strasburg had been closed against goods coming from Vienna. The Mont Cenis route proved inadequate for the cotton trade, and when the Valais was annexed, the Simplon grew in commercial importance.

It remained to be seen whether these supply-routes would be able to carry enough to replace the coastal traffic, which was becoming more and more difficult. There is no doubt that it proved insufficient. France's system of waterways was still very incomplete, whilst elsewhere there were hardly any canals, and the rivers were barely usable. Even on the Rhine, the local tolls set up by the ordinance of 1803 had lessened the burden of the tolls payable for navigation, though they had not altogether removed it. Nor had the privileges controlling certain stretches been abolished, where transhipment had to be carried out for the benefit of certain porters' unions. Wheeled transport enjoyed great prosperity at this time, for instance at Châlons-sur-Saône, for goods being sent to the interior of France, and at Lyons, where the House of Bonnafour became one of the largest concerns of the time. But it was no substitute for water transport where heavy goods were involved; and even if enough vehicles had been built, there would not have been enough horses, and the roads would not have stood up to the traffic, for except in France and a few parts of Southern Germany and Italy they had no hard stone surface.

As there were already a good many centres of industrial production outside the Empire, the best plan would have been to give each of them a sphere of activity and divide the Continental market into customs-zones. The creation of large economic units would even have been an inducement to accept this concentration of territory. The Grand Duchy of Berg, for example, continued to ask for union with the Empire in order to draw on its custom; and Holland would have taken a kinder view of annexation if the customs-barrier had been done away with. Napoleon was in a master position for bringing about commercial unity in Italy; and Beugnot and Bacher repeatedly urged the setting up of a German Customs Union.

But there were various considerations working against, or at any rate delaying, this solution of the problem. In the first place, the vassal and allied states had to be humoured, for they were inclined to be jealous of their sovereignty, and would not have agreed to give up their autonomy in customs. As Napoleon's institutional reforms and military needs were expensive, it was difficult to cut down their resources, and they even put up their customs-tariffs. Territorial arrangements were in a state of constant flux, so that conditions for doing business and exchanging products became worse rather than better. A number of regions naturally belonging together or linked by their histories found themselves cut off from each other: for instance, the Kingdom of Italy from Dalmatia and Istria, from Novara and from Piedmont, from Genoa and Leghorn. Switzerland was cut off from Italy, from Genoa, and from the Black Forest; the Tyrol from Italy and from Austria, and Illyria from Hungary and Vienna, although Fiume would have seen to the matter of transport, and so would Trieste in 1812. The Grand Duchy of Berg, strangled between the French Empire on one side and her German neighbours on the other, was in a pitiful plight. Her sales fell from 55 million currency in 1807 to 39 million currency in 1810. Trade agreements would have provided some relief, but Napoleon did not encourage these, for he wanted to keep all the profits for France.

The reef on which his European policies were wrecked was, to be sure, his failure to see the European market as a thing in itself, and not simply with reference to the French Empire. 'France comes before everything else,' he wrote to Eugène in 1810. Having conceived and planned the Continental System, he would not deviate in his own territory from the Mercantilism he had espoused in the days of the *Consulat*. His frontiers remained strictly closed against allies and vassals, no less than against the English, even for the Swiss or the inhabitants of the Duchy of Berg. In order to avoid all rivalry with his own producers, he even refused to annex the Duchy and kept Holland and North Germany out of the Empire as far as customs were concerned, although he had joined them to France politically. On the other hand he did his utmost to impose against all nations preferential tariffs that benefited his own subjects, and succeeded as far as the Kingdom of Italy and Naples were concerned. This attitude of his can be explained by the position of France. Being the most industrialized of all the Continental peoples, she suffered most of all from the blockade and the war. She had lost both the colonial and the English markets, and then Spain in 1808—Spain, her best remaining customer; and it was from this time onwards that Napoleon made every effort to keep his hold on Italy. France was the heart of the system, and at all costs he felt he must preserve her from economic collapse. Yet political considerations once again saved him from pushing this policy to extremes. He took no steps to prevent the people of Saxony and the Swiss from getting possession of the German market; and at Leipzig fair, France only sold the highest quality goods. On the other hand, he kept a close hold on Italy, where he reigned supreme. In this way he contrived to get a share of the chief three industrial regions. Moreover, pressure from the inhabitants of Lyons made him determined to hold on to this private preserve, and he proceeded to erect progressively a series of impassable customs businesses around the Kingdom of Italy, except on the French side. In 1808 he forced her to accept a commercial treaty, and in 1810 arrogated to himself the sole right to import cotton goods and cloth; he put a tax on the export of raw silk to Austria and Switzerland so as to give Lyons a monopoly; and he insisted on her giving free passage to cotton from Naples and from the Levant, as well as allowing transit between France and Illyria. The Kingdom of Italy bought 43 million worth of goods from France in 1810, and 82 million in 1812, mostly cereals, flax, hemp and silk—73 million in 1810 and 92 million in 1812. But she does not seem to have fared as badly as has sometimes been suggested, for her balance of trade remained favourable. France did not ruin her industries; she simply took the place that had previously been held by England. As she was only in a position to supply her with high-priced goods, local production still provided for the bulk of the population. Nor did Napoleon refuse her all opportunities for improving her own industries. True, he would not send her qualified workers, but he allowed her 200,000 francs for buying spinning machinery. But the country's industrialists only had cause to remember this one fact—that a blockade could have been useful to them if France had not pocketed all the profits. And there was a louder chorus of complaint from those who were the chief sufferers.

Although Industry was in favour of the blockade, especially where the outlook was progressive, this approval was not without serious reservations, particularly with regard to the hindrances to free trade inside the Continent, which the Emperor was accused of maintaining and even reinforcing in the sole interests of France. In agriculture, the problem seemed insoluble. It concerned especially Prussia, Poland, and the Russian provinces bordering on the Baltic, who could find nobody to take the grain surpluses they formerly exported to England. Norway, with her constant demand for imports, was the only country who might have provided a market, but she was inaccessible by land. These countries' timber would have been acceptable in the West, but it was hardly possible to export it without ships. Napoleon himself found it difficult to dispose of his wines and brandies, and in good years he also had too much grain on his hands. The peasants only sold sufficient to provide for local consumption, so this disadvantage must not be exaggerated, for it only applied to a small number of big proprietors among the nobility and large-scale farmers; yet these were influential people, and the fact remains that the blockade tended to depress agricultural prices and rural purchase-power, thus injuring the industries that in other respects benefited from it. The imperfections in the Continental market, the poor economic tone, and the fiscal deficit that resulted from them finally decided the Emperor to reorganize the blockade and to ease it for the time being through a system of licences. However urgent his motives, the effect of this alleviation was nevertheless to revive the centrifugal tendencies that were undermining the system. By closing his ports to the Continent whilst opening them to the Americans, Napoleon gave some justification for the accusations levelled against France for her selfishness. Her allies and vassals claimed the right to follow her example, and Russia gave the lead.

To strengthen the European federation by setting up a single market that was relatively independent would obviously be a long-term policy requiring years of constraint. The first obstacle to be overcome arose from the fragmentation of the lands concerned and the interior customs that went with it; and it was the business of the *Grande Armée* to put an end to these conditions. But in face of world opinion, England had the advantage of being able to show that the Continental System in all its forms was based upon a military dictatorship.

THE CONTINENTAL SYSTEM AND NATIONALITY

The continued existence of the Continental System depended on the campaign against Russia. As a rule, Napoleon would concentrate his attention on the next victory. The rest would follow of its own accord, and would largely depend on circumstances. He therefore had no hard and fast plans for the future of a European federation. All that can be said is that from 1810 onwards he laid more emphasis on the Roman character of the Empire. In the Eternal City, which had now become his second capital, his successors would henceforward be anointed before the tenth year of their reign. He wanted to take Marie-Louise there himself and have her crowned, and preparations for this great event were under way. The Pope would live either in Paris or Rome. Some time or other, Pius VII would be succeeded by a pontiff who would accept this new Babylonish Captivity. As to what would then follow we can give free range to our imagination. After Alexander's army had been destroyed, we could picture the rebuilding of Poland; the creation on Russian soil of new principalities intended to protect this resurrected State; the expulsion of Bernadotte in favour of some reliable successor; the reorganization of Germany; the submission of the Iberian Peninsula; and the conquest of Constantinople, to become the third capital of the Empire. Peace on the Continent would then seem to have been secured, and European civilization as Napoleon conceived it would have made a steady advance.

Attempts have been made to reconcile this extrapolation with the nationalism that was so characteristic of the century, suggesting that Napoleon had planned to transform the Continental System into a society of sovereign nations forming a voluntary association. Certainly the cosmopolitan civilization he envisaged was far from being opposed to such an ideal; but the unity created by conquest was diametrically opposed to the free union of peoples which the Revolution in its early stages looked forward to as the crowning of its endeavours. This illusion can however be explained if we note that Napoleon, ever eager to convert to his own use the forces he found at work, took good care not to neglect national feeling whenever it suited him for the moment. It was to this force that he owed his power in France; and although he sacrificed his country's interests to an Imperial dream, Frenchmen always looked upon him as a national leader, for their interests could no longer be separated from his. Moreover, he carried on the work of the Revolution in strengthening France's internal unity by centralization, by military service, by the wars that fostered a sense of unity in face of the foreigner, and by the victories which exalted the feeling of collective pride. Outside the French Empire, he showed much greater reserve. Though the Poles could not accuse him of treachery—since he never positively promised them anything—he took advantage of their patriotism and there were clearly certain further considerations behind his actions when he first wrote the name of Italy into political geography, revived the name of Illyria, and gave official status to the Slovene and Croatian languages.

Moreover, it can be maintained that his system of government and his policies both tended strongly to advance the cause of nationalism. Although he did not complete the territorial unity of Italy and Germany, he enormously simplified the map in both of them; and he brought a part of the Jugoslavs together—something that had not happened since the fourteenth century. Nor were his reforms less important. By abolishing provincial autonomy, privileges, and feudalism, and replacing them with a central administration, civil equality, and a unified internal market, he created the essential conditions for the expansion of political nationalism. In this sense, he must count as one of the creators of several modern states. But these were consequences he did not intend: a statesman's actions always involve repercussions that were not foreseen by him, and in this respect the Emperor was not above his fellows. It may be replied that he intended Italy to go to his second son, and that it would have been imperative to set up large territorial units in order to administer an empire stretching across the whole Continent. All the same, it is clear that the linking together and the division of its sections among the members of his house had no necessary connection with independent nationalities.

The fact is that, having no contact with national aspirations either in its monarchical or its revolutionary form, Napoleon had no love for it, and even distrusted it. He realized that patriotism in the home country gave the nation an awareness of its own permanent interests and a certain dignity over against its leader, however popular he might be, and a certain impatience with self-centred despotism; and he knew these forces might one day work against his personal power. So he did his best to replace them by 'honour', and individual attachment to his own person and dynasty. It was more important still that this disposition should prevail in external affairs, and from his point of view he was right: nationalist feelings were still more incompatible with the Imperial concept than with despotism; and it was in these feelings that despotism encountered its most formidable foe.

CHAPTER EIGHT

The Independent Forces

THERE WERE OTHER forces—social, spiritual, and economic—in action alongside the genius of Napoleon, combining to help or hinder his work. He was creating a method of government and a society where the revolutionary effects of setting free the forces of individualism blended with the traditions of enlightened despotism, the restoration of a social hierarchy inspired by the *Ancien Régime,* and the fashioning of a new legitimacy. The former dynasties and the old aristocracy would not allow themselves to be dispossessed; the middle classes claimed their freedom; and the nations resisted his attempts at a universal monarchy. Intellectual life, too, preserved its autonomy. Lastly, capitalism continued its advance, and tended to hamper Napoleon's enterprises in more than one respect. It is possible that these forces would have been overthrown or at least kept in check if the *Grande Armée* had not been suddenly destroyed; but the historian can only record that after 1812 they triumphed over the shattered Continental System and continued to dominate the nineteenth century.

THE CONTINENTAL STATES OF THE ANCIEN RÉGIME

Outside the Empire the Napoleonic system came into collision everywhere with the obstinate resistance of the aristocracy, who saw in it a revival of revolutionary egalitarianism. Napoleon offended them by abolishing seignorial power and reducing the nobleman to the level of the subject who tilled the soil. In vain did Napoleon spare the nobility in the vassal states at the expense of the peasants: the nobility merely thought that he was waiting for a more favourable moment to strike. In vain did he establish a hereditary nobility: it only resulted in the *parvenu* rubbing shoulders with the *ci-devant*—and that was intolerable. 'These people are forcing us down to a lower level than dirt,' the comtesse de Voss wrote in 1807; and in the eyes of Wellington and other noble lords Napoleon was never anything else but 'Bony', and the King of Rome was his bastard. The kings too were full of the same haughty pride. Deep down in their hearts they could not admit the legitimacy of a man who had unceremoniously unseated so many of royal line. Moreover, they were afraid of the nobles, and when they felt themselves threatened by Napoleon, they were all the more disposed to retain their services. They also feared that any lowering of the nobility's status would encourage a spirit of insubordination. Nevertheless, the power of the State in France was a constant allurement to them, and persuaded them to adopt certain modifications. Their attitude depended on their intelligence and more particularly on their *entourage*. But whatever novelties were adopted, they had to be consistent with preserving the aristocracy. It was this feature that distinguished the Prussian reform—the only one that succeeded—from the Napoleonic system. Thus the gulf created by the Revolution continued to exist, whatever Napoleon might do: in the eyes of Europe, he was still the soldier of the Revolution.

In Prussia, after the dismissal of Stein, the work of renewal had been concentrated particularly on the army. Scharnhorst had far exceeded the fighting forces that had been contracted for, especially in the country; and additional reserves had been formed with the help of the *Krümper*, and by making use of soldiers given six months' leave, as was customary, in order to train the young generation in the parishes. In 1811, on the pretext of improving the fortifications, he called up the pioneer corps, who in fact spent their time in drilling. It became clear that there had been real technical progress. The army was divided into six corps. Efforts were made—with only relative success, it is true—to accustom the infantry to fighting in skirmishing order; baggage was reduced and tents done away with; the artillery was reconstituted and its equipment renewed, and the necessary requisitioning plans made for the commissariat. All the same, Scharnhorst did not succeed in creating a really national army. Although exemptions were cut down, and corporal punishment abolished in order to make the army appeal to the middle classes, the king refused to decree compulsory service or to set up a militia. Though would-be officers —the *Portepee-Fähnriche*—were obliged to take an examination, and non-commissioned officers were not barred from rising to lieutenant, the nobles' monopoly—apart from certain exceptions made by the king—was in fact confirmed, because officers were authorized to recommend their own candidates for vacancies. Three schools were opened for training the *Fähnriche*, but the cadet schools reserved for noblemen were still kept in being; moreover, the officers were granted a corporate court of honour, and so remained very much a closed aristocratic caste. At least, Scharnhorst was able to form at the General Staff Headquarters, and at the Military Academy, a High Command that was less notable for its technical ability than for its unity of spirit, readiness to take the offensive, and the subordination of all to the common good. As for William de Humboldt, who was recalled from his post as ambassador in Rome in December 1808, to take command of education and the control of the churches, he only held this position for a year and a half. His main task was to create the University of Berlin, which had been projected ever since the loss of the University of Halle. He assembled a famous group of professors —Fichte and Schleiermacher, Wolf, Savigny, Niebuhr, Bückh —and so gave it a prestige that brought great advantages to Prussian policy.

The administrative and social reforms were only resumed after Hardenberg's recall on June 4, 1810. He had himself appointed chancellor, thus at last providing a head for the central government. But this dissolute opportunist did not inspire confidence in all the patriots; yet though he mistrusted the hotheads and the secret societies, he was at one with them in his aims, and had a secret interview with Stein in Silesia. He was much more sensitive than the latter to Napoleon's example, and did not have the same respect for the aristocracy.

As early as 1807, he was saying that Prussia too needed a revolution, but a revolution from above; and he would gladly have taken the kingdom of Westphalia as his model. And so he aroused much more indignation than Stein, and his reputation today does not stand as high. Finance was his first consideration. Although the Trianon tariff and the seizures that followed procured him 12 million thalers, he had to find further new resources. He did not even dare to keep the *Einkommensteuer* in Eastern Prussia, but confined himself to increasing the stamp duty on October 27, as well as the consumption tax on meat, and to extending the milling tax to the lowlands. But he used the occasion to take away the lords' feudal milling, brewing, and distilling rights. He also planned to carry through the agrarian reforms, particularly as there were still disturbances in Silesia. In 1807, it had been necessary to call in the French to restrain the peasants, and there was a new insurrection in 1811. Hardenberg wanted to abolish feudal dues and forced labour, proposing in exchange that the lords should be freed from their obligation to provide aid and protection. The customary rights and the *Bauernschutz* would also disappear, and there would then be nothing to stop a full redistribution of the land, the suppression of compulsory rotation, and a sharing out of the commons. In order to arrange the *Regulierung*, the peasant's obligations would be set against those paid by the lord. If there was a credit balance, the peasant would pay it by giving up a part of his tenure or by paying rent. It was clear that this system, which was in force during the nineteenth century not only in Prussia but in the whole of Eastern Europe, would more or less reduce the peasant to go on working as a day labourer in the service of his lord, and would keep him in a state of subjection. Yet in principle, the State would be the one and only master, and Hardenberg even considered taking the right of policing, if not the right of meting out justice, away from the *Junkers*. In 1812 he borrowed the French *gendarmerie* system and in each district set up a superintendent of police nominated by the king.

Foreseeing that there would be vigorous opposition from the aristocracy, he sought to get support from public opinion. Moreover, like the patriots, he thought that the nation should have a part in the government. To begin with, he was satisfied with an assembly of notables chosen by himself, sitting from February to September 1811. The Junkers, led by Marwitz, protested vigorously: they did not want popular representation, and demanded a return to the Provincial Estates, where they were the sole representatives—apart from a few from the middle classes. The king had to submit, and arrested Marwitz and Finckenstein. It was a straight social conflict. The king could certainly create nobles, as Marwitz observed, but he could not create noble minds and spirits. And as York was to exclaim in front of Prince William: 'If your Highness robs us of our rights, on what then will your own be founded?' The nobles of the Mohrungen district would protest, in 1814, against 'the poisonous influence of French legislation'. Nevertheless, in 1812, an Elective Chamber was called together, comprising two nobles and two deputies representing the towns and the countryside, chosen by the landowners in a two-stage election. This assembly asked for a constitution; but as in the previous one, the nobles were predominant, and their recriminations forced the minister to temporize. The *Regulierungsgesetz* of 1811 transformed the *lassites*, who only enjoyed a right of user on the land, into owners, and abolished their dues and forced labour obligations in return for a relinquishment by the lords of a third of the hand held, if tenure was hereditary, and of half, if the tenure was for life for a limited period. Seignorial protection, feudal customs, and the *Bauernschutz* were of course still in abeyance, without any compensation for the peasant. The law was so burdensome that it did not affect the obligations of the hereditary tenant proper who could prove a title—the *Erbpachtbauer* or the *Erbzinsbauer* (quit-rent tenant). But the Junkers did not like it any the more; and as early as 1812, they began to discuss possible restrictive amendments. In 1815, the law was suspended, and in 1816 annulled as far as most of the peasants were concerned.

The attempts at restricting the seignorial rights of policing were equally unsuccessful. On September 7, 1811, Hardenberg had already done away with the milling-tax in the countryside, restored their feudal rights to the nobility, and fallen back upon direct taxation, capitation fees, taxes on capital and income, and finally licences. This last, which was taken over from France, at any rate involved the abolition of the corporation monopolies. The Junkers' privileges were left intact. They kept their rights of succession and trusts, their powers of justice and patronage, their hunting rights and their fiscal exemptions. Thus Prussia remained very much behind Western Germany, the unity and centralization of the State having only made a very moderate advance. The aristocracy still kept their privileges, and the emancipation of the peasants was little more than nominal. In several respects there had been more modernization even in the Grand Duchy of Warsaw.

Russia, however, had changed still less. After the Peace of Tilsit, Alexander recovered his liking for reform, the war having shown him that the machinery of government called for improvement. From the very outset, the French alliance revived the memories of youth and his taste for liberal catchwords. Although Spéranski had been more definite in his plans and more determined in action than the *comité des amis*, nothing much was left of his efforts. This son of an Orthodox priest, who has gone down in history with the surname given him in the seminary, was a distinguished preacher and professor. The Kourakines had introduced him into the Chancery, and he had then become Kotchoubey's right-hand man in the Ministry of the Interior, entering into direct relationship with the Czar in 1806 and going with him to Erfurt. When they came back Alexander asked him to draw up a constitution, and in 1809 accepted it in principle. The Empire was to be divided into *gouvernements*, *arrondissements*, and *cantons*. The *canton* would have a *duma* elected by the landowners, which would in its turn nominate a directory and a delegate to the *arrondissement duma* —and so on in succession, up to an imperial *duma* which would vote the laws and the budget. There would be a ministry responsible to it, with executive power; and each district would have an elective court supervised by the Senate. The Czar would also appoint a consultative Imperial Council.

This scheme owed something to British influence, for Spéranski had married an English clergyman's daughter, and showed early signs of great admiration for British institutions. His plan originally involved setting up a Parliament with two chambers, one of them representing the landed aristocracy; but he soon realized that the Russian nobility had neither the independence nor the ability of the English lords. All the same it would appear that the territorial divisions he had in mind, the administrative organization and the election of judges, together with a Council of State and ministries, showed that French influence was also at work. It is therefore all the more remarkable that his social reforms were not even honoured with a trial. There was no question of emancipating the serfs, and although the merchant class were not given the power to buy land, the landowners with the right to elect were nearly all nobles. Alexander decided to adopt this plan by stages. In 1810, he set up the council, and in 1811 the ministries. Spéranski became Secretary of State, and required all candidates for public service to have university degrees and to pass an examination. This completed the official machinery, and the result—which was far more on the Napoleonic than on the English model, and more in keeping with Russian development—was all that survived of Spéranski's plan. Although Spéranski had done nothing to impair the nobles' privileges, they viewed him with suspicion, knowing that he was preparing a legal code and a new law for the Jews. He made himself unpopular in his efforts to repair the Empire's decaying finances by increasing taxation and planning an income tax that would not have spared the privileged classes. In Prussia, as in France, the aristocrats put these innovations down to French influence; and when there was a threat of war, he was accused of treason because in obedience to the Czar and in furtherance of his 'secret', he kept up a correspondence with Paris. Alexander needed his nobles in his stand against Napoleon, and therefore sent his friend into exile on March 29, 1812.

When Joseph II came to the throne, his complete change of policy won the admiration of the reactionary aristocracy, for Francis I, who had been equally limited and obstinate in outlook, had refused to contemplate the slightest change in anything at all. All that was left of the Napoleonic regime in Austria was the repression of free thought and speech and indiscriminate power for the police; but these had not been borrowed from outside, and Napoleon, who was not riddled with bigotry and obscurantism, seemed in comparison to be a liberal ruler. The Austrian administration continued to be wholly occupied with finance. In order to pay the war indemnity, it had been necessary to pledge the crown plate and raise forced loans; and even then, there were still 17 million owing in 1811. His son-in-law granted a further respite, and when the King of Rome was born, he was satisfied with undertakings to pay which were not given him till July 4, 1813, and not one penny of which he ever saw. To cover internal expenses, paper money was printed. On February 20, 1811, Count Wallis, successor to O'Donnell who had died in harness, proclaimed a state of bankruptcy. He exchanged notes for a new issue at a fifth of their value, but the new ones soon went down heavily. The Hungarian Diet protested so vigorously that it had to be dissolved; and—clean contrary to the constitution—a dictatorship was set up.

The struggle against France thus never lost its social character. With Napoleon's so-called allies, the *Ancien Régime* aristocracy carefully kept its dominant position, knowing that it was doomed for certain if the Continental System was successful; and the Emperor's downfall was celebrated as a personal triumph. The Holy Alliance was turned into a kind of insurance against the middle classes and the peasants. From now onwards, Austria was the obvious country to take the lead in it.

THE ANGLO-SAXONS AND LIBERALISM

Confronted by a despotic Continental regime in Europe, the Anglo-Saxons held fast to their own traditions. In England, the Tories no longer protested against the parliamentary system. The suspension of *habeas corpus* was not renewed—except in Ireland—and the acts of 1799 were applied with some degree of moderation. As the disciples of Pitt, the Tories had borrowed largely from the eighteenth-century Whigs. They took their stand on the Established Church, but they none the less gave short shrift to any dissidents. They threw open the peerage to upstarts and distinguished soldiers, were lavish in handing out decorations, and wisely welcomed the upper middle classes into the ranks of the old aristocracy. Their social policy was in fact not unlike Napoleon's, for it aimed at keeping a hierarchy, though without establishing any position of legal privilege. But they were none the less opposed to the Napoleonic system because they continued to be attached to their constitutional and liberal ways; and although not unwilling to open their ranks to a certain number of newcomers, they were intent on keeping the power in the hands of the great families of ancient descent.

The Continental nobility, for their part, both feudal or military, were jealous of their own privileges, and reckoned their English counterparts as too unselective, and too inclined to give wealth precedence over birth. There were not many men with the insight of Spéranski or Stein to take them as their model. The chief aristocrats envied the English aristocracy for their skill in keeping their political authority; but they nevertheless agreed with the absolute monarchs and with Napoleon himself that the English were a clear example of the weakness of party government. The Tory party was riddled with personal rivalries, which first brought about the fall of Castlereagh and Canning and then put Perceval and Wellesley at loggerheads. When the Prince of Wales was invested with full royal powers as regent in February 1812, he offered the Whigs—as was to be expected—a place in government (though his own moral authority was at a low ebb, for public sympathy was entirely on the side of his wife Caroline and his daughter Charlotte). But Grey and Grenville stood out for a one-party cabinet. Wellesley retired and when Perceval was assassinated in May, confusion reached its height.

Napoleon was at that moment marching on the Niemen, and a realization of the great danger won the day over internal strife. Castlereagh was called to the Foreign Office, and Vansittart joined him at the Exchequer. Together with Bathurst and under the leadership of Liverpool they formed a government which was to prepare the way for the destruction of the Continental System. In September, Parliament was dissolved, and the new House of Commons was solidly behind them; but they had not as yet won their spurs.

On the other hand there were those on the Continent who wondered whether Parliament would continue to uphold the old regime. Certain symptoms made it doubtful whether the Tories would one day or another come to grief. For whilst they continued to support the Corn Laws, the industrial and trading middle classes were clearly swinging over to free trade, and the youthful Peel was already showing disquieting signs of taking an independent line on this point. In Parliament, its determined opponents—Whitbread and Burdett—were not much of a danger, for they had little support from the Whig leaders, the Russells, the Hollands, and the Greys. But the party was recovering its outside influence thanks to the actions of a growing group in Scotland, centred round Brougham and Sydney Smith. The *Edinburgh Review*, founded by Jeffrey in 1802, and the *Letters of Peter Plymley*, published by Sydney Smith in 1807, were so successful that in 1809 Canning and Southey decided to start the rival *Quarterly Review*. Now that the Tory party changed its policy and came out in favour of war, the Whigs, taking the opposite line, supported the cause of peace, and found it a highly popular platform. These Whigs did not at any rate style themselves democrats. But political radicalism was beginning to crystallize into a party. Cobbett, who had changed his allegiance, was carrying on an impassioned war of words against the government; Major Cartwright was demanding universal suffrage; Francis Place was resuming his propaganda, and James Mill found a valuable recruit for them in the person of Bentham, who was now won over to political action, and in 1812, drew up his *Catechism for Parliamentary Reform*. But in Europe, those who were intent on preserving or recovering their privileges thought that, all things considered, it was better to put their trust in absolutism.

The influence of England therefore had its chief effect on the middle classes and what remained of the liberal nobility. In itself, Toryism did not hold out any particular attraction for them. Its representatives, like the Whigs before them, seemed to be nothing much more than a venal oligarchy, whose reputation was tarnished by many scandals. True, they had made some slight changes in the penal laws, accepted a few improvements in the administration, and in 1807 abolished the slave trade—though this was just as much in order to raise the price of sugar as to placate the religious abolitionists and the humanitarians; but they were more and more disposed to fall in with Walpole's advice—*quieta non movere*. Catholic emancipation was still being held up, and in 1810 O'Connell, who had become president of the Irish committee, had given a lively impetus to propaganda. Grattan had come round to the side of reform, and in 1812 the House of Commons decided to vote for it; but the attempt failed, because O'Connell and the clergy refused the requisite guarantees concerning the choice of bishops. The more modern outlook of the Whigs, however, stood them in good stead; and in any case it was hardly of much consequence, for in the eyes of Royer-Collard, Benjamin Constant, or even Chateaubriand, who were under an iron despotism, England was the home of constitutional government and freedom, all the more attractive because it eschewed democracy and had kept some reverence for lawful monarchy. England became fashionable once again, as it had been a hundred years before.

France towards the end of the Empire was infatuated with the idea of parliamentary government, though without being very certain what it meant—as the sequel of 1815 would show. But enthusiasm outran knowledge, and anglomania, which was to be all the rage in the Restoration period, was already proving an annoyance to the Napoleonic regime.

The Tories showed no inclination to encourage other nations to adopt their country's political institutions. Probably even Castlereagh was in his heart of hearts not too pleased at having to give account of his actions to Parliament. In any case, there was general agreement that other nations were incapable of governing themselves on their own. Among the Whigs there were at least some men who disagreed with Burke and ascribed universal value to British political customs. They even went so far as to think that they should be reformed according to their ideas before export, so as to give them a certain coherence and uniformity that was quite unknown under the old regime in England. It looked as though the various French constitutions had set them thinking. So it came about that in 1812, when Bentinck found himself master of Sicily, he prided himself on presenting it with a constitution on a logical plan and arranging for the election of a chamber on a suffrage based upon property qualifications and valid for the whole country. This Sicilian parliament abolished the feudal system; but when Bentinck had left for Spain, an opposition party demanded still more radical reforms, and under cover of disturbances provoked by a scarcity of food, the king seized the chance of recovering his authority. On his return, Bentinck demanded the removal of the queen, dissolved the parliament, and in spite of new elections made himself dictator. When he was recalled in 1814, his successor,

A'Court by name, used this rather unsatisfactory experiment as an excuse for abandoning the whole project to the vengeance of King Ferdinand.

As far as American democracy was concerned, its calm political life might well have served as an example. Party strife appeared to have ceased. Under Jefferson, the first President, the federalists had disappeared from the scene, and the Republicans seemed gradually to have adopted the views of their opponents. It is true that Jefferson reduced the army and the fleet and paid off half the national debt; but nevertheless he acquired Louisiana, and in order to apply the embargo of 1807, increased control at the centre. Madison, who succeeded him in 1809, finally declared war against England, which forced him to progress still further in the same direction. But in the circumstances of that time, the United States did not strike Europe as a practical example; their influence had a greater effect on South America, when combined with that of England and the French Revolution.

If there were better prospects for liberalism on the Continent and more especially in France, the causes are to be seen in the growth of the middle classes and the development of the ideas of 1789. There can be no doubt that Napoleon only respected religious and economic liberty; but he had none the less kept the sovereignty of the people and the elective principle, and conquered countries were given a constitution on French lines. The framework of political life was thus still in existence, and his very despotism reacted to turn men's minds to it. In England, the Whigs appreciated the liberal quality of his reforms and were quite ready to praise them. On all sides it was freely recognized that they had been inspired by the Revolution; and it was constantly natural enough that everything he had cut away from the revolutionary programme gradually found its way back again. Even in Russia, Spéranski's tentative efforts prepared the way for Russian officers to catch the infection of French ideas when victory turned their steps westwards. From 1812 onwards, events proved how great the influence had been in Spain, although it had risen against France. Jovellanes had managed to induce the central junta to convene the Cortes in 1809, and they met on September 24, 1810, having been in principle elected by the provincial juntas. But the deputies from the invaded areas were chosen in Cadiz, even by the refugees, or nominated by the council or regency, as were the twenty-six American delegates. Now Cadiz contained the most powerful of the middle classes, and those who were the most imbued with the new ideas. There was thus a ready-made liberal majority which certainly did not reflect the opinion of most Spaniards, for in Napoleon they were not only resisting despotism and foreign influence, but also the Revolution. Nevertheless, the constitution of 1812 was an off-print from that of 1791. True, it kept Catholicism as the State religion and forbade the practice of other faiths; but as the clergy and the *serviles* refused all the same to accept it, the liberals decided in 1813 to abolish the Inquisition, reduce the number of convents, and seize the revenues of the monasteries that had been dissolved.

With the fall of the Empire, liberalism would at once resume the battle against the *Ancien Régime.* On his restoration to the throne, Louis XVIII did not dare to refuse a parliament to the middle classes in France, and Spain was to be the first to rise in 1820 against the Holy Alliance.

INTELLECTUAL LIFE

During the Napoleonic period, there was a strange slowing down of intellectual life. On the Continent, despotic governments made it their business to stop men's mouths. The English were more interested in detailed reforms than in ideas, and there was no intellectual activity at all in the United States. Besides, discussion seemed futile during these years when each person had taken up his position and was only awaiting the arbitrament of war. Above all, war called forth youthful energies, whilst the growing political nationalism distracted the attention of a good many minds. Yet in so far as this kind of life went on, it drew no new inspiration from the Napoleonic experiment, and it was between the traditional ideas and the ideas of the eighteenth century that the debate continued in the days to come.

The general state of mental torpor was not favourable to revolutionary thought, and the official papers, the administration, and the churches, which were free to express themselves, more or less openly preached in favour of the counter-revolution. Though Napoleon himself defended a certain part of the heritage of 1789, he did it in his own peculiar way, and he had no intention of enlisting the help of the ideologists. Cabanis died in 1808; but Destutt de Tracy, Ginguené and Fauriel all went on with their labours, and their rationalist positivism still had its faithful adherents, such as Stendhal. All the same, it was increasingly eclipsed by a spiritual outlook in harmony with the religious revival, and taught at the Sorbonne by Royer-Collard. Maine de Biran was concerned to bring back to the process of thinking an intuitive awareness that it existed in its own right, and enable it to construct its own metaphysics. Joubert's thought showed the same development, and even an ideologist such as Laromiguière had made some concessions to the intellectual fashion of the moment. In England, there was Bentham, the father of philosophical radicalism, with a markedly more empirical outlook than the French ideologists. He showed an increasing interest in political and economic reform. In Germany, the reigning philosophy was a transcendental idealism, though it had not made many disciples outside the country. It was becoming more and more imbued with mysticism, especially in the thought of Schelling.

The sciences, however, continued their steady advance. In mathematics, Laplace, Monge, Legendre, Poisson, Poinsot, and Arago kept France very much in the van. The fame of de Gauss in Germany was only in its early stages. French physicists and chemists were equally numerous and distinguished—men such as Malus and Biot, Gay-Lussac and Dulong, Chaptal, Bertholet, and Thénard. But England was not behindhand, for she had men like Dalton and Davy; and there was Berzélius in Sweden, whilst Rumford, although domiciled in France, was Anglo-Saxon in origin. Chemistry had now really come into its own with the formulation of the basic laws of chemical combination. New elements were being constantly isolated, and the new industries based upon these discoveries were rapidly expanding. France enjoyed a striking supremacy in the natural sciences, where such men as Cuvier and Geoffroy-Saint-Hilaire now came in to join the already famous Lamarck. Zoology, comparative anatomy, and palaeontology were ceasing to be purely descriptive; and the controversy that now arose between Lamarck and Geoffroy-Saint-Hilaire, who were working out the first conceptions of the transformation of species, and

Cuvier, who championed the principle of fixed species, was one of the most famous in the whole century. Haüy had established the bases of crystallography, and Candolles was carrying on his botanical research. Bichat had thrown light upon the cellular composition of the tissues, and medicine was turning the discoveries of Broussais, de Laënnec, Corvisart, and Dupuytren to good account. Alexander de Humboldt, famous for his exploration of South America, was the only man to rival the French naturalists. In history and in linguistics, Germany was once again taking the lead, and England was coming to the fore in the sphere of political economy.

In the eighteenth century, there had been a continuous use of scientific knowledge to break down traditional ideas; and its further extension seemed to augur a revival for rationalist positivism. The Emperor involuntarily smoothed the way for its development by giving science a large place in secondary education and by keeping the great institutions of the Convention period through which the scholars saw to it that their discoveries were made widely known. Moreover, Laplace, Lamarck, Cuvier, and Ampère were some of the best writers of the time. Several of these notable men, it is true, were able to reconcile their researches with traditional ideas. Cuvier, for instance, whose training in Stuttgart had accustomed him to think in terms of genera and species like the scholastics, and who saw as the sole purpose of science the discovery in nature of the order that had been established by divine decree, prided himself that his work would form a solid barrier against the positivism of his rivals. But as always, the experts' objective research helped in more or less indirect ways to transform not only men's ideas, but the whole economy, and consequently the structure of society and its habits and morals; with the result that all indirectly helped to bring about the downfall of traditions which were inseparably bound up with it.

The leaders of counter-revolution continued to make use for their own ends of the empirical rationalist movement. In 1802, Bonald had published his *Législation primitive* and in 1810 Maistre his *Essai sur le principe des constitutions politiques*. In 1808, Charles de Haller, by way of prelude to the *Restauration de la science politique* (the first volume of which did not appear till 1816), had produced his *Abrégé de la politique universelle*. Up till then, he had announced a purely positive doctrine, founded, like Bonald's, on the sovereign rights of the head of a family, which was simply stated as a fact. Nevertheless, whilst Bonald and de Maistre justified a hierarchy of authority and held modern kingship to be lawful, Haller took the opposite line, defending the political claims of the aristocracy and questioning the power of the State. The head of the government, he held, was simply one owner among others, an owner who had wrongly encroached on the rights of the *seigneur*; and reason dictated a return to the feudal system.

Bonald and more especially Joseph de Maistre were none the less convinced of the necessity for divine sanctions, and even Haller had recourse to it later on and ended by becoming a Catholic. In the same way, the general thought of the counter-revolutionaries inclined towards traditional religious views when in search of a philosophy, a course in which they were encouraged by the secular power. The temporal interests of the Catholic Church had continued to encounter some severe shocks. Secularization had spread throughout the Empire and through many of the vassal States, even including Bavaria. But these trials had not been without value for the Church's spiritual influence. Pius VII's captivity, following upon his predecessor's, had called forth a sympathy for the Papacy which had been unknown shortly before the Revolution. The lower ranks of the clergy, closely subject as they were to the State and so to the bishops, instinctively turned for help to ultramontanism. The Church had been purified and disciplined by her sufferings, and her ministers were more popularly recruited than in former times. She was now massing her forces for a great offensive, and waiting only for the downfall of the Emperor to give the signal. Yet her system of apologetics was very mediocre in quality, and contaminated by the spirit of the age. Everywhere the State was imbued with a spirit of Josephism, which only saw the catechism as a manual of morality and the priest as a political agent. The Romantic influence, with its hostility to the intellect, was bringing into Catholic thought elements that were foreign to Thomism, and dangerous for Catholic doctrine. Bonald and de Maistre were not altogether free from this tendency, and a school of thought had grown up round Chateaubriand's aesthetic and sentimental Catholicism, whilst

Lammenais' attempts to show the commonsense basis of Christianity, which could not but win universal assent, was unconsciously laying the foundations for future schism. The fact remains that by these various ways people of considerable importance were brought back to the fold. Several German Romantics had had violent conversions, and there was a group of Germanic artists at Rome, called 'the Nazarenes', who were attracted by the primitives, and inclined to the same turbulence of expression. Overbeck, their leader, became a Catholic in 1813. In Germany and in England, a Protestant renaissance was also under way. Schleiermacher was still a reputable pastor; Fichte and Schelling bowed to the conformist spirit. The Methodists, in spite of a fresh internal split in 1812, remained popular; so did the Baptists, who that same year made an opposite move and united in one body. There were now 2 million Dissenters.

Somewhat on the fringe of traditional religion, mysticism continued to flourish and abound. Saint-Martin had died in 1803, but he had left disciples, and so had Antoine de la Salle—people like Azaïs and Gence, later professor at the *École des Chartes*. The centres of mysticism were still Lyons and Alsace. In the former, the printer Ballanche was meditating on the successive interpretations of dogma in the light of an intuitive mysticism; and in Alsace, Oberlin (until his death in 1806), Baron de Turkheim, Salzmann, and the *Préfet* Lezay-Marnésia were all more or less given over to mystical illumination. Some of these speculations had a syncretist and polytheistic tendency, or pursued a cabbalistic line, with research into the magic properties of numbers. Fabre d'Olivet, for instance, had in this way passed from 1805 onwards through ideology to theosophy, and in 1813 had published his *Vers dorés de Pythagore*. In Germany, the oracles of mysticism were Baader and Jung Stilling, who had been professor at Carsruhe since 1803. Like Bergasse in France, he dabbled in millenarianism, Napoleon providing a very convenient figure for antichrist. In Alsace, the French and the German streams tended to merge, and it was here that Mme de Krüdener seems to have become initiated into these mysteries. After meeting Jung Stelling she came into touch with Oberlin and at Sainte-Marie-aux-Mines with Pastor Fontaine. A little later on, we hear of her again at Geneva, from which she was expelled in 1813. She passed on her musings to Mme de Staël, who was already getting Augustus Schlegel to read Saint-Martin to her, and was entertaining Zacharias Werner, a literary figure and renegade mystic who ended by becoming a Catholic priest. In a fit of emulation she began to study the *Imitation* and Mme Cuyon. In Russia, as always, there was a whole host of mystical sects. The *chrétiens spirituels* were fashionable at that time among the aristocracy; and Alexander, who had been won over by Galitzine and Kotschelev, began to read and study the Bible in 1812, preparing himself in this way for playing the part of Mme de Krüdener's angel in white.

In literature and in art, the Romantic movement was the great source of renewal and excitement. Germany, having worked out a philosophy for it and adopted it wholesale, considered that her own genius had created the movement, though it was in fact widespread throughout the West, and owed too much to Rousseau for there to be any doubt about its parentage. The German Romantics were not concerned to be too precise about their metaphysics. The Heidelberg group were chiefly interested in exploring the past, several of them bending their efforts towards an apology for the *Ancien Régime* and for Germanism. Before long, a third generation would only be concerned with interpreting the sentiment of nationality. In particular, what remained from the didactic activities of the initiators of the movement was a disdain for aesthetic conventions and an apologia for creative imagination. Goethe had finally condemned the extravagance and arbitrariness of their literary efforts, and had parted company from them, although their *Affinités électives*, which came out in 1809, had not perhaps gone so far as to disclaim the passionate fatalism which was one of the principal themes of the movement in every country. They did not succeed in producing any great works—unless Kleist is to be numbered among them by reason of his unstable inner life and his inability to fit in with his surroundings, which led him to suicide in 1811; and this remained the permanent central theme of the Romantic movement. But the idealist symbolism expounded by Novalis, with its harmony between the ideal and the visible world as united in the heart of Eternal Being, was very far from answering to his condition, for his own nature and the disasters of the period meant that he could see nothing in this world but insoluble conflicts and universal antagonisms. His dramas are therefore entirely tragic in their genius. In *La famille Schroffenstein*, we have the struggle of the individual against his own kin; in *Robert Guiscard*, the struggle of the hero against hostile forces; in *Penthésilée*, the clash between the sexes and between different races, and between the nations in *La bataille d'Hermann*; and finally the conflict between conscience and law in *Le prince de Hambourg*.

But the German Romantics are to be remembered for something more important than their literary works, namely the impetus they gave to linguistic, historical, and juridical studies. Following on from their friends at Heidelberg, the brothers Grimm had produced their *Fairy Tales* and undertaken the study of their languages while Creuzer was publishing his works on the symbolic interpretation of Greek mythology. The new interest shown in literatures that could be contrasted with the Classics did not stop short at Shakespeare: it went on to include the *romancero*, and Camoëns, as well as the literature of the East and of India. William de Humboldt was also devoting himself to linguistic studies. Philological criticism had been brilliantly represented from the end of the eighteenth century onwards by Wolf's *Prolegomena ad Homerum*, published in 1795. His disciple Böckh went on to add historical research, and in 1811 Niebuhr began to bring out his *History of Rome*. Finally, the Romantic spirit had penetrated the conception of law. Savigny and Eichhorn contrasted what they saw as the unconscious creation of the Volksgeist-age with the *Code Napoléon*. This they considered to be an artificial product of the intellect, and above all a foreign importation having no genuine links with the life of the German nation. This process of exploring the relationship between juridical studies and the general history of societies was to bring new vitality to the whole subject.

In England, famous poets were beginning to be inspired by the Romantic movement. The Lake Poets, Wordsworth and more especially Coleridge, had long been under the influence of a national outlook, and had begun to adopt a preaching tone, whilst Southey had rallied to the Tory cause. He was in receipt of a pension, and became Poet Laureate in 1813. But the increasing influence of a certain puritan outlook was temperamentally repugnant to a number of young aristocrats whom position and fortune exempted from the necessity of earning a living; and they set themselves up as the champions of an anarchical individualism. Though he remained classical in form, Byron became a type of antisocial Romantic. He was an authoritarian aristocrat, impatient of all rules, and in revolt against a caste solidarity: not at all the kind of revolutionary who dreams of coming to the rescue of the oppressed classes, although he did in the end meet his death fighting in the ranks of the Greek insurgents. He was rather the unique figure, alone against the rest of the world, claiming the right to be his own law-giver and choosing as his model the outlaw, or better still, Lucifer in rebellion against God himself. Byron was also the temperamental Romantic who gives himself over with a mixture of delight and torment to the fatal forces of passion, and who feels predestined to misfortune and to death. Or, fleeing from society, from his own country and from himself, he takes refuge in the contemplation of nature and in solitary exile. It was thus that he discovered the East and in 1812 published *Childe Harold*, in 1813 his *Giaour*, and in 1814 the *Corsaire*; and it was these works that were destined in the course of the next few years to have such a powerful effect in making the exotic fashionable, and popularizing the cult of local colour.

Shelley too suffered from a want of social discipline and an unhealthy sensitivity. When sent down from Oxford, he defied the religiously minded by his intellectual pantheism and defence of free love. His first essays came out in 1810 and his *Queen Mab* in 1813. De Quincey, who was—like Coleridge—an opium addict, was likewise bent upon breaking away from his country's conventions. But England repudiated these bold spirits; yet at the same time, Walter Scott was introducing a romanticism not unlike that of the Heidelberg school, at once medieval, conservative and nationalist in outlook, first in his poems, and then in his historical novels, which enjoyed an extraordinary popularity throughout the world, particularly after the publication of his *Waverley* in 1814. In this form, Romanticism could deeply move the common run of men, without irritating the great; for the virtuous rebel or the knight who went about righting wrongs was made acceptable by being adorned with the usual trappings of popular romance, such as mysterious birth, disguises, visions, and dark conspiracies.

In France, literature was still honoured by the *Institut* and sought the approval of Geoffrey, the doyen of critics, not daring to depart from the traditional rules. There were a few graceful writers, among the best of whom was the poet Delille. Benjamin Constant's masterpiece, *Adolphe*, belongs to the classic line; but official doctrine did not reckon the novel among the noble literary *genres*. In spite of his liking for Ossian, Napoleon remained faithful to this aesthetic outlook, for it seemed to him that French influence was suffering from its decadence, and towards the end of his reign he was constantly suspicious of the successes won by the Romantic movement in Germany and England. Yet it was hardly possible to go on deceiving oneself: the Revolution had put the final touches to the decay of classical art by breaking up the old aristocracy who had been its chief patrons, by causing a decline in those studies which alone would enable the middle classes to appreciate it, and by swelling their ranks with uneducated *nouveaux riches* who were more interested in Pixérécourt's dramas, Alexandre Duval's plays, and Pigault-Lebrun's novels. This popular literature bore some of the marks of an ingenuous romanticism, such as unbridled imagination, a mixture of *genres*, and attempts at realism. Official criticism affected to consider the drama as a kind of debased tragedy; but Lemercier's *Pinto* (1801) and *Christophe Colombe* (1809), in which the conventions were isolated, showed—despite their feebleness—that there was a real upheaval coming. Moreover, the pre-romantic tastes of the eighteenth century were still alive. There was still appreciation for the troubador *genre*, as was shown by the welcome given to the so-called Clothilde de Surville, and Ossian was even more popular. Oscar and Malvinia were in favour as Christian names; and Leseur, in his opera *Les Bardes*, drew inspiration from MacPherson's forgeries, as did the painters Gérard and Girodet.

All the same, it was really contemporary events that were chiefly responsible for the Romantic climate. Imaginations had been raised to fever pitch by the disturbances of the Revolution, the rise of Napoleon, and continued warfare. Not everyone could find his niche, and fortune did not favour every temperament alike. Those who were disappointed took their revenge—if they could write—by telling their own story. As early as 1802, in his *Génie du Christianisme*, René laid bare the boredom of the misfit with a disgust that was a mixture of anger and pride. Serancourt's *Obermann* exhibited the same disease, though with an even more mournful despair, whilst in the work of Millevoye and Chênedollé, it was softened down into a Lamartinean melancholy. Besides, although the ideals of liberty and equality had been proclaimed, the customs of the time and the Civil Code had not by any means embodied all their implications. After portraying Atala as the victim of passion in conflict with duty, Mme de Staël gave an equally unhappy portrait of Delphine and Corinne because—in her view—social prejudice refused to allow woman the right to be happy. Horizons were being broadened by returning *émigrés*, full of the memories of strange lands, and by the stories of the Emperor's soldiers and officials; a taste for the exotic was being developed. Chateaubriand's publication in 1811 of his *Itinéraire de Paris à Jerusalem* stirred up the curiosity about the East that had formerly been amused by the Egyptian expedition; and his *Martyrs* had an equally nostalgic effect on those who read it. And lastly, there was a growing closeness of contact with foreign literatures. The ideologists like Fauriel and Gérando, faithful to their objective positivism, condemned the prejudice of Frenchmen and recognized that the works of each nation had their own particular merits and the right to claim a certain beauty. Under the Empire, this eclecticism was of special benefit to the southern nations. Mme de Staël's *Corinne* had already raised the reputation of Italy in French eyes; and from 1811 onwards Guinguené began publishing his *Histoire de la littérature italienne*, whilst in Geneva Sismondi was giving a course on the literatures of the South. All the same, Mme de Staël acted as a kind of spokesman for Germany, and the part played by her was therefore of the first importance, for it was in Germany that Romanticism had first come into its own.

Mme de Staël came of German stock on her father's side. She had married a Swede, and was a Protestant, and with her Genevan connections felt much sympathy for Colonist England and Lutheran Germany. Temperamentally, she was more inclined to be passionate than to exercise the critical spirit, and it was therefore quite natural for her to be taken with the northern literatures. As early as 1801 she had written an essay on *La littérature considérée dans ses rapports avec les institutions sociales* in which she questioned the universal value of the classics, admitted that beauty was relative, and drew a contrast between the different climates of the northern and southern countries, taking Ossian as characteristic of the former and Homer of the latter. She could hardly say too much in praise of the northern nations, with their seriousness, their zeal for liberty, their strong moral sense, and their religious spirit, which yet avoided superstition. Nevertheless, at this period she was still disposed to consider the classics superior, for she had been brought up on them, and she knew nothing as yet of Germany and the German language. But when Napoleon sent her into exile in 1803, she crossed the Rhine, and on her way back she brought Augustus Schlegel along with her. He stayed with her till 1810, initiating her into the mysteries of German Romanticism. Her circle were likewise won over, for Benjamin Constant wrote a *Wallenstein* in 1809, and Mme Necker de Saussure translated Schlegel's *Cours de littérature dramatique* in 1811. It was this development that was the inspiration of her book *De l'Allemagne*, in which French literature now received far less favourable treatment as compared with Shakespeare and the Germans. Here, Mme de Staël repudiated the classical conventions and the critical attitude, and extolled the virtues of enthusiasm, in a spirit of pure Schlegelism. This famous work was printed in Paris in 1810. It was immediately impounded, and only reappeared after the downfall of the Emperor. Nevertheless, during the later years of the Empire criticism came openly face to face with the conflict between classicism and romanticism, and the question was no longer ignored in Italy, where there had been a tendency to favour the nordic literature, either directly or more often indirectly, through French translations. In 1807, its influence was openly shown in Foscolo's *Sepoleri*.

The plastic arts were also beginning to feel the influence of the Romantic Movement, although here the classical tradition put up a much better defence. Napoleon was particularly interested in architecture, and his thirst for prestige was in accord with his personal taste in preferring the majesty of the classical order. 'There is always beauty in grandeur,' as he was accustomed to say. Unconsciously, however, he directed several artists along a new road that led towards the Romantic by suggesting to them—and sometimes ordering—pictures based upon his exploits in contemporary history; but he had little to do with forming the rich and heavy 'Empire style', the roots of which go back to the Etruscan and Egyptian influences of the eighteenth century. Denon, who was the head of his Museums Department, was an artist and a rather eclectic enthusiast. The supporter of classical art as derived from antiquity was Quatremère de Quincy, whose notion of the beautiful went back to ideal platonic archetypes, which must be imitated as closely as possible by eliminating all individual peculiarities and concentrating on design, so that he held sculpture to be the essential form of art. Faithful exponents of this doctrine were Percier and Fontaine in the Louvre, and Gondonin, the designer of the *colonne Vendôme*, together with Chalgrin, who was responsible for the Arc de Triomphe; and David's favourite style was also in accordance with Quatremère's doctrine. But the great sculptors of the period were foreigners such as the Danish Thorwaldsen and particularly Canova, who was a special favourite of Napoleon.

Art was however very far from offering the uniformity that Quatremère desired. Alexandrian influence, which became fashionable in the eighteenth century after the exploration of Pompei, produced a reaction against the firm and somewhat tense lines of David; and there slipped into Girodet and Prudhon's work a kind of tired and melancholy voluptuousness, whilst in Canova, the purity of style was marred by a certain flabby gracefulness and a taste for the picturesque. In decorative art, the Alexandrian style continued to hold its own alongside the imperial fashions. On the other hand, a certain realism was necessary in portraiture, and here there was no one to match Gérard, or better still David. Finally, the subjects taken by Girodet from Ossian or from Chateaubriand or from contemporary history, David's *Consecration*, the battle-scenes by Gros, the soldiers painted by Géricault—all those brought back variety of idea, movement as well as design, and brilliance into the colour-scheme, and were purely Romantic works. There was a still greater freedom about the paintings of Goya and Englishmen such as Lawrence, Romney, and Raeburn, whilst England was at the same time giving birth to the school of landscape painters, led by Constable and Turner, who were to bring into the new style of painting one of its most novel and appealing features.

As far as music was concerned, there was no continuation in France of the new life brought by the Revolution once the revolutionary ideas had been condemned. All that remained was a certain preference for melody and prejudice against 'clever' music, together with some weakness in technique, and a degree of emphasis no longer justified by any supporting ardour or enthusiasm, though not without links with the art of David. Among the chief composers were Frenchmen like Méhul or Italians who had settled in France, like Spontini. *Joseph* and *La Vestale* both appeared in 1807. Then there was Boïeldieu, who returned from Russia in 1811, and was successful in raising the reputation of comic opera. Cherubini, who was Berlioz's teacher, was already showing a truly Romantic productiveness and power, but his music was not popular.

But all other lights were already being eclipsed by Beethoven, who was still in Vienna. While still composing for the piano, he had since the beginning of the century been producing his great instrumental works, his quartets and overtures, and the first eight symphonies. His works often shocked his contemporaries by their daring technique, and by their novel vigour of expression, but they won them over by the richness of their inner life. In many respects, Beethoven was akin to the Romantics. His was a violent and uneven temperament, full of fire and highly sensitive, but cut off from the world by his deafness, and tortured by many a hopeless love affair. He was suspicious and apt to take offence, and condemned by his plebian background and his poverty to all kinds of painful incidents in the aristocratic circles he was obliged to frequent. Like Novalis, he had created through his music a magic world which cushioned him against reality. All the same, there was nothing weak about him. Many of his songs express joy and grace and vigour, and have the light touch of a healthy human being who was full of purpose and buoyancy; others express an aspiration to heroic greatness and to battle with the hostile forces of the universe. Beethoven never sank into fruitless despair, for he was a son of the eighteenth century, on fire with a restless but dogged optimism. He was a natural Republican, with a deep sense of human solidarity and a great confidence in the future of the race. In several respects he was akin to Rousseau, and among the Germans his thought was nearer the classical than the romantic, and particularly near to Schiller's. Fundamentally, he was a tragic figure like Kleist: the deepest pathos in his works centres round the struggle between the heroic soul and a refractory nature, but also—when seen in the light of the times that gave them birth—the stormy conflicts between the Revolution and the old world, between freedom and despotism, and between the rising new nations and the Napoleonic Empire.

THE RISE OF NATIONALITY IN EUROPE AND AMERICA

The progressive expansion of intellectual life among the peoples during the eighteenth century had resulted—especially in Germany—in developing a nationalist culture among the writers and in the universities. Classical civilization was seen as a French creation, which reduced them to a subordinate position. The Napoleonic system reinforced the spiritual influence of France through institutional reform and military conquest, thus strengthening this reaction still further. While not denying the principle of a universal civilization, which is an essential part of Christianity, the nations instinctively guarded their independence in the field of literature, art, and manners, and sought to discover the characteristic features of their original springs of feeling and action—what Jahn in 1810 called *Volkstum*—whether in the past, where there seemed to be no trace of foreign influence, or in the lower classes, whose ignorance kept them apart from all cosmopolitan trends. Herder and Burke had defended this type of nationalism by representing each people as a living being, impossible to assimilate to any other; and the German Romantics crowned this philosophy by endowing each nation with a *Volksgeist*, the most significant expression of which is language. In the Napoleonic period these opinions were shared by Cuoco in Italy and Karamzine in Russia.

The characteristic feature of Italian thought at this period was that it showed much more vigorous resistance to French ascendancy at a time when it seemed that this was likely to be strengthened by Napoleonic rule, and when the writers who had supported the regime, such as Monti and Cesarotti, together with a whole body of official literature, *la littérature des préfets*, had meekly given in to the domination of France. Cesari brought the Tuscan language back to its classic purity, and compiled a dictionary; and without entering into political opposition to France, Cusco, serving under Melzi and Joseph in Milan and Naples and Foscolo at Pavia, showed an uncompromising spirit in any questions of linguistic or literary autonomy. In Florence, Niccolini, who was openly hostile to the victors, published nothing, but went back into the past in search of famous works belonging to his country. Canova's art and Italian music were also a source of national pride, a feeling which Napoleon would seem to have taken into account. Although the re-establishment of the indigenous language in the Italian lawcourts in 1809, in those parts that had been annexed by France, was doubtless a necessary concession in the interests of the administration of justice, literary circles were jubilant when the La Crusca Academy was reconstituted in 1812. In Belgium, there was no resistance to French culture. In the Rhine Provinces, it made little progress, though there was no concerted opposition. In Holland, on the other hand, the literary world gave up all attempts at imitation and simply retreated into itself.

Outside the Empire, Norway obtained a university in 1813. Further east, Russia now had her literary journals, such as the *Messager d'Europe*, founded by Karamzine in 1802, and the *Messager russe*, published by Glinka from 1808 onwards. Karamzine set about producing a literary language and eliminating the classical genres, the ode, and the tragedy. After the Peace of Tilsit, Glinka and Rostopchine came out in vigorous opposition against the foreign manners and modes adopted by the court and the nobles, and Glinka was particularly concerned to uphold the conventional Russian past and to combat western innovations. Karamzine, who had formerly been in sympathy with the *Aufklärung*, was now won over to the national traditions, and began to write a history of the Muscovite State. Among the Hapsburgs, Hungary continued to demand recognition for Magyar as the official language, and the Czechs were also stirring, for there had been a Chair in their language at Prague University since 1792. Dobrovsky was stabilizing its grammar, and Chafaryk (Šafařyk) and Palatzy (Palatsky) were preparing to become writers. After Illyria was conquered, Marmont admitted the Slovene and Croatian languages in public documents and in the elementary schools; and under his protection, Abbot Vodnik wrote elementary books in Slovene. Finally, there were stirrings among the Balkan Christians, the Greeks being the most advanced, and multiplying the number of their *Hetairia*. Among the Serbs, national tradition, supported by the parish priests, kept them loyal to the Orthodox faith; but there was a revival of Rumanian language and history in Transylvania, and in 1813 a Moldavian school was opened at Jassy.

In countries that had long been national states or who had kept a lively memory of their former independence—England and Holland, Switzerland, Poland and Hungary, Spain and Portugal—a national culture was a normal part of political nationalism; but in other countries, it was something that helped to bring political consciousness to birth. The Czechs, the Illyrian Slavs, the Rumanians and even the Greeks did not as yet, like the Serbs, appear to contemplate fighting for their freedom; but in Italy, the transformation of a cultural into a political patriotism, which had begun in the revolutionary period, was making some progress, whilst it had actually taken place in Germany. The Revolution had helped this movement by making sovereignty a national matter, and it was only natural that this principle should have been used against the Napoleonic ascendancy. In practice, the French were equally responsible for preparing the way for the expression of national sentiment by forming a framework for government, with a hierarchy of officials and more especially—at least in Italy—armies which recruited the boldest opponents of the Holy Alliance. In Southern Italy, they also established the societies known as the *bons cousins charbonniers*, originating in Franche-Comté, which had since the beginning of Murat's reign been apparently won over to some extent to the idea of unity.

The influence of these various factors must not, however, be exaggerated: they were none of them as important as the fact of conquest. Whatever idealism the patriot may aspire to, it will only take political shape for extremely practical motives, even among the upper classes, who are the normal exponents of a national culture. At all events, among the bulk of the lower classes, hatred of the foreigner and all new ideas have always been in the forefront, and the appearance of soldiers and foreign administrators had always produced a prompt reaction. The Napoleonic system had its merits; but its benefits had always to be weighed against its burdens, and the balance was hardly a favourable one. In the first place, the Emperor threw the cost of warfare upon the shoulders of the conquered country, which had to bear the demands and depredations of his armies and the requisitions for supply, not to mention the war-taxes. Westphalia, for instance, was taxed at 26 million. Once these arrangements had been made, Napoleon laid it down as a principle that these conquered countries should be self-supporting, even poverty-stricken Illyria. At the very most—as in the case of Naples and Spain—he would produce the ready money for paying the army of occupation as long as the country was not yet pacified, though he did this with extreme reluctance. In 1807, Joseph set aside 44 million for the army, only 6 million of which were repaid. Westphalia had to find 10 million for the 12,500 French who constituted half its army. In 1809, out of expenses amounting to 127 million, the kingdom of Italy had to pay 30 million over to France and only spent 42 million on its own troops. Moreover, the new administrations were expensive. It may be said in general that everywhere taxes rose out of all proportion. The Grand Duchy of Berg paid 6 million in 1808, but 13 million in 1813; and in Venetia the sum was trebled. Moreover, men had to be found as well. The Italian army, for example, was increased from 49,000 in 1810 to 91,000 in 1812; the Duchy of Berg had only 5,000 men in 1806, but 9,400 in 1811. Finally, it may be said that the blockade exasperated more people than it pleased. Apart from Spain, which was largely laid waste by war, it was Germany, and particularly Prussia in 1812, that had the greatest cause for complaint. It was not a purely spiritual fervour that induced this country to become the heart and soul of the national uprising in 1813; for Germany was on the highroad to Russia, and ever since the summer of 1811 she had had to lodge the bulk of the *Grande Armée*. Prussia, like Poland, was the base for the Russian expedition, and had to hand over all she possessed. As early as December 5, 1811, Jerome (whose possessions were nevertheless somewhat to the rear of this area) was already sounding a note of alarm:

Excitement has reached fever pitch. . . . Spain is being held up as an example, and if war breaks out, all the countries between the Rhine and the Oder will rise as one man. The cause of unrest is not simply a strong impatience with the foreign yoke; it lies deeper, in the ruin that faces every class of people, the crushing taxation; the war levies, the billeting of troops, all the military coming and going, and a constant series of harassments. There are good reasons to be afraid of a movement of despair on the part of people who have nothing to lose, because all they had has already been taken from them. . . . The common people are indifferent to affairs of higher policy: they are only concerned with the present evils that weigh so heavily upon them.

The king of Westphalia might well have added that the aristocracy and the middle classes had long been equally affected, which was even more serious. In the vassal countries, the national debt had been left as it was or only partly reduced, retirement and pension agreements had been repudiated, and officials and officers of the old regimes dismissed. The States that had remained independent—in particular Prussia—had been compelled to do the same. And the conquerors were held responsible for all these evils.

On the other hand the Napoleonic system, introduced ruthlessly in the most varied regions, often resulted in a revival of the efforts formerly made by the enlightened despots to improve the lot of their subjects without consulting them; but now they were applied much more decisively, and over a much wider range. All this seemed over-complicated, formal and much too demanding to countries that were not as rich as France and accustomed to very indolent—and often half barbarian—governments, such as existed in Illyria. The Civil Code did even greater harm by upsetting family customs and property arrangements. Its openly lay character, which put all religions on the same footing, introduced a secular state and divorce, gave freedom to the Jews, and protected the Freemasons, ensured the solid opposition of the clergy. In the Protestant States, the equality given to Catholics did not always meet with favour. In Holland, for instance, attempts were made to dismiss them from employment—or so the French authorities maintained. In Illyria, Poland, and Russia, the Orthodox priests looked upon Napoleon as Antichrist. Catholic opposition was specially pronounced because of the secularizations, the abolition of tithe, and the break with the Papacy. Even more formidable was the aristocrat's rage at seeing the feudal system abolished and the secular state introduced. The gentry of Berne and Geneva, the patricians in Holland, and the Hanseatic cities never forgave the French either on this particular point. Nor was there any lack of further grievances for the populace or the middle classes. The artisans were alarmed by the suppression of the corporations; the officials were riled at seeing Frenchmen appointed to the higher posts; and the 'patriots', who had so faithfully supported revolutionary France, were systematically turned down as Jacobins. The peasants complained that agrarian reforms always spared the *seigneurs*. The only people to keep a certain affection for the Napoleonic regime were a number of powerful middle-class citizens who had greedily bought up national property, attained to important positions, and profited by the blockade. In all the countries where Napoleon set up the framework of modern national and social administration, common interests brought the inhabitants together in a strong desire for independence and opposition to France. Poland presents a particularly interesting example, because she owed a great deal to Napoleon, and would have owed more still if he had been victorious over Russia. Yet the Polish clergy remained covertly hostile to him, and the nobles were hesitant, fearing the new reforms that a small nucleus of democrats were already demanding. Moreover, they could not forgive the Emperor for not having remitted the entire mortgaged debt which Prussia had made over to them, consisting of 43 million plus 4 million in arrears of interest, which he reduced to 20 million, payable in three years. The peasants had not gained complete liberty, and were only concerned with the charges that still lay heavy upon them. Like the Prussian peasants, they had suffered from the passage of the *Grande Armée*, and it was to the French that they attributed all they had had to put up with from it. There was no question of Poland doing what Napoleon hoped for, namely to give him enthusiastic and unquestioning support.

In a variety of unforeseen and roundabout ways, the wars of

this period helped on the progress of other nations as well. Finland was separated from Sweden and was given a constitution by Alexander, drawn up by Spérenski, which gave her independence. Norway, cut off from Denmark by the English fleet and reduced to starvation, did in fact become independent, although she had not risen in any way against Frederick VI. In America, the Spanish colonies were in process of forming new nations, and Brazil was no longer willing to pay allegiance to Portugal. The year 1812 is a memorable date in the history of the United States, for it marked the beginning of the Second War of Independence against England, to throw off the yoke of economic dependence that the ex-colony had had to bear up to this time, a dependence from which England had reaped considerable advantage. Madison seems to have been advised to break off relations by a group of new men, such as Clay, Calhoun, and Webster, who wanted to seize Canada and make certain of their country's autonomy by developing industry under the shelter of a customs-barrier. It was a difficult war to fight, for the United States had no army and no money. Funds had to be borrowed for equipping a militia, in spite of protests from the Northern States, who on the very eve of peace threatened to disobey the federal government. The invasion of Canada was a failure: in 1813 and 1814, there were English attacks to be met on Lake Erie and in the direction of Lake Champlain; Baltimore was assailed and Washington burnt down; and again in 1815, Jackson had to repel an attempted assault on New Orleans. At sea, the success of the American frigates and privateers, who captured 2,500 enemy ships, was nevertheless powerless to prevent the ports being blockaded. The losses were reckoned at 30,000 killed, and 200 million in dollars. There were no territorial gains, and the damage to trade was considerable. But industry took advantage of the war to capture the home market, and after peace had been signed, the 1816 tariff ensured its preservation. Moreover, the crisis was responsible for a considerable strengthening of national feeling.

The various national resistances made difficulties for Napoleon. In the Tyrol, insurrections were an embarrassment, and in Spain a source of weakness. But there was no desperate danger as long as his armies remained intact, for the people of

Prussia made no move before they heard the news of disaster in Russia, and when Napoleon's position began to crumble, no other nation followed their example. But it must also be noted that although the discontent aroused by French domination was an undoubted factor in the development of national individuality, only very small minorities were animated by a spirit of pure and disinterested nationalism. This was only a secondary cause as compared with the sufferings of the lower classes and the various interests that had been damaged. The Tyrolean rising is a perfect case in point, for it was a rising against Bavaria, who had in no way infringed its Germanism. The popular exasperation was in fact due to the war, more especially the preparations for the Russian campaign; and it would have calmed down again if the Emperor had won the day and re-established peace on the Continent. All the same, the awakening of nationalism is a hint that the Continental System would not have survived once the Emperor who founded it had gone.

As for the social grievances, they were in part contradictory, with the result that in the countries where the economy had already been modernized, there were obstacles in the way of a united social front. This explains why the coalition between the monarchy and the aristocracy held back from the national movements and turned against them after they had won their own triumph. In the spring of 1812, Alexander was already posing as the protector of downtrodden nations, and from 1813 to 1815, he and his allies were lavish in making vague promises. But they certainly did not intend their own convenient territorial arrangements to be in any way upset. They took it as a matter of course that there should be no reduction in their own power, and that the peasants and middle classes to whom they appealed would have to submit, as they had before, to the superior position of the aristocracy. Austria, obstinately loyal to the *Ancien Régime*, felt very closely threatened by the subjection of so many nations, and was eager to regain her ascendancy over Italy and Germany. Never for one moment did she consent to giving any kind of revolutionary character to the struggle against France. There is thus already revealed in this duplicity of purpose the history of the first half of the nineteenth century, in which the oppressors wreaked a cruel revenge against their subjects who had allowed themselves to be deceived.

THE PROGRESS OF CAPITALISM, AND THE EXPANSION OF EUROPE THROUGHOUT THE WORLD

During the whole of the Napoleonic period, money was abundant. As this book had already several times explained, this was one of the central features of the British economy. From 1809 onwards, there was increasing inflation in Great Britain. The Bank of England dealt with an increasing number of exchequer bills, and in 1811 its commercial discount rate stood at a figure five times as high as in 1795, and there were £28½ million in circulation in the form of banknotes. There was not much increase in the number of private banks in London, with their own issue of notes; but in the provinces there were something like 800 of them in 1809. As the Bank of England issued £1 and £2 notes, coins gradually disappeared and prices continued to rise. In 1814, the index was 198 as compared with 100 in 1790. The Bank of England's gold and silver reserve fell to 2 million in 1815, and the exchange rate dropped from 15 per cent to 20 per cent, though this did not damage the export trade. In France, inflation was less pronounced. There was a continuance of hoarding, and complaints about the scarcity of coin remained frequent; but there can be no doubt that the note-issue increased. The Bank of France's issue rose from 63 million in 1806 to 111 million in 1812. The rate of circulation increased too. From 1809 to 1812, bills rose from 400 to 500 million and reached 747 million in 1810. If it had had the Emperor's support it would have been more lively still, and would have extended greatly in the provinces, where the local banks cannot have done much—though nothing is known about their transactions. Paper credit was as yet only used by a small number of business people, and the increase in metallic coin was of greater importance. This was achieved partly by new minting, partly by the positive funding of the trade balance, chiefly through war indemnities and the income from the foreign territories. The gold and silver brought into France from 1799 to 1814 have been calculated at 755 million. In the Empire, although manufactured products grew dearer, the price of agricultural products sometimes fell; but the general indications are that prices remained perceptibly higher than in 1789. Many of the Continental countries went over to paper-money systems. But as their coin was hidden, or had passed to France or England, these were the two chief countries where the monetary inflation made for economic advance.

Moreover, the extension of the revolutionary reforms to a large part of Europe—freedom for the worker, the abolition of serfdom and feudal dues, the opening up of the land, the abolition of internal customs and tolls, a uniform system of weights and measures—all these were in favour of the growth of capitalism. They were in accordance with Adam Smith's doctrine as popularized by Gamier and especially by J-B. Say, who clarified and supplemented it in his *Traité d'économie politique*, which came out in 1803.

Warfare, too, was a constant stimulant. In England, it forced traders to look for new markets, and on the Continent it ensured effective protection for industry. The Continental blockade only underlined the consequences of incessant hostilities, which makes it impossible to determine its exact effect on the conditions of production. Nevertheless, the havoc wrought by war certainly outweighed the advantages. Political uncertainty and the interference with commercial relationships were a widespread brake upon enterprise; and as industrial progress on the Continent depended particularly on the popular spread of British machinery, it would have been speedier still if Englishmen had continued to come over and install it.

In the economic sphere, the inventive spirit, stirred up by scientific research, did not lose its impetus as much as elsewhere; but as compared with the inventions of the eighteenth century, the results were slender. The expansive power of steam when condensed, which had been thought out by Hornblow in 1792, was taken up again in 1804 by Woolf, who made use of medium steam-pressures to produce a double effect; and this was the origin of the compound steam-engine. In Philadelphia, a workman and mechanic called Evans introduced some remarkable improvements in the construction of boilers. Murdoch, who had succeeded in lighting Boulton's workshops in Birmingham by gas in 1798, installed the first lamps in the streets of London—in Pall Mall—in the year 1807. In France, Philippe Lebon had made the same discovery, but died in 1804 without having been able to get it adopted. Towards the end of the Empire, Philippe de Girard also succeeded in producing a machine for spinning flax. Moreover, the problems of transport were claiming increasing attention. In 1811, MacAdam laid before the House of Commons the process which bears his name for providing roads with a hard stone surface—although it was already in use in France. The English coal industry was making increased use of transport by rail, with improvement in the gradients. Finally, efforts were made to construct a steam-engine to run on an 'iron road', and in 1804 Trewithick achieved a primitive locomotive, and Hedley one in 1803, whilst Stephenson began his researches in 1814. The revolution in water-transport was also in its early stages, though only in America. In 1807, Fulton organized a regular steamship service on the River Hudson, but no one dared as yet to venture on the ocean.

The evidence suggests that the war inclined the manufacturers to rely on military success and on contraband for maintaining their markets, rather than on technical improvements or a reduction in the rate of profit, which would help to explain why there was this slowing down in the progress of inventions. Although in England the use of machinery continued to spread, this took place fairly slowly, even in the cotton industry, where the 'mule' had not yet entirely replaced the 'jenny', and where in 1812 there were not more than 2,000 mechanical looms at work. In the woollen industry, mechanization was in its early stages, and was confined to spinning, though it was more used in lace-making. The metal industries were more advanced. Wood-burning furnaces were dying out, and for smelting cast-iron, the Puddler furnace and the rolling-mill had won the day. Hydraulic power and steam power were still rarely used, except in cotton-spinning and in the mines. Moreover, although there was an undoubted tendency to concentrate industry, it was not so far very marked. Cotton manufacturers only numbered fourteen in 1812, and the first factory in Manchester using steam power only opened in 1806. In the lace industry, the oldest dates only from 1810. The production of metals was still widely dispersed, and other industries even more so, except for distilleries. In London, the working classes undoubtedly held the most prominent position. Taken as a whole, capitalist enterprise was still markedly commercial in character. Merchants had piece-workers engaged in making goods in their own homes out of raw materials supplied them, often on hired looms.

In the Empire, there was still greater weight behind the urge to increase production along traditional lines, in spite of the interest shown in new methods, such as the mule, the *jacquard*, the revolving cylinder for printing calicoes taken over by Mulhouse from Oberkampf in 1805, and Douglas' and Cockerill's machines for wool-spinning. The first reverbatory smelting-furnace appeared at Le Creusot in 1810. Progress was sporadic, and chiefly to be seen in Alsace and the North, at Lyons and Saint-Étienne, in Normandy, and in the State-owned mines of the Sarre: it was most marked in Belgium and the Aix-la-Chapelle region. It was then that the Belgian mines began to be equipped with machinery; and at Liège, Perier—with Napoleon's help—set up a gun foundry. In 1810, Dony established the factory where he used his special process for treating zinc, the origin of the 'Vieille Montagne'. Ghent underwent a revival through the establishment of cotton manufacturies; and at Verviers the beginning of the industrial revolution as far as woollens were concerned was the introduction of English machinery. The town became a very important centre, with 86 manufacturers and 25,000 operatives in 1810. Italy, on the other hand, had few improvements to show; and several regions, deprived—like the West of France—of their traditional markets, devoted themselves more and more to agriculture. Taken as a whole, there was only a very limited installation of new machinery. For cotton-spinning, the spinning-wheel had not disappeared, and the jenny reached its peak in about 1806. The metal industry remained faithful to charcoal smelting, there were few steam-engines, and Belgian mines did not use them until 1807. In spinning, they were not brought in until the end of the Empire, for instance in Alsace, in 1812. There was only a concentration of industry in cotton-spinning and in wool. On the other hand, there was striking progress in commercial concentration. One of the striking features of the period is the increase in the number of big businessmen. There were Bauwens and Richard-Lenoir, the great cotton magnates, at Oberkampf; then Ternaux, who specialized in wool and was a pioneer in the making of cashmere shawls. Dolffus-Mieg at Mulhouse, Japy at Montbéliard,

Peugeot at Audincourt, Cockerill at Liège were all great names. They made no attempt to divide their activities, being at once traders and manufacturers. Though they were the creators of factory products, they still went on employing a whole host of piece-workers in their homes. In comparison with England, the capitalist economy was as behindhand in development as the banking system.

Outside the Empire, the same characteristics recur in Saxony and in Switzerland, the only countries where there were any signs of mechanization and a beginning of the concentration of industry, which was in cotton-spinning and the printing of calicoes. In the United States, there had likewise been great progress in the former, with a rise from four factories in 1804 to 500 in 1815. But weaving was well behind: the first mechanized factory was not set up by Lowel till 1813. The outstanding features in the American economy were the progress in cotton-growing, in which production doubled between 1801 and 1811, and the growth in external trade and in navigation, for it was still the period of magnates like Astor and Girard.

Agriculture remained much more wedded to tradition than industry, except in England, where her superiority over the Continent was even more marked. Only the Low Countries had adopted modern methods, and parts of Northern France. In the Baltic countries and in Prussia, the lords much preferred to evict the peasants and multiply forced labour rather than make any change in their customary methods.

On the Continent, capitalism was making too gradual a progress towards concentration for its social consequences to be for the time being very extensive. Agricultural day-labourers and operatives at the looms went on living much as they had always done, paying more attention to looking for work and keeping an eye on the price of food than on the conditions of work and the rates of wages. They only came into occasional collision with the employers, in certain localities, and only in matters of strictly professional concern. The only attempts at organizing themselves concerned the revival of the trade-guilds and the formation of a certain number of mutual help societies. As in the eighteenth century, their history was chiefly marked by periods of severe unemployment, and high prices caused by bad harvests.

But the case was quite different in England. There, the working classes were growing in numbers and becoming increasingly massed in the black country of the north and northwest. The exodus from the countryside brought about by the enclosures, the employment of women and children, endemic unemployment due to the introduction of machinery, and the periodical economic crises all prevented wages from keeping pace with prices. There was a sinister deterioration in the living conditions of these masses, uprooted from the country, crowded together in insanitary slums, undernourished, uneducated, and altogether lacking in any amusements. In spite of the Act of 1799, Unions continued to be formed. Since they went on appealing to ancient statutory rights, Parliament repealed those which authorized a levy on wages in the year 1813, and in 1814 those which concerned apprenticeship. As in France, all that was left of the ancient laws were the clauses that bore so hardly upon the workers. In 1802, at the instance of Peel's father, Parliament had introduced the first Factory Bill to protect children, but it remained a dead letter. Deprived as they were of all legal redress, it is not surprising that there were periodical outbreaks of violence among them, usually directed against the new machines. The most famous of these Luddite riots in 1811 and 1812 were the result of the economic crisis, although attempts were made to ascribe them to conspiracies and to the influence of French ideas. Maitland, who was entrusted with their suppression, assured the public that 'there was a pernicious spirit abroad', tending 'to subvert the government of the country and destroy all property'. To judge by the speeches made by some men, such as John Baynes of Halifax, there were memories of the democratic agitation that had occurred at the time of the Revolution. He was condemned at the age of 66 for having greeted the recent disturbances as a prelude to revolution:

Too long have these vampires fed upon our blood. . . . They have stirred up wars; they feed on them, nay, they grow fat on them. They have sent us all over the world to fight in order to stamp out freedom in France and maintain despotism over the whole of Europe. . . . I have waited a long while for the dawn to break; but old as I am, may I still live to see the glorious triumph of democracy.

But if the masses in Great Britain had been filled with revolutionary fire, they would at least have demanded universal suffrage: as it was, these events can only be seen as the writhings of a tortured people who had lost all political sense. It is possible —as some have maintained—that there were certain influences at work holding the populace in check, such as the Dissenters, Hannah More's Sunday School movement, and the schools for self-help instruction recommended by a young Quaker called Lancaster in 1798, and fostered by an organization from 1810 onwards. Nevertheless, the absence of any general uprising was essentially due to the fact that as yet the working classes were not very closely massed together; and since 1795, wages had been made up to a certain figure in proportion to the price of bread. For the property-owning classes, the poor-law was an insurance premium.

Some thinkers, however, were beginning to have new ideas in the face of these social developments. Although the British economists found no fault with the existing system on the score of justice, it filled them with a profound pessimism, as already exemplified by Malthus. The banker Ricardo, who began to write in 1810, founded all value upon work; but he noted that in England the cultivation of the less and less profitable land, made necessary by the increasing population, insured a differential income to the owners of the better land, whilst he also confirmed the iron law of supply and demand which controlled wages. Man's attempts to ward off famine would become more and more desperate, labour would absorb an increasing proportion of the cost of production, and the capitalist's profits would continually decrease. The final result would be that no new land would be taken into cultivation, and Malthus' law would exercise its inexorable sway over the whole situation. On the Continent, Sismondi, adopting a moral standpoint altogether absent from Ricardo's thought, was working out his *Principes d'économie politique*, which appeared in 1819. It contained a sharp criticism of the new organization of labour in which the wage-earner became a mere chattel whose value was constantly being lowered by the competition of the machine. As early as Year XII, Fourier had denounced the state of social chaos that had arisen from the individualism of the Revolution. Saint-Simon, taking an opposite line, retained the eighteenth-century enthusiasm for the productive capacity of modern industry; but he proposed to organize it in such a way as to increase production still further.

These men were no champions of democracy, and Fourier and Saint-Simon's violent attacks on the effects of the Revolution were quite in keeping with the reaction of contemporary thought. Saint-Simon, for example, claimed that society should be run by 'the really capable people', that is to say, by the experts and the technicians, so that the 'ruling class' should be 'always more enlightened than those whom they ruled'. It was thus his intention to reconstitute an aristocracy invested with absolute power. But he realized that this new aristocracy would, in order to continue to deserve its privileged position, have to be constantly renewed by fresh blood; and he was therefore against the principle of inheritance. Like Saint Simon, Sismondi and Fourier attacked economic liberty and competition. Their ideal was that all men, regardless of politics, should be concerned solely with creating wealth for the benefit of all mankind. Socialism could afford to disregard the noise and tumult of war, for it was the inevitable outcome of capitalism; and it was about to infuse new life into the democratic movement. By this time, Robert Owen was already planning his experiments in community.

Outside Europe, capitalism pursued its conquering career by the English spirit of commercial progress shown in America; but it continued to be a brake upon white expansion. In the Far East, the agents of the East India Company continued their efforts to establish trading centres. As early as 1802, the Portuguese were asked to admit a British garrison at Macao, and in 1808 a squadron put in an appearance there, though still without success; whilst in Canton a series of incidents produced continual friction between the Chinese and the English. Gia-long also had to repel attacks on Cochin China in 1804 and against Hanoi in 1808. In Japan, a ship appeared at Nagasaki in 1808 in an attempt to capture the Dutch ships; and later on Raffles, who had established himself in Java, tried to get his authority recognized by the Batavian trade-settlement of Deshima. In China, K'ia-king was increasingly threatened by secret societies, and in 1813, a great insurrection broke out in Shantung. Japan could not have put up any serious resistance, and the appearance of Captain Pellew in 1808 had struck terror into the leading spirits. It was only the internal struggles of Europe that gave the Far East more than a quarter of a century of respite.

As far as colonization was concerned, it did not make more than very modest progress in the British Empire. Emigrants were few, and preferred to go to the United States. None came to the Cape till 1808, and Canada hardly accepted any. In Australia about the year 1815 there were only some 600 to 700 colonists, 400 of whom were convicts, cultivating about 20,000 acres. Canada showed the most favourable advance. At the end of the period, Lower Canada had about 250,000 inhabitants, 20,000 to 30,000 of them English, and Upper Canada 70,000. American contraband was very profitable to Halifax, and the needs of the Admiralty gave an advantage to timber export, thus laying the foundation of a prosperous industry. In Java, Stamford Raffles went in for new methods, transforming the native chiefs into officials, renting land to the inhabitants, and allowing them freedom to work it and to engage in trade; but they did not have the necessary time or money.

White expansion continued to prosper, particularly in the United States. This was less due to immigration than to the excessive birthrate, which led to a continuous trek from the Atlantic coast to the north-western territories. Ohio had become a State in 1802, and Indiana and Illinois were to be admitted soon after 1815. In the south, on the other hand, the negroes were increasing in numbers with the growth of the cotton plantations, and were now reckoned at more than 1½ million. Louisiana was admitted to the federation in 1812, and Florida was having greedy eyes cast upon it. Madison occupied the western part of it along with Pensacola, which was debatable territory; and Jackson, at the head of the Tennessee militia, was conducting operations against the Creeks.

The only serious rivals to the Anglo-Saxons were the Russians. They had entered Transcaucasia, conquered the Persians, and by the treaty of Gulistan in 1813 been recognized as the possessors of Daghestan and Baku, with the sole right of having a fleet on the Caspian. They tried unsuccessfully to establish relationships with China; and in 1805 an embassy from Alexander was arrested in Mongolia. The Behring Company, established in

1799, was expanding in Alaska, and in 1803 they sent the cruisers Razanov and Kruzenstern round Cape Horn. The first appeared at Nagasaki in 1804, but was not admitted to harbour; and in 1806 proceeded from Alaska as far as San Francisco. From Okhotskh, the Russians attempted to seize Sakhalin and attacked the Kunle Islands and Yeso, to the great consternation of the Japanese. A little later on, they were planning to establish a colony in California as a supply-base for Alaska, and in 1811 set up a fort north of San Francisco, coming into contact at this point with the Canadian company that was beginning to work in Colombia and Oregon.

The part played by the missions remained a very subordinate one. In China, the Apostolic Vicar Dufresne had called the first synod together in 1803; but it was not attended by any priest from Europe. In 1805, persecution broke out again, and Dufresne himself was beheaded in 1815. In 1807, a Protestant missionary called Morrison landed at Canton, and Baptists had also begun to work in Burma. The Bible Society was founded in 1804, but conditions did not so far allow it to engage in much activity.

In the minds of Europeans, the colonies were still playing the part assigned to them by the Mercantile Theory; but the old colonial system was already threatened. France had at a particular juncture abolished slavery, thus giving up one of her chief advantages, and she lost Saint Domingo in an attempt to reintroduce it. In 1807, England abolished the Slave Trade, which was bound to cut off the supply of negroes. On the other hand, the United States took a distinctive line, for the colonists and the half-castes had made up their minds to have done with exclusiveness, and to separate from Europe to get rid of it. Spain was in a fair way to lose her colonial possessions. After recognizing Ferdinand VII, the colonies had not been slow to remember that they were only his personal possessions, and that during his captivity they were their own masters. In 1810, when the news came through that Andalusia had fallen and that the Junta were shut up in Cadiz, they took a further step. Caracas deposed its viceroy on April 19; Buenos Aires on May 20. New Granada rose in July, Quito in August, Chile and Mexico in September. The colonies offered to sign a commercial treaty with England, and Bolivar went to London. Wellesley intervened, but the Cortes refused to abolish the trade monopoly, and declared their American subjects to be rebels. Bolivar returned home again, followed by Miranda. They called together a congress which declared Venezuela independent on July 7, 1811, and voted a constitution. New Granada did the same. In the Argentine, the leaders were already at odds, and one of them, Moreno by name, had been expelled. The Constituent Assembly did not meet till 1813. Everywhere the rights of man were proclaimed, whilst keeping for Catholicism its privileged position as the religion of the State; but slavery, the *mita* and the *comiendas* were suppressed.

Discord promptly broke out in the new States. The half-castes cold-shouldered the Spaniards. The moderates took alarm at the appeal to the negroes and the half-breeds, while the leaders quarrelled, and the towns, in their jealousy of one another, changed sides in order to defend their independence. The mountain-dwellers, led by the clergy, supported the Spaniards; and in Venezuela, the *llaneros* were prepared to fight for anyone who would pay them. But Spain succeeded in retaining some solid advantages. In Mexico, they shot the parish priest Hidalgo in 1811; and his confederate, Morales, who made a new attempt in 1813, suffered the same fate in 1815. The Spaniards retained possession of Lima, from which point they could successfully contest Quito with the Granadinos; and after varying fortunes, they recaptured High Peru from the Argentinians. Paraguay finally slipped from their grasp, but Elio put up a long resistance at Montevideo and called in the Portuguese to his assistance. The town was not finally freed until 1814, under Alvéar. In Chile, Rosas, Carrera, and O'Higgins were rivals for power; and in 1813, the Spaniards, concentrating their forces in the south, recaptured the offensive and reconquered the whole country. But the struggle took its most dramatic turn in Venezuela and New Granada. The Spaniards had been able to hold out in the region of Maracaïbo and in the Orinoco valley; and in 1812, they fairly easily got the better of Miranda, who capitulated on July 25. He was sent to Cadiz, where he died in 1816. Bolivar managed to escape and reached Carthagena. The following year, the Gradadinos authorized him to invade Venezuela, and he entered Caracas on August 6. His enemies once more retreated eastwards, whence in 1814 they renewed their attack and defeated him, forcing him to retire to New Granada. Just at this moment, Ferdinand VII, restored to power, despatched reinforcements, and in the spring of 1815 his fleet appeared and Bolivar embarked for Jamaica. The Argentine alone remained free; but it was weakened by dissensions, and Alvéar, who was elected governor in 1814, and had asked for English protection, was overthrown in April 1815. There was thus still some uncertainty about the eventual destiny of Spanish America; but it was certain that the mother country could never fully re-establish the old colonial regime.

Since the objective of capitalist production was profit, it represented a power that was quite foreign to Napoleon's political and military ideals. It is true that in its most developed forms it is inimical to national barriers, which are a hindrance to the exploitation of natural wealth and prevent a rational division of labour among the different regions of the earth; and in this sense, a universal empire might have been favourable to it. But capitalism was only just beginning, and its champions, who were thoroughly imbued with the Mercantile doctrine, simply viewed their own country as a preserve to be guarded at all costs. Moreover, in their human capacity as patriots, they were devoted to its independence; and the favours Napoleon reserved for France would sooner or later have turned them into partisans of nationality in opposition to the Empire, until such time as national feelings set them at odds with one another. Nevertheless, this was not the worst aspect of things for Napoleon. More serious for him was the fact that England was the country where industrial capitalism had originated, and where it had acquired the greatest resources and power. It alone enabled England to finance the war: in this sense, Great Britain's victory over the Emperor was a victory for capitalism.

III

THE FALL OF NAPOLEON
(1812–1815)

CHAPTER NINE

The Disintegration of the Continental System (1812–1814)

THE CONTINENTAL SYSTEM had been created and upheld by the victories of the *Grande Armée*. But each new war made its continuance more and more doubtful. The Russian campaign was intended to put the finishing touches to it; instead, its outcome was disaster. After the disintegration of the *Grande Armée*, all the Emperor's efforts were set upon rebuilding it; and although it had lost its cohesion, and with it the chief secret of its strength, it would again have been victorious if it had only had to fight against one or two of the Continental powers, as in the previous struggles.

But on this occasion, remembering the lessons of the last twenty years, the powers united to fall upon him. The Continental System disintegrated, Napoleon vanished from the scene, and France was left to pay for his failures.

THE RUSSIAN CAMPAIGN

To bring against Russia, Napoleon had over 700,000 men, more than 611,000 of whom successively crossed the frontier in the course of the campaign. These forces followed the pattern of the *Grand Empire*. There were 300,000 French, including those from the annexed territories; 180,000 Germans, including 30,000 Austrians from Schwarzenberg and York's 20,000

Prussians; 9,000 Swiss; 90,000 Poles and Lithuanians; 32,000 Italians, Illyrians, Spaniards, and Portuguese. These contingents proved to be of very variable loyalty. Never had the *Grand Armée* been so large, and never of such motley composition and with so little cohesion; Frenchmen of France proper hardly constituted a third of the total.

The shock troops, who had taken up positions beyond the Vistula, consisting of 450,000 men and 1,146 guns, were divided into nine corps, plus the Guards, four cavalry corps and the allies. With this customary division of forces, the army seemed unwieldy enough because of its very size, the length of the front, and the difficulties of liaison. Napoleon did in fact group these corps into armies. He was on the Niemen with 227,000 men. Eugene was a little to the rear with 80,000. Jerome was in command of the right wing, with 76,000; beyond him were Schwarzenberg, and on the extreme left, Macdonald and York. But really good army commanders were needed, and Jerome could hardly be reckoned as such. In choosing him, Napoleon had been swayed by dynastic reasons. Never again was there to be the same precision of manœuvre.

As usual, Napoleon intended this to be a short war. Up to June 20, he hoped that it would be fought in Poland. Whilst he was making for Kovno with the bulk of his forces, he refused to give battle with his right wing towards Warsaw, where Jerome's mediocre generalship was a positive snare. If the enemy made a massed attack on the Grand Duchy, he would fall back on his right flank and disperse them, and there would be a quick peace. But the Russians made no move, and it was therefore necessary to attack them on their own ground. His soldiers took a four-day bread ration, and the convoys followed them with a flour-supply for three weeks. By the end of this period, a decisive blow would have brought Alexander to his knees.

It is certain that there was no lack of voices advising Alexander to take a conciliatory line, men like the Grand Duke Constantine and Rumiantzov. On June 28, Balachov was despatched to Napoleon to offer negotiations if he would evacuate Russian territory. The enemies of France, such as Armfelt and Stein, never ceased to fear that their sovereign might give in, and perhaps they had good grounds for their anxiety. At all events, pride won the day. Nevertheless, the

Russian army's inferiority seemed quite irremediable. Behind the Niemen, Barclay de Tolly had 120,000 men at his disposal, while, on the Bug, Bagration had less than 40,000. Further south, Tormasov could bring up rather more; and in the second line of defence, Wittgenstein was advancing to protect the Duna and the Riga. In the interior, there remained 300,000 to 400,000 recruits, Cossacks, and militiamen, and Tchitchagov was getting under way with the Danube army, but still needed time. Time could be gained by concealment, and those who—like Rostoptchine—considered the distances and the winter to be their best allies, saw nothing but advantage in this delay. The majority, however, could not stomach the idea of invasion, or were afraid that it would break their master's resolve. In the end, the plan adopted was that of Phull, a German *émigré*, according to which either Barclay or Bagration—whichever of them was attacked by Napoleon—would resist, while the other would fall upon the assailants' flank. Alexander had no thought of the war being carried to the heart of the country. But that could scarcely fail to happen, because his generals knew they were weaker than their enemies, and were very much afraid of them. They were given a good deal of latitude as to their movements, fell back in order to avoid disaster, and thus condemned their opponents to wear themselves out in pursuit.

Napoleon's army crossed the Niemen on June 24 and 25, 1812, and on the 26th reached Vilna by a forced march of twenty-five miles, with the intention of crushing Barclay. But it struck thin air, for Barclay had retreated towards the entrenched camp at Drissa, behind the Duna. So Bagration remained to be dealt with. Davout set out from Vilna towards Minsk, in order to cut off his retreat, whilst Jerome went in pursuit. But Jerome had a long way to go, and did not hurry. Bagration, seeing that he was not directly pressed, slipped out of Davout's way by turning south, crossed the Dnieper, and then went on up stream. Jerome, deprived of his objective, turned back towards Westphalia. Davout defeated Bagration at Mohilev, but was unable to stop him. The Vilna manœuvre had failed.

On July 3, Napoleon set out again for Vitebsk, in order to come between the two Russian armies, but when he arrived on the 24th it was too late. Barclay had evacuated Drissa and then

Vitebsk, and was withdrawing towards Smolensk, where he managed to join forces with Bagration.

The two Russian armies being thus united, Barclay agreed to take the offensive towards Vitebsk. Napoleon immediately put a third plan into action. He slipped away southwards, crossed the Dnieper, and appeared before Smolensk on August 16. But his attack failed, and Barclay, who had been forewarned and had begun to withdraw on the 12th, arrived in time to defend the town. On the 17th, as the result of a bloody battle, the French only managed to capture the suburbs. Again the Russian army retired, and on the 19th its rearguard covered the retreat at Valoutina. Would the French follow it to Moscow?

From the start, it was clear that this was to be a new kind of war. Napoleon's strategy had proved faulty: the enemy were shamelessly withdrawing, and there were no natural obstacles to bring it to bay, nor was it possible to catch it by surprise, because in these deserted plains the cavalry wore itself out without collecting any information, and because the sheer distances deprived the French rapid marches of their usual effectiveness. And the marches had been more than usually exhausting. As early as June 26, there had been many stragglers and deserters in the advance on Vilna, and these had assumed alarming proportions. The convoys were unable to keep pace, and almost from the start the army had to live on the country—and the country produced absolutely nothing. Deprived of their fodder, the horses died by the thousand. Then the weather took a hand in the game, with storms, rain, and cold nights at the end of June, followed by sweltering heat. At Smolensk, the available troops were reduced to 160,000 men. How many of these would be left by the time Moscow was reached? The foreign troops in particular were visibly melting away. The Wurtemberg divison, 16,000 strong, only had 1,456 men left by September 4. On the flanks and in the rear, the situation was far from promising. Macdonald had failed to take Riga, and Gouvion-Saint-Cyr, who had been victorious at Polotsk, saw Wittgenstein's army visibly increasing in size to bar his path. Reynier and Schwarzenberg were making Tormasov move cautiously; but Tchitchagov was moving towards them. Napoleon had counted on the Poles to rise as one man and invade the Ukraine. But on June 28 the Diet gave way to a confederation presided over by Czartoryski's father, which immediately re-established the Kingdom of Poland. The Emperor gave a cold reception to this news and remained silent, realizing that it was not wise to irritate Prussia and Austria, nor to drive Alexander to despair before having beaten him. He did not even join Lithuania onto the Duchy, but handed it over, like Courland, to French officials. The Poles were in a state of disappointment and unrest. Moreover, they were exhausted, and Napoleon's ambassador, De Pradt, Archbishop of Malines, did not arouse much enthusiasm. They were waiting to show their hand until victory was well on the way. In these circumstances, would it not be wiser to stop and organize the country so far conquered, and arrange to provision the army while it went into winter quarters on the spot? Napoleon had already asked himself this question at Vitebsk. There was one way of making a radical change in the whole complexion of the war, and in the chances of success, and that was to promise the peasants the abolition of serfdom. The Emperor was well aware of this; but the revolutionary tradition was now too much against the grain with him for this expedient to seem anything but hateful. From this time onwards, he decided that the efforts demanded from the Empire could not continue without damage to his own prestige. In Germany more particularly, the consequences might well be incalculable. Moreover, he was convinced that the fall of Moscow would bring Alexander to his knees, and he decided to go forward.

On September 5, he suddenly came up against the Russian army on the outskirts of the River Moskva. Kutusov had replaced Barclay, and did not intend to give up Moscow without a struggle. His right flank was covered by the river, and was therefore protected: his left, resting on a forest, was only turned at a later stage. Napoleon attacked in the centre on September 7, and carried the redoubts after a long and bloody battle. The French lost 30,000 men and the Russians 50,000. At the critical moment, Napoleon had refused to throw the Guards into the battle, and Kutusov was able to withdraw without a breach in his line behind the Nara, south of Moscow, whilst Napoleon entered the capital on September 14. From the 15th to the 18th it was devastated by fires, kindled at least in part on the orders of Rostopchine.

Alexander meanwhile had come back from Drissa to St. Petersburg. He made peace with England and handed over his fleet. At the end of August, his alliance with Bernadotte was confirmed in an interview at Abo. But although Bernadotte had now obtained a subsidy from Great Britain, he was in no mind to risk anything in Germany without first conquering Norway, and then only so long as Napoleon remained victorious. It was clear that the Czar must rely simply upon his own efforts. His sister Catherine, and the *émigrés*, joined by Arndt, d'Ivernois, and Mme de Staël, insisted on fighting to the bitter end. If Alexander had capitulated, he would no doubt have been in great danger from the nobility, who were beside themselves with anxiety and rage. But it would appear that what finally prevailed with him was the attraction of striking a heroic attitude. The international circle surrounding him saw in him their last hope and greeted him as the liberator of Europe; and he was secretly sure that victory would make him its master. He had always dreamed of playing this part, which suited his vanity, his lip-service to liberty, and his deep-down instinct for domination. With his increasing tendency to mysticism, he was easily persuaded that he was God's chosen vessel in the fight against Antichrist. Having thus put himself at the head of this crusade which Burke had formerly preached, he remained deaf to all Napoleon's suggestions.

Napoleon did not possess the means to go any further into Russia. In Moscow, the army was in no immediate danger: nevertheless, it only held the ground it occupied, and its lines of communication were far from secure. Official tradition has no doubt exaggerated the national character of this war; but the serfs, like everyone else, could only flee before a starving foe, and, reduced to despair, they could only reply by guerilla warfare. The Cossacks, with their usual elusiveness, kept a close watch on all the French detachments. If Napoleon allowed winter to hem him in, he might lose Europe and even France in the general uncertainty about his fate. Up to the middle of October, he continued hopeful. Kutusov was keeping Murat happily occupied by negotiating for an armistice; but he suddenly took his enemy by surprise at Winkovo. The next day Napoleon, thoroughly disillusioned, gave the order to retreat.

Kutusov could reckon on several days' start from Taratino

to Smolensk. In order to intimidate him, Napoleon advanced southwards and defeated him on the 24th at Malo-Yaroslavetz, after which he slipped away and continued to make for Smolensk, while Davout—not without some difficulty—covered him against Miloradovitch. When he set out, it was still fine weather; but quite abruptly snow began to fall. The countryside had been devastated on the forward march, and now offered no shelter and nothing in the way of resources. The horses fell by the wayside, vehicles and guns were abandoned, the trail of stragglers grew constantly longer under the daily scourge of the frost and the Cossacks. From November 9 to 13 the army entered Smolensk, and from the 14th to the 18th they left it in successive stages. The Russians went ahead and cut the road to Krasnoi. On the 15th, Napoleon got by without much resistance; but on the 16th Eugène, and on the 17th Davout, had to give battle. On the 18th, Ney was stopped, and only managed to escape by miraculously crossing the frozen Dnieper. The army regrouped, and reached the Beresina, though now reduced to about 30,000 men. At this point, a serious danger confronted it. Chitchagov, having rejoined Tormasov, had moved northwards, and without being pursued by Schwarzenberg had taken Minsk, and then Borisov. Wittgenstein, for his part, had crossed the Duna and was driving back Oudinot and Victor. Oudinot hastened back to recapture Borisov, but found the bridge had been destroyed. In the night of the 25th to 26th, Éblé's sappers built two new bridges. Napoleon crossed on the 27th, and the next day there was a furious battle on both sides of the river. On the right, Chitchagov was held; but Kutusov's weakness allowed Victor to escape, though he had to sacrifice his stragglers. At this point the cold, which had up till then been relatively moderate, since the Beresina was not frozen over, grew desperately severe, and finished off what was left of the *Grande Armée*. Some 12,000 men reached Vilna on December 9 and retreated by way of Kovno to Königsberg, to be gradually joined by 40,000 stragglers who had been cut off. Macdonald, falling back towards Tilsit, and Reynier and Schwarzenberg towards the Bug, had between them no more than 55,000 men. Napoleon had lost 400,000, plus 100,000 prisoners.

The *Grande Armée*, the shield of Europe, no longer existed, and would take a long time to rebuild. There was no longer any possibility of the binding-force that had held the French armies together since 1793, nor could new cavalry be improvised. Nevertheless, Napoleon was not altogether shattered by this catastrophe, and was already giving his whole mind to the problem of rebuilding an army. On December 5, before Vilna, Napoleon had received the news of General Malet's attempt to seize the government in Paris on October 23, which all but succeeded; but he and his accomplices had been shot on the 29th. Yet Napoleon realized it was high time to go and take over the reins again before the terrible news from Russia became generally known. He handed over command to Murat and hastened back to France by sledge, accompanied by Caulaincourt. He was full of illusions, demanding new contingents from Prussia and Austria, and counting on Murat to hold the Russians at a safe distance on the Vistula, whilst he himself would reappear there in the spring with new legions.

THE DEFECTION OF PRUSSIA AND THE FIRST CAMPAIGN OF 1813

If the Prussians and Austrians had remained faithful, Murat might perhaps have been able to hold on. Kutusov was exhausted and did not venture across the frontier, thinking that his country had no interest in prolonging the war, an opinion shared by many of his countrymen. It was Alexander who decided to resume the offensive. Dismissing Rumiantzov in disgrace, he appeared at Vilna with Nesselrode on December 23. He was spurred on by Stein, who had been imploring him since November 17 to set Germany free. The people would be called upon to rise, and the princes would be urged to join the right side on pain of losing their thrones. Overtures had already been made to York by the Italian Paulucei and the German *émigrés*. York asked for instructions, and it is possible that none reached him. But, separated as he was from Macdonald by the Russians, he made no attempt to force his way through—which he could easily have done—but signed a convention of neutrality at Tauroggen on December 30. The Russians invaded Prussia, and with Bulow refusing to work with Murat, Macdonald had some difficulty in regaining the Vistula.

Frederick William dismissed York; but York pretended to be unaware of the fact and followed the Russians, who had good reason to count upon the Polish aristocracy. In December, Czartoryski had asked the Czar to re-establish Poland under the sceptre of one of his sons. Several members of the Warsaw government offered the Grand Duchy to Russia, asking for reunion with Lithuania and the granting of a constitution. Nesselrode and Stein opposed this plan, the former in his country's interest, the latter on the plea that the coalition would then become impossible. On January 13, 1813, Alexander did not do more than assure the Poles of his good intentions; but they were satisfied with this, and offered no resistance. Schwarzenberg for his part began to enter into discussions and withdrew without a fight. Warsaw was occupied on February 9.

The French retreated towards Posen, Eugène taking the place of Murat, who had left for Naples. On January 30, Schwarzenberg signed a separate armistice, as a result of which he withdrew towards Warsaw, followed by Poniatovski, thus exposing Reynier, whose army corps was partly destroyed. On February 12, Eugène left Posen, and at the end of the month he prematurely abandoned the line of the Oder. From this time onwards, the desertion of Prussia was more or less an accomplished fact.

Frederick William took time to convince himself that the ruin of the *Grande Armée* set him free; and if Napoleon had offered him the Duchy of Warsaw, he would perhaps have been satisfied. He was afraid of Austria, whom he thought to be in league with France, and suspected Russia of wishing to annex the whole of Poland, and even Eastern Prussia. His entourage were very divided. Knesebeck—followed more tentatively by Hardenberg—was in favour of an immediate alliance with Alexander. Ancillon would have preferred an agreement with Metternich to impose a mediation which should deliver Germany without offering an entry to the Russians. At the end of December, the king was inclined to put off a decision till the spring, and then to desert in the rear of the Emperor if he made a new entry into Russia. In Vienna, Knesebeck learnt that Prussia had nothing to fear from Austria; when he was surreptitiously advised to make an agreement with the Czar. His proposals for an alliance were rejected.

The decision was finally swayed by the revolutionary actions of the patriots. York's desertion set matters in motion. The king at first met the news with consternation. He decided to send the Czar an agent who promised to 'reconstitute' Prussia and follow up his urgent request by threats. Reckoning moreover that he had incurred the wrath of Napoleon, Frederick William allowed himself to be persuaded on January 22 that it was better to leave Berlin and establish himself instead at Breslau. During this time, York had gone ahead in to Prussia; Stein appeared at Königsberg as the Czar's commissary and had taken the initiative of calling together the Estates. The officials were frightened and in the end took offence, and he had to give way to York; but basically it was realized that the two parties were in agreement. Subject to royal approval, the Estates set up a *Landwehr* which York was commissioned to organize, without prejudice to ordinary recruiting. In default of volunteers, all men between 18 and 45 were compelled to serve in a contingent; but provision was made for substitutes. The Estates were careful to reserve to themselves the choice of officers, in order to deprive this arming of the people of any possible menace to the nobility. The king did not take kindly to this illegal step; but it might have cost him his crown to resist it; besides, the war party at Breslau, led by Scharnhorst, had been considerably strengthened by this measure. For his part, Frederick William sent out on February 3 an invitation to those of his subjects who could equip themselves to form volunteer corps in support of the regular troops; and in order to give this movement some impetus, he abolished on February 9, for the duration of the war, all rights to exemption for men between the ages of 17 and 24. On the 10th, he sent out a first appeal to his people. At the same time, he sent Knesebeck to the Czar. The talks dragged on because Prussia wanted to be given back her frontiers of 1806, at any rate on the east, whilst Alexander would only promise to give an equivalent in territory. Stein resolved the difficulty by going with Anstett to Breslau, where the king gave in. The alliance was concluded on February 28 at Kalisch. Alexander joined Frederick William on March 15; on the 16th, a declaration of war against France was despatched, and on the 17th the king instituted the *Landwehr* through the kingdom for all men between 17 and 40 years of age, with no right of substitution. The officers were to be appointed by district councils, with two nobles and a representative of the peasants. On April 21, there was a further call-up of men over 40 to form a *Landsturm*, but it was scarcely put into operation. In order to conquer France Prussia was thus borrowing from her the system of wholesale levies, as Scharnhorst and Gneisenau had long wished to do; and as she had only 5 million inhabitants, she applied it with a rigour that even the Committee of Public Safety had not thought necessary.

This alliance was of outstanding importance to the Russians. They could hardly produce more than 70,000 front line troops. Although the *Landwehr* was not ready for the front before August, and only 7,000 to 8,000 volunteers joined up in May, the regular army—thanks to the recall of 30,000 to 40,000 *Krümper* and officers who had been commissioned in 1807, as well as to the recruits—was able to send 35,000 men straight away to the front, and to play its part in the sieges. As early as March 4, Eugène had left Berlin and retired behind the Elbe. The enemy immediately crossed this river. Hamburg had risen in revolt on February 24 and the Russians entered it on March 18. That same day, Davout evacuated Dresden. Saxony was thus immediately overrun and the French pushed back behind the Saale.

This national movement on the part of Prussia also had a great moral effect, for it gave the war the character of a struggle for freedom, which had been Alexander's dream; and in German histories, it still goes down as the *Befreiungskrieg*. There was particularly marked enthusiasm among the university students, the middle classes, and the nobility. In Berlin, Fichte interrupted his course of lectures and joined with Steffens and Schleiermacher in giving ardent support to the king's appeal. There was a very uneven response in the different provinces. In Silesia and West Prussia, the Poles refused to obey, or deserted; in East Prussia, there was considerable use of the substitute system. In the country especially, the obedience which the peasants were accustomed to give to the *Junkers* and officials—for they had barely emerged from serfdom—was responsible for bringing more men to the colours than any patriotic fervour. Moreover, the nobility contrived only to admit the middle classes to the lower grades, and so one of the chief stimulants that had given strength to the revolutionary armies no longer made itself felt. Nevertheless, the results were considerable: from March to April, 15,000 volunteers enrolled in the free corps, not to mention the *Landwehr*, which finally numbered some 120,000 to 130,000 men. In August, it first saw fire, and formed more than half the operational force; it made a real change in the character of the Prussian army. It need hardly be said that the professional soldiers had not much use for the *Landwehr*, for, like the early revolutionary levies, it was somewhat untrained and inclined to panic.

The rising in Prussia had a stirring effect on all Germany. Since the end of 1812, the patriots had been more and more active in their propaganda, for which Paulucci had made use of Merkel, whilst Arndt wrote leaflet after leaflet, in particular a *Catéchisme du soldat allemand*, calling upon all Germans to fight against 'the spirit of evil' if need be, even if not supported by their princes. Stein wanted to go further still. He wanted Alexander and Frederick William to decree and organize a national war, which would rally the cautious and the indifferent. Sure enough, on March 19, the sovereigns addressed a proclamation to all Germans, in which they declared the Confederation of the Rhine at an end and summoned the princes to change sides on pain of being unseated from office as unworthy to rule their subjects. They set up a council to administer the territories to be occupied, empowered to organize a *Landwehr* in them, and Stein was made its president. The excitement immediately spread to Hamburg and Saxony; and further afield—for instance at Hanau and in the Duchy of Berg—Napoleon's new levies caused disturbances, which assisted the propaganda against the French. Mecklenburg deserted, and the majority of the princes would certainly have done likewise if they had not still been afraid of the Emperor. Stein's threats and exhortations to rebellion had the effect of estranging them, and were not at all helpful to the influence of Prussia: the result was rather to make them look to Austria for support.

The national enthusiasm gave rise to a new generation of poets who despised all dreams and speculations, and whose only thought was to celebrate the heroism of the soldier. One of these was Theodor Körner, who fell in action, leaving behind him a famous collection of poems entitled *La lyre et l'epée*; others were Rückert, whose *Sonnets cuirassés* appeared in 1814, Schenkendorf, and Uhland. Nevertheless, although a great change was clearly coming over German patriotism, it was very far from complete. The Germans could not help feeling at one in their desire to get rid of the French who had made life so hard for them; but for the most part, this was the limit of their vision, and they had no clear idea of a political nationalism. Even the patriotic leaders did not always make a clear distinction between this and a purely cultural nationalism. Gneisenau, for example, had no feelings against the idea of England setting up to her own advantage a great state between the Rhine and the Elbe. Those who were all for unity, like Stein, did not always succeed, because of the historical circumstances, in forming a clear conception of it. It mattered little to them whether the leadership fell to Prussia or to Austria; and Stein did not even see any disadvantage in the complete disappearance of Prussia. But this indifference did nothing to solve the problem, and was in fact an expression of their powerlessness to solve it. And what was more, these men realized that the Germans would not manage to achieve freedom without the help of Europe; and they were therefore coming round to the view that Europe should organize the new state and place it under a European guarantee as a protectorate. Moreover, the middle classes' patriotism was blended with more or less advanced liberal ideas, whilst the nobles associated the thought with the maintenance or restoration of the *Ancien Régime*, both politically and socially. As for the princes, they were not interested in any unity that would diminish their sovereign rights, nor in any constitution that would put restraint upon their authority.

National union came about in equivocal circumstances, in which each party looked to turn the victory to its own advantage. As long as it was necessary, the common people were left with the hopes that would encourage them to fight; but Austria's intervention was destined to ensure that the princes and the nobles were to reap the advantages.

This intervention was being prepared for by Metternich with an equal degree of circumspection and resolution. The disaster to the *Grande Armée* having set Austria free, her alliance with

France had been virtually dissolved, for she could not willingly help the *Grand Empire* to remain in being when it had largely grown rich by despoiling Austria. Bubna was sent to Paris at the end of December to inform Napoleon that his master would not increase his contingent; then Schwarzenberg withdrew from the front line. 'This is the first step towards desertion!' Napoleon exclaimed. It was a cruel disappointment for him, when he had built such hopes upon this dynastic alliance. But he calmed down, and did his best to put a good face upon a gloomy situation. He would first deal with the Russians and the Prussians: after that he would settle accounts with Austria. Metternich had no doubts about this. People have wondered whether Napoeon could not have reaffirmed the alliance by offering to strike some sort of bargain. But this was not possible, for if Austria had helped him to defeat Russia and Prussia, she would then have found herself entirely at his mercy. Metternich could accept no terms that had not been agreed at least with the Prussians in order to re-establish a balance of power and a lasting peace by holding both Alexander and Napoleon in check. That is why he sent Bubna to offer his assistance in persuading France to make some concessions. As a statesman, he would have perhaps viewed such a solution with some satisfaction, for he was not anxious to increase the size of Prussia, and he was even more distrustful than Frederick William of the Czar, whom he suspected of having ambitions not only in Poland, but also in Turkey. He mistrusted the effervescent mood of Germany as equally threatening to the *Ancien Régime* and to Austria. But in order to restore the former powers in Germany, France would have to consent to the limits fixed at the Peace of Lunéville, and Metternich was convinced that Napoleon would never agree to this. It only remained then for Austria to join the coalition at the opportune moment in order to overthrow it. As an aristocrat and a victim of the Revolution, Metternich personally viewed the prospect with some pleasure, as did the whole Austrian nobility. Lebzeltern, his ambassador to Alexander, boasted that 'he had always acted in agreement' with the Russians and the Prussians 'to crush the Revolution and bring victory to the righteous cause'.

In fact, the Emperor did not go further than to make Bubna the generous offer of Illyria. He was also willing to re-establish the throne of Portugal. But he would abandon none of the countries constitutionally united to the Empire, nor the Grand Duchy of Warsaw. And he publicly reaffirmed this declaration before the *Corps Législatif*. True, he would agree to negotiate through the Austrians; but by that time Metternich had made up his mind and only entered into discussion in order to gain time and be able to mobilize with perfect safety. This game was not altogether easy, for the aristocracy were growing impatient, and Gentz himself was not happy about these delaying tactics. Meanwhile, Hormayr was again up to his tricks, causing an insurrection in the Tyrol, and had to be arrested in March. In April, Schwarzenberg was sent to Paris. This time, Metternich announced his conditions: Napoleon must relinquish Illyria, the Grand Duchy, and the whole of Germany. In the end, Napoleon agreed to partition the Duchy between Austria, Prussia, and the Duke of Oldenburg; but by way of compensation, Saxony was to annex the Prussian provinces between the Elbe and the Oder. Austria gave notice that she would now no longer be an ally and intermediary, but would go over to armed mediation, with the firm resolve to intervene against the party that refused to accept what she considered to be satisfactory conditions. This attitude was already enough to disturb a good number of loyalties. In February, the King of Saxony had left Dresden and finally took refuge in Austria, thoroughly frightened by Stein's threats. On March 26, Metternich offered to guarantee the integrity of his states, and to see that he was compensated for the loss of the Grand Duchy. On April 26, the agreement was signed, and the army of Saxony undertook to join the Austrian forces if the negotiations failed. At this moment, Metternich was also negotiating with Bavaria, which from now on only gave very halting support to Napoleon. On arrival in Naples Murat had sent an envoy to Vienna to offer his co-operation, provided only that he could retain his kingdom. He was well received, and his act of treachery was only postponed because Bentinck, who had just occupied the Ponza islands and had visions of an Italian national movement under English protection, reserved the rights of Ferdinand, demanded that he should have Gaëta and claimed the right to land 25,000 men. Murat was upset, and once more rejoined the *Grande Armée*.

There is no reason to be surprised at Napoleon's refusal to capitulate without a fight. He had not been defeated, and as in 1807, a devastating campaign might well put the Russians and the Prussians *hors de combat* before Austria had made up her mind about her policy. And if he had capitulated, what would the French have thought of him? They would willingly have forgiven him if he had agreed simply to become once more their national leader; but if he had confessed himself beaten he would no longer have been their master, and rather than compromise, he preferred to risk disappearing from the scene. He has been criticized for his selfishness; but having for so long lost all sense of his nation's true interests, he could scarcely reason in any other way. Besides, if he had accepted Metternich's conditions, there was no guarantee that his opponents would not have taken advantage of this respite to make increased demands; and this would certainly have happened. The Czar only accepted mediation on March 11, and then with a bad grace, and solely to spare the Austrians, who assured him it would fail, and that their assistance would then follow as a matter of course. At the beginning of April, Wessenberg saw Castlereagh in London; but he roundly refused all idea of Austrian mediation, and quoted the declarations made by Napoleon. Metternich was willing to admit that there could be peace on the Continent if nothing but British interests were at stake. But now Castlereagh, who had held his hand since the beginning of the Russian campaign, realizing how helpless he was, proceeded to go into action in the new situation that was taking shape, without concerning himself in the least with Metternich. On March 3, he promised Bernadotte Norway and Guadeloupe provided he could bring the Czar 30,000 men. There was still some hope of enlisting the help of Denmark, who had signed a treaty of neutrality with Alexander.

The treaty of Kalisch had made England decide to go to the aid of the coalition. At Alexander's headquarters she was already represented by Lord Cathcart and Wilson; and in April Castlereagh sent the King of Prussia his own brother, Lord Stewart, accompanied by Jackson. He made an offer of subsidies, on condition that Hanover was enlarged and more especially that the Prussians and Russians should undertake not to treat with Napoleon without the English. As to the frontiers to be offered to France, he made no stipulations: it all depended on the military outcome of events. But it is clear that the conditions agreed upon between Metternich and Napoleon would have come up for scrutiny as soon as the treaty proposed by Castlereagh was signed. It was therefore necessary to win a new victory. The only objection was that it might well be no more than a modest one; but this would be enough to ensure peace if it was decided in advance to make certain reasonable sacrifices. In Napoleon's mind, however, no victory must be allowed to call for any concessions on his part.

Austria was not yet ready. Since 1809, her army had been reduced to 150,000 men, and for lack of money she had not at the beginning of 1813 more than 60,000 in a state to undertake a campaign. On February 9, it had been decided to mobilize a further 40,000, but there was no equipment for them. On April 16, it was agreed to issue new paper money over and above what had been created in 1811. Not till the beginning of May was it possible to undertake the formation of an army in Bohemia. Napoleon thus had time to defeat the Russians and the Prussians—and it was his last chance.

With his usual energy he set about this attempt. From Moscow, on September 22, 1812, he had called up the 1813 class and raised the contingent from 80,000 to 137,000 men. He recalled some troops from Spain and sent the Paris municipal guard to Germany. On January 11, he transferred to the regular army the 100,000 men of the National Guard of the first draft which he had formed into cohorts in the spring of 1812. At the same time he called up the 1814 class, the effective strength of which was brought up to 150,000 conscripts and 100,000 men from the 1809 and 1812 classes. On April 3, he asked for a further 90,000 men from the 1814 class and 80,000 from the first draft of the National Guard. There was a reappearance, too, of the guards of honour, and it was intended to get them to provide 10,000 mounted men. The troops in Germany were reorganized, and provided the units for incorporating the recruits in Thuringia and on the Rhine. Napoleon managed without too much difficulty to find the guns, rifles, munitions, and vehicles, but not the horses, so that he had to begin the campaign with only a few thousand cavalry. Finance was a great source of worry to him. Gaudin had estimated for

1813 more than a thousand million in expenses against 906 million in receipts. The Emperor sacrificed the 80 million reserves he had accumulated from his private treasury; he exchanged property of communes for treasury stock, and against the probable proceeds of the sale was able to issue 131 million worth of bonds. He laid more stress on the fiscal character of the blockade by issuing hundreds of licences, and by authorizing exporters to import freely once more, subject to a 6 per cent tax. But confidence had been shaken, and economic enterprise upset. Money was shy and became very dear. The amount of colonial goods decreased because it looked as though the days of the blockade were numbered. There was a panic on the Stock Exchange from May 20 to 23; and by June it had become very difficult to provide funds for the treasury.

Napoleon thought he would both strengthen the dynasty and flatter Austria by organizing a regency and entrusting it to Marie-Louise. He also tried to conciliate the Catholics by coming to an arrangement with the Pope, whom he had brought to Fontainebleau in the summer of 1812. He went and talked to him and on January 25 persuaded him to sign the preliminaries of a *concordat* published as a State law on February 13. There was to be a canonical investiture according to the scheme put forward by the National Council in 1811. But there were representations from several cardinals, and on March 24 the Pope withdrew his consent. The conflict broke out once again, and numerous and rigorous steps were taken against the opposition parties. The *Corps Législatif* met in February, and as usual kept silence. All the same, there was no mistaking the mood of the nation. Never had the Emperor called upon it to make such sacrifices. The 1814 class was called to the front in its entirety, and even the conscripts who had already found substitutes were recalled to the colours, and in the cohorts married men were being enrolled. Although Frenchmen remained faithful to Napoleon, they followed him without enthusiasm, as if this war were no longer any concern of theirs.

Napoleon left Paris on April 15 and rejoined the army of the Main which was marching on the Saale, whilst Eugène was marching up the Elbe with part of his troops. On the evening of the 28th they joined forces, and on the 29th and 30th the French crossed the Saale at Merseberg and Weissenfels. They had a crushing superiority in numbers—150,000 men against 43,000 Prussians and 58,000 Russians. But having practically no cavalry, they were unable either to scout ahead or pursue; and the chief difficulty was that several of their commanders proved to be of poor quality: Bertrand and Lauriston had never commanded an army corps. As far as the allies were concerned, Wittgenstein, their commander-in-chief, had purely nominal authority. On the 27th, they were once more dispersing, Blücher in front of the Mulde, and Miloradovitch and Tormasov to the rear, when the former gave the order to concentrate south of Leipzig so as to attack the French at the mouth of the Saale. On the 29th the Czar, taking Toll's advice, adopted another plan, namely to wait for Napoleon at the foot of the mountains, and if he marched on Leipzig, to attach his flank.

Napoleon's tactics, which he reckoned as one of his most skilful displays, was to bear down towards Leipzig in order to overwhelm the enemy, cunningly arranging his corps in echelon so that they could support one another in case of attack. Once the city had been taken the whole army would swing round to the south in order to drive the enemy back on Bohemia, trap them there, and wipe them out. On May 2, he was directing the attack on Leipzig, when Ney's corps, who were not on the look-out, were surprised in front of Lützen and vigorously attacked by Blücher, only receiving weak support from Marmont. The Emperor hastened on the scene and redressed the situation while waiting for Bertrand to intervene on the allies' left flank, and more especially for Eugène to come and cut off their retreat to the east. But both of them were late in arriving, and then only came with part of their forces. Thus Wittgenstein was able to get clear and retire towards the Elbe, with the loss of far fewer men than the French—only some 12,000 against 20,000 to 22,000. The plan had failed. There was at least this compensation, that the King of Saxony decided to change sides. He handed over Torgau and his army to Napoleon.

Whilst the Russians were making for the Spree, the Prussians were moving north, pursued by Ney, and finally decided to rejoin their allies, leaving only Bülow to cover Berlin. Napoleon, reinforced by Victor and Sebastiani, engaged battle on May 20, crossing the Spree and taking Bautzen, in order to pin the enemy down and give Ney, who was hurrying up from the north, time to take them on the flank, and in the rear. The general attack was launched on the 21st. Once again, Ney arrived too late, manœuvred clumsily, and restricted the movement that was to have overwhelmed the enemy. The coalition forces were once more able to escape and retire to Silesia, along the mountains and beyond the Weistritz, abandoning Breslau to its fate. But they were badly off from the material point of view, and Napoleon, in spite of his losses, was still numerically superior. The *Landwehr* still needed some time to enter the front line, and the Austrian army far more. Fearing that Metternich would persist in his neutrality if they marched away from his frontier, they had made a risky move between the Riesengebirge and the Oder. Napoleon was thus given a last chance; he did not take it, but instead proposed an armistice.

Little did he know that the enemy were so weak, and Austria so unprepared. The intentions of Metternich had been communicated to him by Saxony, for Bubna had arrived on May 11 to confirm his master's conditions and propose a congress in Prague. Napoleon had agreed to the congress, but had made no offer; yet he was clearly ill at ease, for at the same time he was making unsuccessful attempts to enter into negotiation with Alexander. And so the unlooked-for retreat by the allies seemed to him to be a trap arranged with Metternich. Now he did not reckon himself for the moment to be capable to standing up to the three powers. His army was not in good condition; he could not manage to feed them; and the regiments were apt to melt away because of the excessive proportion of conscripts, who could not stand the incessant marches. There were 30,000 on the sick-list, and the 3rd corps, which had stood at 47,000 on April 25, now had no more than 24,000 men. Munitions too were running short. An armistice would give a chance for reinforcements, particularly of cavalry; in fact, it did enable him to double the strength of his army. No doubt it would be useful to the enemy as well; but, given equal force, Napoleon felt he could win. Moreover, he did not give up hope of keeping Austria or winning round Russia by negotiation. In short, on May 25 Caulaincourt was commissioned to get in touch with the allies, and made proposals which surprised them. 'Do you realize that an armistice will be to our advantage? . . . If you are sure that Austria is with you, it would be better for you not to consider making peace with us.' They were only willing to suspend hostilities for a month, and only accepted the date of July 20 on the advice of Metternich, who needed this respite. The agreement was signed at Pleiswitz, on June 4.

THE AUTUMN CAMPAIGN

Diplomatically speaking, the armistice turned out badly for Napoleon. The English plenipotentiaries had just joined the allied sovereigns at Reichenbach. They signed treaties on June 14 with the King of Prussia and on the 15th with the Czar, under conditions fixed by Castlereagh, namely the restoration and enlargement of Hanover, the reconstitution of Prussia, and no separate peace. Subject to these conditions, they promised a subsidy of £2 million—a third of it for Prussia and the rest for Russia, and guaranteed up to half a £5 million loan. From now onwards, Prussia and Russia could not treat without English consent, though England's intentions with regard to France had yet to be defined. Castlereagh's deep-laid scheme, which was not finally realized till 1814, was to unite in one unbreakable block all the enemies of France; and in this he had just scored a first success. But Austria still had to be won over.

Meanwhile, Metternich had brought his master to Gitschin, where Nesselrode saw them on June 3. Francis was still averse to the idea of war, but he nevertheless consented to seek agreement on the conditions of peace, and to conclude an alliance in case his mediation should fail. Metternich went to Reichenbach, where the Prussians and Russians were obliged to agree to the stipulations Austria had made to Napoleon—the division of the Grand Duchy, the renunciation of Illyria and the Hanseatic *départements*, and the reconstitution of Prussia; the only point they added was to demand immediate evacuation of the Pomeranian fortresses. Metternich on his side promised to support the immediate dissolution of the Rhine Confederation, and admitted that once England was brought in to the debate she might clearly put forward other demands. The alliance between the three Continental powers was signed at Reichenbach on June 27; but it was only to come into force if Napoleon refused the mediation of Austria. In that case, she would align herself with Prussia and Russia's maximum demands, resume her frontiers of 1805, and require the evacuation of the whole of Germany, Spain, Italy, and Holland.

Metternich had not changed his position; for on the one hand he was still just as uneasy about the Czar, and on the other he was less and less convinced that it was possible to come to an arrangement with Napoleon. Napoleon summoned him to Dresden, where he saw him on the 26th. They had a stormy interview. To the offer of Illyria in return for neutrality, Metternich simply replied that Austria insisted on mediation, and would join the coalition if her terms were rejected. On the 30th, as he was about to leave, Napoleon changed his mind. He accepted the mediation and the congress, and the armistice was extended till August 10. This was only to gain time, for he gave Caulaincourt no instructions before July 22, required him to claim the *status quo ante bellum*, and refused to give him full powers while he himself was away at Mainz up till August 5, seeing Marie-Louise. When Caulaincourt at last appeared at Prague on the 28th, the allied plenipotentiaries refused to enter into any plenary conference and referred him to Metternich. The language he used was much the same as at Pleiswitz: 'Just tell me if you have enough troops to make us once and for all see reason. . . . I am as good a European as you. . . . Make us confine ourselves once more to France, whether it be by peaceful or by warlike means . . .' Metternich did not need any such encouragement, for he had made up his mind, and demanded an outright acceptance of the preliminary terms. On August 5, Napoleon resigned himself to asking for an official notification of them, which he received at three o'clock on the 9th. But his reply did not arrive till the 13th. He was willing to give up the Duchy of Warsaw, except for Danzig, and accepted the re-establishment of Prussia, on condition that she compensated the King of Saxony by handing over to him half a million subjects. He was also willing to part with Illyria, except for Trieste and Istria. Yet even if Napoleon had given way unconditionally, the situation would have been completely changed, for on July 5, Castlereagh, spurred up by Wellington's victory at Vittoria, had espoused the maximum Russian and Prussian programme, reserving Sicily for Ferdinand and stipulating for Bernadotte certain advantages he had promised to him. But at midnight on August 10 Metternich pronounced the congress to be at an end; and on the 12th he declared war. On September 9, the Continental alliance was confirmed at Teplitz, and on October 9 England joined Austria, and made her a grant of £500,000.

All the belligerents had taken military advantage of the armistice. With part of the *Landwehr* coming into the front line, Prussia now had 100,000 men; the Russians had 184,000 and the Austrians 127,000. Bernadotte contributed 23,000, having lost all hopes of any further support from Napoleon since Denmark had once more ranged herself on the French side. In addition, Wallmoden was in command of 9,000 Anglo-Germans, and Mecklenburg provided 6,000 soldiers. Against this total of 512,000 Napoleon could only set 442,000, without counting the 26,000 men in the garrisons along the Elbe. But in the second line, his enemies' reserves were far superior to his own. All the same, he now had 40,000 cavalry.

The coalition plan had been adopted on July 12 at Trachenberg, to which place Alexander had summoned Bernadotte. The first suggestion had been to enter Saxony in Napoleon's rear, Bernadotte and Blücher from the north and Schwarzenberg from the south. But as Blücher preferred to operate on his own, it was finally agreed to form three armies, the Prussians and Russians figuring in each of them so as to encourage Bernadotte and Schwarzenberg and also be able to keep an eye on them. To make up the army of Bohemia, the 127,000 Austrians were joined by 82,000 Russians and 45,000 Prussians, who crossed the frontier from August 11 onwards. The army of Silesia, under Blücher's command, included 66,000 Russians and 38,000 Prussians. Bernadotte took command of the northern army consisting of 73,000 Prussians, 29,000 Russians, and 23,000 Swedes. The first army was to march on Dresden along the left bank of the Elbe; Bernadotte, covering Berlin, was to advance towards Wittenberg; Blücher would bear towards one or the other, depending on the movements of the French. It was moreover decided at the pressing request of Bernadotte that they should keep systematically out of the Emperor's way and only give battle to his lieutenants. This strategy—which had nothing Napoleonic about it—can be explained by the Austrian and Prussian desire to protect their own territory, but also by the terror which the great war-lord inspired. Instead of seeking for decisive encounters, they would have recourse to the eighteenth-century tradition of forcing the enemy back by manœuvring so as to threaten his line of communications, thus wearing him down bit by bit. The astonishing thing is that this method succeeded. Although military writers have expressed admiration for the genius and vigour displayed by Napoleon in the course of the various incidents in this campaign, it must be admitted that his grasp of the whole did not show its usual perfection—perhaps because the difficulties were insuperable.

The Emperor's situation was now very like the one he had faced in August 1796, at the outset of his career, which he turned into one of his most brilliant triumphs. It might have been expected that he would fall with almost his entire strength on the northern army, which might have been taken in the flank by Girard, setting out from Magdeburg, and Davout from Hamburg, as well as by the Danes. In this event, it would surely have been defeated and Berlin occupied. Blücher and Schwarzenberg would have joined forces, but this would not seriously have mattered. All the same, they would have captured Dresden; and this was what Napoleon, in his desire to spare the King of Saxony, could not bring himself to face. Moreover, he left Davout in Hamburg—the French having reoccupied it—and this deprived him of 40,000 men. In thus tying himself down to fortresses, which he had never done before, he reduced his freedom of movement, and this was the initial cause of the disaster. True, the distances to be covered between one enemy and another were two or three times greater than in 1796, and that with a much more numerous and much less seasoned army. The early events of the Russian campaign had perhaps convinced Napoleon that an offensive in the grand manner would exhaust his troops and lead to no result. Finally, there can be no doubt that he was mistaken as to the importance of the northern army, for he thought that Oudinot with 70,000 men would easily contain it and would even be able to occupy Berlin. He himself took up a position that would allow him to wait for his enemies and yet take the offensive against the one that should prove to be the boldest. As he knew nothing of the massing of forces in Bohemia, he was not afraid of Schwarzenberg, imagining that to go to the help of Blücher he would come by way of the Bautzen gap. Two army corps were detailed to keep watch on him, whilst four others were disposed towards the Bober. He himself remained in reserve with the Guards and the cavalry in the neighbourhood of Bautzen. But Oudinot proved much too far off for him to be supported or recalled. Quite contrary to all his principles, Napoleon was infringing the rule of unified action. Besides, the formation of the large army in Bohemia and the attack delivered by it to the west of the Elbe deprived Napoleon's dispositions of all their effectiveness.

As always, it was the impetuous Blücher who first took the offensive. Napoleon at once fell upon him, and was surprised to see him hurriedly retreat. On August 23, without having been able to engage him in battle, he suddenly learnt that Schwarzenberg had driven Gouvion-Saint-Cyr back into the suburbs of Dresden. He immediately disengaged himself to go to the rescue of this city, leaving Macdonald 75,000 to keep Blücher in check, a step which made his mobile forces too weak. His first plan was to advance by way of Pirna to take Schwarzenberg in the rear, a move that might well have proved decisive. But he heard that Dresden was about to fall! Yet he only sent Vandamme in this direction. At three o'clock on the 26th the redoubts covering the town had in fact just been taken when the Young Guard appeared and barred the enemy's path. On the 27th, the army of Bohemia, with both its wings turned and its centre almost driven in, lost 10,000 men, and retired in disorder in several columns. Torrential rain was falling, and the French army was utterly spent. There was only a very ineffective pursuit, all the more so because Napoleon himself was ill, and soon returned to Dresden. Vandamme, who had boldly pushed on to Teplitz to cut off the enemy retreat, suddenly realized at Kulm that he was surrounded, and surrendered with 7,000 men and 48 guns. This terrible reverse cancelled out the moral effect of the recent victory.

Nor was this the only check. Bernadotte, uneasy about his rear communications, and not at all anxious to risk a reverse that would shake his prestige in Sweden, had not adopted the offensive; besides, he was probably not very keen to fight his fellow-countrymen as he had not given up hopes of being accepted as their sovereign if Napoleon were to fall. Nevertheless, since Oudinot had attacked Bülow at Gross-Beeren on

August 23, Bernadotte had to support his subordinate. The forces of Saxony gave way, and Oudinot, finding himself driven back, had to retire behind the Elbe. Macdonald, who had gone in to attack on August 26 on the Katzbach, saw his left flank and centre being threatened and thrown back by Blücher, and retired on the Bober, where one of his divisions was cut off and then destroyed, with a loss of 20,000 men and 100 guns. Napoleon sent Ney against Bernadotte and hastened to attack Blücher, who also retreated. Once again Schwarzenberg threatened Dresden, and once more Napoleon turned back to it, only to see the Austrians slip out of his way. During this time Ney, who had crossed the Elbe, was being beaten at Dennewitz on September 6, with the loss of 15,000 men. Bernadotte only marched southwards with great deliberation and by a very roundabout route; nevertheless his cavalry entered Westphalia and on the 30th occupied Cassel.

The situation was becoming serious. The French army was dwindling at a frightening rate. This was not chiefly due to battles, but to the continual comings and goings and forced marches, and to hunger, for the soldier was only getting half a pound of bread a day and there was no more meat to be had. There were 90,000 men sick, and the 3rd corps, 38,000 strong on August 15, was reduced to 17,000 by October 1. The enemy's numerical superiority was gradually becoming a formidable factor. The Emperor made one last but unsuccessful effort to reach Blücher, then he abandoned Lusatia and retired behind the Elbe. Meanwhile the allies, going back to their original plan, were bearing down upon Leipzig, Bernadotte on the one side and Schwarzenberg on the other. The former crossed the Elbe on October 4, pushing back Ney as he went; the latter born down upon Chemnitz as early as September 26, and Murat was told to harass his advance. As they were moving cautiously forward, Napoleon, covering 80 kilometres in two days, fell upon Blücher, who had also just crossed the Elbe at Wartenburg. But once again, he failed. Blücher had escaped westwards, and, like Bernadotte, had taken shelter behind the Saale. For a moment, the Emperor himself thought of crossing to the right bank of the Elbe, and switching his basis of operations; but when he learnt of Blücher's movement, he made for Leipzig, where there was a risk of Murat being caught between two fires. Even then, however, he would not make up his mind either to evacuate Dresden, where he had left Gouvion, or to recall Davout. And so he could only muster some 160,000 men around Leipzig against the 320,000 allies closing in on it.

Nevertheless, the allied forces were very widely spaced. Blücher was approaching from the north, but Bernadotte only arrived on the 18th. Schwarzenberg, astride the Elster and the Pleisse, was in a most exposed situation. If the French had managed to mass their forces by the 14th, they could have crushed him the following day. But nothing of the kind took place. On the morning of the 16th, Macdonald had still not arrived; and as Blücher with his usual zeal was pressing on Marmont to the north, Ney could not make up his mind to detach the divisions requested by the Emperor. The battle was joined in the morning, on the heights of Wachau, to the south of the city. Schwarzenberg was the first to attack; but he met with a sharp counter-thrust, realized his danger, and called on his reserves, while Napoleon was waiting in vain for reinforcements so that he could give the word for a decisive attack. Macdonald appeared at last—but it was too late: he could not turn the enemy flank, and the day ended with an unsuccessful frontal attack. Napoleon could still retreat, and this was his only chance of avoiding disaster. But he chose rather to stand and bear the full allied attack. On October 18, his troops were thrown back right into the city. Bernadotte had debouched on the north-east, and the forces of Saxony deserted, thus hastening the defeat. The French only had one bridge they could use for retreat, the Lindenau bridge. On the 19th the attack was renewed and the bridge blown up, though this meant sacrificing the rear-guard. The French had lost 60,000 men, 23,000 of them prisoners; the allies had 60,000 killed and wounded.

After the conclusion of an armistice as from September 17, Bavaria had gone over to the coalition on October 8 by the treaty of Ried, and Wurtemberg did the same on the 23rd. But while Napoleon was moving by way of Erfurt and Fulda, Wrede lost time in reducing Würzburg and only blocked his advance at Hanau on October 30. He attempted this most ineptly, and was driven back. What remained of the *Grande Armée* recrossed the Rhine at Mainz from November 2 to 4, and to complete the disaster, typhus broke out. The German fortresses held another 120,000 men, uselessly blocked in.

At this moment Eugène, threatened by the Austrians, who had occupied Illyria and who were advancing by way of the Drave and the Tyrol—thanks to the defection of Bavaria—was completing his retreat on the Adige. On November 15, he scored a useless success at Galdiero; but the enemy proceeded to occupy the Romagna and the Marches. Murat, who had left Napoleon at Erfurt, resumed his talks with Metternich as soon as he had come back to Naples.

Spain was by this time as good as lost. In the spring of 1813, the insurrection had made headway in Biscay and Navarre and occupied the forces of Clausel. Joseph had no more than 75,000 men, and they were scattered between Madrid and Salamanca. On May 15, Wellington took the offensive with 70,000 men, and forced the French back on Salamanca with his right wing, whilst his left, crossing the Douro, joined hands with the Spanish from Galicia and turned the enemy front. Joseph evacuated Madrid and concentrated his forces behind the Carion, but then retreated as far as the Ebro. By this clever manœuvre Wellington had without striking a blow freed the whole Biscay coast, and thanks to the English fleet, who were cruising off the coast, he thus acquired a base of operations much nearer at hand. On June 21 he launched an attack with 80,000 men against the 55,000 French lined up behind the Zadorra, in front of Vittoria, and completely defeated them. The enemy retired behind the Bidassoa, where Foy and Clausel contrived to join them. Suchet, left on his own, managed to hold the Spaniards; but after Vittoria he had to fall back on the Ebro. Saragossa fell and Bentinck arrived from Sicily to attack Tortosa and Tarragona. Suchet retreated across Catalonia as far as Figuères.

This was the end of the *Grand Empire*; and as in 1723, France was now to experience invasion.

THE CAMPAIGN IN FRANCE AND NAPOLEON'S ABDICATION

A bare 60,000 Frenchmen formed a very thin screen from Switzerland to the North Sea. Having reached the Rhine with 140,000 men, the allies could march on Paris with practically no resistance. On the other hand, if they let the winter slip by, Napoleon would collect a new army and the whole situation would be changed. This was certainly the view of Alexander and Blücher; but others, moved by memories of 1792 and fearing a national resistance, did not wish to enter France except with overwhelming forces. Their advice was to call a halt till spring, so as to be able to bring up the reserves and wait for Bernadotte. Instead of marching on Holland, as the English had begged him to do, he entered Holstein on January 14, 1814, and forced the Danes to surrender Norway to him. Besides, the troops were in an appallingly destitute state. All the sovereigns were short of money, for up till now England had supplied full consignments of arms and clothing, but no funds, because she was so afraid of weakening the pound as long as her trade with Germany was still suspended. The loan agreed upon at Reichenbach appeared to be impossible. During the summer, d'Ivernois had studied the possibility of issuing a federal paper money, but without success, because he rejected the idea of an artificial rate of exchange recommended by Stein, and also because the English refused to give it complete backing, on the grounds that if it was thus put on a par with banknotes, it would have found its way back to England and ruined their own currency. In the end, England had agreed on September 20 to offer the allies bonds at 6 per cent, but the German banks had great difficulty in discounting them. In the council of war held on November 7 and 8, Schwarzenberg obtained consent to a middle course. No date was fixed for an offensive, but it was agreed to begin it as soon as possible. This would mean a winter campaign—a decision that was to prove fatal for Napoleon.

Meanwhile, however, Metternich insisted on one more attempt to negotiate. On October 17 at Leipzig, Napoleon had conversations with General Merfeldt, whom he had just taken prisoner and was liberating for an express purpose. The Emperor showed that he was prepared to give up the Grand Duchy, Germany, Holland, Spain, and perhaps even Italy, provided that England would give back the French colonies and restore freedom of the seas. He evidently still hoped to divide the allies and especially to win over Austria. Metternich himself got into touch at Weimar with Saint-Aignan, the

French Minister of Finance, and on November 9 the Russians and Prussians reluctantly consented to send him with an offer of peace on the basis of the natural frontiers. Moreover, they seemed inclined to require some concessions and guarantees from England, whose ascendancy on the seas was not at all to their liking.

It will always be a matter of dispute how far Metternich was sincere: the probability is that he did not really know himself. His relations with the allies were bad; but he knew they could not get on without his help, and so openly pursued his personal policy, the prime object of which was to restore the power of the Hapsburgs. In Germany, he was determined to bar the path of the revolutionary patriots by coming to an arrangement with the southern princes, and on October 21 he subordinated the work of the commission on the occupied countries presided over by Stein to a diplomatic committee set up in the chief allied headquarters. He was manœuvring to make himself master of Italy, and during the autumn campaign he was continuously negotiating with Caroline. On December 10, he approved the decision to send Neipperg as an envoy to Murat. It was apparently a question of driving out Eugène; but Metternich's real purpose was to despoil the Pope in concert with the Neapolitans. He likewise wanted to get a footing in Switzerland, bring about a counter-revolution, and establish his influence there, so making it possible to approach Italy from the north and cut it off from France by a threat to Lyons. And finally, he was more than ever intent upon preventing Russian expansion in Poland and Turkey. His duel with Alexander was just beginning. The Czar had made a bargain with Prussia to give up Saxony, whose king was a prisoner, in return for the Grand Duchy. He was prepared to defend the Italian sovereigns, and at Laharpe's instance posed as the protector of the Swiss. While determined to dethrone Napoleon in order to satisfy his hatred, he fancied that he could replace him by Bernadotte, who would then become his underling. It only needed the barest suggestion of this kind to set Metternich planning the opposite and considering with some satisfaction how to save the Emperor or at least his dynasty, using Marie-Louise's regency to tie France to Austria. He could hardly think it likely that Napoleon would be content with the natural frontiers, but it was an opportune offer, for at least it would involve the Emperor in difficulties with his own subjects.

Napoleon received Saint-Aignan on November 15. The next day he authorized Caulaincourt to negotiate, but he kept silence as to the conditions fixed by the allies. The rumour of this spread abroad and there was an outburst of opinion against him and against Maret, who remained to the last an advocate of war to the bitter end, sensing how flattering this was to his master's instincts. Either because he wished to spare Maret, or more likely because he hoped to gain time, the Emperor appeared to change his mind. He replaced Maret by Caulaincourt in the Foreign Office and on December 2 the new minister accepted the preliminaries of Frankfurt.

But it was too late. On November 16, Lebrun had evacuated Amsterdam. On the 17th, the Hague had risen in revolt, and the first concern of a triumvirate set up by Hogendorp was to ask for help from London and to recall the Prince of Orange, who answered the call at once. On December 4 the allies, noting the silence of Napoleon, put out a proclamation in which they appeared to separate his cause from the cause of France. They again offered her peace, this time without mentioning the natural frontiers, which had been already invaded in Holland. As Metternich had reckoned, many Frenchmen held their leader responsible for the disasters. He would surely never consent to acknowledging his personal defeat, even if it cost the nation nothing. Yet even if he had resigned himself to this, what guarantee could be given him? Metternich's offer seemed even more suspect than his previous ones. The Continental powers were tied to England, and could decide nothing without her; yet at this point she was avowedly opposed to these suggestions. The youthful Aberdeen had been accredited to Metternich in August, and proved fairly docile in his hands; but on September 18 Castlereagh, making Pitt's policy his own, had demanded that Holland should have a suitable barrier on the French side, and was giving a favourable hearing to the Prince of Orange, who wished for Belgium. As England intended to keep several of the Dutch colonies, she would gain doubly by reconstituting the unity of the Low Countries. Castlereagh was also thinking of giving them part of the left bank of the Rhine, and refused on November 5 to allow this to go to France.

Nevertheless, it may be presumed that at this point the French nation, who were negotiating under the wing of Austria, would have managed to retain some of the conquests made by the Republic.

The allied offensive was held up for a while by the disagreement about Switzerland. At the urgent request of Alexander, Francis revoked the order he had given to invade Switzerland, on December 11. Metternich, however, was trying to persuade the cantons to make their own appeal to the allies. He did not succeed, but one of the agents, Senft by name, who had formerly been a minister in Saxony, induced General Watteville to make some rather ambiguous statements and provoked an aristocratic counter-revolution in Bern. The chancellor used it as a pretext for returning to the attack in agreement with Schwarzenberg, and on the 16th the latter was authorized to enter Switzerland. His army crossed the Rhine on the 21st from Schaffhausen to Kehl and entered Basle. Bubna made for Geneva in order to attack Lyons, whilst Schwarzenberg moved his troops forward towards Besançon, Dijon, and Langres. On the 29th, Switzerland denounced the Act of Mediation. At the beginning of January, Blücher too crossed the Rhine, between Coblenz and Mannheim, penetrated into Lorraine, and turned the Argonne by way of Bar-le-Duc. The Marshals retired before the invaders, falling back upon the Marne. By the end of the month, Schwarzenberg was marching on Troyes and Blücher was about to reach Saint-Dizier. Meanwhile, Caulaincourt had set out and wrote from Lunéville on the 6th to Metternich, expressing surprise that he had been left without information for a month. In reply, he was informed that the allies were waiting for Castlereagh, who arrived at Basle on the 18th—an event of the greatest importance.

In the year 1813, England had still only taken a very modest part in affairs on the Continent. She had only kept contingents of any size in Spain, and she had not sent any ready money. Up to the autumn, she continued to labour under great internal difficulties. But the evacuation of Germany and Holland, together with the excellent harvest of 1813, produced a tremendous change in the situation. The blockade was coming to an end and Central Europe was being reopened to colonial produce and to manufactured goods, which poured into it.

Prices recovered, the index figure rising from 158 in 1811 to 185 in 1813 and 198 in 1814. A fever of speculation ran through the business world, in a recovery which put an end to unemployment and restored the level of wages. In 1814, the export trade produced more than £70 million, much more than in 1802 (£60·2 million), which had been the best year up till then. At the same time, the resumption of corn imports and the abundant harvest brought back the price of bread to the level of 1808, and the working-class agitation died down. Thus reassured, England was now able to contemplate new efforts of financial aid. Under Vansittart new taxes were voted and in 1813 a loan of £105 million was negotiated. Expenses in that year were the greatest in this period, reading £177 million; subsidies rose sharply from £3 million to more than £8 million, and payments abroad to more than £26 million. At this point, the National Debt was nearly £834 million. The only difficulty was the rate of exchange, which remained low. In 1813, the Spanish piastre gained 38 per cent, and in order to provide for Wellington's campaign, the Bank of England had to set aside £1,400,000 in gold from its cash reserves. Once again, the Rothschilds came to the rescue. Nathan in Holland, James in Paris, and their brothers in Frankfurt drew heavily on their French funds, and thanks to what they made available, Wellington was able as he entered France to pay cash for all his purchases. In 1814, the Rothschilds also acted as intermediaries for transmitting the promised subsidies to the Allies; and it was for these services that the Rothschilds of Frankfurt were raised to the nobility by the Emperor of Austria in 1817. From now onwards England, although she lacked troops, could make her will prevail by arguing with good ringing coin.

In Castlereagh's opinion, it was high time for England to make her influence felt. Although the Continental powers had promised not to treat without England, they had kept her out of their Prague and Frankfurt negotiations, and appeared to be ignoring her colonial and maritime claims. Metternich was negotiating with Murat without much regard for King Ferdinand. Several of the English diplomats were proving ineffective, and it was not possible at that distance to change their instructions in order to keep pace with the ups and downs of the war. The Government were of the opinion that Castlereagh ought to be on the spot. He drew up his own instructions on December 26. England was to demand that peace with France should be concluded in concert, in which case she would offer £5 million for 1814. She ruled out any discussion of the freedom of the seas, and would make the restitution of the conquered colonies depend upon the solution adopted for the Low Countries. Spain and Portugal were to be restored, and Ferdinand was to receive compensation. Nothing was said about the rest of the Continent, so that Castlereagh had a free hand, enabling him to pose as a mediator between the Continental powers and to see that the traditional policy of the Foreign Office—in effect, Pitt's policy—should prevail. He now at last stood on the threshold of the career that was to bring him so much fame. On arrival in Basle, he at once set up a barrier against France. Holland should have Belgium under a European guarantee and Prussia should take possession of the territory between the Meuse and the Moselle, which would make it impossible for her in the future to have any underhand dealings with France. At this juncture, however, Castlereagh was still prepared for France to advance as far as Treves if the military situation required it.

On January 14, in company with the Austrians, he joined the Russians at Langres. Immediately he had to intervene between Alexander and Metternich. The general opinion was that Napoleon's cause was lost. The Czar refused to negotiate and wanted to dethrone him in favour of Bernadotte, whilst Metternich was willing to negotiate with the Emperor, and wished to open the conference promised to Caulaincourt at Châtillon-sur-Seine. In any case, he ruled out Bernadotte in favour of a regency. As to the wisdom of treating with Napoleon, the British government were divided. Although Castlereagh would take no definite line, he knew that the Regent and public opinion were becoming more and more hostile to the Corsican. He succeeded in turning down Bernadotte, and in exchange managed to persuade Metternich to give up the regency, in the firm belief that this would make the restoration of the Bourbons inevitable. In this way, he obliged the Czar to put up with the conference, postponing its opening till February 5 in order to leave the way open for the decisive battle that was generally expected. Finally, he insisted on agreement about the conditions of peace, and on January 29 succeeded in reducing France to the boundaries of 1792. At this point, the diplomats left for Châtillon, just as the campaign in France was beginning.

This time Napoleon had neither the breathing-space nor the means to improvise a new army, though there was no absolute dearth of man power. As from October 9, he called for 120,000 men from the 1808 to 1814 classes, who had already on August 24 provided 30,000 for the army in Spain. There does not seem to have been any particular difficulty about this levy; but he had also called on the 1815 class to the extent of 160,000 conscripts, and this operation, which had scarcely begun when he came back from Germany, needed a good deal more time to complete. On November 15, he recalled 150,000 men from the 1803 to 1814 classes, plus 150,000 in the last resort if the eastern frontier was forced; and on the 20th he added 40,000 to the quota from the 1808 to 1814 classes. The National Guard was set on an active footing in the fortified places on December 17, and in Paris on January 8, 1814; and he then decided to form volunteer regiments that would take in the Paris unemployed, and even considered wholesale conscription. By the end of January, about 125,000 men had been collected in the depots, but were quite untrained. Most of them moreover were without equipment or weapons, for the magazines and arsenals were empty. As in 1793, requisitioning of arms, horses, fodder, and corn was set in train in a rather haphazard fashion. Above all, there was a lack of money. In November and January, Napoleon announced tremendous increases in taxation: but when would they be collected? Even the receipts from indirect taxation were becoming almost negligible. There was no money coming into the Treasury. Government stock had fallen from 74 to 52 francs after the battle of Leipzig; money was being hoarded and the notes simply passed back to the Bank of France. Salaries and pensions above the level of 2,000 francs were cut by a quarter, and contractors were now paid in sinking fund bonds which were nothing more than promissory notes, like the *assignats* of the Revolution. Enclosed once more within her old frontiers, the France of the Empire was on the same level as the much-abused Directory, and this was natural enough. No longer able to make war at the expense of the foreigner, Napoleon was reduced to seeking the wherewithal from his own nation.

The nation did not take at all kindly to this process, and for the first time there was resistance. The Imperial aristocracy and the notables whose ranks the Emperor had filled considered his downfall inevitable and were thinking how to snatch the political power he had always refused to give them by coming to terms with his successor, whoever he might be. When the *Corps Législatif* assembled on December 19, it dared to ask that the allied conditions should be communicated to it, and the Emperor gave way. In the name of the committee, Lainé declared that France would fight no more except to defend her independence and the integrity of her territory. At the same time, he asked the sovereign to guarantee his subjects' civil and political liberties. On December 29, the *Corps Législatif* gave its approval, and was at once adjourned. The pact that Bonaparte had made with the middle classes in Brumaire was finally at an end.

As for the people, they thought it monstrous that the Emperor, after losing two huge armies in successive disasters, should presume to form another. In the course of a few months, Napoleon became downright unpopular. The nation wanted peace, and was rapidly coming to the conclusion that its master did not want to give it. With a running commentary from the royalists, the allied proclamation was having its effect. There was no thought of preferring the Bourbons to Napoleon, for they symbolized the *Ancien Régime*; but the French were weary and discouraged, and they began to offer passive resistance—the only right that he had left them. The malcontents, who had been growing in number since 1812, were now beyond computation. People stopped paying taxes; requisition orders were not obeyed. The population looked on at the invasion and took no action, at any rate, as long as the allies managed to hold their troops in check; and in the south the English were quite well received, for they could be relied upon to pay their way.

In normal times, the Imperial administration would have had no difficulty in punishing the recalcitrant. But the overwhelming invasion left it no time to act, and—what was worse—paralysed its machinery. The officials who had rallied to Napoleon's cause realized how powerless they now were and foresaw the Emperor's downfall. They were therefore anxious to provide for their future, and made common cause with the royalists or even came to terms with the enemy. Napoleon tried to get the machinery working again by sending Extraordinary Commissioners into the *départements*, as the Committee of Public Safety had done in its day; but the pitiable result of their efforts as compared with the work done by the committee's travelling representatives shows how low the public morale had sunk. The royalists put the finishing touches to the disintegration. As in the days of the Republic, the country's misfortunes gave them new hope, and they did their best to help 'our good friends the enemy'. Their announcements and public notices spread discouragement and fostered the spirit of disobedience. Once again the West was stirring. In Flanders, Fouchart armed the recalcitrants in order to help the invasion, and everywhere the allies found guides, spies, and traitors. By December 3, Count de Scey had reached Freiburg and in the name of the royalists of Franche-Comté was offering his province to Austria. On March 12, the Mayor of Bordeaux handed the city over to the English, who had brought the Duke of Angoulême along with them. At moments, Napoleon would talk of once again becoming the soldier of the Revolution and rekindling the national spirit; but it was hardly more than words. How could he reconcile the memories of 1793 with the aristocratic monarchy he had undertaken to set up? His subservient ministers might remind him imperiously that it was his duty to see to the preservation of the social order and warn him against the 'dregs of the people'; yet the only national resistance was in Champagne, where in the heat of battle the foreign troops ran riot in appalling excesses. But the resistance had no time to develop, and no one came forward as a leader.

When Napoleon left Paris on January 25, he handed over to the care of Joseph, as Lieutenant-General, his wife and his son, whom he was destined never to see again. He had at his disposal only about 60,000 men, and even these were not in a concentrated formation. He hastened to meet the Prussians, whom he thought to be at Saint-Dizier; but Blücher was already reaching the Aube, well on the way towards linking up with Schwarzenberg. The Emperor pursued him and beat him at Brienne on the 29th, but was unable to prevent his joining up with the Austrians. On February 1, he was overwhelmed by a force three times as large at La Rothière. He fell back on Troyes, then on Nogent. But it was a hopeless contest: there was only one thing for him to do if he wished to save his throne—to negotiate unconditionally. During the night of February 4, he gave Caulaincourt a free hand; and on the 7th at Châtillon Caulaincourt was given the allied conditions, which reduced France to her frontiers of 1792. He protested, appealing to the preliminary negotiations at Frankfurt, though he had no illusions about the probable result. Here, then, was a unique opportunity offered to this statesman, who had always been a man of peace, and who was this time—most unusually—armed with full powers, to settle his country's destiny. But he dared not take the responsibility, not through fear of being a traitor, but because he was a little man: he referred the decision to his master. In the night of the 7th, after hours of anguish, Napoleon finally gave in. But by the morning he had changed his mind, for he had just discovered the enemy's military mistake. There was a new situation, and with it, new hope.

To satisfy Blücher and to facilitate their progress and their supplies, the allies had in fact once more separated. Leaving Schwarzenberg to follow the Seine, Blücher had advanced on February 2 by way of Sézanne and the Petit Morin valley, where his divisions were strung out in Indian file. He was aiming at cutting off the retreat of Macdonald, who was falling back before York on the Marne and succeeded in reaching the Ourcq. During this time, Napoleon was hurrying towards them. On February 10, at Champaubert, he routed Olsoufief's corps and cut the enemy's army in two. He then made for Montmirail, and on the 11th completely defeated Sacken's corps there. Its remnants rejoined York in front of Château-Thierry. York was attacked and his front driven in on the 12th, forcing him to recross the Marne with all speed, whilst Napoleon turned back against Blücher, who was pressing on Marmont at Vauchamps. On the 14th Blücher, finding himself under attack, retreated; but his forces were cut through in retreat, and he lost some 10,000 men. Napoleon had won a brilliant victory; but he had not destroyed the enemy, for their divisions managed to join up again at Châlons. Moreover, Schwarzenberg's troops were crossing the Seine, driving Victor and Oudinot as far back as the Yerres, where Macdonald joined them, and also on to the Yonne and the Loing, till he had reached Montargis and Fontainebleau.

By marching on Montereaux from Vauchamps, Napoleon could have carried out one of his favourite manœuvres, but he lacked the necessary forces. He made for the Yerres, throwing the enemy back on the Seine, and on the 18th managed with difficulty to recapture Montereau. Schwarzenberg had time to reassemble his forces and retire on Troyes, continuing his retreat via Chaumont and Langres, although Blücher had already withdrawn to the Aube.

These checks disconcerted the allies. On the 17th, the Austrians took it upon them to offer an armistice, and repeated the attempt they had made on the 24th. In the letter he addressed to his father-in-law on the 22nd and in his instructions to Flahaut, commissioned to go and negotiate at Lussigny, Napoleon declared that he would only treat on the basis of the Frankfurt proposals, for he could not reduce France to smaller proportions than when he had assumed control. Moreover, Castlereagh had protested against the Austrians' separately taking the initiative. Although Schwarzenberg had sent 50,000 men to the rescue of Bubna, who could not get the better of Augereau, final success was no longer in doubt now that Bernadotte's army was approaching. Bülow and Wintzingerode were already entering Champagne, whilst Langeron and Saint-Priest were bringing two fresh army corps from Germany. On February 24, Blücher set out again, this time with the valley of the Grand Morin as his objective. Castlereagh did not despair, but on the contrary pressed on with the final discussions. It had already been agreed on the 15th that if Napoleon would not negotiate before the fall of Paris, it might be necessary to consider a possible 'vote' of the capital in order to refuse to treat with him. It was agreed at Chaumont on the 26th to make a last communication of these conditions to Caulaincourt, fixing March 10 as the final date for reply. On March 9, just as this fatal respite was about to expire, Castlereagh obtained the signature of a pact which bound the four powers together against France for a period of twenty years. In order to ensure respect for the new European order they intended to work out by themselves, they agreed each to provide 150,000 men. Only at this point did Castlereagh grant the £5 million he had offered in 1814—now that he had at last formed the coalition which he had been hoping for for over twenty years. On March 10, Caulaincourt, who had not succeeded in making Napoleon give in, asked for further time, and on the 15th produced a counter-plan, by which France would retain Eugène in Italy, keep Saxony in the hands of its king, and have a voice in a congress which should reorganize Europe. Negotiations were finally broken off at Châtillon on the 19th. Vitrolles, who had come from Paris, had already been received by the allies. They had authorized him to go to the Count of Artois, whom he met at Nancy. Meanwhile, the royalist demonstrations in the occupied countries were more or less openly encouraged. On March 22, the English government finally decided not to negotiate any further with Napoleon.

The drama was now drawing to its close. On February 28, Napoleon had once again dashed off in pursuit of Blücher, who was driving Marmont and Mortier before him until he was brought up short by the Ourcq on March 1. Realizing that he was in danger of being caught between two fires, he turned northwards to join Bülow and Wintzingerode, who were attacking Soissons. But he would not have escaped disaster if the place had not suddenly capitulated on the 3rd, making it possible for his whole army to reform behind the Aisne around Laon, whilst the French were compelled to look for a crossing-place at Berry-au-Bac. After repulsing an attack by Blücher at Craonne, Napoleon divided his forces into two columns and marched upon Laon, where the enemy had now massed 100,000 men. On the 9th, he was thrown back to the south of the town. Marmont, who had been held up to the east, was surprised during the night and put to rout. And now, on the 10th, the attack fell upon Napoleon, who withdrew towards Soissons, giving Saint-Priest's corps a pounding at Reims. None the less, the manœuvre had failed. Thereupon Schwarzenberg, who now only faced Macdonald and Oudinot, had slowly recovered all the lost ground. From the 17th to the 19th, Napoleon left Blücher and hastened from Reims to Méry in an attempt to take him in the flank. But once again his enemy made off, this time with even greater speed; and by the 19th he was in safe shelter between the Seine and the Aube.

At this juncture, Napoleon did not give up the fight, but ceased any attempt to prevent the allies marching on Paris. He decided to make for Lorraine, where he would regroup the garrison forces and cut the enemy's communications, after which he would come back and attack them under the walls of a beleaguered Paris. But Schwarzenberg suddenly made up his mind to act, and overwhelmed him on the 20th and 21st as he was crossing the Aube at Arcis, while Blücher was also on the way via Châlons. Napoleon managed to cut free, though not without some difficulty, and retired to Saint-Dizier. Now that they had come together again, the two generals agreed to march on Paris side by side along the valleys of the two Morins. Mortier and Marmont, whose troops had been decimated on the 25th at Fère-Champenoise, fell back onto the outskirts of the town, which had just been abandoned by Marie-Louise on the 29th. After being attacked on the 30th and slowly driven back, they surrendered during the night. Napoleon was hurrying to their assistance in a state of agitation, and when he reached Fontainebleau on the 31st, he still would not admit defeat, but set about making arrangements for continuing the struggle. Already, however, he had been betrayed and deserted.

On March 31, an allied proclamation invited the inhabitants of Paris to pronounce on the kind of government France wished to have, and pointed to the example of Bordeaux, which had greeted the Duke of Angoulême with acclamations. The royalists went out to applaud their enemies' entry into the city and wore the white cockade, though they were few in number. On the evening of the 31st, at Talleyrand's house, the sovereigns confirmed their resolve not to treat with Napoleon and required the Senate to set up a provisional government, of which Talleyrand naturally became the head. The municipal council and the various constitutional bodies immediately began to call for the return of the Bourbons. On April 2, the Senate decided that the Emperor was deposed, and this was proclaimed on the 3rd with the agreement of the *Corps Législatif*. The Senators hastily patched together a constitution, taking good care to preserve their own hereditary status and endowments; and on the 6th they called Louis XVIII to the throne. Meanwhile, the Marshals at Fontainebleau were refusing to follow their chief and were urging him to abdicate in favour of his son. Napoleon gave way, and on April 4 sent Caulaincourt, Ney, and Macdonald to the Czar, picking up on the way Marmont, who had withdrawn to Essones. Alexander would not give an immediate answer. But Marmont had accepted Schwarzenberg's offer to go over to the allies; and though he had put off taking this step, he went over to the enemy with his forces in the night of the 4th, thus leaving Fontainebleau undefended. There and then the Czar demanded outright abdication; and on the 6th, Napoleon finally gave his consent.

But the war still went on in Italy and in the south. In January, Murat had thrown off the mask and occupied Rome, then Tuscany, and had finally invaded the Romagna. He then hesitated, indignant at the actions of Bentinck, who had only agreed to an armistice with him on Castlereagh's orders, and, feigning ignorance, was landing troops at Leghorn in order to march on Genoa. Eugene was able to halt Bellegarde on the Mincio. In the hope of keeping the kingdom of Italy for himself, he began to negotiate with Murat. But no agreement was reached and on April 13 the king launched an offensive towards the Taro, and an insurrection broke out in Milan. On the 16th, Eugène signed a convention allowing him to leave Italy. In the Pyrenees, Soult, after a fruitless attempt to free Pampeluna and San Sebastian, had successively lost the line of the Bidassoa in October 1813, the Nivelle in November, and the Nive in December. He had then fallen back on the Gave at Pau, leaving the road to Bordeaux open to Wellington. Though he was beaten at Orthez at the end of February, he manœuvred around Tarbes for the whole of March, and then retreated on Toulouse, where he was finally defeated on April 10.

The treaty of Fontainebleau, signed on the 11th, sealed the fate of Napoleon. He was given the island of Elba and an annual allowance, Parma was given to Marie-Louise and his son, and his relatives were granted an income in national funds. On the 20th, he said farewell to the troops that he had driven so relentlessly, who were yet the only people to remain faithful to the last.

CHAPTER TEN

The Restoration and the Hundred Days

THE VICTORIOUS SOVEREIGNS assembled in Vienna to reorganize Europe according to their desires. In France, Louis XVIII confirmed the principles of 1789 and the institutions of Napoleon; but it was not long before the protests of a disappointed aristocracy began to be an embarrassment to his government. This was just what Napoleon had hoped for. He was incapable of resigning himself to his fate, and afraid that his conditions would be made worse; and so he resolved to make one last bid for fortune. His return involved France in a fresh catastrophe, and led to his permanent captivity in Saint Helena.

THE CONGRESS OF VIENNA AND THE SUCCESS OF THE COUNTER-REVOLUTION

The allies, who were now complete masters of France, began by imposing their conditions on the Bourbons. On April 20, the Count of Artois, who had just been appointed lieutenant-general by the Senate, signed an armistice surrendering the fortified ports still occupied by the French, together with all their equipment and stores. Peace was signed in Paris on May 30. As well as Montbéliard and Mulhouse, Talleyrand managed to save Chambéry and Annecy, together with part of the Saar region, where he had special interests. The allies did not ask for any war indemnity, and did not even claim return of the artistic treasures removed by Napoleon from the conquered countries. As the boundaries of 1792 to which the allies had decided to confine France did not include the colonies, England took over Tobago, Saint Lucia, the Île-de-France, Roderigo, and the Seychelles, whilst Spain was given back her part of Saint Domingo. France accepted in advance any decisions the allies might make as to the territories she had seized in the congress that would meet at Vienna.

This gathering was the most important that Europe had so far held, and aroused great hopes, first and foremost among the old 'legitimate' authorities. The more important among the dispossessed princes resumed their places. Napoleon had himself set Ferdinand VII free by the treaty of Valençay as early as December 11, 1813, and had sent the Pope back to his Papal States in January, 1814. The Elector of Hesse, the King of Sardinia, and the Dukes of Modena and Tuscany all went back to their capitals, and the King of England resumed possession of Hanover, which now became a kingdom. But would Napoleon's former allies restore what he had given them? In Germany more especially, the *Ritterschaft* and the ecclesiastical princes were asserting their rights. There was no less anxiety on the part of the peoples who had fought for their independence, and not in order to re-establish the *Ancien Régime*, especially as they had been promised their freedom. The German patriots claimed unity, though without quite knowing how to define it, and from the beginning of the year Görres had been conducting a vigorous campaign in the *Rheinische Merkur* against the selfishness of the princes. The Italians were delighted to have got rid of the French, but were afraid the Austrians might return. Moreover, the middle classes and peasants set free by the French did not intend to sink back into a state of dependence. On May 22, 1815, on the eve of the new campaign against Napoleon, the King of Prussia himself promised a constitution. But whether it was those who adored the past, such as Baader, who urged the sovereigns to base the new political order on the principles of religion, or those who looked to the future, like Saint-Simon and Augustin Thierry, and who wanted at last to organize a European society, there was common agreement that what was required of the congress was peace—a long, if not an everlasting, period of peace.

Castlereagh, Metternich, and the Prussians did not look so far ahead. Even the Czar, though he might listen to the vaticinations of Jung Stilling and Mme de Krüdener which reached him through one of the Czarina's ladies-in-waiting, followed his usual habit of using the mysticism to further his ambitions. He was to say to Talleyrand before long: 'The habits of Europe constitute its law.' The four powers intended the congress to limit itself to ratifying their decisions, and England, still claiming the right to mediate, invited the allies to come and settle them in London. Alexander interposed in a lordly fashion, annoying the Tories by flattering the Whigs, and offending the Regent. The discussion broke up without reaching agreement, and the September meeting in Vienna was no more successful. The congress was then adjourned, and although Talleyrand, with the support of Spain, won a moral victory by fixing the opening for November 1, the congress never really came together. Everything took place in committee and the important questions were decided by the four. The chief bone of contention continued to be the Duchy of Warsaw, which Russia wanted to keep, and Saxony, which she intended to make over to Prussia. There was steady resistance from Metternich, whilst the English government showed itself indifferent, merely insisting on avoiding all discussion on the freedom of the seas and reserving its rights to decide the colonial question. England appropriated Malta and Heligoland, and took over from the Dutch the Cape, Singapore, and a part of Guiana. She also obtained the condemnation of the slave trade, without however being able to secure its immediate abolition, owing to the non-co-operation of Spain and Portugal. On Continental matters, she was prepared to leave Castlereagh a free hand.

Castlereagh did not think it possible for his country to stand aside: of all British statesmen, he was the most European-minded there had ever been. His first concern was to encircle France by organizing the Low Countries, installing Prussia on the Rhine, and settling Austria in Italy; yet he also thought it advisable not to allow the Czar to assume the hegemony. He thought it essential to fortify Germany against France and Russia by bringing Austria and Prussia together. At first, he seemed to be succeeding, and Metternich agreed to leave Saxony to Prussia if the Prussians would desert Alexander. But Frederick William, overwhelmed by his friend's reproaches, disowned his ministers' decisions. The situation seemed so serious that Castlereagh took it upon him to sign a treaty of alliance with Metternich and Talleyrand on January 3, 1815. 'The coalition has been dissolved,' wrote Talleyrand, who took the credit for this success, and has since persuaded a good many people to believe him. To be sure, he showed great adroitness; but the principles of territorial impartiality and legitimacy with which he made such play did not have as much effect as has commonly been believed. No one dreamt of granting him anything, and if he defended legitimacy, everyone knew that this was only in order to flatter Louis XVIII, who wanted to reinstate his relations in Naples and Parma. The truth is that he complied with Castlereagh and Metternich in order to get them to throw over Murat. Moreover, the allies had no intention of breaking up their coalition. Castlereagh was prepared to make concessions, and quickly persuaded Alexander to agree. Thorn and Posen were given back to the Prussians, who had to be satisfied with a third of Saxony, and only obtained Eupen and Malmédy on the Dutch side. Failing any better offer, they accepted the Rhine Provinces. Castlereagh thus followed Napoleon's footsteps in the unification of Germany. By agreeing with Talleyrand in his refusal to let the King of Saxony be brought onto the Rhine, he effectively prepared the way for him to pass under Prussian influence. Once this matter had been settled, he left Vienna. Napoleon's return did not interrupt the work of the committees, and the final treaty was signed on June 9.

This settlement has been looked upon as a masterpiece, but in fact it left the way open for rivalries in the East, which might well lead to further wars. The Turks seized this favourable moment to reoccupy Serbia between July and October 1813. Then in November 1814, as a result of a fresh revolt, they found themselves shut up in the fortresses. Now the Czar maintained that by virtue of the Treaty of Bucharest, the Serbs had a right to autonomy; besides which, the Sultan persisted in disputing the Czar's right to his conquests in the Caucasus. It was easy to foresee that some time or other the Czar would demand Constantinople in return for the services he claimed to have rendered to Europe. This was why Metternich had suggested to Mahmoud that he should get the Powers to guarantee his territories. But the Russians opposed the suggestion, and the English, oblivious of future dangers, also refused to give their consent.

Furthermore, it was natural that the diplomats of the *Ancien Régime* should be proud of their work, since they had divided the various lands and 'souls', according to their cherished principles of equilibrium. For that very reason, the work of the congress ran counter to the new European tendencies, for it completely ignored the feelings of nationality which the revolutionary wars had aroused. In spite of the Whigs' protestations, on this particular point Castlereagh was just as blind as Metternich. With the Lombards and Venetians handed over to Austria, the Belgians unwillingly subjected to the Dutch, Poland once again partitioned, and even the Germans brought together into a paralytic confederation torn between Austria and Prussia, it was obvious that the victims would not be long in reasserting their rights.

The political administrative and social reaction was also taking its course. In May 1814, Ferdinand VII had annulled the constitution of 1812 before entering Madrid, and Ferdinand of Sicily followed his example. The Pope and the Italian princes, and the sovereigns of Central and Northern Germany all set about destroying the work of Napoleon; whilst the King of Prussia suspended the agrarian reforms that were so hateful to the *Junkers*. Metternich reckoned that he would certainly also be able to make Southern Germany return to sound doctrine. In this respect, Castlereagh and the Tories agreed with him: freedom was a perquisite of the British aristocracy, and the Continental rabble had no claims to it. They were soon destined to discover that the spirit of the Revolution, which had been carried abroad by Napoleon's troops, had survived their defeat. Even at the present moment, the aristocrats of Europe were furious to observe that the revolutionary spirit was being given its share of good things. Several usurpers were allowed to keep their thrones, which to the aristocrats seemed symbolic. True, Murat was condemned, because he obstinately insisted on retaining the Marches, thus alienating Metternich, who handed him over secretly to Castlereagh and Talleyrand in January

1815. But Bernadotte remained in possession of Sweden, and with English support compelled Christian of Denmark, who had been elected king by the Norwegians, to cede him the crown in November 1814. Bonaparte himself reigned over Elba, and his 'bastard', as Wellington called him, would one day be Duke of Parma. The reactionary party considered it to be far more serious still that in the Low Countries, the Rhine Provinces, Southern Germany, and Switzerland there should be an apparent obligation to respect the whole or at least part of the French innovations. In order to oblige William of Orange to have some regard for the Belgians, Castlereagh had thought it necessary to make him give them a constitution. The Czar had also promised one to the Poles. In France, the legitimate king who had been restored with so much difficulty was very far from re-establishing the old absolutism and all its privileges. He had resigned himself to preserving the results of the Revolution and the Empire, and intended to share the work of government with the middle classes.

The lightning return of Napoleon was to be another proof of the frailty of this 'moderate' restoration regime.

THE FIRST RESTORATION IN FRANCE AND THE RETURN FROM ELBA

Louis XVIII had reached Calais on April 24, 1814. It was hardly possible for him to accept the constitution drawn up by the Senate who had called him to the throne in the name of the nation. In a declaration made at Saint-Ouen on May 2 he treated it as no more than a preliminary sketch. He was prepared to keep its essential points, such as civil liberty and equality, the sale of national property, the retention of the imperial institutions, and the principles of constitutional government; but the sovereignty of the people disappeared from the constitution, and in its place the king 'would grant a charter'. This was drawn up by a commission sitting from the 22nd to the 27th. The political organization was borrowed from the English. The king exercised executive power through responsible ministers. He also had the sole power to initiate legislation. The taxes were voted and the laws passed by a Chamber of Peers and a Chamber of Deputies, the first chosen by the king, with the possibility of hereditary seats, the latter elected by a suffrage based on property qualifications. Anyone paying direct taxes of 300 francs or more would have a vote, and at 1,000 francs a man became eligible as a deputy. But for the time being, the *Corps Législatif* of the Empire became as it stood the Chamber of Deputies. The new aristocracy also provided the majority of the peers—84 senators and several marshals. The charter was read before the Chambers on June 4.

The upper middle classes received the new constitution with some satisfaction, for on the one hand it was a barrier against a counter-revolution, and on the other it deprived the common people of all political influence. All the same, it remained to be seen whether Louis XVIII would hand the government over to the notables, that is, whether he would choose his ministers according to the wishes of the parliamentary majority, like the King of England. Well, he intended to do nothing of the sort: he had reconstituted the old *conseils* '*d'en haut*' and '*des parties*', and his ministers were nothing but superior clerks who dealt with him separately and did not form a like-minded cabinet with collective responsibility. The middle classes were disappointed. And to make matters worse, Louis XVIII showed no interest in affairs, and foreign ambassadors—particularly Wellington and Pozzo di Borgo—aspired to have a hand in the game. The regime had no proper government, and consequently lost power.

The mass of the nation remained indifferent, for the Bourbons no longer counted for anything in their eyes, as the allies and *émigrés* had been astonished to note. After all, Louis had returned without their being consulted, and they only accepted him because foreigners seemed to be imposing him on them as a condition of peace and the evacuation of French territory. Naturally enough, they were not at all grateful to him for this peace—quite the contrary, in fact: the white flag seemed to them to be a symbol of national humiliation. Nothing in the charter could rouse their interest, for they did not care about the seat of political power once it had been decided not to reintroduce the ancient privileges, or the tithe, or the feudal dues.

This was precisely what the nobles and the priests could not resign themselves to accept. The latter in particular, having proclaimed the Catholic faith as the religion of the State, did not intend it to be a mere hollow formula. These two classes looked upon the charter as a temporary concession, an opinion that was shared by the Count of Artois. Louis XVIII, moreover, owed them certain satisfactions. To the nobles he dealt out places at court, in his household guard, in the administration and in the army, whilst thousands of officers found themselves discharged on half pay, at a time when the financial state of the country was being made an excuse for maintaining the 'combined excise' which the Count of Artois had promised to abolish. The clergy procured a decree requiring the observance of Sunday, the exemption of Church schools from all dues and all control, and the abolition of the office of Grand Master in the University of Paris. The government could hardly refuse to make certain symbolical gestures, such as the erection of a monument to the dead at Quiberon, and the elevation of Cadoudal to the nobility. There was all the more excuse for showing indulgence to the nobles' pleas and the priests' sermons; and all Frenchmen soon realized that nothing less than a return to the *Ancien Régime* would satisfy these interests. Resignation was now succeeded by anger, and the regime could certainly not rely on the loyalty of the soldiers.

Before long, there were conspiracies on foot. Fouché was confident that Europe would not tolerate the return of Napoleon and so was inclined to look to the Duke of Orleans, or a regency under Marie-Louise with the support of Austria. Maret, on the other hand, was working for the Emperor, and in February 1815 sent Fleury de Chaboulan to inform him of the state of affairs. Some generals were preparing a military rebellion, and Lallenand and Drouet tried to provoke one in the north. They failed, but at the same moment the news spread that '*he*' had returned.

Napoleon, for his part, had never resigned himself to his fate, and he had good reasons for complaint. The authorities refused to give him back his son, and Marie-Louise had already taken Neipperg as her lover. Louis XVIII declared he would not pay him the allowance that had been promised. Napoleon probably knew that there was talk at Vienna of banishing him to Saint Helena. On February 26, two days after Chaboulon's visit, Napoleon embarked for France, on an adventure which could only bring him new misfortunes.

On March 1, he reached the Gulf of Juan without let or hindrance. From there he marched upon Grenoble, where he was awaited by Colonel La Bedoyère, who surrendered the place to him. On the 10th, the workers of Lyons greeted him in triumph. Ney, who had promised to recapture him, also went over to his side on the 14th at Lous-le-Saulnier and joined up with him at Auxerre. In face of this blow Louis XVIII, who up till now had appeared to be confident, came to the conclusion that the game was lost, and in the night of the 19th left for Lille, from which he reached Ghent. The eagle and the tricolour were flying once more from belfry after belfry, and even from the towers of Notre-Dame.

THE HUNDRED DAYS

Napoleon met with no serious resistance. The Duke of Bourbon and the Duchess of Angoulême tried in vain to draw the troops away from the Emperor. The Duke of Angoulême advanced from Languedoc as far as la Drôme; but he was soon surrounded, and found himself being shipped off to Spain. Although Napoleon met with few avowed enemies, he found France considerably changed. During the Hundred Days political life gave signs of a revival that disconcerted Napoleon.

The spirit of the Revolution once more walked openly abroad and revived its traditions. In the course of his lightning journey, Napoleon had not scrupled to make use of it and to launch violent attacks upon the nobles and priests who wished to restore the *Ancien Régime*. 'I shall string them up to the lamp-posts,' he exclaimed at Autun. There was, in fact, a lively popular reaction against both these classes. Moreover, the Jacobin bourgeoisie revived the federations, which proved successful in Brittany at the end of April, in Paris on May 14, and more especially in the east—in Lorraine, at Strasbourg, in Burgundy, and in Dauphiné. They brought back memories of the Committee of Public Safety and the army in Year II. There was even singing of the *Marseillaise* and the *Chant du départ*. The government took alarm and conscientiously set about measures to ensure that this revival did not have any practical results. But Napoleon gave it his approval, though without the smallest intention of restarting the Revolution. Hereditary and absolute monarchy had returned for good: all the people had to do was to keep quiet till they were required to fight.

But he did not dare to treat the liberals so cavalierly. From the moment of his arrival at Lyons he began to hand out lavish promises—no doubt at the instance of La Bédoyère, though probably without attaching much importance to them. But in Paris the newspapers, the constitutional bodies and even the Council of State demanded a constitutional government. 'That blackguard has ruined France for me,' he remarked of Louis XVIII. But the king had in fact been powerless: he had had to bow in spite of himself to the power which the notables partly owed to the imperial policy; and Napoleon, reluctant to base himself on popular support, was obliged to do likewise. In order not to have to eat his own words, he merely agreed to promulgate a 'decree to supplement the imperial constitutions'. This supplementary decree was fairly close to the Charter, and was likewise a compromise. He signed it himself along with Benjamin Constant, who had as lately as March 19 published a violent article against him in the *Débats*, but had yielded to the Emperor's first appeal. The liberal middle classes did not manage to retain the property qualification for the suffrage. Napoleon re-established universal suffrage and the electoral colleges; but he conceded hereditary peerage to the Senate, though he had refused it in Year XII. The results satisfied nobody. There were few voters at the plebiscite, and more than half the electorate failed to vote at the election of the deputies. The granting of hereditary peerage had frozen the zeal of the patriotic party and robbed them of all their initiative. As for the liberal middle classes, they did not trust Napoleon, and soon resumed the offensive against him. After the promulgation of the decree with all due pomp in a *Champ de mai* which had to be postponed till June 1, the deputies undertook to transform themselves into constituent assemblies and to revise the decree. In short, Napoleon alienated the Frenchmen who were disposed to support him warmly, without managing to conciliate the notables.

The liberal opposition proved a source of annoyance to the government. Fouché, in control of the police, was lenient towards all parties, and was in addition secretly negotiating with Metternich. At the Ministry of the Interior, Carnot did not make many ministerial changes. The extraordinary commissions were no more energetic in their actions than in 1814. The censorship—which had been retained by Louis XVIII—had now been abolished, and the royalists took advantage of the fact to exploit the economic crisis, the fear of conscription, and the inevitability of war. At the beginning of May, la Vendée rose once again, and the chouans reappeared in Brittany. The rebels took Bressuire and Cholet, and Napoleon had to put a western army in charge of Lamarque. The rebellion was quickly suppressed. The Vendean leaders were crushed near Légé on June 20 and made peace on the 25th. Nevertheless, they had pinned down a force of 30,000, and had done good service to the coalition, for Lamarque's troops would have made all the difference between victory and defeat at Waterloo.

Whatever interest the historian may find in these movements of opinion, Frenchmen themselves were more occupied during these months with the threats from abroad. During his march on Paris, Napoleon had given an assurance that he was acting in concert with Austria; but it is difficult to believe that he can really have been under such an illusion. When he reassumed the title of Emperor, he sent the allies an offer of peace and despatched some envoys to them. But he received no answer. As early as March 13, he was declared a European outlaw at Vienna, and on the 25th the alliance of Chaumont was confirmed. In this supreme and final struggle, the kings and the aristocracy once more posed as the defenders of popular independence and even the freedom of the French nation, which had been subjugated by a tyrant. They were in fact well aware that this was no longer the question at issue: the vital thing was to crush the Revolution once and for all by striking down the man who personified it in their eyes. Pozzo di Borgo had written:

> Napoleon is advancing on Paris, holding aloft the torch of revolution. He is accompanied by the dregs of the populace and by the army. . . . The foreign powers must make haste to nip this evil in the bud, or it will once more undermine all the foundations of social order, for it represents the lust for pillage and violence pitted against the rights of property and law.

Europe was about to come down on France like an avalanche. She had from 700,000 to 800,000 men on foot, considerable reserves, and all the resources of England at her disposal.

The Restoration had an army of 160,000 men, and there were another 100,000 at home, with or without leave. Napoleon called them all up and mixed them with the 1815 conscripts, who had been summoned to the ranks on October 9, 1813. He also appealed for volunteers and for officers of the reserve, preserved the organization of the National Guard which he had initiated, and set a part of them on to guarding the fortresses or forming reserve divisions. Unfortunately, there was no great abundance of arms, munitions, or horses, and still less money. The worst part of it was that the national spirit, though better than in 1814, did not show much enthusiasm. Those who were called up were slow to respond, and by no means all of them put in an appearance. Napoleon might perhaps have rekindled some enthusiasm if he had supported the federations. But he disclaimed the revolutionary ardour and the example of the Committee of Public Safety, and did not dare to restore either conscription or a mixed system which would have joined the national guards in with the army and thus have made it easily possible to take 200,000 men to Belgium. It must however be admitted that he would not have had time to make better arrangements, for it was imperative to take the offensive and reconquer the Rhine before the coalition was organized for action.

In his last army there was thus a breach with the traditions of the Revolution. It was composed of trained men, who had mostly already fought a campaign; it was more reliable than the 1813 army, and better provided with artillery and cavalry, but it was too small. Leaving out of account the National Guard and the forces assigned to the different frontiers, the northern army only numbered 126,000 men—that is, six army corps, the Guards and four cavalry groups. The staff and higher command did not prove to be of the first order, and on the very eve of Ligny Bourmont went over to the enemy. In spite of what has been said to the contrary, it would seem that the Emperor's health, energy, and confidence were no longer what they had been in former days.

Two of the armies that had evacuated France were still quartered in Belgium. One of these, composed of English, Hanoverians, Belgians, and Dutch, numbered 96,000 men; and Wellington had come to take command of it. The other—

Blücher's troops—consisted of 124,000 Prussians. Between them, these two armies were therefore superior in strength; but they were still in scattered groups and there might well be a chance of surprising them, or at least defeating them one at a time: this at any rate was the only card Napoleon had to play. Besides, even an overwhelming victory would not have decided the issue.

From June 6 onwards, Napoleon began to move his troops from Lille to Metz in order to concentrate them south of the Sambre, and on the 15th he debouched at Charleroi and threw himself between the two enemy armies. But his orders were rather ineffectively carried out, and Ligny and Quatre-Bras were not taken. He for his part allowed the enemy to retreat and lost the whole morning of the 16th. In actual fact, Blücher and Gneisenau, having collected 84,000 men, had made up their minds to risk a battle. Wellington, who had made no move until the 12th and was still waiting for an attack from the Mons direction on the 15th, was quickly moving his divisions eastwards in order to catch the French in the flank. At last, in the early afternoon of the 16th, Napoleon realized that the Prussians were present in force at Ligny. He gave battle, instructing Ney and Drouet to fall back from Quatre-Bras on their right, but he had left Lobau's corps at Charleroi, which did not rejoin him till the evening, and he only had 68,000 men. Ney was under increasing pressure from Wellington, and could not disengage himself. Orders were inefficiently passed on, with the result that Drouet manœuvred between the two battlefields without being of any use in either. Blücher's army was driven in at the centre and forced to retreat, though not destroyed. Napoleon was unwell, and left the field of battle; there was no pursuit of the enemy until at the end of the morning of the 17th, when Grouchy was at last sent to see what had happened to their retreating forces. In the course of the night he discovered that far from retiring on Namur, they were marching on Wavre; and instead of crossing the Dyle and blocking their path he followed them to such purpose that there was now nothing to prevent Blücher marching to the assistance of Wellington.

Meanwhile, Wellington had retired northwards, and had taken up a position in front of the forest of Soignes, on the Mont-Saint-Jean plateau, with 67,000 men, his right strongly protected by the Château de Hougoumont and the Haie-Sainte farm, and his centre was well covered. His left was more exposed, but he expected Prussian support on this side. Napoleon turned back against him in the course of the 17th with 74,000 men; but rain impeded operations, and he did not launch an attack against him till about midday on June 18, with the result that by one o'clock Bülow had appeared on the French flank. The frontal attack on the English positions, which had been left to Ney, was deplorably carried out. Launched to begin with against the enemy's right, it was held up at the Château de Hougoumont; then it was transferred to the centre, where it was caught up until three-thirty in front of la Haie-Sainte. After this, the infantry advanced in deep column and were mown down by grape-shot, then charged and thoroughly mauled. The cavalry, charging in its turn at the English squares, was repulsed; then in a final rally the infantry came back to the assault and shook the enemy line. Ney called for the Guards to deal a final blow. But Napoleon had been obliged to use a large part of them to support Lobau, who had slowly been thrust back by Bülow's growing forces, and was only able to send five battalions of the Old Guard, whose attack was held by the English Guards—Wellington's last reserves. At this moment Ziethen appeared on the extreme right of the French, and the English took up the offensive. The whole of Napoleon's army wavered, and then broke and fled in panic, losing 30,000 men and 7,500 prisoners. Grouchy, who had been treated with some circumspection at Wavre, was able to disengage his forces; then the remnants of the army gathered together at Laon and retired behind the Seine.

Returning to Paris on the 21st, Napoleon wanted to organize further resistance. But the Chamber showed their hostility, and he abdicated the next day. An executive commission was elected, with Fouché as its moving spirit, and he succeeded in inducing Napoleon to leave Malmaison on the 29th. The Chamber declared against the Bourbons and sent a delegation to Wellington, who arrived outside the capital on June 30. The general inclination was to substitute the Duke of Orleans for Louis XVIII, and Talleyrand (who had remained in Vienna) was inclined to assent. The allies had some difficulty in agreeing to restore the fallen king, and Alexander remained strongly opposed to him. But Alexander was not there: the unexpected disaster to Napoleon left the solution largely in the hands of Louis XVIII and Wellington. The king had set out at once, and from Cambrai he promised to proclaim an amnesty on the 28th. Wellington's reply to the deputies was that a change of dynasty would be a revolutionary act entailing the dismemberment of France, whereupon the Chambers and the commission broke up. Davout, who had been put in command of the army, signed the capitulation of Paris on July 2, and then retired behind the Loire. Louis XVIII took possession once more on the 8th.

Meanwhile, Napoleon had arrived at Rochefort on the 3rd. He had asked for frigates to take him to the United States; but the executive commission, intimating that there was an English cruiser in waiting, directed that he should go on board, and in fact held him as a prisoner. On the 15th, he surrendered to them on board the *Bellerophon.*

The English Government, the Prussians, and even Metternich were in favour of taking several provinces away from France. But Castlereagh, with Wellington and Alexander's support, was firmly against this course. In the end, he won over Liverpool, while the Czar persuaded Austria to change her mind. The Prussians found themselves alone, and had to give way. The draft treaty, produced on September 26, was rejected by Talleyrand; but Louis XVIII dismissed him and on November 20 signed the second Treaty of Paris, which took away from France Philippeville and Marienbourg, Sarrelouis, Landau, and the Saar and all that was left of Savoy. An indemnity of 700 million francs was imposed upon her, in addition to 240 million in private claims; she was to be occupied by the allies for from three to five years; and this time she was also obliged to give back the art treasures she had taken from other countries. On the same day the allies confirmed their alliance and excluded the Bonapartes from the French throne in perpetuity. Castlereagh inserted the additional proviso that the congress should meet together from time to time to examine the situation in Europe. As from September 26, Alexander had concluded a mystical pact with Prussia and Austria, the Holy Alliance, to preserve peace and ensure good government in Europe according to the principles of Christianity.

Meanwhile, Napoleon was sailing towards Saint Helena, where the allies had decided that he should be interned. This tragic exile in a distant island, lost in the ocean, beneath a tropical sun, put the finishing touches to that romantic prestige which will always exercise such a fascination on the minds of men. It also helped to give birth to the legend which transformed the role he had played in history. In French eyes he became a victim of the kings, and was once again looked upon as the hero of a revolutionary nation. His captivity was not only due to the terrifying effects of his very name; it was also an expression of vengeance against the upstart soldier who had presumed to take an archduchess to wife.

With the last—but by no means the least of his strokes of genius, he succeeded in dictating his memoirs with a complete forgetfulness of everything personal in his policies, seeing himself simply and solely as the leader of a revolutionary army come to set mankind and all the nations free, an army which he had in the end persuaded to throw away its sword.

CONCLUDING REMARKS

The great Napoleonic achievement—the establishment of a new dynasty and the building of a universal empire—ended in failure. Hence the imagination of the poet has tended to see the Emperor as a second Prometheus whose daring was punished by the heavenly powers, and as a symbol of human genius at grips with Fate. On the other hand, some have seen him as the sport of historical determinism, on the pretext that the Revolution was bound to lead to a dictatorship, and that the acquisition of her natural frontiers was bound to lead France on to perpetual war. Without rashly launching into metaphysical speculation, the historian would be inclined to agree with the former thesis. It would seem to him a fact that an authoritarian government was indispensable to save the Revolution as long as its enemies were in league with the foreigner, and that the middle classes needed Napoleon to give this authority. It would also seem at least probable that the annexation of Belgium and the left bank of the Rhine would expose France to new attacks. But a military dictatorship did not in itself necessitate the re-establishment of an hereditary monarchy, still less an aristocratic nobility. Nor was the best means of defending the natural frontiers to be found in expanding beyond them and so giving rise to coalitions in self-defence. Yet this was what Napoleon was personally responsible for setting in train. Circumstances were certainly favourable to his efforts, but they none the less arose from the depths of his own essential nature. Moreover, there is a widely held view that Napoleon's work was doomed to fail; and it would perhaps be salutary for all would-be Caesars and for the good of the human race if this judgment could be held beyond a doubt. But this cannot for one moment be admitted: Alexander's will-power might well have failed at Moscow, and the allied army might have been destroyed at Lützen. The only solid certainty is that the risks were tremendous, and that France, hazarding her all, lost all that the Revolution had conquered in her name.

Although Napoleon's individual ambitions were not realized, his actions have nevertheless left the deepest impress on society. In France, the new State had not yet taken definite shape, and it was Napoleon who gave it an administrative framework that bore the marks of a master hand. The Revolution of 1789 had thrust the middle classes forward into power, but this power had then been disputed by a rising democracy. Under the protection of the Emperor, the notables succeeded in recovering it, and grew in wealth and influence. Once they had got rid of the menace of the common people, they were prepared to govern and to restore liberalism. In Europe, the spread of French ideas, the influence of England, the advance of capitalism, and the consequent rise of the middle classes, all tended in the same direction and resulted in a marked speeding up of evolution and the introduction of the modern order. The expansion of culture, the proclamation of the sovereignty of the people, and the spread of romanticism foreshadowed the awakening of nationalism, and Napoleon's territorial rearrangements and reforms encouraged these trends. Capitalism was taking root in the West, and the blockade provided protection for its early stages. Romanticism had long been fermenting in Europe, and Napoleon provided its poets with the perfect hero. But though Napoleon's influence was considerable, this was only in so far as it followed the currents that were already carrying European civilization along with them. If historical determinism is to be brought into the picture, this is where its effects may be observed.

Since he was in this respect, a man of his century, one can understand the swift growth of the Napoleonic legend, and the deep roots that it struck. Nevertheless, there is a glaring contradiction between his personal tendencies and the durable elements in his achievement, which only legend preserved. He had in fact become more and more hostile to the Revolution, to such a degree that if he had had the time he would in the end have partly repudiated even civil equality; yet in the popular imagination, he was the hero of the Revolution. He who dreamt of universal empire remained in the eyes of Frenchmen the defender of his country's 'natural frontiers' whilst the European liberals saw him as the defender of nationality against the kings of the Holy Alliance. He had instituted the most rigorous despotism; yet it was in his name that the constitutional reign of the Bourbons was opposed. The Romantics had idolized him, yet his methods of thought and his literary and artistic tastes ranged him on the side of the purest classicism. From the political and national point of view, this ambivalence was to lead in the end to Napolcon III.

Yet the Romantics were not wholly wrong about him, for his classicism was only one of culture and cast of mind. His springs of action, his unconquerable energy of temperament, arose from the depths of his imagination. Here lay the secret of the fascination that he will exercise for ever more on the individual person. For men will always be haunted by romantic dreams of power, even if only in the passing fires and disturbances of youth; and there will thus never be wanting those who will come, like Barres' heroes, to stand in ecstasy before the tomb.

BIBLIOGRAPHY

Bibliography

PART ONE. THE IMPERIAL CONQUESTS AFTER TILSIT (1807–1812)

Chapter 1. The Continental System (1807–1809)

For general works see those cited in the bibliography in *Napoleon 1799–1807:* pp. 279, 281, 294, 302.

ENGLAND AWAKENS

See works relating to England cited in Vol. I, pp. 286–7, 289, 290; G. Brodrick and J. Fotheringham, 'The History of England from Addington's Administration to the Close of William IV's Reign, 1801–1837' (London, 1906; Vol. XI of *Political History of England*, ed. Hunt and Poole); for finance see N. J. Silberling, 'Financial and Monetary Policy of Great Britain during the Napoleonic Wars', *Quarterly Journal of Economics*, Vol. XXXVIII (1924), pp. 214–333 and 397–439; A. Hope-Jones, *Income Tax in the Napoleonic Wars* (Cambridge, 1939); for military strength see J. W. Fortescue, *History of the British Army*, Vol. IV (London, 1906); for economy see F. Crouzet, *L'économie britannique et le blocus continental, 1806–1813* (Paris, 1958).

EUROPE CLOSED TO ENGLAND (1807–1808)

See Vol. I, p. 289. Most important is H. Butterfield, *The Peace Tactics of Napoleon I, 1806–1808* (Cambridge, 1929). For Prussia see P. Hassel, *Geschichte der preussischen Politik, 1807–1815*, Vol. I, '1807–1808' (Leipzig, 1881).

AFFAIRS IN PORTUGAL AND SPAIN (1807–1808)

See Vol. I, pp. 281, 292, 302, and those works about Spain cited p. 287. A most important work is A. Fugier's *Napoléon et l'Espagne* (Paris, 1930), but it stops at the eve of the interview at Bayonne; C. de Grandmaison's *L'Espagne et Napoléon* (Paris, 1908–31, 3 vols.) deals with the whole Spanish affair but is not so good. The works cited in the section below deal with the events that led up to the peninsular war. See also P. Conrad, *La constitution de Bayonne* (Paris, 1909).

Bibliography

THE SPANISH INSURRECTION (1808)

See Comte de Toreno, *Histoire du soulèvement de la guerre et de la Révolution d'Espagne* (Paris, 1836–38, 5 vols.); J. S. Arteche y Moro, *Guerra de la independencia* (Madrid, 1868–96, 10 vols.); W. F. P. Napier, *History of the War in the Peninsular and in the South of France from the Year 1807 to the Year 1814* (London, 1828–40, 6 vols., 2nd. ed., 1890), written from the Whig point of view; Fortescue, *History of the British Army* (London, 1906). An authoritative account is that by C. W. C. Oman, *History of the Peninsular War* (Oxford, 1902–30, 7 vols.). Among those works written for the 150th anniversary of the revolt see C. E. Corona, *Precedentes ideologicos de la guerra de independencia;* F. Suarez-Verdeguer, *Las tendencias politicas durante la guerra de independencia;* L. C. Rodriguez, *La evolucion institucional, Las Cortes de Cadiz: precedentes y consecuencias* (Saragossa, 1959); J. M. Recasens Cornes, *El corregimiento de Tarragona y su junta en la guerra de independencia, 1808–1811* (Tarragona, 1958); C. G. Etchegaray, *Coleción de documentos ineditos de la Guerra de independencia existantes en el Archivo de la Deputacion de Vizcaya* (Bilbao, 1959); J. Perez Villanueva, *Planteamiento ideologico inicial de la guerra de independencia* (Valladolid, 1960). For military aspects see S. Amado Loriga, *Aspectos militares de la guerra de independencia;* F. Solano Costa, *El guerillero y sa transcendencia* (Saragossa, 1959), *La guerra de independencia y los sitios de Zaragoza* (Saragossa, 1958). For England's role and Canning see J. Holland Rose, 'Canning and the Spanish Patriots in 1808', *The American Historical Review*, Vol. XII (1906–7) pp. 39–52; C. Petrie, *Great Britain and the War of Independence* (Saragossa, 1959). The French point of view is given by Grasset, *La guerre d'Espagne* (Paris, 1914–32, 3 vols.), 'L'Eglise et le soulèvement de l'Espagne', *Revue de Paris*, Vol. III (1923) pp. 410–31. There is no social and economic study of Spain in 1808. Nor is there one of the conditions in which preparations for the revolt were made. Gasset is the only one to have attempted to research into these subjects. The others subscribe to the myth of a purely patriotic and spontaneous revolt. For the Baylen affair see Lt.-Col. Titeux, *Le général Dupont* (Paris, 1903–4, 3 vols.); Lt.-Col. Clerc, *La capitulation de Baylen* (Paris, 1903); G. Pariset, 'La capitulation de Baylen', *Journal des Savants*, 1905, pp. 81–94; M. Leproux, *Le général Dupont, 1763–1840* (Paris, 1934); see T. Geisendorf des Gouttes, *Les prisonniers de guerre au temps du premier Empire. L'expédition et la captivité d'Andalousie, 1808–1810* (Geneva, 1930), for the pontoons at Cadiz.

THE BEGINNINGS OF THE FRANCO-RUSSIAN ALLIANCE AND THE INTERVIEW AT ERFURT (1808)

See Vol. I, pp. 281, 292, 302. Most important is A. Vandal, *Napoléon Ier et Alexandre Ier* (Paris, 1891–6, 3 vols.); Grand Duke Mikhailovitch, *Les relations de la Russie et de la France d'après les rapports des ambassadeurs d'Alexandre 1er et de Napoléon Ier* (St. Petersburg, 1905), *Le tsar Alexandre Ier* (trans. into French by Baron Wrangel, Paris, 1931); K. Waliszewski, *Le règne d'Alexandre Ier* (Paris, 1923–5, 3 vols.). On the Prussian indemnity see C. Lesage, *Napoléon Ier créancier de la Prusse, 1807–1814* (Paris, 1924) and, for the Prussian point of view, see H. Haussheer, *Erfüllung und Befreiung. Der Kampf um die*

Durchführung des Tilsiter Friedens, 1807–1808 (Hamburg, 1936). For Talleyrand see Vol. I, p. 295. For oriental politics see N. Iorga, *Geschichte des osmanischen Reiches*, Vol. V (Gotha, 1913, Vol. 37 of the series 'Geschichte der europäischen Staaten', founded by Heeren and Ukert) and Vol. I, p. 310.

NAPOLEON IN SPAIN (NOVEMBER 1808–JANUARY 1809)

See Commandant Balagny, *Campagne de l'empereur Napoléon en Espagne* (Paris, 1902–7, 5 vols.).

Chapter II. The War of 1809

See Vol. I, pp. 281, 292, 302.

THE AWAKENING OF GERMANY

See A. Rambaud, *La domination française en Allemagne*, Vol. II, 'Allemagne sous Napoléon Ier' (Paris, 1874, 4th ed., 1897); E. Denis, *L'Allemagne de 1789 à 1810: fin de l'ancienne Allemagne* (Paris, 1896); H. von Zwiedineck-Südenhorst, *Deutsche Geschichte von der Auflösung des alten bis zur Errichtung des neuen Kaiserreiches*, Vol. I, 'Die Zeit der Rheinbundes, 1806–1815' (Stuttgart, 1897); F. Meinecke, *Weltbürgertum und Nationalstaat* (Berlin, 1908, 4th ed., 1917), *Geschichte des Historismus im XVIIIten und XIXten Jahrhundert* (Berlin, 1927); O. Tschirch, *Geschichte der öffentlichen Meinung in Preussen im Friedensjahrzehnt vom Baster Frieden bis zum Zusammenbruch des Staates* (Weimar, 1933); F. Schnabel, *Deutsche Geschichte im neunzehnten Jahrhundert* (Freiburg im Breisgau, 1929, 4th ed., 1949); R. Aris, *History of Political Thought in Germany from 1789 to 1815* (London, 1936); H. von Treitschke, *Deutsche Geschichte im neunzehnten Jahrhundert*, Vol. I (Leipzig, 1879), this stops at 1814; F. Meinecke, *Das Zeitalter der deutschen Erhebung* (Bielefeld, 1906, 2nd ed., 1913), an excellent account; A. Berney, 'Reichstradition und Nationalstaatsgedanke, 1789–1815', *Historische Zeitschrift*, Vol. CXL (1929), pp. 57–86. See also those works relating to German romanticism cited in Vol. I, pp. 282–3; K. Schmitt-Dorotic, *Die politische Romantik* (Munich, 1925), partially translated into French under the title *Romantisme politique* (Paris, 1928); Eva Feisel, *Die Sprachphilosophie der deutschen Romantik, 1801–1816* (Tübingen, 1927); E. Tonnelat, *Les frères Grimm; leur œuvre de jeunesse* (Paris, 1912); E. Müsebeck, *E. M. Arndt*, Vol. I, '1769–1815' (Gotha, 1914); R. Steig and H. Grimm, *Achim von Arnim und die ihm nahestanden* (Stuttgart, 1894–1904, 2 vols.); J. Uhlmann, *Joseph Goerres und die deutsche Einheits- und Verfassungsfrage bis zum Jahre 1824* (Leipzig, 1912); H. Dänehardt, *Joseph Goerres politische Frühentwicklung* (Hamburg, 1926); J. Baxa, *A. Müller* (Jena, 1921); R. Aris, *Die Staatslehre Ad. Müllers in ihrem Verhältnis zur deutschen Romantik* (Tübingen, 1929); L. Sauzin, *Adam-Heinrich Müller, 1779–1829. Sa vie et son œuvre* (Paris, 1937); for Müller see also Meinecke, *Weltbürgertum und Nationalstaat* and Schmitt-Dorotic cited above. See also *Le romantisme politique en Allemagne*, selected texts by J. Droz (Paris, 1963). On the general question of the influence of the 'French wars' on the evolution of Germany see the symposium *Die französische Kriege und Deutschland 1792 bis 1815* (Berlin, 1958).

PRUSSIA

See Treitschke, and Meinecke, *Das Zeitalter*, cited in the section above; G. Cavaignac, *La formation de la Prusse contemporaine* (Paris, 1891–7, 2 vols.); E. N. Anderson, *Nationalism and the Cultural Crisis in Prussia, 1801–1815* (New York, 1939); J. Vidal de la Blache, *La régénération de la Prusse après Iéna* (Paris, 1910). For Stein's reforms see M. Lehmann, *Freiherr von Stein* (Leipzig, 1902–5, 3 vols.), and, even better, G. Ritter, *Stein, eine politische Biographie* (Berlin, 1931), who corrects Lehmann on a number of points and fills in his omissions. The Prussian State Archives has published documents relating to the Prussian reform: C. Winter, *Die Reorganisation des preussischen Staates unter Stein und Hardenberg*, Vol. I (Leipzig, 1931); W. Görlitz, *Stein, Staatsmann und Reformator* (Frankfurt, 1949). The question of French influence has been the subject of lively controversy in Germany: E. von Meier, *Preussen und die französische Revolution* (Leipzig, 1908), denies it completely; Lehmann thinks it was very great; Ritter considers that it played a certain part, see also 'Der Freiherr von Stein und das politische Reformprogramm des Ancien Regime in Frankreich', *Historische Zeitschrift*, Vol. CXXXVII (1927), pp. 442–97, and Vol. CXXXVIII (1928), pp. 24–46; he takes up the subject again in the symposium *Die französische Kriege und Deutschland* cited in the section above. On agrarian reform see G. Knapp, *Die Bauernbefreiung und der Ursprung des Landarbeiters in den älteren Theilen Preussens* (Leipzig, 1887); H. Sée, *Esquisse d'une histoire du régime agraire en Europe aux XVIIIe et XIXe siècles* (Paris, 1921). On the army, see documents published by R. Vaupel in the series 'Preussische Staatsarchive': *Das preussische Heer von Tilsiter Frieden bis zur Befreiung, 1807–1814*, Vol. I (Leipzig, 1938); M. Lehmann, *Scharnhorst* (Leipzig, 1886–7, 2 vols.); S. Stadelmann, *Scharnhorst. Schicksal und geistige Welt* (Wiesbaden, 1952); H. Delbrück, *Das Leben des Feldmarschalls Grafen N. von Gneisenau* (Berlin, 1882, 3rd ed., 1908); W. von Unger, *Blücher* (Berlin, 1907–8, 2 vols.); P. Roques, *Adversaires prussiens de Napoléon* (Paris, 1928).

AUSTRIA

See Vol. I, p. 286; M. von Angeli, *Erzherzog Karl als Feldherr und Heeresorganisator* (Vienna, 1895–7, 6 vols.). On Gentz see Vol. I, p. 284; V. Bibl, *Oesterreich, 1800–1809* (Leipzig, 1939); H. Rössler, *Oesterreichskampf in Deutschlandsbefreiung* (Hamburg, 1940); J. Mayer, *Wien im Zeitalter Napoleons. Staatsfinanzen, Lebensverhältnisse, Beamte und Militär* (Vienna, 1940); W. C. Langsam, *The Napoleonic Wars and German Nationalism in Austria* (New York, 1930); A. Robert, *L'idée nationale autrichienne et les guerres de Napoléon* (Paris, 1933). For Hungary see K. Kecskemeti, *Témoignages français sur la Hongrie à l'époque de Napoléon, 1802–1809* (Brussels, 1960): 'Fontes rerum historiae hungaricae in archivis extraneis', I, 1.

Bibliography

THE CAMPAIGN OF 1809

On the state of France see Vol. I, pp. 281, 292; G. Lacour-Gayet, *Talleyrand* (Paris, 1930–4, 3 vols.); L. Madelin, *Fouché* (Paris, 1901), Fouché's *Mémoires*, re-edited and annotated (Paris, 1945); G. Lenôtre, *La chouannerie normande au temps de l'Empire. Tournebut. 1804–1809* (Paris, 1901); E. Herpin, *Armand de Chateaubriand* (Paris, 1910). For the campaign see E. Bordeau, *Campagnes modernes, 1792–1815* (Paris, 1912–21, 2 vols. and an atlas); General Descoins, *Étude synthétique des principales campagnes modernes* (Paris, 1901, 7th ed. revised with sketches by General Chanoine, 1928); J. Colin, *Napoléon Ier* (Paris, 1914); Commandant Saski, *Campagne de 1809 en Allemagne et en Autriche* (Paris, 1899–1902, 3 vols.), up to Essling; A. Veltze, *Das Kriegsjahr 1809 in Einzeldarstellungen* (Vienna, 1905–9, 9 vols.); Mayerhoffer von Vedropolye *et al.*, *Der Krieg von 1809* (Vienna, 1907–9, 4 vols.) up to Essling; M. von Angeli cited in the section above; O. Criste, *Erzherzog Carl* (Vienna and Leipzig, 1912); General Derrécagaix, *Nos campagnes au Tyrol* (Paris, 1910); J. Hirn, *Tirols Erhebung im Jahre 1809* (Innsbruck, 1909); von Voltelini, *Forschungen und Beiträge zur Geschichte des Tirolaufstandes im Jahre 1809* (Gotha, 1909); M. Doeberl, *Die Entwicklungsgeschichte Bayerns*, Vol. II (Munich, 1912); W. de Fédorovicz, *1809. Compagne de Pologne depuis le commencement jusqu'à l'occupation de Varsovie*, Vol. I, 'Documents et matériaux français' (Paris, 1911).

THE AUSTRIAN MARRIAGE

See Vol. I, pp. 281, 292, 302; Vandal, *Napoléon Ier et Alexandre Ier* (Paris, 1891–6, 3 vols.); A. (or C.?) Latreille, *L'église catholique et la Révolution française*, Vol. I, 'Le pontificat de Pie VI et la crise française, 1775–1799' (Paris, 1946), *L'opposition religieuse au Concordat* (Paris, 1910); J. Leflon, 'La crise révolutionnaire, 1789–1846' (Paris, 1949, Vol. XX of the *Histoire de l'Église*, ed. A. Fiche and V. Mostim), *Monsieur Émery*, Vol. I, 'L'Église d'Ancien Régime et la Révolution' (Paris, 1944), Vol. II, 'L'Église concordataire et impériale' (Paris, 1947), *Étienne-Alexandre Bernier, évêque d'Orléans, et l'application du Concordat* (Paris, 1938); H. Welschinger, *Le divorce de Napoléon* (Paris, 1889); P. Dudon, 'Napoléon devant l'officialité de Paris', *Études*, Vol. XCI (1902), pp. 480–98. The divorce papers have been examined by L. Grégoire, *Le 'divorce' de Napoléon et de l'impératrice Joséphine; étude du dossier canonique* (Paris, 1957): the annulment of the marriage between Napoleon and Josephine was declared according to the canons of the church, and was not a matter of whim; the members of the Parisian ecclesiastical tribunals, both diocesan and metropolitan, were imbued with the traditions of the Gallic Church and applied them to this case as to others of marriage annulment which were submitted to them during this period. F. Masson, *Napoléon et sa famille*, Vols. IX, X, and XI (Paris, 1897–1919, 13 vols.), *Napoléon et son fils* (Paris, 1922), *L'impératrice Marie-Louise* (Paris, 1902); Baron de Bourgoing, *Marie-Louise, impératrice des Français* (Paris, 1938); *Lettres inédites de Napoléon Ier à Marie-Louise, écrites de 1810 à 1814*, collected by L. Madelin (Paris, 1935); *Marie-Louise et Napoléon. Lettres inédites (1813–1814)*, with a commentary by C. F. Palmstierna (Paris,

1955); É. Driault, *Le roi de Rome* (Paris, 1932). For Metternich see F. von Demelitsch, *Metternich und seine auswärtige Politik*, Vol. I, '1809–1812' (Stuttgart, 1898); F. Strohl von Ravensberg, *Metternich und seine Zeit* (Vienna, 1907); H. von Srbik, *Metternich* (Munich, 1925–6, 2 vols.); Marie Sadrain, *La réunion du Valais à la France en 1810* (Bourges, 1936).

Chapter III. England's Successes (1807–1811)

See works cited at the beginning of Ch. I.

THE COMMAND OF THE SEAS AND ITS CONSEQUENCES

See Vol. I, pp. 286–7, 304–5; the works on the British Empire and India cited Vol. I, p. 290. For the English in Sicily see H. Acton, *The Bourbon of Naples (1734–1825)* (London, 1956); P. Mackesy, *The War in the Mediterranean* (London, 1957); A. Capograssi, *Gl'Inglesi in Italia durante le campagne napoleoniche (Lord W. Bentinck)* (Paris, 1949); C. W. Crawley, 'England and the Sicilian Constitution', *The English Historical Review*, Vol. LV (1940), pp. 251–74; J. Rosselli, *Lord William Bentinck and the British Occupation of Sicily, 1811–1814* (Cambridge, 1956); G. Falzone, *Il problema economico della Sicilia tra 1700 e 1800* (Palermo, 1960); see also the articles by Miss H. M. Lackland cited in the section 'The Anglo-Saxons and Liberalism' below (p. 390). On the French colonies see J. Saintoyant, *La colonisation française pendant la période napoléonienne* (Paris, 1931); H. Prentout, *L'île de France sous Decaen* (Paris, 1901). For Latin America see B. Moses, *Spain's Declining Power in South America, 1730–1806* (Berkeley, Calif., 1919), *The Intellectual Background of the Revolution in South America* (New York, 1926); J. Mancini, *Bolivar et l'émancipation des colonies espagnoles des origines à 1815* (Paris, 1912); W. S. Robertson, *The Life of Miranda* (Chapel Hill, N. Carolina, 1929); P. Groussac, 'Un Français vice-roi de la Plata: Jacques de Liniers', *Revue des Deux Mondes*, Vol. III (1912), pp. 140–72; Fortescue, *History of the British Army*, Vol. V (London, 1906); M. Belgrano, *Belgrano* (Buenos Aires, 1927).

WELLINGTON'S CAMPAIGNS

See works cited in the section 'The Spanish Insurrection (1808)' above (p. 374); L. Guedalla, *The Duke* (London, 1931); R. Aldington, *Wellington* (London, 1946); T. Lucke, *Wellington der eiserne Herzog* (Berlin, 1938); H. Brett-James, *Wellington at War, 1794–1815, A selection of his wartime letters* (London, 1961): 175 letters or orders, 83 concerning the war in Spain, 26 about the operations in France and Belgium in 1814–15, the rest general. See also S. G. P. Ward, *Wellington's Headquarters. A study of the administrative problems in the Peninsula, 1809–1814* (London, 1957). For the French point of view see *Mémoires du maréchal Soult. Espagne et Portugal*, presented by L. and A. de Saint-Pierre (Paris, 1955). For the economic and social situation in Catalonia on the eve of the French occupation see P. Vilar, *La Catalogne dans l'Espagne moderne*, Vols. II and III (Paris, 1962); P. Conard, *Napoléon et la Catalogne* (Paris, 1909); Lt.-Col. Grasset, *Malaga province française* (Paris, 1910); J. Vidal de la Blache, 'La préfecture des Bouches-de-l'Èbre',

Revue de Paris, Vol. VI (1912), pp. 165–87; J. Mercader Riba, *La organización administrativa francesa en España* (Saragossa, 1959); M. Artola, *Los Afrancesados* (Madrid, 1953), with a preface by G. Marañon; J. Lucas-Dubreton, *Napoléon devant l'Espagne. Ce qu'a vu Goya* (Paris, 1946); A. Fugier, *La junte supérieure des Asturies et l'invasion française, 1810–1811* (Paris, 1930).

Chapter IV. The Continental Blockade

See A. T. Mahan, *The Influence of Sea Power upon the French Revolution and Empire* (London, 1892); E. F. Heckshér, *The Continental System* (Oxford, 1922); E. Tarlé, *Kontinentalnaia Blodaka* (Moscow, 1913); F. E. Melvin, *Napoleon's Navigation System* (New York, 1919)—the last two works quote from unpublished documents; Betrand de Jouvenel, *Napoléon et l'économie dirigée. Le blocus continental* (Paris, 1942). See also Vol. I, pp. 290, 305. There is no general work on the history of the blockade in France. For Northern Italy see E. Tarlé, *Le blocus continental et le royaume d'Italie* (Paris, 1928); for Germany, F. L.'Huillier, *Étude sur le blocus continental. La mise en vigueur des décrets de Trianon et de Fontainebleau dans le grand-duché de Bade* (1951); for Spain, J. Mercader Riba, 'España en el Bloqueo continental', *Estudios de Historia Moderna*, Vol. II (1952), pp. 233–78; Crouzet's work is the most important for England, *L'économie britannique* (Paris, 1958).

ENGLISH COMMERCE DURING THE EARLY YEARS OF THE BLOCKADE

Crouzet is again essential (see above). See also his 'Groupes de pression et politique de blocus: Remarques sur les origines des ordres en Conseil de novembre 1807', *Revue historique*, Vol. CCXXVIII (1962), pp. 45–72. See also the works cited in the preceding section. W. Freeman Galpin, *The Grain Supply of England during the Napoleonic Period*, Publications of the University of Michigan, History and Political Sciences, Vol. VI (New York, 1925); R. Greenhalg Albion, *Forests and Sea Power; the Timber Power of the Royal Navy, 1652–1862*, 'Economical Harvard Studies' 29 (Cambridge, U.S.A., 1926); W. E. Lingelbach, 'L'Angleterre et le commerce des neutres à l'époque napoléonienne, et depuis', *Revue des études napoléoniennes*, Vol. XIII (1918), pp. 129–55; J. Holland Rose, 'Napoleon and the British Commerce' and 'British Food Supply in the Napoleonic Wars', in his *Napoleonic Studies* (London, 1904), pp. 166–203 and 204–21; 'British West-India Commerce as a Factor in the Napoleonic Wars', *Cambridge Historical Journal*, Vol. III (1929), pp. 34–46; W. S. Galpin, 'The American Grains Trade under the Embargo of 1808', *Journal of Economic and Business History*, Vol. II (1924), pp. 71–100; D. B. Gœbdel, 'British Trade to the Spanish Colonies', *The American Historical Review*, Vol. XLIII (1938), pp. 288–320; H. Heaton, 'Non-importation, 1806–1812', *The Journal of Economic History*, Vol. I (1941), pp. 178–98; F. Birlandi, 'Relazioni politico-economiche fra Inghilterra e Sardegna durante la Rivoluzione e l'Impero', *Rivista storica italiana*, 1933, pp. 165–210. Holland Rose has shown the importance of the grain question, but Heckshér and Galpin do not consider it decisive since they do not take into account the psychological factor and do not look at the overall situation. The general opinion concerning England's difficulties in her struggle with France is that the internal crises and clashes which were capable of bringing Great Britain into conflict with other powers were not of a nature to favour her adversary. Heckshe has calculated British trade figures. He produces a table of imports in weight (p. 242) and a table of exports in real values (p. 245) without explaining how he has arrived at them. They are a little better than those of A. H. Imlah, 'Real Values in British Foreign Trade', *The Journal of Economic History*, Vol. VIII (1948), pp. 133–52.

THE DEVELOPMENT OF THE CONTINENTAL BLOCKADE

Since there is no general work on France and the Empire, see Vol. I, p. 303, and those works which deal with French economic history cited in Vol. I, p. 287, especially E. Levasseur, *Histoire des classes ouvrières et de l'industrie en France depuis 1789 jusqu'à nos jours* (Paris, 1862, 2nd ed., 1903), *Histoire du commerce en France*, Vol. II (Paris, 1912); P. Darmstädter, 'Studien zur napoleonischen Wirtschaftspolitik', *Vierteljahrschrift für Sozial- und Wirtschaftsgeschichte*, Vol. II (1904), pp. 559–615, Vol. III (1905), pp. 112–141; E. Tarlé, 'Napoléon Ier et les intérêts économiques de la France', *Revue des études napoléoniennes*, Vol. XXVI (1926), pp. 117–37; Rose, 'Napoleon and the British Commerce', cited in the section above. See also these sections below: 'Finances and the National Economy' (p. 382), 'Social Development and Public Opinion' (p. 384), 'The Continental Economy' (p. 388), particularly the works by C. Schmidt. See also F. Crouzet, 'Le commerce des vins et eaux-de-vie entre la France et l'Angleterre pendant le blocus continental', *Annales du Midi*, 1953, No. 1. For German economics see S. Schnabel, *Deutsche Geschichte im neunzehnten Jahrhundert*, Vol. III, 'Erfahrungswissenschaften und Technik' (Freiburg im Breisgau, 2nd ed., 1950); L'Huillier Étude sur le blocus continental (1951); for Denmark see R. Ruppenthal, 'Denmark and the Continental System', *Journal of Modern History*, Vol. XV (1943), pp. 7–23. For the Emperor's policy towards the United States, see Phoebe-Anne Heath, *Napoleon and the Origins of the Anglo-American War of 1812* (Toulouse, 1929); U. Bonnel, *La France, les États-unis et la guerre de course, 1797–1815* (Paris, 1961), does not deal solely with the war over privateering (between 1800 and 1815 the French captured 500 American ships), but also the Franco-American trade war and that of the Continental blockade. On smuggling see F. Ponteil, 'La contrabande sur le Rhin au temps du Premier Empire', *Revue historique*, Vol. CLXXV (1935), pp. 257–86.

THE CRISIS OF 1811

Essential for the study of England is Crouzet's *L'économie britannique* (Paris, 1958). See also Vol. I, p. 290, and those works cited at the beginning of this chapter, particularly the article by Silberling. On the Bullion Report see E. Fossati, 'Ricardo und die Entstehung des Bullion Report', *Zeitschrift für Nationalökonomie*, Vol. II (1933), pp. 433–500; J. Viner,

Studies in the Theory of International Trade (London, 1937); E. Morgan, 'Some Aspects of the Bank Restrictive Period', *The Economic History Review*, Vol. III (1939), pp. 205–21; F. Fetter, 'The Bullion Report Re-examined', *The Quarterly Journal of Economics*, Vol. LVI (1942), pp. 655–65. For France see those works cited in the section above and those cited below in the section 'Finances and the National Economy' (p. 382); C. Ballot, 'Les prêts aux manufactures', *Revue des études napoléoniennes*, Vol. II (1912), pp. 42–77; the best accounts are those by L. de Lanzac de Laborie, *Paris sous Napoléon*, Vol. VI (Paris, 1910) and Darmstädter's article; Odette Viennet, *Napoléon et l'industrie française. La crise de 1810–1811* (Paris, 1947). For regional information see P. Léon, 'La crise des subsistances de 1810–1812 dans le département de l'Isère', *Annales historique de la Révolution française*, 1952, No. 3, J. Vidalenc, 'La crise économique dans les départements méditerranéens pendant l'Empire', *Revue d'histoire moderne et contemporaine*, 1954, No. 3; J. Labasse, *Le commerce des soies à Lyon sous Napoléon et la crise de 1811* (Paris, 1957).

Chapter V. The Preliminaries of the Russian Campaign (1811–1812)

See Vol. I, pp. 281, 292, 302; Vandal, *Napoléon Ier et Alexandre Ier* (Paris, 1891–6); Waliszewski and the other works cited in Vol. I, p. 305, about Alexander I and oriental history.

THE SCARE OF 1811

See above.

THE DIPLOMATIC CAMPAIGN AND THE MARCH OF THE 'GRANDE ARMÉE'

See the works cited in the preceding note, particularly Vandal. For Austria see C. S. B. Buckland, *Metternich and the British Government* (London, 1932) and those works about Metternich cited above in the section 'The Austrian marriage' (p. 377). On Sweden see C. Schefer, *Bernadotte roi* (Paris, 1899); D. P. Barton, *Bernadotte, Prince and King, 1810–1844* (London, 1925), *The Amazing Career of Bernadotte* (London, 1929); T. Höjer, *Bernadotte maréchal de France*, translated from the Swedish by L. Maury (Paris, 1943). On the correspondence between Benjamin Constant and Bernadotte see B. Hasselbrot, *Benjamin Constant, Lettres à Bernadotte* (Geneva and Lille, 1952).

PART TWO. THE WORLD IN 1812

Chapter VI. Imperial France

See Vol. I, p. 294. For a good general reference see the bibliographies in G. Pariset, 'Le Consulat et l'Empire' (Paris, 1921), Vol. III of the *Histoire de France Contemporaine*, ed. E. Lavisse.

Bibliography

AUTHORITARIAN GOVERNMENT

See those works about Napoleon's private and family life cited in Vol. I, pp. 292, 294, above in the section 'The Austrian Marriage' (p. 377) and below in the section 'The Political Organization of the System' (p. 385). See also Masson, *Napoléon et sa famille* (Paris, 1897–1919), and *Joséphine, impératrice et reine* (Paris, 1899). See also J. Godechot, *Les Institutions de la France sous la Révolution et l'Empire* (Paris, 1951, from the series 'Histoire des institutions', ed. L. Halphen). On the evolution of the government and administration see those works cited in Vol. I, p. 294, especially C. Durand, *L'exercice de la fonction législative de 1800 à 1814* (Aix-en-Provence, 1955), *La fin du Conseil d'État napoléonien* (Aix-en-Provence, 1959). On justice see P. Poullet, *Les institutions françaises de 1795 à 1814* (Brussels and Paris, 1907); G. Vauthier, 'L'épuration de la magistrature en 1808', *Revue des études napoléoniennes*, Vol. XV (1919), pp. 218–23; H. Welschinger, *La censure sous le premier Empire* (Paris, 1882); V. Coffin, 'Censorship and Literature under Napoleon I', *The American Historical Review*, Vol. XXII (1916–17), pp. 288–308; E. d'Hauterive, *La police secrète du premier Empire. Bulletins quotidiens adressés par Fouché à l'empereur* (Paris, 1908–22, 3 vols., up to 1807, Vol. IV, J. Grassion, '1808–1809' (Paris, 1963), Vol. V, '1809–1810' (in preparation). G. Vauthier, 'Les prisons d'état en 1812', *Revue historique de la Révolution et de l'Empire*, Vol. IX (1916), pp. 84–94; L. Deries, 'Le régime des fiches sous le premier Empire, *Revue des études historiques*, Vol. XCII (1926), pp. 153–96; M. Albert, 'Napoléon et les théâtres populaires', *Revue de Paris*, Vol. III (1902), pp. 806–27; R. Holtman, *Napoleonic Propaganda* (Bâton-Rouge, 1950).

FINANCES AND THE NATIONAL ECONOMY

See M. Marion, *Histoire financière de la France depuis 1815*, Vol. IV (Paris, 1921–5); H. de Grimouard, 'Les origines du domaine extraordinaire', *Revue des questions historiques*, 1908, pp. 160–92. On economy see F. Simiand, *Recherches anciennes et nouvelles sur le mouvement général des prix du XVIe au XIXe siècle* (Paris, 1931), *Le salaire, L'évolution sociale et la monnaie* (Paris, 1932); Levasseur, *Histoire des classes ouvrières* (Paris, 1862), *Histoire du commerce en France* (Paris, 1912); Darmstädter, 'Studien zur napoleonischen Wirtschaftspolitik', *Vierteljahrschrift für Sozial- und Wirtschaftsgeschichte*, Vol. II (1904), pp. 559–615, Vol. III (1905), pp. 112–41; Tarlé, 'Napoléon Ier', *Revue des études napoléoniennes*, Vol. XXVI (1926), pp. 117–37; Pariset, *Le Consulat et l'Empire* (Paris, 1921); Chaptal, (Paris, 1945 and 1949, 2 vols.). For the administration of the economy see J. Petot, *Histoire de l'administration des Ponts et Chaussées, 1599–1815* (Paris, 1958) Pt. 3, Chs. IV, V, VI; B. Gille, *Le Conseil général des manufactures* (*Inventaire analytique des procès-verbaux*) *1810–1829* (1961). On agrarian problems see R. Laurent, 'La lutte pour individualisme agraire dans la France du Premier Empire', *Annales de Bourgogne*, 1952, No. 3 (the question of collective rights has a large part to play in the preparation of a rural code which Napoleon did not promulgate). For regional aspects, apart from studies which do not deal exclusively with the Napoleonic era, such as Camille Jullian, *Histoire de Bordeaux* (Bordeaux, 1895); R. Lévy, *Histoire économique et l'industrie cotonnière en Alsace* (Paris,

1912); *Les Bouches-du-Rhône*, encyclopaedia ed. P. Masson, Vol. VIII, 'L'industrie' (Marseilles, 1926), Vol. IX, 'Le commerce' (1922); P. Léon, *La naissance de la grande industrie en Dauphiné (fin du XVIIe siècle—1869)* (Paris, 1954); F. Dornic, *L'industrie textile dans le Maine et ses débochés internationaux. 1650–1815* (Paris, 1955); P. Leuillot, *L'Alsace au début du XIXe siècle, Essais d'histoire politique, économique et religieuse, 1815–1830*, Vol. II, 'Les transformations économiques' (Paris, 1959), goes up to the end of the Empire; see these works which deal specially with the period under discussion: S. Charlety, 'La vie économique à Lyon sous Napoléon', *Vierteljarhschrift für Sozial- und Wirtschaftsgeschichte*, Vol. IV (1906), pp. 365–79; P. Masson, 'Le commerce de Marseille de 1789 a 1814', *Annales de l'Université d'Aix-Marseille*, Vol. X (1916), 'Marseille et Napoléon', Vol. XI (1918); L. de Lanzac de Laborie, *Paris sous Napoléon*, Vol. VI, 'Le monde des affaires et du travail' (Paris, 1910); D. Pinkney, 'Paris capitale du coton sous le Premier Empire', *Annales*, Vol. V (1950), pp. 56–60; P. Viard, 'Les conséquences économiques du blocus continental en Ille-et-Vilaine', *Revue des études napoléoniennes*, Vol. XXVI (1926), pp. 52–67 and 138–55; Baron de Warengheim, 'Histoire des origines de la fabrication du sucre dans le département du Nord', *Mémoires de la Société d'agriculture, sciences et arts du Nord*, Vol. XII (1909–10), pp. 215–627; G. Vauthier, 'Une manufacture de sucre a Rambouillet', *Revue des études napoléoniennes*, Vol. II (1913), pp. 148–60; F. Roques, *Aspects de la vie économique niçoise sous le Consulat et l'Empire* (Aix-en-Provence, 1957); G. Thuillier, *Georges Dufand et les débuts du grand capitalisme dans la métallurgie en Nivernais au XIXe siècle* (Paris, 1959); E. Baux, 'Les draperies audoises sous le Premier Empire', *Revue d'histoire économique et sociale*, 1960, No. 4; G. Dumas, 'Situation économique du département de l'Aisne à la fin de l'Empire', *Mémoires de la Federation des Soc. sav. de l'Aisne*, 1961; C. Schmidt, 'Sismondi et le blocus continental', *Revue historique*, Vol. CXV (1914), pp. 85–91; the works of M. Blanchard cited below in the section 'The Continental Economy' (p. 388).

THE CONTROL OF MEN'S MINDS

G. Constant, *L'Église de France sous le Consulat et l'Empire* (Paris, 1928); Latreille, *L'Église catholique* (Paris, 1946), *Napoléon et le Saint-Siège* (Paris, 1935), *L'opposition religieuse au Concordat* (Paris, 1910); Leflon, *La crise revolutionnaire* (Paris, 1949), *Étienne-Alexandre Bernier* (Paris, 1938), *Monsieur Émery* (Paris, 1947); L. Lévy-Schneider, *L'application du Concordat par un prélat d'Ancien Régime. Monseigneur Champion de Cicé, archevêque d'Aix et d'Arles, 1802–1810* (Paris, 1921); Mgr. Ricard, *Le cardinal Fesch* (Paris, 1893); J. Hergenröther, *Cardinal Maury* (Würzburg, 1878); A. Mathiez, 'Le cardinal Cambacérès, archevêque de Rouen', *Revue des études napoléoniennes*, Vol. IX (1916), pp. 25–64; C. Ledré, *Le cardinal Cambacérès, archeveque de Rouen, 1802–1818* (Paris, 1947); Canon Mahieu, *Monseigneur Louis Belmas, ancien évêque constitutionnel de l'Aude, évêque de Cambrai, 1757–1841* (Paris, 1934); J. Berti-Langermin, *Le cardinal du Belloy* (Paris, 1951, typewritten thesis); P. Genevray, *L'administration et la vie ecclésiastique dans le grand diocèse de Toulouse (Ariège, Haute-Garonne, arrondissement de Castel-sarrasin) pendant les dernières années de l'Empire et sous la Restauration* (Paris, 1940); L. Deries, *Les congrégations religieuses au temps de Napoléon Ier* (Paris, 1929); G. de Grandmaison, *La Congrégation* (Paris, 1889); A. Latreille, *Le catéchisme impérial* (Paris, 1935); Comte d'Haussonville, *L'Église romaine et le Premier Empire* (Paris, 1868–9, 5 vols.); H. Welschinger, *Le pape et l'empereur* (Paris, 1905); Abbé Féret, *Le Premier Empire et le Saint-Siège* (Paris, 1911); Mgr. Ricard, *Le concile de 1811* (Paris, 1894); G. de Grandmaison, *Napoléon et les cardinaux noirs* (Paris, 1895); E. Dousset, *L'abbé de Pradt, grand aumônier de Napoléon* (Paris, 1959). For the conflict between the papacy and the Empire see E. de Levis-Mirepoix, *Un collaborateur de Metternich. Mémoires et papiers de Lebzeltern* (Paris, 1949). R. Anchel, *Napoléon et les Juifs* (Paris, 1928); P. Leuilliot, 'L'usure judaïque en Alsace sous l'Empire et la Restauration', *Annales historiques de la Révolution française*, 1930, pp. 231–51; Gaston-Martin, *Manuel d'histoire de la franc-maçonnerie francaise* (Paris, 1926, 2nd ed., 1932); A. Bouton et M. Lepage, *Histoire de la franc-maçonnerie dans la Mayenne, 1756–1951* (Le Mans, 1951); A. Bouton, *Les francs-maçons manceaux et la Révolution française, 1741–1815* (Le Mans, 1958). For education see Pariset; A. Aulard, *Napolèon et le monopole universitaire* (Paris, 1911); L. de Lanzac de Laborie, *Paris sous Napoléon*, Vol. IV (Paris, 1907), 'La haute administration de l'enseignement sous le Consulat et l'Empire', *Revue des études napoléoniennes*, Vol. X (1916), pp. 185–219; M. Gontard, *L'enseignement primaire en France de la Révolution à la loi Guizot, 1789–1833* (Paris, 1959); C. Schmidt, *Le réforme de l'Université impériale en 1811* (Paris, 1905); M. Halbwachs, 'Les programmes des premiers lycées de 1802 à 1809', *Bulletin de la Faculté des Lettres de Strasbourg*, 1930, pp. 132–6; Aileen Wilson, *Fontanes* (Paris, 1928). For a regional example see R. Boudard, *L'organisation de l'Université et de l'enseignement secondaire dans l'Académie impériale de Gênes entre 1805 et 1814* (Guéret, 1962). For the artistic and intellectual movements see the section below 'Intellectual Life' (p. 390); also Pariset. For propaganda see Holtman.

SOCIAL DEVELOPMENT AND PUBLIC OPINION

See Vol. I, p. 301; E. Levasseur, *La population française* (Paris, 1889–92, 3 vols.); M. Reinhard, 'La statistique de la population sous le Consulat et l'Empire. Le bureau de statistique', *Population*, 1950, pp. 103–20; for a regional example see R. Rousseau, *La population de la Savioe jusqu'en 1861, nombre d'habitants pour chaque commune des deux actuels départements savoyards, du milieu du XVIIIe au milieu du XIXe siècle* (Paris, 1960); G. Vallée, *Population et conscription 1798–1814* (Rodez, 1938); Levasseur, *Histoire des classes ouvrières* (Paris, 1862); G. Vauthier, 'Les ouvriers de Paris sous le premier Empire', *Revue des études napoléoniennes*, Vol. II (1913), pp. 426–51; G. Mauco, *Les migrations ouvrières en France au début du XIXe siècle* (Paris, 1932); P. Leuilliot, 'L'émigration alsacienne sous l'Empire et au début de la Restauration', *Revue historique*, Vol. CLXV (1930), pp. 274–9; A. Gain, 'La Lorraine allemande foyer d'émigration au début du XIXe siècle', *Le pays lorrain*, Vol. XVIII (1926), pp. 193–205, 259–66; O. Festy, 'La société philanthropique de Paris', *Revue d'histoire moderne et contemporaine*, Vol. XVI (1913), pp. 170–96; G. Weill, 'Un groupe de philanthropes français', *Revue des études napoléoniennes*, Vol. XI (1917), pp. 189–218; G. Vauthier, 'La société maternelle sous l'Empire', *Revue des études napoléoniennes*, Vol. II (1914), pp. 70–83; H. Troclet, *La première expérience de sécurité sociale. Liège, décret de Napoléon de 1813* (Brussels, 1953), concerns the setting-up in 1813 of a fund for minors who suffered industrial injury. On the food shortage in 1812 see Lanzac de Laborie, *Paris sous Napoléon*, Vol. V (Paris, 1908); P. Viard, 'Les subsistances en Ille-et-Vilaine sous le Consulat et l'Empire', *Annales de Bretagne*, Vol. XXII (1917), pp. 328–52, 471–88, Vol. XXIII (1918), pp. 131–54; G. Lavalley, *Napoléon et la disette de 1812* (Caen, 1896), deals with the shortage at Caen; F. L'Huillier, 'Une crise des subsistances dans le Bas-Rhin, 1810–1812', *Annales historiques de la Révolution française*, 1937, pp. 518–36; P. Léon, 'La crise des subsistances de 1810–1812 dans le département de l'Isère', *Annales historiques de la Révolution française*, 1952, No. 3. For public opinion see A. Cassagne, *La vie politique de R. de Chateaubriand* (Paris, 1911); P. Gautier, *Madame de Staël et Napoléon* (Paris, 1902); Lady Blennerhasset, *Frau von Staël* (Berlin, 1887–9, 2 vols.), translated into French by A. Dietrich (Paris, 1891); P. S. Larg, *Madame de Staël* (Paris, 1924); B. Hasselbrot, *Nouveaux documents sur Benjamin Constant et Mme de Staël* (Copenhagen, 1952), deals with Benjamin Constant's *L'esprit de conquête et d'usurpation*; H. Guillemin, *Mme de Staël, Benjamin Constant et Napoléon* (Paris, 1959); C. H. Pouthas, *La jeunesse de Guizot, 1797–1814* (Paris, 1936). For the royalist conspiracy see G. de Bertier de Sauvigny, *Le comte Ferdinand de Bertier (1782–1864) et l'énigme de la Congrégation* (Paris, 1949). On the reunified *départements* see Vol. I, pp. 287–9; L. Dechesne, *Histoire économique et sociale de la Belgique* (Paris, 1943); P. Lebrun, *L'industrie de la laine à Verviers pendant le XVIIIe siècle et au début de XIXe* (Liège, 1948); R. Zeyss, *Die Entstehung der Handelskammer und die Industrie am Niederrhein während der französischen Herrschaft* (Leipzig, 1907); C. Schmidt, 'Anvers et le blocus continental', *Revue de Paris*, Vol. I (1915), pp. 634–51; A. Fischer, *Napoléon et Anvers* (Anvers, 1933); M. Deneckère, *Histoire de la langue française dans les Flandres* (Ghent, 1954); E. Chapuisat, *Le commerce de Genève pendant la domination française* (Geneva, 1908), publication of the Société historique et archéologique de Genève, 'Mémoires et documents', Vol. XXVIII; A. Fugier, *Napoléon et l'Italie* (Paris, 1947); J. Borel, *Gênes sous Napoléon* (Paris, 1929).

Chapter VII. The Continental System

For general works see those cited in Vol. I, pp. 281, 292, 302.

THE POLITICAL ORGANIZATION OF THE SYSTEM

See those works cited below in the following four sections. For the vassal princes see Masson, *Napoléon et sa famille* (Paris, 1897–1919); B. Nabonne, *Joseph Bonaparte, le roi philosophe* (Paris, 1949), *Pauline Bonaparte* (Paris, 1948); F. Rocquain, *Napoléon Ier et le roi Louis* (Paris, 1875); A. Duboscq, *Louis-Bonaparte en Hollande* (Paris, 1911); P. de Lacretelle, *Secrets et malheurs de la reine Hortense* (Paris, 1936); Arthur-Lévy, *Napoléon et Eugène de Beauharnais* (Paris, 1926); Prince Adalbert of Bavaria, *Eugène de Beauharnais, beau-fils de Napoléon*, translated by Marguerite Vabre, adapted by A. de Gouyon (Paris, 1939); T. Jung, *Lucien Bonaparte et ses mémoires* (Paris, 1882–3, 3 vols.); A. Vandal, 'Le roi et la reine de Naples', *Revue des Deux Mondes*, Vol. LV (1910), pp. 481–514, 757–88, Vol. LVI (1910), pp. 42–75; M.-A. Fabre, *Jérôme Bonaparte, roi de Westphalie* (Paris, 1952); Abel Mansuy, *Jérôme Napoléon et la Pologne en 1812* (Paris, 1930); *Fürstenbriefe* (Stuttgart and Berlin, 1929); Prince Napoléon and J. Hanoteau, *Lettres personnelles des souverains à l'empereur Napoléon Ier* (Paris, 1939); J. Valynseele, *Les princes et ducs du Premier Empire non maréchaux* (Paris, 1959).

THE NAPOLEONIC REFORMS

See the next three sections.

THE MEDITERRANEAN COUNTRIES; ITALY; THE ILLYRIAN PROVINCES AND CATALONIA

Fugier, *Napoléon et l'Italie* (Paris, 1947); A. Pingaud, 'La politique italienne de Napoléon Ier', *Revue historique*, Vol. CLIV (1927), pp. 20–33, 'Le premier royaume d'Italie', *Revue des études napoléoniennes*, Vol. XX (1923), XXI (1923), XXV (1925), then in the *Revue d'histoire diplomatique*, Vol. XL (1926) to XLIV (1930), XLVI (1932), XLVII (1933), totalling about 400 pages. For a reappraisal of the administrative history of the realm of Italy see M. Roberti, *Milano capitule napoleonica; la formazione di un stato moderno, 1796–1814* (Milan, 1946–7). A valuable work in social and economic history is that by R. Zangheri, *Misure della popolazione e della produzione agricola nel dipartimento del Reno* (Bologna, 1958), which is based on the returns of 1812 for the *dipartimento* of Reno; see also his *Prime recerche sulla distribuzione della proprieta fondiaria nella pianura bologuese, 1789–1835* (Bologna, 1957), *La proprieta terriera e le origini del Risorgimento del Bolognese*, Vol. I, '1789–1804' (Bologna, 1961); U. Marcelli, *La vendita dei beni ecclesiastici a Bologna e nelle Romagne, 1787–1815* (Bologna, 1961). For Tuscany see P. Marmottan, *Le royaume d'Étrurie* (Paris, 1896), *Bonaparte et la république de Lucques* (Paris, 1896); G. Drei, *Il regno d'Etruria, 1801–1807* (Modena, 1937); E. Rodocanacchi, *Élisa Bacciocchi en Italie* (Paris, 1900); A von Reumont, *Geschichte Toscanas*, Vol. II, '1737–1859' (Gotha, 1877) in Heeren and Ukert's 'Geschichte der europäischen Staaten'; A. Ingold, *Bénévent sous la domination de Talleyrand* (Paris, 1916); L. Madelin, *Rome sous Napoléon*, (Paris, 1906); J. Moulard, *Le comte C. de Tournon*, Vol. II (Paris, 1930); J. Rambaud, *Naples sous Joseph Bonaparte* (Paris, 1911); G. La Volpe, 'Gioachino Murat, re di Napoli'. Amministrazione e reforme economiche', *Nuova rivista storica*, Vol. XIV (1930), pp. 538–59 and Vol. XV (1931), pp. 124–41; R. Trifone, *Feudi e domani. Eversione della feudalità nelle province napolitane* (Milan, 1909); A. Valente, *Murat e l'Italia meridionale* (Turin, 1941); M. Caldora, *Calabria napoleonica, 1806–1815* (Naples, 1960); P. Villani, *Mezzogiorno tra riforme e revoluzione* (Bari, 1962); on the economic situation in the Bari region at the end of the Empire see *Le relazioni alla Societa economica di terra di Bari* (Molfetta, 1959). On Illyria see P. Pisani, *La Dalmatie de 1797 à 1815* (Paris, 1893); M. Pivec-Stellé, *La vie économique des provinces illyriennes, 1809–1813* (Paris, 1931); G. Cassi, 'Les populations juliennes-illyriennes pendant la domination napoléonienne', *Revue des études napoléoniennes*, Vol. XXXI (1930), pp. 193–214, 257–75, 335–69. For Catalonia see Vilar, *La Catalogue dans l'Espagne moderne* (Paris, 1962); J. Mercader Riba, *Barcelona durante la occupacion francesa* (Madrid, 1949), 'El mariscal Suchet "virrey" de Aragon, Valencia y Cataluña', *Cuadernos de Historia Jeronimo Zurita* (Saragossa, 1954), pp. 127–42, 'L'oficialitat del Català soto la dominació napoléónica', *Bulletit de la Societat catalana d'estudis* (1953), pp. 7–22, 'La ideologia dels Catalans del 1808', *Anuari de l'Institut d'estudis catalans*, 1953, pp. 1–16. See also J. Vicens Vives, 'Conjunctura economica y reformismo burgues, dos factores en la evolución de la España del antiquo regimen', *Estudios de Historia moderna*, 1954, pp. 349–93.

HOLLAND AND GERMANY

On Holland see P. Blok, *Geschiedenis van het nederlandsche volk*, Vol. VII (Groningen, 1907), translated into English under the title *History of the People of the Netherlands* (London, 1908–12, 5 vols.); H. F. Colenbrander, *Gedenstukken der algemeene geschiedenis van Nederland van 1785 tot 1840* (The Hague, 1905–13, 7 vols.); Marquis de Caumont-La Force, *L'architrésorier Lebrun, gouverneur de la Hollande* (Paris, 1907). For Germany see Rambaud; E. Denis, *L'Allemagne de 1789 à 1810: fin de l'ancienne Allemagne* (Paris, 1896); E. Höltzle, 'Das napoleonische Staatssystem in Deutschland', *Historische Zeitschrift*, Vol. CXLVIII (1933), pp. 277–93; H. A. L. Fisher, *Studies in Napoleonic Statesmanship. Germany* (Oxford, 1903); C. Schmidt, *Le grand-duché de Berg* (Paris, 1905); R. Gœcke and T. Ilgen, *Das Königreich Westphalen* (Düsseldorf, 1888); A. Kleinschmidt, *Geschichte des Königreichs Westfalen* (Gotha, 1893); F. Thimme, *Die inneren Zustände des Kurfürstentums Hannover unter der französisch-westfälischen Herrschaft* (Hanover, 1893–5, 2 vols.); Mansuy, *Jérôme Napoléon* (Paris, 1930); W. Kohl, *Die Verwaltung der östlichen Departements des Königreichs Westphalen, 1807–1814* (Berlin 1937, Pt. 323 of Ebering's 'Historische Studien'); G. Servières, *L'Allemagne française sous Napoléon Ier* (Paris, 1904), deals with the Hanseatic towns during the annexation; H. Schnepel, *Die Reichstadt Bremen und Frankreich von 1789 bis 1813* (Bremen, 1935); P. Darmstädter, *Das Grossherzogthum Frankfurt* (Frankfurt, 1911); R. Leroux, *La théorie du despotisme éclairé chez K. Th. von Dalberg* (Strasbourg, 1932); K. von Beaulieu-Marconnay, *K. von Dalberg und seine Zeit* (Weimar, 1879); E. Gerhard, *Geschichte der Säkularisation in Frankfurt-am-Main* (Paderborn, 1935); T. Scherg, *Das Schulwesen und der Fürst Theodor von Dalberg* (Munich, 1939); A. Chroust, *Das Grossherzogthum Würzburg* (Würzburg, 1913), *Die äussere Politik des Grossherzogthums* (Würzburg, 1932); M. Döberl, *Entwickelungsgeschichte Bayerns*, Vol. II (Munich, 1912); M. Dunan, *Napoléon et l'Allemagne. Le système continental et les débuts du royaume de Bavière, 1806–1810* (Paris, 1942); F. Zimmermann, *Bayerische Verfassungsgeschichte vom Ausgang der Landschaft bis zur Verfassungskunde von 1818*, Pt. I, 'Vorgeschichte und Entstehung der Konstitution von 1808'

(Munich, 1940), Bavarian Academy publications, Vol. XXXV; E. Höltzle, *Das alte Recht und die Revolution. Eine politische Geschichte Württembergs in der Revolutionszeit, 1789–1815* (Munich and Berlin, 1931), *Württemberg im Zeitalter Napoleons und der deutschen Erhebung* (Stuttgart, 1937); F. Wintterlin, *Geschichte der württembergischen Behördenorganisation*, Vol. I (Stuttgart, 1904), up to 1914; W. Andreas, *Die Geschichte der bädischen Verwaltungsorganisation und Verfassung in den Jahren 1802–1818* (Leipzig, 1913); Abbé Moulard, *Le comte de Tournon*, cited in the section above—Tournon was the *intendant* of Bayreuth. For the administration of a principality see J. Courvoisier, *Le maréchal Berthier et sa principauté de Neuchatel, 1806–1814* (Neuchatel, 1959)—in seven years Berthier extracted about 850,000 francs.

THE GRAND DUCHY OF WARSAW

See M. Handelsman, 'Napoléon et la Pologne (étude du régime)', *Revue des études napoléoniennes*, Vol. V (1914), pp. 162–80; Abel Mansuy, *Jérôme Napoléon* (see above), which contains an extensive bibliography—I would like to express my thanks to M. Mansuy for having lent me his notes concerning Poland and Russia, 'Le clerge et le régime napoléonien dans le grand-duché de Varsovie', *Revue d'histoire moderne et contemporaine*, Vol. V (1903–4), pp. 97–106, 161–71; H. Grinwasser, 'Le Code Napoléon et le grand-duché de Varsovie', *Revue des études napoléoniennes*, Vol. XII (1917), pp. 129–70; T. Mencel, 'L'introduction de Code Napoléon dans le duché de Varsovie', *Annales d'histoire du droit* (Poznan; article in French) 1949, pp. 141–98; S. Askenazy, *Le prince Joseph Poniatovski* (Warsaw, 1912) in Polish—the Society of the Friends of Science in Poznan has published, under A. Skalkowski's editorship, *Correspondance du prince Pontiatovski avec la France* (Poznan, 1921–9, 5 vols.) in French. See also B. Grochulska, 'Recherches sur la structure économique du duché de Varsovie', W. Sobocinski, 'Le duché de Varsovie et le Grand Empire', M. Senkowska, 'Les majorats français dans le duché de Varsovie', *Annales historiques de la Révolution français*, 1964, a special issue dealing exclusively with Poland during the era of the Revolution and the Empire, with a bibliography of recent Polish works on the period.

EUROPEAN CIVILIZATION

Vol. XI of F. Brunot's *Histoire de la langue française des origines à 1900*, 'Le français au-dehors sous la Révolution, le Consulat et l'Empire', mentioned as being in the course of preparation, has not yet appeared. For a regional example see Deneckère, *Histoire de la langue française dans les Flandres* (Ghent, 1954), who describes the adoption of French by the upper classes during imperial times; French became the language of administration, secondary education, the press and the theatre. The degradation of Flemish followed the decline of primary education.

THE CONTINENTAL ECONOMY

See those works cited above in the section 'The Development of the Continental Blockade' (p. 380); E. Tarlé, 'L'unité économique du continent européeen sous Napoléon Ier', *Revue historique*, Vol. CLXVI (1931), pp. 239–55; P. Darmstädter, 'Studien zur napoleonischen Wirtschaftspolitik'; E. Tarlé, 'Napoléon Ier et les intérêts économiques de la France'; M. Blanchard, *Les routes des Alpes occidentales à l'époque napoléonienne* (Grenoble, 1920), 'Enquête administrative sur le roulage en 1811', *Revue de géographie alpine*, Vol. VIII (1920), pp. 585–626; F. Evrard, 'Le commerce des laines d'Espagne sous le premier Empire', *Revue d'histoire moderne*, Vol. XII (1937), pp. 197–227; Y. Roustit, 'Raymond Durand, commerçant à Barcelone (1808–1819)' *Estudios de Historia moderna*, Vol. VI (1956–9), pp. 313–410. For the effects of the blockade on the vassal states see the account given by Hecksher, *The Continental System* (Oxford, 1922), and also, for Holland, see E. Baasch, *Holländische Wirtschaftsgeschichte* (Jena, 1925); for Northern Italy see E. Tarlé, *Le blocus continental et le royaume d'Italie* (Paris, 1928); for Switzerland see B. de Cérenville, *Le blocus continental et la Suisse* (Lausanne, 1906); for Germany, P. Darmstädter, *Geschichte der Handelskammer zu Frankfurt am Main* (Frankfurt, 1908); E. Hasse, *Geschichte der Leipziger Messen* (Leipzig, 1885); A. König, *Die sächsische Baumwollenindustrie am Ende des vorigen Jahrhunderts und während der Kontinentalsperre* (Leipzig, 1899, Pt. 3 of the 'Leipziger Studien auf dem Gebiete der Geschichte', ed. Buchholtz, Lamprecht, Marcks, and Seeliger, Vol. V); A. Wohlwill, *Neuere Geschichte der Freien und Hansestadt Hamburg, inbesondere von 1789 bis 1815* (Gotha, 1914); K. Bockenheiwer, *Mainzer Handel. Der Zoll und Binnenhafen zu Mainz, 1648–1831* (Berlin, 1887); W. Vogel, 'Die Hansestädte und die Kontinentalsperre', *Pfingstblätter des Hansischen Geschichtsvereins*, 1913, Pt. 18; M. Schaefer, 'Bremen und die Kontinentalsperre', *Pfingstblätter*, Vol. XX (1914), pp. 413–62; E. Gothein, *Wirtschaftsgeschichte des Schwartzwaldes und der angrenzenden Landschaften* (Strasbourg, 1892); C. Schmidt, *Le grand-duché de Berg*; A. Wollner, 'Handel, Industrie und Gewerbe in der ehemaligen Stiftsgebieten Essen und Werden sowie in der Reichstadt Essen zur Zeit der französischen Herrschaft, 1806–1813', *Beiträge zur Geschichte von Stadt und Stift Essen*, 1909, pp. 97–311; L. Bein, *Die Industrie der sächsischen Voigtlandes* (Leipzig, 1884, Vol. II); W. Stieda, *F. K. Archard und die Frühzeit der deutschen Zuckerindustrie* (Leipzig, 1928, from 'Abhandlungen der philologisch-historischen Klasse der sächsischen Akademie der Wissenschaft', Vol. XXXIX); F. L'Huillier, *Le blocus continental* (s.l., 1951).

THE CONTINENTAL SYSTEM AND NATIONALITY

See Vol. I, p. 285 and the section 'The Napoleonic Reforms' (p. 386). See also F. Brunot, *Histoire de la langue française*, Vol. IX, 'La Révolution et l'Empire', Pt. I: Le français, langue nationale (Paris, 1927); E. Robin, *Le séquestre des biens ennemis sous la Révolution française* (Paris, 1929); M. Handelsman, *Les idées françaises et la mentalité politique en Pologne au XIXe siècle* (Paris, 1927); J. Prijatelj, *Sloventchina pod Napoleonom* (Ljubljana, 1911), is summarized in French in the *Revue des études napoléoniennes*, Vol. XXV (1925), pp. 269–70; F. Zwitter, 'Illyrisme et sentiment yougoslave', *Le monde slave*, 1933, pp. 39–71, 161–85, 358–75.

Chapter VIII. The Independent Forces

THE CONTINENTAL STATES OF THE 'ANCIEN RÉGIME'

For Prussia see Cavaignac, *La formation de la Prusse contemporaine* (Paris, 1891–7); de la Blache, *La régénération de la Prusse après Iéna* (Paris, 1910); Knapp, *Die Bauernbefreiung* (Leipzig, 1887); Sée, *Esquisse d'une histoire du régime agraire en Europe* (Paris, 1921); G. Rambow, *L. von der Marwitz und die Anfänge der konservativer Politik und Staatsanschauung in Preussen* (Berlin, 1930, Pt. 195 of Ebering's 'Historische Studien'); W. Kayser, *Marwitz* (Hamburg, 1936). For Austria see above Bk. IV, Ch. 2, Pt. III and Pt. V; Johanna Kraft, *Die Finanzreform des Grafen Wallis und der Staatsbankerott von 1811* (Graz, 1927, Pt. 5 of the 'Publications du séminaire d'histoire de l'Université de Graz'); for Russia see Vol. I, p. 286, those works dealing with the reign of Alexander I cited in Vol. I, p. 305; A. Pypin, *Die geistigen Bewegungen in Russland in der ersten Hälfte des XIX^{ten} Jahrhunderts*, Vol. I, translated from the Russian by B. Minzes (Berlin, 1894); V. R. Iatsounski, 'De l'influence du blocus continental sur l'industrie cotonnière russe', *Annales historiques de la Révolution française*, 1964, p. 65.

THE ANGLO-SAXONS AND LIBERALISM

See the general works on England cited in Vol. I, pp. 286–7, 289–92, 305; A. Chevrillon, *Sydney Smith et la Renaissance des idées libérales en Angleterre au XIXe siècle* (Paris, 1894); M. Roberts, *The Whig Party, 1807–1812* (London, 1939); M. D. George, *English Political Caricature, A study of opinion and propaganda*, Vol. II, '1793–1832' (Oxford, 1959). On Sicily apart from the works cited in the section above, 'The Command of the Seas and its Consequences' (p. 378), see H. M. Lackland, 'Lord W. Bentinck in Sicily, 1811–1812', *The English Historical Review*, Vol. XLII (1927), pp. 371–96, 'The Failure of the Constitutional Experiment in Sicily', Vol. XLI (1926), pp. 210–35. On France see the section above, 'Social Development and Public Opinion' (p. 384). On Spain see the sections above, 'The Spanish Insurrection' (p. 374), 'The Mediterranean Countries' (p. 386), particularly the article by J. Vincens Vives. On the United States see Vol. I, p. 289; G. Chinard, *Jefferson* (Boston, 1929).

INTELLECTUAL LIFE

See Vol. I, pp. 282–5, and above to Bk. V, Ch. I, Pt. IV. See also for England, A. H. Koszul, *La jeunesse de Shelley* (Paris, 1910); E. Estève, *Byron et le romantisme français* (Paris, 1907). On Germany see those works cited in the section above, 'The Awakening of Germany' (p. 375); G. Gromaire, *La littérature politique en Allemagne de 1800 à 1815* (Paris, 1911); R. Ayrault, *H. von Kleist* (Paris, 1934); F. Büchler, *Die geistigen Wurzeln der heiligen Allianz* (Freiburg-im-Breisgau, 1929). For Italy see A. Caraccio, *Ugo Foscolo* (Paris, 1934); F. Battaglia, *L'opera de V. Cuoco e la formazione dello spirito nazionale in Italia* (Florence, 1925). For France see F. Brunot, *Histoire de la langue française*, Vol. X, Pt. 2, 'Le retour a l'ordre et à la discipline' (Paris, 1943); L. Merlet, *Tableau de la littérature française pendant la Révolution et l'Empire* (Paris, 1878–83, 3 vols.); P. Alfaric, *Laromiguière et son école* (Paris, 1929 Pt. 5 of the second series of the 'Publications de la Faculté des Lettres de Strasbourg'); R. Bray, 'Chronologie du romantisme', I, *Revue des cours et conférences*, 1931–2, pp. 17–31; C. Desgranges, *Geoffroy et la critique dramatique sous le Consulat et l'Empire* (Paris, 1897); A. Viatte, *Le romantisme chez les catholiques* (Paris, 1922); P. Gautier, 'Un grand roman oublié: Corinne' *Revue des Deux Mondes*, Vol. III (1927), pp. 435–51; Comte d'Haussonville, *Madame de Staël et l'Allemagne* (Paris, 1928); J. Gibelin, *L'esthétique de Schelling et l'Allemagne de Madame de Staël* (Paris, 1934); Béatrix d'Andlau, *Chateaubriand et 'Les Martyrs', naissance d'une épopée* (Paris, 1952), with a bibliography; J. B. Galley, *Claude Fauriel* (Paris, 1909); J. de Salis, *Sismondi* (Paris, 1932). For a regional example see L. Trénard, *Histoire sociale des idées. Lyon, De l'Encyclopédie au préromantisme*, Vol. II, 'L'éclosion du mysticisme, 1794–1815' (Paris, 1958). For the sciences see Vol. I, pp. 282–5; J. Fayet, *La Révolution française et la science*, 1789–1815 (Paris, 1960). For the arts see those works cited in Vol. I, pp. 282–5, by Michel, Benoit, Lavedan, Combarieu, and Rolland; P. Lelièvre, *Vivant Denon* (Angers, 1942); L. Hautecœur, 'Les origines de l'art Empire', *Revue des études napoléoniennes*, Vol. V (1914), pp. 145–61, *Histoire de l'architecture classique en France*, Vol. V, 'Révolution et Empire, 1792–1815' (Paris, 1953); É. Bourgeois, *Le style Empire, ses origines et ses caractères* (Paris, 1930); F. Benoit, 'David et la révolution dans la peinture', *Revue de Paris*, Vol. III (1913), pp. 47–60; L. Hautecœur, *Louis David* (Paris, 1954); R. Schneider, *L'esthétique classique chez Quatremère de Quincy* (Paris, 1910), 'L'art anacréontique et alexandrin sous l'Empire', *Revue des études napoléoniennes*, Vol. X (1916), pp. 257–71, 'L'art de Canova et la France impériale', *Revue des études napoléoniennes*, Vol. III (1912), pp. 36–57; A. Venturi, 'Canova', *La vita italiana durante la Revoluzione francese e l'Impero* (Rome, 1906). For the Emperor's activities and responsibilities in the realm of the arts see the special issue of *Apollo*, September 1964.

THE RISE OF NATIONALITY IN EUROPE AND AMERICA

See Vol. I, p. 285; E. Fournol, *Les nations romantiques* (Paris, 1931). For Germany see those works cited above in the sections 'The Awakening of Germany' (p. 375), 'Prussia' (p. 376), 'Austria' (p. 376), 'The Continental States of the *Ancien Régime*' (p. 390); M. Antonovytsch, *F. L. Jahn* (Berlin, 1933, Pt. 230 of Ebering's 'Historische Studien'), contains a bibliography; P. Rühlmann, *Die öffentliche Meinung in Sachsen, 1806–1812* (Gotha, 1902). For Italy see P. Hazard, *La Révolution française et les lettres italiennes* (Paris, 1910); R. M. Johnson, *The Napoleonic Empire in Southern Italy and the Rise of the Secret Societies* (London, 1904); D. Spadoni, 'La conversione italiana del Murat', *Nuova rivista storica*, Vol. XIV (1930), pp. 217–52; A. Mathiez, 'L'origine franc-comtoise de la charbonnerie italienne', *Annales historiques de la Révolution française*, 1928, pp. 551–61. For Russia see A. Koyré, *La philosophie et le problème national en Russie au début du XIXe siècle*

(Paris, 1929). For Norway see E. Bull, 'Formation de la nationalité norvégienne', *Revue des études napoléoniennes*, Vol. X (1916), pp. 5–54. For the United States see Vol. I, p. 289; A. T. Mahan, *Sea Power in its Relations to the War of 1812* (Boston, 1905).

THE PROGRESS OF CAPITALISM AND THE EXPANSION OF EUROPE THROUGHOUT THE WORLD

See Vol. I, pp. 290–2, in particular E. Cannan, *A History of the Theories of Production and Distribution in English Political Economy from 1776 to 1848* (London, 1893), and those works cited above in the sections 'Finances and the National Economy' (p. 382), 'The Continental Economy' (p. 388). See also C. Gide and C. Rist, *Histoires des doctrines économiques depuis les physiocrates* (Paris, 1909, 3rd ed., 1920), and E. Allix, 'La methode et la conception de l'économie politique dans l'œuvre de J. B. Say', *Revue d'histoire des doctrines économiques et sociales*, Vol. IV (1911), pp. 321–60. On European expansion see Vol. I, pp. 290–2; on Latin America see those works cited above in the section 'The Command of the Seas and its Consequences' (p. 378). On Malaysia see R. Coupland, *Sir T. Stamford Raffles* (Oxford, 1926); on the Pacific see J.-P. Fabre, *L'expansion française dans le Pacifique, 1800–1842* (Paris, 1953); the first book deals with the Empire, particularly the Baudin expedition along the Australian coastlands, an account of which was previously given by R. Bouvier and E. Meynial from the museum manuscripts to which Fabre adds the marine archives. On the expansion of European population, see the second part of M. R. Reinhard and A. Armengaud, *Histoire générale de la population mondiale* (Paris, 1961).

PART THREE. THE FALL OF NAPOLEON

Chapter IX. The Disintegration of the Continental System (1812–1814)

See Vol. I, pp. 281, 292, 302.

THE RUSSIAN CAMPAIGN

La guerre nationale de 1812 (St. Petersburg, 1901–14), translated into French by Cazalas (Paris, 1903–11, 8 vols.), covers the ground up to the end of 1811; M. Bogdanovitch, *Geschichte des Krieges von 1812*, translated from the Russian by G. Baumgarten (Leipzig, 1861–3, 3 vols.); M. Kukiel, *Wojna 1812 roku* (Cracow, 1937); E. Tarlé, *Našestvie Napoleona na Rossiju 1812 g.* (Moscow, 1938), translated into French under the title *La campagne de Russie, 1812* (Paris, 1941, 2nd ed., 1950); Commandant Magueron, *Campagne de Russie* (Paris, 1897–1906, 4 vols.); Lt.-Col. Fabry, *Campagne de Russie* (Paris, 1900–3, 5 vols.), up to August 19; State publications: *Documents relatifs à l'aile gauche, 20 août–4 décembre* (Paris, 1912) and *Documents relatifs à l'aile droite* (Paris, 1913); P. Gronsky, 'L'administration civile des gouvernements russes occupés par l'armée française en 1812', *Revue d'histoire moderne*, 1928, pp. 401–12; P. Dundulis, *Napoléon et la Lithuanie en 1812* (Paris, 1940); Mansuy; H. Schmidt, *Die Urheber des Brandes von Moskau* (Greifswald, 1904). For the whole of the campaign see Caulaincourt, *Mémoires* (Paris, 1933); comte de Ségur, *La campagne de Russie*, Vol. I, 'La marche vers Moscou', Vol. II, 'La retraite', with extracts from General Gourgaud's refutation, preface, and notes by J. Burnat (Paris, 1960); A. de Montesquiou, *Souvenirs sur la Révolution, l'Empire, la Restauration et le règne de Louis-Philippe*, presented and annotated by R. Burnand (Paris, 1961)—Montesquiou participated in the retreat from Russia and was charged by Napoleon to bear to France the famous bulletin of the *Grande Armée* announcing the disaster. De Lort de Serignan, *Le général Malet* (Paris, 1925); L. Le Barbier, *Le général Lahorie* (Paris, 1904).

THE DEFECTION OF PRUSSIA AND THE FIRST CAMPAIGN

See Vol. I, pp. 281, 292, 302. J. d'Ursel, *La defection de la Prusse* (Paris, 1907). For the polemic on York's defection see W. Elze, *Der Streit um Tauroggen* (Breslau, 1926). For Austria see J. d'Ursel, *La defection de l'Autriche* (Paris, 1912), and those works about Metternich cited in the section above, 'The Austrian Marriage' (p. 377). See also C. Buckland, *Metternich and the British Government from 1809 to 1813* (London, 1932); de Lévis-Mirepoix, *Un collabarateur de Metternich* (Paris, 1949). For the Prussian national movement see Lehmann, *Freiherr von Stein* (Leipzig, 1902–5); Ritter, *Stein* (Berlin, 1931); Cavaignac, *La Formation de la Prusse* (Paris, 1891–7); D. Czygan, *Geschichte der Tagesliteratur während des Freiheitskrieges* (Leipzig, 1909–10, 3 vols.); Aris, *History of Political Thought* (London, 1936); Gromaire, *La littérature politique* (Paris, 1911); K. Wolff, *Die deutsche Publizistik in der Zeit der Freiheitskämpfe und des Wiener Kongress, 1813–1815* (Plauen, 1934). On the campaign see *Das preussische Heer des Befreiungskrieges* (Berlin, 1912–14, 3 vols.); *Geschichte des Befreiungskrieges*, Pt. I, A. von Holleben and R. von Caemmerer, 'Geschichte des Frühjahrsfeldzuges 1813 und seine Vorgeschichte' (Berlin, 1904–7, 2 vols.); von der Osten-Sacken, *Militärischpolitische Geschichte des Befreiungskrieges im Jahre 1813* (Berlin, 1903–6, 2 vols.); A. F. Reboul, *Campagne de 1813, Les préliminaires* (Paris, 1910–12, 2 vols.) is a study of Eugène and Murat's command. G. Fabry, *Journal des opérations des 3e et 5e corps en 1813* (Paris, 1902); R. Tournès, *Lützen* (Paris, 1931); P. Foucart, *Bautzen* (Paris, 1893–1901, 2 vols.).

THE AUTUMN CAMPAIGN

See those works cited in the previous section. See also *Geschichte des Befreiungskrieges*, Pt. 2, Major Friederich, 'Herbstfeldzug' (Berlin, 1903–6, 3 vols.); General von Woinovitch and Major Veltze, *Oesterreich in den Befreiungskriegen* (Vienna, 1911); O. Karmin, 'Autour des négociations financières anglo-prussiennes de 1813', *Revue historique de la Révolution et de l'Empire*, Vol. XI (1917), pp. 177–297; Vol. XII (1917), pp. 24–49, 216–52; M. Doeberl, *Bayern und die deutsche Erhebung wider Napoleon I* (Munich, 1907, Vol. XXIV of the 'Historische Abhandlungen der k. Akademie der Wissenschaften'). For Castlereagh's policy see A. W. Ward and G. P. Gooch,

The Cambridge History of British Foreign Policy, Vol. I (Cambridge, 1912), J. Holland Rose, *The Life of Napoleon I* (London, 1901; 11th ed., 1929); the most important is C. K. Webster, *British Diplomacy, 1812–1815* (London, 1921), republished in 1931 under the title, *The Foreign Policy of Castlereagh. Britain and the Reconstruction of Europe*; for relations with Prussia see K. Goldmann, *Die preussisch-britischen Beziehungen in den Jahren 1812–1815* (Würzburg, 1934). For Bernadotte see those works cited above in the footnote to 'The Diplomatic Campaign and the March of the *Grande Armée*' (p. 381); K. Lehmann, *Die Rettung Berlins im Jahre 1813* (Berlin, 1934, Pt. 244 of Ebering's 'Historische Studien'); E. Wiehr, *Napoleon und Bernadotte in Herbstfeldzuge 1813* (Berlin, 1893); B. von Quistorp, *Geschichte der Nordarmee im Jahre 1813* (Berlin, 1894); F. D. Scott, *Bernadotte and the Fall of Napoleon* (Cambridge, Mass., 1935, Harvard Historical Monographs, 7); T. Höjer has written in Swedish about Bernadotte, *Car Johan i den stora koalitionen mot Napoleon* (Upsala, 1935); B. Hasselbrot, *Benjamin Constant. Lettres à Bernadotte* (Geneva and Lille, 1952). For the Bavarian defection see H. W. Schwartz, *Die Vorgeschichte des Vertrages von Ried* (Munich, 1933, Pt. 2 of the first series of the 'Münchener historische Abhandlungen', ed. A. Meyer and K. von Müller). For the French retreat see Lefebvre de Béhaine, *La campagne de France*, Vol. I, 'Napoléon et les allies sur le Rhin' (Paris, 1913).

THE CAMPAIGN IN FRANCE AND NAPOLEON'S ABDICATION

See Vol. I, pp. 281, 292, 302. For thc beginnings see de Behaine, Vol. II, 'La défense de la ligne du Rhin', Vols. III and IV, 'L'invasion' (Paris, 1933 and 1935); J. Thiry, *La chute de Napoléon*, Vol. I, 'Campagne de France', Vol. II, 'La première abdication' (Paris, 1938 and 1939); the classic work for general background is Henry Houssaye, *1814* (Paris, 1888); 'Geschichte des Befreiungskrieges', Pt. 3: von Janson, *Geschichte des Feldzuges 1814 in Frankreich* (Berlin, 1903–5, 2 vols.); A. Fournier, *Der Kongress von Chatillon* (Vienna, 1900); Caulaincourt, *Mémoires* (Paris, 1933); L. Bénaerts, *Les commissaires extraordinaires de Napoléon Ier en 1814* (Paris, 1915); Captain Borrey, *La Franche-Comté en 1814* (Paris, 1912), *L'esprit publique chez les prêtres franc-comtois pendant la crise de 1813–1815* (Paris, 1912); G. Bourgin, 'Les ouvriers et la défense nationale en 1814', *Revue des études napoléoniennes*, Vol. X (1916), pp. 55–65; T. Höjer, *Charles-Jean (Bernadotte) au Congrès de Chatillon* (in Swedish; summarized in French; Upsala, 1940); J. Vidal de la Blache, *L'évacuation de l'Espagne et l'invasion dans le midi* (Paris, 1914); H. Weil, *Le prince Eugèn et Murat* (Paris, 1902); *J. Murat, roi de Naples; La dernière année du règne* (Paris, 1909–10, 5 vols.); R. Rath, *The Fall of the Napoleonic Kingdom cf Italy, 1814* (New York, 1941); Capograssi; W. Martin, *La Suisse et l'Europe, 1813–1814* (Geneva, 1931). On the abdication and recalling of Louis XVIII, see those works about Talleyrand cited in Vol. I, pp. 294–7, and Fahmy Scandar Naguib, *La France en 1814 et le gouvernement provisoire* (Paris, 1934). See also G. de Bertier de Sauvigny, 'The American Press and the Fall of Napoleon in 1814', *Proceedings of the American Philosophical Society*, Vol. 98 (1954), pp. 367–76.

Bibliography

Chapter X. The Restoration and the Hundred Days

For general background see *Histoire de France contemporaine*, ed. E. Lavisse, Vol. IV, 'La Restauration' by S. Charléty (Paris, 1921), which contains a good bibliography.

THE CONGRESS OF VIENNA AND THE SUCCESS OF THE COUNTER-REVOLUTION

On the question of the Gex district in the 1814 negotiations see J. Biaudet, 'Le traité de Paris du 30 mai 1814 et la question du pays de Gex', *Revue suisse d'histoire*, 1952. For the Vienna Congress see the next volume in the present series, 'L'éveil des nationalités et le mouvement liberal, 1815–1848' by G. Weill (Paris, 1930), a new edition by F. Ponteil (Paris, 1960) with a bibliography.

THE FIRST RESTORATION IN FRANCE AND THE RETURN FROM ELBA

See Chariéty, *La Restauration* (Paris, 1921); Thiry, Vol. III, 'La première Restauration', Vol. IV, 'Le vol de l'aigle' (Paris, 1941 and 1942); P. Bartel, *Napoléon à l'île d'Elbe* (Paris, 1947); de Marchand, *Mémoires*, Vol. I, 'L'île d'Elbe. Les Cent Jours', ed. J. Bourguignon (Paris, 1952). For a regional example see P. Leuilliot, *La première Restauration et les Cent Jours en Alsace* (Paris, 1959). For Carnot and his role see the last chapters of his biography by M. Reinhard, *Le grand Carnot*, Vol. II, 'L'organisateur de la victoire, 1792–1823' (Paris, 1952).

THE HUNDRED DAYS

See Charléty, cited above. The classic work is Henry Houssaye, *1815* (Paris, 1895–1905, 3 vols.); Thiry, Vol. V, 'Les Cents Jours', Vol. VI, 'Waterloo', Vol. VII, 'La seconde abdication' (Paris, 1943 and 1945). For the history of internal affairs see E. Le Gallo, *Les Cents Jours* (Paris, 1924); L. Radiguet, *L'acte additionnel aux constitutions de l'Empire* (Caen, 1911); C. Durand, *La fin du Conseil d'État napoléonien* (Aix-en-Provence, 1959, from the 'Annales de la Faculté de Droit d'Aix-en-Provence', new series No. 51)—the Council rallied practically unanimously to Napoleon at the time of the Hundred Days; it began to function again according to the pre-1814 system, but it made absolutely no contribution to the preparation of the additional Act, due to Benjamin Constant's being elected Council member on that occasion; C. Alleaume, *Les Cent Jours dans le Var* (Draguignan, 1938, 'Mémoires de la Société d'études scientifiques et archéologiques de Draguignan', Vol. XLIX); Leuillot, *La première Restauration* (Paris, 1941). For the campaign see Couderc de Saint-Chamant, *Les dernières armées de Napoléon* (Paris, 1902); J. Regnault, *La campagne de 1815. Mobilisation et concentration* (Paris, 1935); A. Grouard, *La critique de la campagne de 1815* (Paris, 1904), *La critique de la campagne de 1815. Réponse à Monsieur Huossaye* (Paris, 1907), 'Les derniers historiens de 1815', *Revue des études napoléoniennes*, Vol. III (1913), pp. 235–58, 367–90, Vols. XI and

XII (1917), pp. 163–98, 180–206, 300–23; E. Lenient, *La solution des énigmes de Waterloo* (Paris, 1915–18, 2 vols.); A. F. Becke, *Napoleon and Waterloo* (London, 1915, new ed., 1936); J. Holland Rose, 'Wellington dans la campagne de Waterloo', *Revue des études napoléoniennes*, Vol. VIII (1915), pp. 44–55, 'The Prussian Co-operation at Waterloo' in his *Napoleonic Studies*, pp. 274–304; Cavalie Mercer, *Journal of the Waterloo Campaign* (London, 1927)—the author was an artillery officer in the British army. *Napoleon a bord du Bellerophon* and *Napoleon a bord du Northumberland*, works by British officers translated by H. Borjane (Paris, 1934 and 1936). For St. Helena see Frederic Masson, *Napoléon à Saint Hélène* (Paris, 1912), 'L'énigme de Saint-Hélène', *Revue des Deux Mondes*, Vol. II (1917), pp. 756–788; O. Aubry, *Saint Hélène* (Paris, 1935); D. M. Brookes, *St. Helena Story* (London, 1960)—a work partly founded on family documents, the author being a descendant of William Balcombe, representative of the India Company in whose house Napoleon spent the first months of his captivity. See also Napoleon's writings on St. Helena cited in Vol. I, p. 292; Comte de Las Cases, *Mémorial de Sainte-Hélène* (Paris, 1823; the most recent editions by M. Dunan in 1951 and by A. Fugier in 1961); see also E. de Las Cases, *Las Cases, le mémorialiste de Napoléon* (Paris, 1959), based on unpublished documents from the family archives; Gourgaud, *Journal* (Paris, 1899); *Cahiers de Sainte-Hélène*, General Bertrand's diary annotated by P. Fleuriot de Langle, Vol. I, '1816–1817', Vol. II, '1818–1819', Vol. III, '1821' (Paris, 1951, 1959, 1949); P. Gonnard, *Les origines de la legende napoléonienne. L'œuvre historique de Napoléon à Saint-Hélène* (Paris, 1906); J. Dechamps, *Sur la légende napoléonienne* (Paris, 1931); J. Lucas-Dubreton, *Le culte de Napoléon, 1814–1848* (Paris, 1960); P. Holzhausen, *H. Heine und Napoleon I* (Frankfurt, 1903); G. Lote, 'Napoleon und die französische Romantik', *Romanische Forschungen*, Vol. XXXVIII (1913), Pt. 1; W. Klein, *Der Napoleonkult in der Pfaltz* (Munich, 1934, Pt. 5 of the 'Münchener historische Abhandlungen'); Maria dell'Isola, *Napoléon dans la poésie italienne à partir de 1821* (Paris, 1927).

Index

Index

Index